Praise for *Do Glaciers Listen?*

I0876601

Narrative, encounter, and locality come alive in this exquisitely written account about the sentient quality of glaciers ... This book is exceptional for its style, prose, the quality of research and, perhaps most of all, for the passion the author brings to her subject.

– Andrew Baldwin, *Environmental History*

Cruikshank's ... project is sociologically complex and historically satisfying for she concretely demonstrates how the local and global are not two "locations," but different aspects or moments of ongoing processes of conquest and resistance ... as Cruikshank reconstructs the past encounters and the selectivity of scientific reporting, one increasingly appreciates the historical intermingling of ideas and practices and her insistence that we listen to other voices – including even the glaciers that are listening to us.

– Paul K. Gellert, *Contemporary Sociology*

This is a beautifully written and thoughtful book, a pleasure to read. Focused on a small area while drawing on a complex, interdisciplinary literature, it offers a grounded yet connected account of a sort that postcolonial scholarship often advocates and rarely achieves.

– Cole Harris, *BC Studies*

Author Julie Cruikshank weaves a complex and engaging work that explores the intersections of history, culture, science, environmental change, theory, and methodology ... *Do Glaciers Listen?* is an elegant interdisciplinary work.

– Michele Hartlev, *Western Folklore*

Drawing on a lifetime of work amongst Aboriginal groups in the southern Yukon, ethnohistoric research on early explorations into the region, and analyses of current debates around the designation of the UNESCO World Heritage Site, Cruikshank contrasts the central divide between nature and culture in the Western imagination with those of indigenous groups where the two are intimately intertwined.

– Anne Henshaw, *The Journal of the Royal Anthropological Institute*

Cruikshank's book is not for those with fixed theoretical convictions. If you are confident that the causal forces of history operate independently of peoples' understanding, then this book will be of little interest, serving only to further demonstrate how inconvenient the people of history are in our understanding of their past. If, however, you are willing to recognize the historical influence of both the shadowy world of perception and the real world of existence, you will find here a gazetteer on the construction of social landscapes.

– ANDREW MARTÍNDALE, *Canadian Journal of Archaeology*

Reading this book was as exhilarating as taking a raft trip down the Alsek River, dodging melting icebergs and sailing under ice bridges ... Although this book will particularly delight those familiar with cultures of Alaska and the Yukon, it holds much interest for a broader audience.

– RACHEL MASON, *American Anthropologist*

[Cruikshank's] book is a vital contribution to today's scientific and popular debates about how best to respect nature and preserve wilderness.

– ADRIENNE MAYOR, *Journal of Folklore Research Reviews*

This remarkable book is the latest in Professor Cruikshank's expositions of oral history and local knowledge in the Yukon, Alaska, and British Columbia border region. In this volume she is concerned equally with native knowledge and traditions and with explorers' and colonizers' knowledge and assertions.

– NELSON H.H. GRABURN, *The American Review of Canadian Studies*

Perhaps the crucial word in the title is "Listen." The reader must listen carefully to the words as spoken by others in this beautifully crafted book. *Do Glaciers Listen?* is a fascinating read. Cruikshank's discussion of how encounters shape and create perceptions of the world, and how layers of meaning are forced onto landscapes by peoples is thoroughly thought provoking. This book is highly recommended for scientist, anthropologists, historians, and everyone with an interest in the social construction of landscapes.

– SUSAN ROWLEY, Canadian Polar Commission, *Meridian*

Cruikshank's book marks a significant contribution to the growing scholarship on animism, reclaiming this key anthropological concept, and *Do Glaciers Listen?* is essential reading for anthropologists, geographers, archaeologists, and all those interested in Native ontologies and the interface of the indigenous world with colonial encounters.

– Robert J. Wallis, *Time and Mind: The Journal of Archaeology, Consciousness and Culture*

Cruikshank presents the reader with several occasionally overlapping narratives, which come from Dene elders, European and American travellers, and modern mapmakers, about the glaciers and ice fields that define this corner of the Western Subarctic ... Dr. Cruikshank has produced a work that should be important not only to students of culture history in Pacific Northwest, but also to all who grapple with the cultural complexities of traditional knowledge.

– George W. Wenzel, *Arctic*

Do Glaciers Listen? is an exploration of nature and culture in encounter that builds upon Julie Cruikshank's deep and unrivalled knowledge of indigenous tradition. It focuses on an area that is, by most people's reckoning, "off the beaten track" and probably thus, by extension, unpropitious space for such an inquiry. But this is its triumph. It brings liminal space to the very centre of several important concerns of contemporary scholarship.

– Graeme Wynn, Department of Geography, University of British Columbia

This fascinating book weaves together a study of memory, oral history and transformations through a series of encounters between people and glaciers in the region where the Saint Elias Mountains and the Alsek River converge in the southwest Yukon Territory and Alaska.

– Rebecca K. Zarger, *Journal of Ecological Anthropology*

Do Glaciers Listen?

McLean Family
Canadian Studies Series

UBC Press is proud to publish the McLean Family Canadian Studies Series. Each volume is written by a distinguished Canadianist appointed as a McLean Fellow at the University of British Columbia, and reflects on an issue or theme of profound import to the study of Canada.

Borderlands: How We Talk about Canada
W.H. New

Citizens Plus: Aboriginal Peoples and the Canadian State
Alan C. Cairns

Making Native Space: Colonialism, Resistance, and Reserves in British Columbia
Cole Harris

Globalization and Well-Being
John F. Helliwell

Do Glaciers Listen? Local Knowledge, Colonial Encounters, and Social Imagination
Julie Cruikshank

On the Art of Being Canadian
Sherrill Grace

Big Tent Politics: The Liberal Party's Long Mastery of Canada's Public Life
R. Kenneth Carty

Moved by the State: Forced Relocation and Making a Good Life in Postwar Canada
Tina Loo

The Bomb in the Wilderness: Photography and the Nuclear Era in Canada
John O'Brian

Do Glaciers Listen?

Local Knowledge, Colonial Encounters, and Social Imagination

ANNIVERSARY EDITION

JULIE CRUIKSHANK

Foreword by Paul Nadasdy

UBCPress · Vancouver

© UBC Press 2026

All rights reserved. No part of this publication may be reproduced, stored in a retrieval system, text or data mined, used for training machine-learning or generative artificial intelligence (AI) systems or similar technologies, or transmitted in any form or by any means, without prior written permission of the publisher, or, in the case of photocopying or other reprographic copying in Canada, a licence from Access Copyright, www.accesscopyright.ca.

Printed in Canada, this book is made of FSC-certified and recycled (forest-based) material. The FSC-certified materials meet FSC's standards for responsible forestry, and recycled materials are used instead of virgin forest materials. www.fsc.org.

UBC Press is an eBOUND Digital Certified publisher. The epub version of this book meets stringent accessibility standards, ensuring it is available to people with diverse needs.

Library and Archives Canada Cataloguing in Publication

Title: Do glaciers listen? : local knowledge, colonial encounters, and social imagination / Julie Cruikshank ; foreword by Paul Nadasdy.

Names: Cruikshank, Julie, author. | Nadasdy, Paul, writer of foreword.

Description: Anniversary edition. | Includes bibliographical references and index.

Identifiers: Canadiana (print) 20260235261 | Canadiana (ebook) 20260235296 | ISBN 9780774874090 (softcover) | ISBN 9780774874106 (PDF) | ISBN 9780774874113 (EPUB)

Subjects: LCSH: Indigenous peoples—Saint Elias Mountains—Folklore. | LCSH: Glaciers—Saint Elias Mountains—Folklore. | LCSH: Ice fields—Saint Elias Mountains—Folklore. | LCSH: Human ecology—Saint Elias Mountains. | LCSH: Oral tradition—Saint Elias Mountains. | LCSH: Saint Elias Mountains—Discovery and exploration. | LCSH: Saint Elias Mountains—Folklore. | LCSH: Saint Elias Mountains—Environmental conditions. | LCSH: Glaciers—Social aspects—Saint Elias Mountains. | LCSH: Climatic changes—Saint Elias Mountains.

Classification: LCC GB2403.2 .C78 2026 | DDC 979.8/3—dc23

Canada | Canada Council for the Arts | Conseil des arts du Canada

British Columbia Arts Council | British Columbia

UBC Press gratefully acknowledges the financial support for our publishing program of the Government of Canada, the Canada Council for the Arts, and the British Columbia Arts Council.

UBC Press is situated on the traditional, ancestral, and unceded territory of the xʷməθkʷəy̓əm (Musqueam) people. This land has always been a place of learning for the xʷməθkʷəy̓əm, who have passed on their culture, history, and traditions for millennia, from one generation to the next.

UBC Press
The University of British Columbia
www.ubcpress.ca

Dedicated to the memory of Annie Ned, Angela Sidney, and Kitty Smith

The glaciers creep
Like snakes that watch their prey, from their far fountains,
Slow rolling on.

– Percy Shelley, "Mont Blanc," 1816

In one place Alsek River runs under a glacier. People can pass beneath in their canoes, but, if anyone speaks while they are under it, the glacier comes down on them. They say that in those times this glacier was like an animal, and could hear what was said to it.

– Deikinaak'w, speaking to John Swanton
at Sitka, Alaska, 1904

The climate system is an angry beast and we are poking at it with sticks!

– Wallace S. Broecker, 1998

We were always told that a giant worm, gyu shäw, lives under the glaciers. Therefore we have always been counseled to avoid cooking any grease or fat meat when in the mountains near glaciers. Glaciers will surge and collapse on you if you cook any fat meat in the vicinity.

– Daniel Tlen, 2004

Contents

Illustrations

Maps

Figures

Foreword

It has been just over twenty years since the publication of Julie Cruikshank's *Do Glaciers Listen?* but already it has the feel of a classic. Beautifully written and a pleasure to read, the book is as relevant today as it was when it first came out. Indeed, as I reread the book in preparation for writing this foreword, I found myself reflecting on its ongoing – even increasing – relevance at a time when struggles over Indigenous lands and epistemologies figure ever more prominently in global efforts to understand and address accelerating climate change. Yet, *Do Glaciers Listen?* was also clearly a product of its time, and it made important – if understated – theoretical interventions into then contemporary debates. When it came out, for instance, anthropologists, geographers, and others were engaged in vigorous discussions about ontology and other-than-human agency, and the book's compelling account of Tlingit and Athapaskan people's reciprocal social relations with sentient landscapes in the Yukon–Alaska borderlands became a vital part of those conversations. Twenty years on, those ontological debates have quieted, yet the book retains all its considerable intellectual and moral force.

Do Glaciers Listen? is a rich and nuanced work that grapples with the full complexity of its ethnographic and historical material. Notably, Julie refuses to draw any sharp distinction between Indigenous and western/scientific ways of knowing/being, and she explores the heterogeneity on both sides of this supposed ontological divide. This distinguishes the book from many others associated with the so-called ontological turn, whose proponents often flattened ethnographic complexity in their quest to produce clean examples of "radical alterity."[1] *Do Glaciers Listen?* shows us that there is no single unified "Indigenous" understanding of – or way of interacting with – glacial landscapes. Rather, the various stories told by Tlingit and Athapaskan storytellers enact glaciers in different ways. In some, glaciers appear as sentient beings who are quick to anger when not treated with the proper respect (by, for example, cooking with grease in their vicinity or speaking to them in insulting ways); in others, glaciers serve as dens for giant animals, and it is those creatures – and not the glaciers themselves – who demand respect and pose a danger to human travellers. In yet another story, it is an offended shaman – rather than sentient ice or a giant animal – who causes a glacier to surge and retreat. One set of stories suggests that glaciers are part of a "winter world" that exists beyond the horizon, a home to white or colourless beings that includes, perhaps, Europeans; another set focuses – somewhat more mundanely – on glaciers as critically important though dangerous travel routes between the coast and the interior, routes that facilitated migration and trade prior to the arrival of Europeans. Although all of these various stories are built upon a set of shared cultural assumptions (that landscapes and animals are sentient and can interact socially with humans), they are not strictly compatible with one another, and Julie makes no attempt to tie them together into a single unified "Indigenous" perspective on glaciers. Instead, she encourages us to embrace the ambiguity and to consider how, taken together, the stories disturb taken-for-granted boundaries between categories like place, personhood, and kinship.

Julie also subverts the idea that there is some unitary "scientific" or "Euro-American" perspective on glaciers. Jean-François de La Pérouse's glaciers are different from John Muir's, which are different again from those of Edward Glave, the Alaska boundary surveyors, and contemporary glaciologists. Importantly, Julie also disabuses us of the commonplace notion that "modern" Euro-American views of a "disenchanted" nature are separated by an Enlightenment divide from Indigenous ideas about sentient landscapes. After all, John Muir was nothing if not a child of the Enlightenment, yet he engaged in serious discussions with his Tlingit guides about whether wolves have souls, and he was receptive to the idea that elements of the landscape – and glaciers in particular – possess a kind of sentience and spiritual power.[2] Central to Muir's natural theology was the idea that nature reveals the character of God; and he argued, in what he referred to as his "glacial gospel," that glaciers were especially potent sources of divine revelation.[3] In Julie's book, however, we learn that Muir's editor convinced him to delete from his published accounts most of his "philosophical digressions" about the Tlingit worldview, as well as his own ideas about the sentience and power of natural landscapes.[4] To be sure, his ideas were not the same as those of his Tlingit guides, but neither were they consistent with the views of glaciologists. Nor was Muir, in his openness to the non-material and agentic dimensions of nature, a complete outlier among Euro-Americans. From the Romantic poets to Aldo Leopold's later exhortation to "think like a mountain," there is a long tradition in Euro-American environmentalist thought of attributing agency and/or spiritual power to the land.[5]

In *Do Glaciers Listen?,* Julie embraces all this heterogeneity. Rather than sorting into two opposing camps the many ways people have known and interacted with the glacial landscapes of the southern Alaska–Yukon borderlands, she allows each to stand on its own. The dynamic masses of ice studied by glaciologists stand in juxtaposition to the forbidding symbols of sublime nature celebrated by the Romantic poets and the powerful sentient beings encountered by Tlingit and Athapaskan travellers. In her analysis, she refuses to privilege – or dismiss – any of these views, arguing that the erasure of worlds entailed in such an act is the essence of colonialism. Indeed, she treats the glaciers evoked by Tlingit storytellers as having the same ontological status as those conjured by the narratives of glaciologists. By explicitly refusing to privilege glaciologists' "knowledge" about glaciers over Indigenous people's "superstitious" beliefs about them, she moves beyond the standard ethnographic suspension of disbelief and embraces instead a principle of methodological symmetry,[6] a fairly standard approach in science and technology studies, which rejects a priori judgments about the truth of different knowledge systems, subjecting them all to similar analytic treatment.[7] Taking this approach enables Julie to trace multiple perceptions, understandings, and interactions with glaciers both cross-culturally and over time, while attending to the different social and cultural assumptions upon which each is based and showing how they shaped colonial encounters and continue to shape ongoing debates over protected areas and the creation of a World Heritage site.

Not everyone has found this approach completely satisfying. In his otherwise positive review of *Do Glaciers Listen?,* eminent geographer Cole Harris called Julie to task for not answering the book's eponymous question, taking it upon himself to seek the answer: "I asked a colleague, an expert on snow, why glaciers surged, and he spoke of ground water, friction, and the laws of physics. Is it possible, I asked, that they surge because they don't like being spoken about or because they don't like the smell of grease? He looked at me blankly, slowly shook his head, and retreated into his office."[8] Reflecting on his colleague's reaction, Harris went on: "Can we avoid the conclusion ... that my colleague offers a more robust explanation for glacial surges than do Tlingit and Tutchone storytellers? I doubt we can."[9] In short, he concludes, glaciers do not *really* listen. Tellingly, though, apart from his colleague's reaction, Harris offers no evidence to support his conclusion that stories about glaciers told by geophysicists and glaciologists have "more explanatory power" than those told by Indigenous elders. Nor is it apparent in his review why we should take the word of an "expert on snow" at the University of British Columbia over that of Indigenous experts who have lived their lives near the glaciers in question. Indeed, the principle of methodological symmetry requires that we consider not only a glaciologist's reaction to Tlingit stories but also Tlingit elders' reaction to glaciologists' own culturally specific explanation for why glaciers surge. For those who lack the necessary and taken-for-granted cultural background, stories – whether those told by Indigenous elders or geophysical scientists – can seem nonsensical. This is no reason to dismiss them.

On another level, Harris's critique misses the whole point of *Do Glaciers Listen?* Throughout her career-long exploration of storytelling and its role in society, Julie has taken a dynamic approach that challenges long-standing notions that there is a single authoritative version of any story. Instead of trying to determine in some abstract sense which story is the truest, most efficacious, or most authentic, she has focused instead on the practice of storytelling. Storytellers themselves, she shows us, never tell stories in quite the same way; rather, they adapt and deploy their stories differently – and to different ends – depending on the social and political context. Every telling, then, is a creative social act. This is, of course, as true for scientist-explorers and environmentalists as it is for Tlingit and Athapaskan elders. Indeed, one of the profound implications of Julie's work is that we are all storytellers; it is through the stories we tell – whether around the campfire or in academic journal articles – that we make sense of our place in the world. Of course, the medium matters; whether we tell our stories orally or in written form, in the pages of academic journals, through photos, or on social media affects how they will be received and by whom. The point of *Do Glaciers Listen?* is not to judge whose stories about glaciers are better (truer, more efficacious, etc.), but rather to explore the sensibilities and assumptions about the world that make those stories meaningful to some people and not others ... and then to consider what happens when those in power valorize some stories as true (and therefore not as stories at all), while consigning others to the dustbin of superstition.

In a subsequent article (perhaps in response to critiques like Harris's), Julie addresses the question of veracity explicitly and notes that Indigenous narratives often get cast as "traditional ecological knowledge" (TEK), and in that form can be of interest to scientists looking for "evidence" of historical environmental change.[10] And, indeed, she observes that "oral traditions helped to establish the mid-nineteenth century date when the Nàlùdi (Lowell Glacier) ice dam deformed, releasing a giant outburst flood that swept down the Tatshenshini-Alsek River Valley to the coast." But, she asks, "what is gained and what is lost in this translation when stories are assessed for veracity, and when instrumentality and utility become TEK's goal? The process, invariably selective, narrows the register of what knowledge is deemed to be ... In translation to data what disappears are the relationships through which entities in the world come into being as well as the capacities we might gain if we could actually learn to think with such stories."[11] This suggests that notions like "veracity" or "explanatory power" are not neutral yardsticks against which all stories can be assessed. After all, how much explanatory power any story possesses depends on what exactly one wants to explain.

In *Do Glaciers Listen?*, Julie tells us that as John Muir's expedition approached the mouth of Glacier Bay, his Tlingit guides told stories of Devilfish (a giant octopus) and other giant animals who dwell within various arms of the bay and who lie in wait to attack and eat people foolish enough to enter. It was clear to Samuel Hall Young, Muir's companion – if not to the sometimes-oblivious Muir himself – that their guides were relaying these stories at least in part to warn them about the considerable dangers posed by the active glaciers they would encounter within the bay.[12] More than a hundred years later, Tlingit elders told these stories again, but this time in the Portland Museum of Art. In this later telling, however, the Devilfish blocking the entrance to Glacier Bay had become a symbol for the government agencies that had long denied Tlingit people access to Glacier Bay (designated a National Monument in 1925, a National Park in 1980, and a UNESCO World Heritage Site in 1992). In this context, Julie points out, the "ancient story takes on precise political meanings in terms of contemporary struggles."[13] A narrow focus on "veracity" misses the vital social and political work people do when they tell such stories, and an exclusive focus on some kinds of "explanatory power" (e.g., the physical causes of glacial surge) obscures other forms of explanation (e.g., the political relations illuminated by likening government agencies to inhuman man-eating monsters).

With its focus on narrative, *Do Glaciers Listen?* paved the way for what some have begun to call the "ice humanities," an avalanche of recent studies focusing on what glaciers/ice *mean*.[14] These studies foreground the many different kinds of stories that Indigenous peoples, scientists, and others tell about ice, and they explore the various media in which they do so – from oral histories to repeat photography to computer models.[15] In the process, they are extending Julie's insights into how such stories inform prevalent ideas about climate change and human–land relations, and how they have shaped – and continue to shape – colonial relations with lands and peoples.

In their call for a feminist glaciology, Carey et al. draw extensively on *Do Glaciers Listen?* and conclude that, "the goal is neither to force glaciologists to believe that glaciers listen nor to make indigenous peoples put their full faith in scientists' mathematical equations and computer-generated models ... Rather, the goal is to understand that environmental knowledge is always based in systems of power discrepancies and unequal social relations, and overcoming these disparities requires accepting that multiple knowledges exist and are valid within their own contexts."[16] This captures the general thrust of the book, yet I think Julie would also push back gently on the suggestion that knowledge and narrative are only "valid within their own contexts." She has shown, after all, that stories can do important work in social and political contexts far removed from those that spawned them, and she has written with grace and humility about how her longtime collaborators Kitty Smith, Annie Ned, and Angela Sidney – and their stories – helped decentre her own preconceived ideas about history, nature, personhood, and life. This is why she exhorts us to heed Annie Ned's advice – not just to listen *to* stories, but to listen *for* them.

Paul Nadasdy
Author of *Sovereignty's Entailments* (2017)
and *Hunters and Bureaucrats* (2003)

Notes

1 See, for example, critiques by Michael Cepek, "There Might Be Blood: Oil, Humility, and the Cosmopolitics of a Cofán Petro-Being," *American Ethnologist* 43, 4 (2016): 623–35, https://doi.org/10.1111/amet.12379; David Graeber, "Radical Alterity is Just Another Way of Saying 'Reality': A Reply to Eduardo Viveiros de Castro," *HAU: Journal of Ethnographic Theory* 5, 2 (2015): 1–41, https://doi.org/10.14318/hau5.2.003; and Sarah Hunt, "Ontologies of Indigeneity: The Politics of Embodying a Concept," *cultural geographies* 21, 1 (2014): 27–32, https://doi.org/10.1177/1474474013500226.

2 Julie Cruikshank, *Do Glaciers Listen? Local Knowledge, Colonial Encounters, and Social Imagination* (UBC Press, 2005), 166–67, 174–75.

3 Cruikshank, *Do Glaciers Listen?*, 161.

4 Cruikshank, *Do Glaciers Listen?*, 174–75.

5 Aldo Leopold, *A Sand County Almanac: And Sketches Here and There* (Oxford University Press, 1949).

6 Cruikshank, *Do Glaciers Listen?*, 129.

7 There are, however, multiple versions of the principle of methodological symmetry, see Michael Lynch, "STS, Symmetry and Post-truth," *Social Studies of Science* 47, 4 (2017): 593–99, https://doi.org/10.1177/0306312717720308.

8 Cole Harris, "Do Glaciers Really Listen? A Review Essay," *BC Studies* 148 (2005): 103–6, https://doi.org/10.14288/bcs.v0i148.

9 Harris, "Do Glaciers Really Listen?," 106.

10 Julie Cruikshank, "Are Glaciers 'Good to Think With'? Recognising Indigenous Environmental Knowledge," *Anthropological Forum* 22, 3 (2012): 239–50, https://doi.org/10.1080/00664677.2012.707972.

11 Cruikshank, "Are Glaciers 'Good to Think With'?," 248.

12 Cruikshank, *Do Glaciers Listen?*, 170–71.

13 Cruikshank, *Do Glaciers Listen?*, 175.

14 Klaus Dodds and Sverker Sörlin, *Ice Humanities: Living, Working, and Thinking in a Melting World* (Manchester University Press, 2022).

15 See Karine Gagné and Georgina Drew, eds., "Vital Matter: Icy Liveliness in the Anthropocene," special issue, *Social Anthropology/Anthropologie sociale* 32, 1 (2024); Dani Inkpen, *Capturing Glaciers: A History of Repeat Photography and Global Warming* (University of Washington Press, 2024); and Jen Rose Smith, *Ice Geographies: The Colonial Politics of Race and Indigeneity in the Arctic* (Duke University Press, 2025).

16 Mark Carey, M. Jackson, Alessandro Antonello, and Jaclyn Rushing, "Glaciers, Gender, and Science: A Feminist Glaciology Framework for Global Environmental Change Research," *Progress in Human Geography* 40, 6 (2016): 770–93, https://doi.org/10.1177/0309132515623368.

Note from the Publisher

First published in 2005, *Do Glaciers Listen?* contains terminology and viewpoints that reflect the perspectives and language of the early twenty-first century and may be considered outdated or inappropriate by some modern readers. The content of this seminal work, however, is as relevant today as it was then; so, rather than revising the text to meet contemporary and constantly changing standards, we have chosen to reissue it in its original form with the exception of the front matter, which includes new and updated material.

Acknowledgments

My first and enduring debt of gratitude is to Kitty Smith, Annie Ned, and Angela Sidney who made me think about glaciers thirty years ago before I had ever seen one. I learned about Yukon landscapes first through their stories and then during our travels together between 1974 and 1989, as we followed out-of-the-way roads and trails in the southwest Yukon, recording place names and mapping stories associated with those places. The Council for Yukon Indians (now Council for Yukon First Nations) and the Yukon Native Languages Project (now Yukon Native Language Centre) originally encouraged and then funded our work during the late 1970s and early 1980s. I especially thank Paul Birckel and John Ritter for their confidence in and support for our work.

In the Yukon, I also thank daughters of my mentors – Ida Calmegane, daughter of Angela Sidney; Stella Jim, daughter of Annie Ned; and May Hume, daughter of Kitty Smith. All have continued to share with me memories of their mothers. I am grateful to Champagne-Aishihik First Nation for including me in a visit their members made to Yakutat, Alaska, in June 1999. I am especially indebted to Marge Jackson, Diane Strand, Sarah Gaunt, Lawrence Joe, John Fingland, Steven Reid, and Sheila Greer, who have helped me to understand the local complexities of issues discussed in this book from the perspectives of Champagne-Aishihik members.

Kluane First Nation invited me to attend Indian Claims Commission hearings in their community in February 2002 and enlarged my understanding of struggles their community has faced while living on the edge of a national park. I thank Mary Jane Johnson, Robin Bradasch, and Dave Joe for this invitation.

I thank Elaine Abraham and George and David Ramos, for hospitality at Yakutat both in June 1999 and when I returned again in June 2002. In Sitka, Bob Sam has long been a helpful colleague. Paul Jackson, a L'uknax.ádi clan member living in Sitka, was very generous with his time and advice when

I visited in June 2000. Paul Johnson, surely one of the most skilful boat pilots on the Gulf of Alaska, made it possible for me to visit Lituya Bay in summer 2002, and he, Tami Mulick, and their family at Gull Cove made me so welcome in their home. National Park Service staff in Glacier Bay, Copper Center, and Anchorage, Alaska, were generous with their time and hospitality, and they gave me helpful perspectives on parks issues; I especially thank Karen Gaul, Barbara Cellarius, and Geoff Bleakley.

Jim Katz invited me to join his raft trips down the Tatshenshini River from Dalton Post to the Gulf of Alaska as a historical guide in summer 2003 and again in 2004. He and his accomplished crew made these trips an extraordinary experience.

Armed with questions from oral history, I delved into archives. There, I made connections with other stories that began elsewhere and became enmeshed with North America's northwestern glaciers. Those accounts began in France, where La Pérouse prepared his trip to the Gulf of Alaska; in equatorial Africa, where Edward Glave worked before he came to the Tatshenshini and Alsek rivers; and on a small farm in Wisconsin, where John Muir spent a childhood that fired his interest in glacial processes. I thank the Scott Polar Research Institute at the University of Cambridge, where I was welcomed for a sabbatical year in 2001–2; the Rare Books Room in the University of Cambridge Library; the Yukon Archives in Whitehorse; the Newberry Library in Chicago; and the Special Collections division of the University of British Columbia Library.

A research grant from the Social Sciences and Humanities Research Council of Canada made the initial research possible. Time to write this book was enabled by the generosity of David and Brenda McLean, who endow a Chair in Canadian Studies, which I held from 2001–3 in the Faculty of Arts at the University of British Columbia. Richard Cavell and John O'Brian, successive heads of UBC's Canadian Studies Program, were consistently encouraging and thoughtful in their support.

An earlier version of Chapter 1 was published in *Arctic* 54, 4 (December 2001), by the Arctic Institute of North America and appears here in revised form, with permission. An earlier version of Chapter 4 was published in *Research in Science and Technology Studies: Knowledge and Technology Transfer*, edited by Marianne de Laet, Volume 13 of *Knowledge and Society* (2002); this revised version appears with permission from Elsevier Science, Oxford, UK.

Elizabeth Povinelli's fine paper "Do Rocks Listen?" and her approach to her subject originally inspired the way I framed this project, including its title. Colleagues with whom I discussed parts of this manuscript or who have made helpful suggestions include David Anderson, Alexia Bloch, Barbara

Bodenhorn, Michael Bravo, Mary Burns, Dara Culhane, Richard and Nora Dauenhauer, Frank Duerden, Frederica de Laguna, Marianne de Laet, Margery Fee, Harvey Feit, Robert Galois, Carol Geddes, Ken George, Ken Hewitt, Tim Ingold, Linda Johnson, Leanne Lennon, Catharine McClellan, Karen McCullough, Bruce Miller, Patrick Moore, Blanca Muratorio, Paul Nadasdy, Kirin Narayan, David Neufeld, Beth O'Leary, Ben Orlove, Frances Pine, John Ritter, Leslie Robertson, Tom Thornton, Daniel Tlen, Charlotte Towsend-Gault, Piers Vitebsky, Nancy Wachowich, and Wendy Wickwire. Particular thanks are owed to Eric Leinberger for his careful preparation of maps.

I thank Jennifer Brown and Graeme Wynn for their thoughtful reading of this manuscript and their immensely helpful suggestions. Any errors are entirely my own responsibility.

Kluane National Park staff were consistently supportive. The facilities provided by the Arctic Institute's Kluane Research Station, and conversations there with David Hik, Peter Johnson, and Andy and Carole Williams have helped push my questions along. Thanks to UBC Press, especially to Darcy Cullen and Jean Wilson for perceptive comments and for moving this manuscript smoothly through successive stages. Mostly, I thank my long-time companion, Garry Clarke, for his good-humoured interest in glacier research so very different from his own.

Do Glaciers Listen?

INTRODUCTION

The Stubborn Particulars of Voice

Glaciers and their intangible connections to recent human history provide this book's unifying theme. I draw on climate histories, colonial records, Aboriginal oral traditions from the Yukon and Alaska,[1] and a personal fascination with the imaginative force that glaciers exert on regional histories in northwestern North America. The icefields in question flow from the craggy mountain spine where Canada and the United States meet at their least-known boundary, the Saint Elias Mountain divide. Far below that serrated crest, Tlingit peoples on the Gulf of Alaska coast and inland speakers of Athapaskan languages came to know this glacial landscape during successive generations. Their experiences reinforced a vision that humans and nature mutually make and maintain the habitable world, a view now echoed by environmental historians.

Glaciers appear as actors in this book. In accounts we will hear from Athapaskan and Tlingit oral tradition, glaciers take action and respond to their surroundings. They are sensitive to smells and they listen. They make moral judgments and they punish infractions. Some elders who know them well describe them as both animate (endowed with life) and as animating (giving life to) landscapes they inhabit. Glaciers also enter accounts left by early North Atlantic visitors who wrote in a different idiom and brought distinctive environmental visions to their interpretations.

English is a language rich in nouns but lacking verb forms that distinguish animate from inanimate subjects. Both Athapaskan and Tlingit languages have comparatively fewer nouns but are verb-rich and hence often define landscape in terms of its actions. The Tlingit noun for glacier is *sít'*; in Southern Tutchone, an inland Athapaskan language spoken on the Canadian side of the mountains, the words are *tän shäw* (*tän* "ice" + *shäw* "big") or *tän shi* (beneath the front of glacier). Both languages emphasize activity and motion, making no distinction between animate and inanimate. In Athapaskan languages, you know something is animate if the verb signals that it has the power to act on other things or to move, and actions are often attributed to entities, such as glaciers, that English speakers would define as inanimate. Linguistic anthropologists discuss this "enlivening" influence of the Tlingit verbs and how this results in "action-oriented naming."[2] In Athapaskan languages, an elaborate system of verb stems means that different stems are used for singular, dual, and plural verb forms. Furthermore, directional clues situate characters and their actions so that if a speaker is orienting herself to a glacier, for instance, one verb stem will be used to indicate travelling upstream, another for going downstream, another for crossing away from a point of reference, another for crossing toward a point of reference, and so on.[3] Clearly, the varied ways of speaking about glaciers are sometimes difficult to capture in English.

"A country that listens," as anthropologist Elizabeth Povinelli has shown, was not unfamiliar in Europe before conditions underpinning the Industrial Revolution began to spill over into everyday lives, language, and beliefs. It is not surprising, she observes, that we now find it difficult to believe that rocks, mountains, and other landscape features like glaciers might listen, when the very conditions of the Western material and cultural world are underpinned by language that rejects that possibility.[4] The question, *Do Glaciers Listen?* is less straightforward than it may at first seem.

An enduring theme of oral traditions told in northwestern North America is the inclusion of nature in human affairs. One of my objectives in the following chapters is to provide an account of how interpretations of natural, social, and cultural worlds became gradually disaggregated in a place where they were formerly viewed as unified, and to examine consequences of that fragmentation. Many disciplines are re-evaluating reciprocal relationships between humankind and the natural world, and some now identify nature as a category of social analysis as important as (and entangled with) class, race, and gender.[5] My aim in this book, then, is twofold. First, I argue that local knowledge is never crudely encapsulated in closed traditions, but is produced during human encounters, rather than "discovered." It is dynamic and complex, and it often links biophysical and social processes. Second, I trace how long-contested views of nature weave uneasily through a history of encounters among humans and glaciers and into contemporary discussions about Protected Areas, parks, and a new World Heritage site that now encompasses the region. While my focus here is on a very specific corner of the globe, I contend that themes discussed in the following chapters, by no means limited to this location, speak to other arenas of colonial encounter. In that sense, I hope that this work may contribute to what Michel Foucault once called "histories of the present."

The stories I trace in this book begin during the late stages of a period some scientists refer to as the Little Ice Age. Spanning roughly AD 1550-1850, this Little Ice Age was characterized by cooler and more variable temperatures over much of the globe, with pronounced consequences at high latitude. Jean Grove, the physical geographer who coined this term for an interval of global cooling between the Middle Ages and the early twentieth century, traces some of its slipperiness in her classic volume *The Little Ice Age,* and notes that chronologies vary from region to region. Archaeologist Brian Fagan's recent book of the same title suggests dates of 1300-1850 for Western Europe, but he also notes that scientists strongly disagree about dates.[6] In the Pacific Northwest, the years between 1550 and 1900 are commonly cited.

In Europe, French historian Emmanuel LeRoy Ladurie traces records from medieval archives that chronicle the destruction of European villages by advancing glaciers during the Little Ice Age. Descriptions abound of "great and horrible glacier[s] of great and incalculable volume which can promise nothing but the destruction of houses and lands which still remain."[7] Terrified sixteenth-century villagers entered glacial caves with swords drawn, and they mounted crosses at the edge of terminal moraines in vain attempts to halt these advances. Volcanic activity also enhanced northern hemispheric cooling. Evidence from temperate regions of North America and Europe demonstrates that the summer of 1816 – the year after the volcanic eruption of Tambora in Java – was exceptionally cold. Reports from Connecticut, southern England, and Switzerland show that it was the coldest year for which records exist.[8] At higher latitudes, the impact of volcanic dust in the upper atmosphere may have been even more significant. Romantic poets were especially captivated by Little Ice Age changes and drew on opportune cultural metaphors to portray expanding glaciers. Samuel Coleridge wrote what he called a devotional poem, "Hymn before Sunrise," addressing glaciers at Chamonix as "motionless torrents, silent cataracts."[9] Victor Hugo's portrayal of Mer de Glace was more aggressive, "a bent arm [that] overhangs and hurls down great blocks of marble whiteness."[10] John Turner's ruddy skies may have mirrored effects of volcanic dust.

Glaciers also inspired aesthetic forms passed on orally and in writing from the Pacific Northwest, where global cooling was accompanied by significant glacier activity on coastal shores and inland mountain passes. The icefields supported by the Saint Elias Mountains are the largest non-polar icefields in the world and they include a significant number of glaciers that surge quite independently of climate. Scientists now think that surges are triggered by subsurface deformation – processes involving water and

Figure 1 Trapridge Glacier, in the Saint Elias Mountains, is one of approximately two hundred surging glaciers in northwestern North America. *Trapridge Glacier Project Archives*

subglacial deposits, or till, under high pressure. Surging glaciers differ from the torrents and cataracts that inspired Coleridge in Europe, being neither motionless nor silent. They may advance without warning after years of stability, sometimes several kilometres, and as we will see in following chapters, they frequently create ice-dammed lakes that build up and burst out with catastrophic consequences when the ice eventually thins and the dam breaks. The impact of glaciers on regional history, I suggest, lies not simply in their immense physical presence but also in their contributions to social imagination.

Concerns about global climate change are giving glaciers new meaning for many people who may previously have considered them eternally frozen, safely distant, and largely inert. Most of the world's glaciers now seem to be melting rather than reproducing themselves, becoming a new kind of endangered species, a cryospheric weather vane for potential natural and social upheaval. Encounters with glaciers during times of rapid environmental change produce diverse interpretations. In the Andes, for instance, anthropologist Michael Sallnow has documented an age-old practice where thousands of contemporary pilgrims make their way up to the towering glaciers of Mount Sinakara during the fiesta of Señor de Qoyllur Rit'i. They light candles, reclaim crosses placed there a few days earlier, and carve out blocks of ice and laboriously carry them back down to a sanctuary. Or so they did, that is, until the 1990s when this practice was discontinued in order to stop the glacier from losing even more of its ice.[11] In Asia, geoscientist Ken Hewitt first heard accounts of gendered ice and artificial glaciers in 1961 when he began working in the Karakoram Range. In October of that year, a small group of local men bearing baskets lined with leather and straw began filling them with ice from the snout of the Biafo Glacier where he was working. He learned that specialists had determined that fetching ice from this glacier to "plant" at the opposite-gendered glacier overlooking their village could alleviate a drought affecting the village. The village headman gave the young scientists permission to visit the site, where they found a somewhat active remnant of a cirque glacier covered with broken rock. They were shown a hole where some half-dozen alternate layers of "male" and "female" ice were laid, each layer covered with special twigs, straw, and cloth.[12] And in his ongoing historical work in Peru's Cordillera Blanca, Mark Carey reports that in one glacier location, campesinos recently confiscated measuring devices scientists were using to monitor changes in glaciers because they suspected that the instruments might be causing a drought.[13] Imaginative possibilities from such differing locations and historical periods suggest that glaciers (and stories about them) may provide one lens through which to assess current cross-disciplinary discussions about the relevance of local knowledge to environmental policies.[14] As historian Richard White observes, there is a tangible physical world out there that sometimes affirms but often mocks the representations we design to constrain it.[15]

Romantic poets, Tlingit elders, scientists, and linguists, such as those cited in the opening epigraph, bring contrasting approaches to understanding climate change, and they all deserve attention. Percy Shelley wrote his poem "Mont Blanc"[16] when he was visiting the Alps in 1816, the reputed "year without a summer" when Mary Shelley also wrote *Frankenstein*, sending her protagonist deep into Alpine glaciers during his tormented struggle to become human. Deikinaak'w, a senior Tlingit orator, spoke at length with ethnographer John Swanton in 1904 and reflected on accounts he had heard about glacier surges on the Alsek River during the previous century.[17] Wallace Broecker, a prestigious geophysicist from Columbia University's Lamont-Doherty Earth Observatory, was addressing a *New York*

Times readership concerned about future climate change at the end of the twentieth century.[18] Daniel Tlen, linguist and member of Kluane First Nation, records oral histories with elders in the southern Yukon and teaches at Yukon College in Whitehorse.[19]

I first encountered these glaciers in stories told by elderly First Nation women who spent their lives inland from the Saint Elias Mountains in what is now the Yukon Territory. Three women in particular, Kitty Smith and Annie Ned, both born in the early 1890s, and Angela Sidney, born in 1902, unexpectedly forced me to think more carefully about glaciers. Their extraordinary lives spanned the century that began with the 1896-98 Klondike gold rush and ended just before the turn of the millennium. In the 1970s, they began our conversations with chronicles of ancestors who had lived within the shadow of these mountains as glaciers advanced and receded during the Little Ice Age, and whose stories flowed into their own. They spoke about glaciers familiarly and often by name, well aware of their dangers, and they integrated accounts of glacier behaviour into narratives of their own experiences.

The women I knew portrayed glaciers as conscious and responsive to humans. Glaciers, they insisted, are wilful, sometimes capricious, easily excited by human intemperance but equally placated by quick-witted human responses. Glaciers engage all the senses. I was informed, for instance, of firm taboos against "cooking with grease" near glaciers, which are offended by such smells. I heard concerns expressed about hikers who embark on overnight camping trips in Kluane National Park and might inadvertently trigger a glacier surge of ear-splitting force and great danger by cooking bacon for breakfast. Other stories dramatize consequences of improper treatment of cooked food, especially fat, that might grow into a glacier overnight. The narratives sometimes seemed to be less about actual glaciers than about the imaginative possibilities they provide. Glaciers portrayed as sentient beings in these stories seemed to be, in the felicitous phrase of French anthropologist Claude Lévi-Strauss, "good to think with." What most clearly differentiates the stories these women tell from written accounts left by early travellers whose accounts we will read in later chapters is the way Yukon storytellers *merge* natural histories of landscape with social histories and pursue their analogies in a local human ecology.

What happens during colonial encounters when matters of locality confront unfamiliar practices of exploration? I approach this as a problem in the anthropology of encounter that can be retrospectively investigated through narrative traces, which accumulate from such meetings. The idea of encounter seems especially useful because of what it reveals about scale and subjectivity. Initially, the actors in this region were relatively few, and their motives, intentions, and imaginings can be traced partially in diaries and reports, but also in orally narrated stories still told. These stories may originate in the past, but they continue to resonate with contemporary debates about history, science, and colonial practices as well as with current struggles surrounding environmentalism, land rights, nationhood, and national parks.

Anthropologists have recently addressed the need for more differentiated portrayals of colonial encounters. A postcolonial metanarrative that depicts coherent, homogeneous colonialism as an intractable template with predictable outcomes, they point out, now seems too globalizing and too ahistorical. Such representations of history also err in their apparent relegation of colonialism safely to the past.[20] Geographers point to the intellectual sleight of hand that can occur when urban scholars, settled in universities far from places they study, cautiously eschew speaking directly about "Others," yet casually bring a shaky sense of the colonial setting (without history or context) to their analysis of European imperial practices, presumably on such Others' behalf. Postcolonial literature inclines increasingly to theoretical concerns that seem ever more distant from detailed knowledge of local practices and power relations on the ground. This underlying universalism can be interpreted as refuelling an intellectual imperialism that once again presents Europe as the key historical agent, as though no other actors existed. Yet the aftermaths of colonialism are always local.[21] Taking up these themes, I focus on early encounters where transfers of knowledge seem to have occurred on both sides, before the balance of power in such exchanges shifted and state infrastructure made "difference" a rationale for inequality. Because narratives energize both exploration practices and local meanings, it is worth paying attention to what such stories accomplish, how they move, and why they persist – my ongoing preoccupation in this book.

Environmental Change, Local Knowledge, and Human Encounters

This work will, I hope, contribute to literature about environmental change, local knowledge, and human encounters – three themes often central to historical struggles in places depicted as "remote" despite long entanglements with world markets. *Changing environments* figure prominently in oral and written accounts passed on from late stages of the Little Ice Age. Environmental historians advise us to examine nature as a continuing force in history, not in a determining role but as one actor in relation to others.[22] *Local knowledge,* as I use the term, refers to tacit knowledge embodied in life experiences and reproduced in everyday behaviour and speech. In the early twenty-first century, local knowledge has become a commonsense term, couched in acronyms like TEK (traditional ecological knowledge) or IK (indigenous knowledge), gaining new visibility in management-science studies, but too often depicted as static, timeless, and hermetically sealed.[23] A historical approach reveals how socially situated but also how porous knowledge practices are. As the field of science studies shows, all knowledge is incontrovertibly local. *Encounters* come in many forms. We hear of human encounters among strangers, but also of encounters between those same people and transforming landscapes. Stories that participants tell orally or in writing about their experiences, in turn, encounter successive audiences whose interpretations of what they hear or read are shaped by their own contemporary concerns. In some cases, meetings between humans or landscapes may generate insights on all sides. But encounters, as Gillian Beer notes, do not guarantee understanding and may instead emphasize what is incommensurate.[24] Such themes connect chapters in this book.

Briefly, my argument is this. In northwestern North America, two fundamental processes that are often discussed independently coincided in the late eighteenth and nineteenth centuries: geophysical changes associated with late stages of the Little Ice Age and European colonial incursions. Raymond Williams's observation that the concept of nature always contains an extraordinary amount of human history is especially relevant here.[25] When glaciers on the North Pacific coast began to melt and recede, they released new lands that were gradually occupied by ancestors of contemporary Tlingit and Athapaskan peoples. But late stages of this Little Ice Age also coincided with European mercantile forays, initially on coastal shores and eventually across mountains into the interior uplands. A time of significant geophysical change, then, coincided with dramatic social upheaval, causing both readjustments and realignments among resident peoples and the permanent problem of powerful strangers who came to stay. Natural and cultural histories, in other words, are objectively entangled in this place.

Second, interpretations by participants struggling to make sense of both geophysical changes and social encounters often diverged dramatically. Eighteenth-century European visitors were especially excited by ideas of an inanimate nature subject to empirical investigation and measurement. They were heartened by the possibility that their Enlightenment categories and scientific instruments might help them to pry nature from culture. They imported these ideas to places like the Arctic and Africa, where local cultural meanings were framed very differently. Visitors wrote about glaciers, for instance, as *natural* spaces – pristine, wild, and remote from human influence, "on the verge of the world" in the words of one early French voyager, Jean-François de La Pérouse.[26] This local North Atlantic idea of a self-evident divide neatly separating natural from social phenomena contrasted sharply with Tlingit and Athapaskan understandings. Their oral traditions frame glaciers as intensely *social* spaces where human behaviour, especially casual hubris or arrogance, can trigger dramatic and unpleasant consequences in the physical world. In other words, Tlingit and Athapaskan oral traditions explore the connections between nature and culture as carefully as early exploration projects tried to disentangle them. Later, we will hear parallel distinctions from Central Africa, where jungles (like glaciers) evoke local connections with ancestors and historical knowledge about particular forest places. There, too, local visions contrast sharply with an iconography of jungles and savagery that provided the groundwork for colonial expansion.

Third, conflicting depictions of glaciers in oral histories and historical records have twenty-first-century consequences. They seem to typify or even model classic and continuing struggles over cultural meanings replicated in contemporary debates. The consequences of what Bruno Latour calls this "Great Divide"[27] differentiating nature from culture continue to cascade internationally through debates about environmentalism, biodiversity, global climate change, and indigenous rights. It is the contemporary anthropocentric implications of these historical understandings that especially interest me. Anthropologist Paul Nadasdy argues that a growing number of terms crucial to ongoing land claims negotiations, wildlife-management debates, and environmental conflicts in northwestern Canada – terms like "land," "hunting," "resources," and "property" that may initially seem straightforward – are actually fundamentally contested. All parties may agree on their importance, yet negotiating parties may mean very different things when they use the same terms. Participants predictably take their own meanings to represent "common sense," but the more powerful parties regularly build their meanings into legal agreements.[28] Distinct though glaciers may seem from such daily negotiations, observations about their behaviour and qualities resonate with current debates about local environmental knowledge. Glaciers' temporal and spatial strangeness for most of us may actually enable local ideas about them to better resist metropolitan interpretive schemes.

Fourth and finally, these themes all concern memory, stability, and change in human affairs. Anthropologists, geographers, and historians have demonstrated the enduring power of landscape features to act as points of reference for communicating tacit knowledge. Humans persist in transforming seemingly neutral spaces into places of significance. A growing body of research about social memory argues that landscapes are places of remembrance and that culturally significant landforms may provide a kind of archive where memories can be mentally stored.[29] In the Saint Elias Mountains, though, we can see also how changing landscape features, such as fluctuating glaciers, have provided imaginative grist for comprehending and interpreting *shifting* social circumstances. Orally narrated stories do indeed provide empirical observations about geophysical changes and their consequences. But they also demonstrate how glaciers provide substantive material for evaluating changes wrought by colonial histories.

It is hardly surprising that local knowledge in the notebooks of Euro-American scientists and travellers often differs from that passed on in Aboriginal traditions, yet the lines are not always so sharp. Ideas develop in relationship with others and emerge from encounters in particular places at specific times. The various approaches to knowledge brought to bear on these northwest borderlands contribute perspectives on Canadian history from a location that often remains a mere footnote in canonical accounts proceeding from east to west, with only occasional glances north.

North America's Towering Ridge

Encounters discussed in the following chapters centre on a location that has long been portrayed both as physically remote and internationally connected. Its axis is the most inaccessible region of Canada's northwest border with the United States, and it is also the spine of a recently designated UNESCO international World Heritage site. The precise location of this international border is not especially well known to residents of either Canada or the United States, and following its tortuous route can be disorienting (see Map 1). The southern perimeter crosses Dixon Entrance, skimming the southern edge of Prince of Wales Island. It reaches the mainland at the Portland Canal and swings northward to the head of this narrow fiord. From there, the border follows the mountain crest in a relatively smooth contour along the coast to a point near the head of Lynn Canal, where it veers precipitously southwest toward the pinnacle of Mount Fairweather, retrieving a triangle of British Columbia for Canada. It then clings to the jagged mountain ridge that separates the high inland plateau from the Gulf of Alaska for more than two hundred kilometres before turning sharply north at the 141st meridian on its unswerving course to the Arctic Ocean.

I focus here on a restricted portion of that border, the part anchored by the Saint Elias Mountains separating the coastal Gulf of Alaska from the high-country Yukon Plateau. In cross-section, this boundary lurches from peak to peak as it traverses some of North America's highest peaks. Crossing enormous icefields, it typifies immoderation. Delineated more conventionally on a two-dimensional map, it resembles a child's concentrated efforts

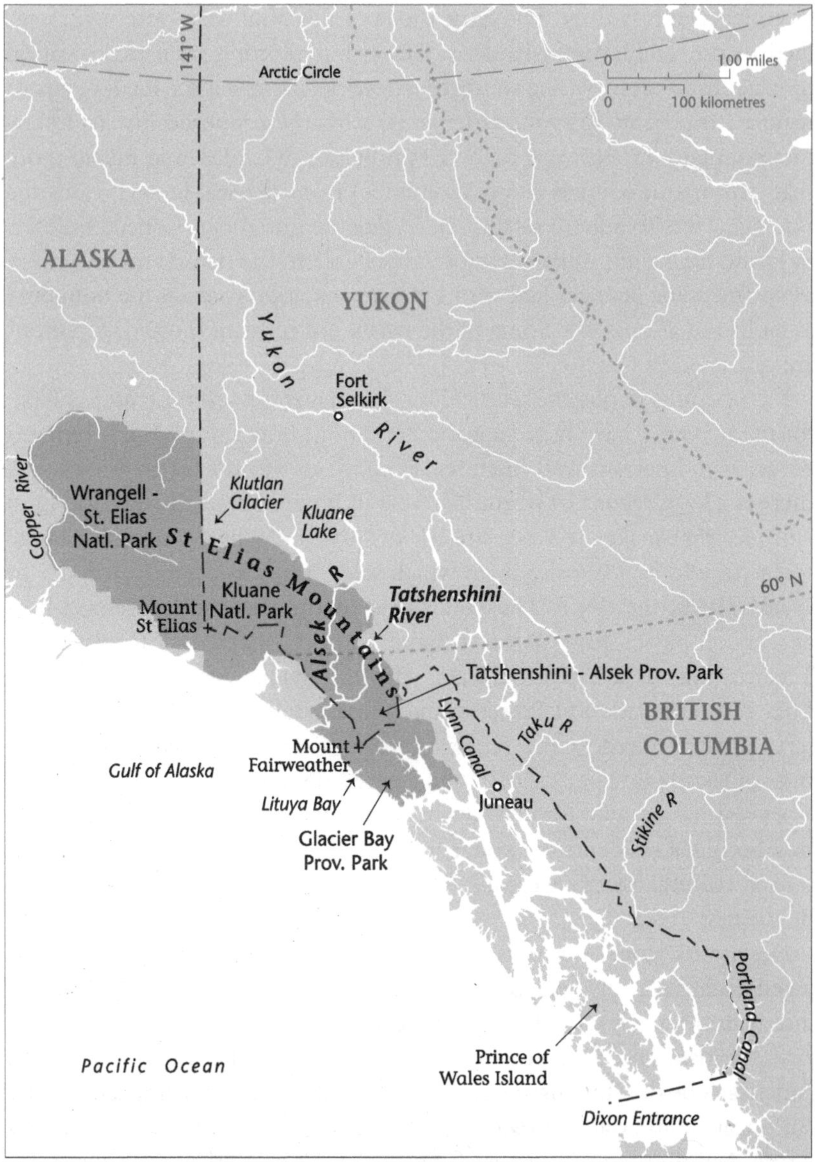

Map 1 The northwest Canada-United States border. A World Heritage site (shaded) now straddles this border, encompassing four parks. Over the years, park names have altered with status changes. In 2005 the parks on the Canadian side are named Kluane National Park and Reserve and Tatshenshini-Alsek Provincial Park; and those in the United States are officially known as Wrangell-Saint Elias National Park and Preserve and Glacier Bay National Park and Preserve.

to connect unruly dots. The dimensions of this boundary were first imagined in the 1825 Anglo-Russian Treaty, but plotting its actual location took almost a century. The southern extension was given the form of a panhandle (to protect Russian settlements) with the proposed line to follow the mountain divide, except where that height of land swung inland more than ten marine leagues (55.6 kilometres) from the sea; in such cases the boundary was to adhere to this ten-league measurement. Canada's efforts to locate the height of land as close as possible to the ocean and to capture a North Pacific port clashed with US determination to push the boundary as far inland as possible. Some of the twists and turns of those negotiations are discussed in Chapter 7.

I am curious about the Saint Elias Mountains for several reasons. First, for many years I have heard a good deal about how this region is remembered in indigenous oral histories. Second, as we will see in Chapter 1, there is a long record of scientific research here, at high altitude and high latitude, that makes it a key site for twenty-first century climate change research, and hence a site from which scientists now claim legitimacy to speak. Third, the World Heritage site spanning the Alaska/Canada border encompasses four parks: Kluane National Park and Reserve and Tatshenshini-Alsek Provincial Park on the Canadian side; Wrangell-Saint Elias National Park and Preserve and Glacier Bay National Park and Preserve in the United States. Here, unproblematized representations of nature as "aesthetic landscape," "endangered/pristine wilderness," or even as a giant jungle-gym for eco-tourists now compete with conceptions held by Aboriginal residents who once lived and hunted in these parks. If natural and cultural history were enmeshed here in the past, this also seems to be the case today.

Despite its iconic status as America's "wildest" wilderness[30] and its alleged distance from metropolitan affairs, this region was already a hub of international activity by the late eighteenth century, when Russians, Spaniards, British, and French competed for access to the interior of North America. The dominating mountain ridge made a dramatic impact on early European visitors and provided imaginative resources for accounts they wrote. Naval expeditions approaching the Gulf of Alaska consistently singled out (when they could see it through rain or above fog) the mountain that Vitus Bering named "Saint Elias" in 1741 after he reached land on 20 July, that saint's feast day,[31] and another that Captain James Cook optimistically called "Fair Weather" (now Fairweather) to commemorate a rare sunny day in 1778. When Jean-François de La Pérouse identified a coastal bay he named "Port des Français" (now Lituya Bay) between these two mountains a few years later, he hoped that he had discovered the Northwest Passage. Commercial traders, attracted initially by furs and subsequently by fish, later moved inland across the mountains once they had exhausted coastal ecologies. Close behind came natural scientists, mountain climbers, and boundary surveyors, many of whom also recorded their impressions.

For much longer, though, this region has been homeland to indigenous peoples – speakers of Eyak, Tlingit, and Athapaskan languages who inhabited the coastline, the valleys, and the high inland plateaus that fell away from these peaks. Tlingit traditions also single out the Saint Elias Mountains, though they attend to features different from those recorded by ships' captains. George Thornton Emmons, collector of artifacts for American museums, heard from Tlingit narrators in the early 1900s that Mounts Fairweather and Saint Elias had once been united in marriage but that following a domestic quarrel, Saint Elias journeyed west, taking the household slaves (now the range of mountains separating the two) and leaving behind their children, who became the lesser ranges extending inland for 150 kilometres.[32]

If mountain ridges provide one axis of this region, the Alsek River defines another. Rising in what is now the Yukon Territory, its two branches slice through the eastern edge of the Saint Elias Mountains, race past surging glaciers, and drop roughly six hundred metres before emptying into the Pacific Ocean. Oral histories indicate that by the time Europeans arrived, inland Athapaskan peoples were using glacier passages and the Alsek River to travel from the high interior plateau to the coast. Edward James Glave, whose story appears in Chapter 6, provided the first detailed written description of the Tatshenshini-Alsek's challenges in 1890, but he needed local people who knew that river well to transport him down its length in a dugout canoe.

Mountains ornamented with glaciers and crosscut by rivers have contributed to local stories that show how imaginative practices diverged. If eighteenth-century visitors saw these territories through lenses of the Sublime,[33] whether as innocent and empty or as vast and terrible, local residents' accounts begin with stories of pre-given places. Annie Ned, born on the inland side of the mountains during the early 1890s, describes how Raven, also known as Crow, originally configured the drainages from interior to coast at the beginning of time, tipping his wings to orient them in opposite directions; some lakes and rivers now flow north to the Yukon River and hence to the Bering Sea and others pour south to the Gulf of Alaska through the Alsek and Tatshenshini drainage. Distinctions between stories sometimes blur as they circle back on one another. Vitus Bering's

Saint Elias is the same as Elijah, the Old Testament prophet whose story is told in Kings I and II. Bering may not have appreciated how Elijah's story resonates with those already told in the Pacific Northwest when he named Mount Saint Elias. That prophet undertook long journeys, and on one occasion God commanded ravens to feed him twice daily, which they did; on another, Elijah travelled for forty days and forty nights clad in skin clothing and took refuge in mountain caves where he endured strong winds, an earthquake, and fire.[34] There is no Romantic wilderness in the Old Testament. Ancient symbolism surrounding Saint Elias thus evokes ravens, mountains, earthquakes, water, and the clothing of a hunter named Kwäday Dän Ts'ínchi (of whom we will hear more later) claimed by a glacier in these same mountains some three centuries before Bering's arrival.

Encounters and Consequences

Encounters take diverse forms that are explored in subsequent chapters. First, actual meetings between strangers were usually characterized by mutual caution and recounted on all sides in terms of difference – in appearance, language, habits, and imagined beliefs. Imbalances in knowledge drove such meetings. Inevitably, strangers relied on practical navigational assistance that only local residents could provide over mountains, across tundra, down rivers, and through glaciated landscapes.

Second, encounters between humans and a rapidly changing landscape were often perilous. Some glaciers were growing, while others were wasting and new land became habitable. Local knowledge that had been acquired painstakingly over generations in active engagement with the non-human environment was being put to surprising tests just as strangers began to arrive – Russians, Spaniards, British, and French on the Gulf of Alaska coast, and later British and Americans pressing on to the interior plateau. Encounters with glaciers seem to have influenced how all participants imagined one another and interpreted human relationships, particularly with strangers.

A third and different encounter concerns ongoing exchanges between stories and their subsequent readers and listeners, as they are taken up in different knowledge traditions.[35] Enlightenment scientists and Victorian travellers interpreted glaciers as alternately terrifying and inspirational. Their accounts represented places and people as exotic and frequently portrayed humans as extensions of landscape, as a background for their own story. Their writings, in turn, attracted other visitors – scientists, climbers, government agents, conservationists, and tourists. Such old accounts continue to have consequences as they encounter new audiences, including Aboriginal residents, academics, environmentalists, lawyers, judges, and land claims negotiators, to mention only a few, who inevitably rework them into new narratives of coherence. A growing literature about "first contact" narratives, for example, seems to resonate more often with European imaginings than with those of local indigenous traditions. As we will see in the stories that follow, the arrival of Europeans on the far northwest Pacific coast is frequently included only as a minor episode in Tlingit and Athapaskan oral histories.[36] Oral traditions continue to be told in local contexts where they also attract new audiences; for example, at the Yukon International Storytelling Festival.[37] In successive settings, then, old encounters continue to undergo reinterpretation as they are debated and re-evaluated in locations where they still have consequences. The stubborn particulars of voice persist through time.

Practices of Exploration, Matters of Locality

The book is organized in three overlapping parts. Part 1, *Matters of Locality,* examines contributions that Aboriginal oral traditions make to ongoing debates about local knowledge. Chapter 1 discusses memories from late stages of the Little Ice Age when both indigenous peoples and eighteenth-century Europeans were becoming familiar with newly habitable territories. I rely on both written and oral accounts, trying to privilege neither but rather to see how both kinds of accounts illuminate past worlds and shed light on present interpretations. The rich ethnographic record of oral traditions from coastal regions extends back more than a century and provides historical depth for narratives still told. Some of the accounts we will hear in this chapter reappear later from quite different perspectives, rather like a prism viewed from various angles. Chapter 2 moves inland. It provides a framework for listening to oral traditions told by three Yukon elders, all women, setting their concerns within a modernity that shaped their twentieth-century lives. Chapter 3 presents glacier narratives told by Kitty Smith, Annie Ned, and Angela Sidney in their own words and with brief references to the contexts in which they were recorded.

Part 2, *Practices of Exploration,* centres on stories about glaciers that reverberate through the literature of exploration and science. In the late eighteenth century and again at the end of the nineteenth, strangers made brief appearances in northwestern North America, but they left significant traces. I follow those traces – written records left behind, memories transmitted and transformed in oral tradition, social legacies we still encounter – and examine what they reveal collectively about practices of exploration and matters of locality. Three travellers, each an exemplar of a kind, were in some way changed by the experience of meeting Aboriginal residents here. Chapter 4 examines the encounter between eighteenth-century French expedition leader Jean-François de La Pérouse and local Tlingit people he met at Lituya Bay in 1786. Chapter 5 considers encounters between American environmentalist and moral crusader John Muir and the Tlingit guides who influenced his views in 1879 and again in 1880. Chapter 6 follows two trips that British writer and traveller Edward Glave made to what is now the southwest Yukon in 1890 and again in 1891, shortly before he returned to Africa where his faith in "civilization" was ultimately shattered in the Belgian Congo.

Part 3, *Scientific Research in Sentient Places*, takes as its theme the imposition of boundaries and the new stories of nationhood they enforce. Intrusion of emerging nation states into regions already populated inevitably involved the displacement of indigenous populations, as elsewhere. Those boundaries and their consequences are part of the modern history of Aboriginal peoples in northwestern North America. Chapter 7 looks at the mapping and making of the international boundary, including hints of human experience that emerge in surveyors' accounts. Chapter 8 concludes with an overview of debates, now reinvigorated both by land claims negotiations and by evidence of human history emerging from melting glaciers. Those debates continue to echo themes of encounter, knowledge, unequal power, and issues now surrounding scientific research in sentient places.

The earliest historical encounters in northwestern North America occurred at a time when local knowledge in Europe was in ferment. Travellers were motivated by new and powerful concepts of science, religion, and economics that provided modernity's motor. They often took for granted the universal applicability of these concepts as organizing principles and were eager to put them to work, repeatedly advocating agriculture and trade as appropriate models for indigenous economies. Visitors, though, were encountering inhabited places where knowledge traditions had their own long histories that paid close attention to tangible reference points – people, places, and landscape features. Principles governing indigenous social life and economic exchange centred on reciprocity: among humans, with non-human animals, and with a responsive landscape. Observant behaviour was crucial to well-being, and disastrous consequences might follow thoughtless lapses or wilful disregard. Initially, visitors were quick to grasp the importance of the local empirical expertise needed to traverse unfamiliar territories.[38] But opportunities for transferring more foundational knowledge rapidly narrowed as the alleged universality of one set of concepts began to squeeze out alternatives that could then be disparaged as "belief" or "superstition."

I conclude this introduction with a vignette that illustrates shifting ideas about local knowledge in this region. When strangers began crossing the mountains to the Yukon interior in the late nineteenth century, they were eager to tell stories about travels on ice. One brief account captures the contrast. Frederick Schwatka, a veteran of the United States Army who took up "exploration," passed through this region in the summer of 1891. Schwatka's accounts seem to typify a kind of exploration that geographer Felix Driver, borrowing from Joseph Conrad, has called "Geography Militant," characterized by aggressive naming practices, crude census taking, detailed mapping, and extravagant military metaphor.[39] This was not Schwatka's first trip to the Yukon River: in 1883, he had led down the Yukon River a United States-sponsored expedition framed as a military reconnaissance in search of "hostile Indians," of whom he found none.[40] His legacy today largely consists of many place names, those intangible wormcasts of exploration, that he left along the Yukon River.

By 1891, Schwatka was back, this time with a young geologist named Willard Hayes who was later to assume the position of chief geologist with the US Geological Survey.[41] They travelled inland from Juneau up the Taku River, through the southern lakes to the Yukon River, and down that river to Fort Selkirk, then overland toward the Copper River (see Map 1). With difficulty, they found local guides who would agree to take them through glacier country, and as they prepared to cross the Klutlan Glacier, Schwatka reported that their guides insisted "we must not fry grease in our pans ... or the ice of the glaciers will tumble in as we cross and kill us all." He noted somewhat dismissively that, "we easily catered to this and told them we would forbear oleaginous condiments rather than have a ton of ice tumble upon us." During a glacier crossing that he describes as "simply frightful," he noted that the guides "besought us to make no noise while on the ice or the crevasses would open wider and swallow us up ... They firmly resented even our whispering, so fearful were they of the consequences." His conclusion conveys both his relief after their safe crossing and a sense of how ideas were already being differentiated hierarchically. "Before crossing, they all 'made medicine' and no doubt it saved many valuable lives. Their fear of glacial ice is too pronounced and manifest to be based on any general physical reasons, and must be accounted for wholly by superstition."[42]

Here, then, we have a pivotal moment in the history of encounters between residents and strangers. From the perspective of indigenous residents steeped in familiar places, glaciers provide scaffolding both for close empirical observation and interpretation of the dangers of hubris in a complex and unpredictable world. From the vantage point of the transient explorer immersed in a *fin de siècle* myth of modernity that segregated nature from culture, matters of locality could be casually dismissed as "superstition."[43] My intention here is not to single out Schwatka, whose hubris would undoubtedly have been praised as "pluck" by his nineteenth-century colleagues. More telling is the persistence of such ideas. Notably, Schwatka's 1891 journals were republished in 1996, and the contemporary editor adds a footnote at this point indicating that Schwatka's comments about "superstition" can be taken as straightforward common sense: "The origin of the Pelly River Natives' unreasonable or superstitious fear of glacier ice and the connection with frying with grease is not known."[44] It is clear from this note that, even a century after Schwatka wrote his journal, some kinds of local knowledge are still dismissed as "superstition."

What is remarkable is how speedily such new stories take root, displace local knowledge, and gain authority as official "common sense." Addressing this issue, anthropologist Michael Taussig has observed that social sciences pay considerable attention to ideology and rather less to the fact that people delineate their understandings in stories, or story-like creations, such as gossip and small talk – rarely in full-blown ideologies.[45] Anthropologists working in Africa, the Americas, and the South Pacific have likewise observed that colonial practices are mediated largely by convincing narratives.[46] Such encounters are full of complexity and contradiction on all sides. Inevitably they involve exchanges – of substance and of symbols, whether objects or ideas. Characteristically, exchanges involve struggles over conflicting meanings that are often sharpest on the frontiers of empire where matters of locality collide with global practices. North America's far northwest, then, contributes to a history of local knowledge from liminal locations once at the edges of colonial empire.

Overlapping stories emerging from early colonial encounters provide a trap door to a history of local knowledge, with tunnels leading in various directions. In subsequent chapters, I follow persistent historical traces of knowledge practices as they connect and endure in stories where glaciers have a role.

PART 1

Matters of Locality

1

Memories of the Little Ice Age

Evidence that global climate change will be amplified at arctic and subarctic latitudes now seems overwhelming. Scientists may argue about the magnitude of globally averaged temperature changes, the rates at which change may occur, or the role of humans in the process, but they agree that, as in the past, extreme values will be experienced in arctic regions during the twenty-first century.[1]

The potential for scientific modelling of past climates has increased enormously during the last decade, but so has our understanding about the richness of oral traditions from circumpolar northern regions. Increasingly, cross-disciplinary research on human dimensions of climate change is extending beyond debates among scientists to include local perspectives on the making, meaning, and evaluation of scientific knowledge.[2] One emerging nexus of cultural anthropology, environmental earth sciences, and Athapaskan and Tlingit oral traditions especially interests me because of conversations I have had over the years with elders from the Yukon and Alaska whose immediate ancestors had direct experience with climate variability during late stages of the Little Ice Age. Memories of eighteenth-century clan migrations involving glacier travel remain vivid in oral traditions from northwestern North America.

This chapter provides an overview of the region and its glacial history, background for the chapters that follow. My sources include expedition narratives written by eighteenth- and nineteenth-century North Atlantic travellers as well as oral traditions from northwestern North America. They provide both contrasting views of place and a point of reference for appreciating how diverging ways of organizing knowledge affected colonial encounters. What do indigenous residents living near North America's highest mountains have to say about human ecology in this region, and how do their concerns overlap with or differ from those of scientists? I begin with a discussion of intersecting narratives, some conventionally labelled "myth" and others framed as science. Geological stratigraphy is well documented in the Saint Elias Icefields, but layered memories have also accumulated through centuries of oral tradition. Both perspectives provide clues about changing habitat along the Gulf of Alaska as melting glaciers released new lands during late stages of the Little Ice Age. Oral traditions about these "lands reborn"[3] form the core of this chapter. As ice melted, Athapaskan and Tlingit migrants arrived from three directions: southward from Copper River in central Alaska, northward from the archipelago (now southeast Alaska), and coastward across glacier passes and down rivers from the interior. I conclude the chapter with some reflections about how environmental knowledge becomes authorized in different contexts, who gets to control that knowledge, and how this changes over time.

Glaciers that flow from mountain ranges separating the Gulf of Alaska from the inland Yukon Plateau have been in the same place for thousands of years and have survived successive ice ages. The ice is continuously replaced by precipitation. Glaciologists now believe that at very high altitudes, where moisture and flow are minimal, ice cores will provide a record from which thousands of years of climate history may be "read" – a metaphor harkening back to Plato's concept and St. Augustine's elaboration of the "Book of Nature."[4] A number of these glaciers also surge periodically. Of some four thousand glaciers in northwestern North America, an unusually high concentration – approximately two hundred – have this characteristic. They may remain dormant for decades and then suddenly begin to advance, often quickly and for distances of several kilometres. Visually, glaciers conventionally suggest antiquity and permanence, so the term "surging glacier" initially sounds like an oxymoron. For scientists, though, understanding the physics of surging glaciers is one of the many puzzles of modern geophysics. Surging glaciers are also a prominent feature in Antarctica and Greenland, but scale and accessibility make it easier to study their behaviour in the Saint Elias ranges.

The very act of studying glaciers exposes differing approaches to knowledge. Scientists conceptualize climate change as a global process, not limited to particular field sites where they do their research. They are particularly interested in mountainous subarctic regions where combinations of low sun angle, strong seasonal differences in radiation, extreme ecological changes with altitude, and extensive snow and ice cover focus and exaggerate climate impacts.[5] They recognize that social and natural factors are profoundly linked, but they define their own role as disentangling what they call "natural forcing mechanisms" from anthropogenic factors driving climate change.[6]

Athapaskan and Tlingit oral traditions attribute to glaciers characteristics rather different from those discovered through science. Glaciers have long provided travel routes that enabled human connections between coast and interior, and they are characterized by sentience. They listen, pay attention, and respond to human behaviour – especially to indiscretion. One serious prohibition against "cooking with grease" near glaciers on the inland side of the icefields is woven into Southern Tutchone narratives as an example of hubris that courts disaster. The historical and cultural crevasses separating indigenous oral traditions from narratives of geophysical science seem so deep that they rarely intersect. Yet, glaciers figure prominently in both conventions, and approaches sometimes collide unexpectedly in contemporary discussions about climate change.

If climate change is indeed global, its consequences are profoundly local. Projections about global warming raise critical concerns for residents of Yukon communities currently implementing economic and political planning processes mandated by land claims and self-governance agreements. In contemporary debates about climate, the universalizing discourse of science plays a significant role. However, resident peoples are aware that science is used both to attack and to defend local participation in management. They know that local knowledge is both advocated and opposed as a basis for making decisions. Reflections by indigenous northerners on the nature of science and scientists are recurring issues throughout the circumpolar North.[7]

Gulf of Alaska: Layered Perspectives

Some of the highest mountains in North America, undergirding the northern hemisphere's most extensive glaciation outside Greenland, overlook the Gulf of Alaska and extend inland for 150 kilometres before levelling off as the Yukon Plateau (see Map 2). Mount Saint Elias towers almost fifty-five hundred metres above the coast, some eight hundred metres higher than the massive Mount Fairweather, two hundred and fifty kilometres to the southeast.[8] Each plays a significant role in both Tlingit oral traditions and European exploration narratives. The Tlingit Waas'eita Shaa or Yaas'eita Shaa (mountain at the head of Icy Bay),[9] which Bering named Mount Saint Elias, and Tsalx̱aan, Cook's Mount Fair Weather, served as compasses for Tlingit mariners, providing both navigational orientation and guides to weather. European navigators working from ships in the late 1700s were inclined to see mountains walling off the Gulf of Alaska as impediments to inland travel, and they clung to the shore as their axis. From Tlingit and Athapaskan perspectives, mountains provided passages

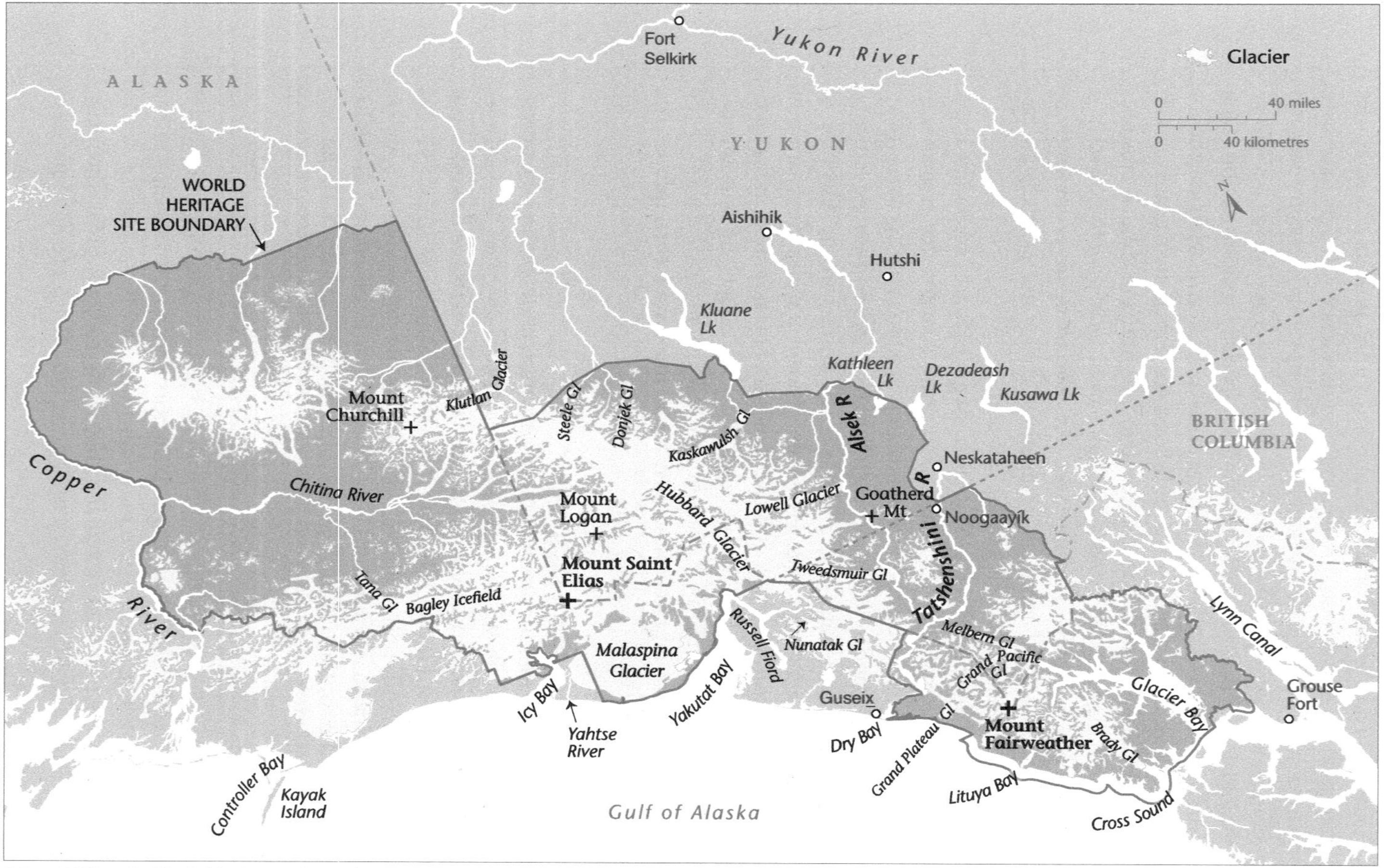

Map 2 The Gulf of Alaska and southwest Yukon, indicating the approximate extent of present glaciers in the Saint Elias Mountains and the boundaries of the World Heritage site. Geographical features mentioned in Chapter 1 are also shown.

as well as boundaries, scaffolding for travel routes connecting peoples who traded between coast and interior.

Those two towering and measurable summits offered attractive anchors when an international boundary was first proposed in 1825. Almost a century later, they provided benchmarks for surveyors who doggedly partitioned this narrow coastal strip of the United States from Canada. Another century on, the same two mountains became anchors for the world's largest UNESCO-designated World Heritage site. Mount Saint Elias serves as the linchpin for the two parks originally accorded this status in 1979 – Kluane National Park and Reserve (Yukon Territory) and Wrangell-Saint Elias National Park and Preserve (Alaska) – just as Mount Fairweather secures both Glacier Bay National Park and Preserve (Alaska) and Tatshenshini-Alsek Provincial Park (British Columbia) added in 1992 and 1994 respectively. The foreshore between Yakutat Bay and Dry Bay is notably exempted from Glacier Bay National Park and from the World Heritage site because of its continuous human occupation since glacial recession released habitable lands.

Ethnographic, scientific, and historical literature from northwestern North America provides an intriguing narrative of how exploration and science proceeded shoulder to shoulder and how canonical historical and scientific knowledge emerged here over two centuries. A dominant narrative of northern science has long portrayed the Arctic and Subarctic as a kind of superlaboratory where experimental moments might occur. Yet environmental sciences – geophysics, geography, geology, biology, and botany – are more accurately characterized as field sciences than as closed, controlled laboratory sciences. Like the idea of the laboratory, the notion of the field, inhabited by articulate, politically situated resident peoples, has always been complicated.[10]

Both geophysical scientists and indigenous residents speak figuratively of memory and sedimentation, but they express these concepts differently. The storyline of geology is framed by narrative every bit as much as oral tradition, and both are engaged in discovering a reality that includes more than the merely human.[11] Scientists are confident that ice cores from near the summit of Mount Logan, Canada's highest mountain, reveal the shadow of the Industrial Revolution and retain a memory of climate that may soon allow them to interpret Holocene history.[12] They anticipate that, in combination with tree-ring records (dendrochronology) and the sedimentary record in lakes and glacial deposits, ice cores will tell a detailed story about the early Holocene cooling event some 8,200 years ago. Cores also show traces of the two volcanic eruptions at Mount Churchill on the upper White

River near the present Canada-Alaska border – one in approximately AD 100 and a second about AD 800. Ash from these events blanketed the central Yukon and is still visible along river-cut banks. Ice cores should also yield information about melting, trace metals, and biological organisms.

Memories of the Little Ice Age also play a significant role in indigenous oral traditions, and – like geophysical processes – they are also sedimented on the land. Raven, the Trickster and world-maker, left evidence of his travels in geographical features he transformed. He once strategically disappeared down the blowhole of a whale and spent the winter feasting comfortably on the finest blubber, eventually piloting his dying host ashore to the mouth of the Alsek River, where it remains an island resembling a beached whale. At Mount Fairweather, Tsalxaan, Raven slashed one side of that mountain where Echo offended him by mimicking him.[13] Further north at Controller Bay, where Bering landed in 1741, Cook in 1778, and a Spanish expedition in 1779, Raven harpooned a whale and transformed it into an island now known as Kayak Island. A nearby island is remembered as "Raven's kayak," and the long spit just to the northeast is "Raven's harpoon line."[14] In his sculpting of landscape features, Raven brings to mind the journeys of another famous Pacific traveller, Pele, who made her fitful way among the Hawaiian islands with her digging-stick, opening volcanic craters wherever she struck the earth. A temperamental being, she is easily goaded into sending floods of lava that permanently mark her trail across that archipelago but can sometimes be placated by offers of food and tobacco.[15]

Both oral accounts and scientific evidence suggest that as land and ice stabilized in the North Pacific following Wisconsinan glacial recessions, salmon began moving inland up the Alsek-Tatshenshini river system, while glacial barriers, forming and breaking on the Alsek, prevented animals from moving downriver to the coast until much later.[16] Humans began moving in both directions, as did their stories. The Saint Elias ranges and their icefields undoubtedly posed serious barriers to human and animal movements, but glaciers flowing from them seem also to have connected people by providing efficient travel routes. Early geologists referred to these glaciers as "ice flooded valleys"[17] and coined the term "through glaciers," referring to glacial plateaus leading inland.[18] Anthropologist Frederica de Laguna described the Alsek River as a "highway" to the interior, accessible from Yakutat Bay via the Nunatak Glacier, from Glacier Bay via Melbern and Grand Pacific glaciers, and from Lituya Bay by a route across the Grand Plateau Glacier.[19] Geologist Israel Russell observed in 1892 that this was a "land of nunataks,"[20] and indeed those knobs of bedrock poking through the icefields reportedly provided navigational guides for Aboriginal travellers, as we will hear shortly. Well before the European fur trade was established, there was brisk trade between the coast and interior in such marine products as fish oil and seaweed, exchanged for native copper and tanned hides.[21]

Subsequent international boundaries, imbricated by parks, preserves, sanctuaries, and national forests, have proven more divisive to travel, sociability, and exchange than mountains and glaciers ever were.[22] Tlingit people living on the Gulf foreshore became separated from interior Southern Tutchone Athapaskan speakers by federal, state, territorial, and provincial boundaries, and the bureaucracies charged with administering lands that straddled multiple jurisdictions. "Now no one goes up [the Alsek]," a Tlingit man, Jack Ellis, told Goldschmidt and Haas in 1946. "There are good hunting grounds, but they are on the Canadian side of the line."[23] Inland, Southern Tutchone were less able to maintain their everyday connections with coastal territories after they were prohibited from hunting in the newly designated Kluane Game Sanctuary in 1942, a topic we will return to in Chapter 8. It remains to be seen how the settlement of Yukon land claims at the end of the twentieth century, three decades after the Alaska Native Claims and Settlement Act, may enable coastal and interior people to re-establish new and modern economic agreements.

Little Ice Age Habitat in the Gulf of Alaska

Glacial activity has severely eroded the archaeological record in the Gulf of Alaska, but archaeologists agree that human habitation was possible at least nine thousand years ago.[24] Subsequent pulsations have erased any record of early human history – an advance five thousand years ago, then a recession two thousand years later, followed by another advance. One thousand years ago, a combined Malaspina and Hubbard Glacier, joined by lesser glaciers, descended slowly and continuously from Mount Saint Elias, filling Icy Bay and Yakutat Bay. Swelling into tidewater beyond present-day mouths of these bays, a thousand-metre-thick continuous wall of ice extended northwest of Yakutat Bay for more than one hundred kilometres. Closer to historical times, forests took root six hundred years ago when ice again wasted behind present-day limits. We know this because carbon-dated wood shards preserved in moraines indicate that mature forests at Yakutat Bay were crushed in the sixteenth-century Little Ice Age advance.[25] South of Dry Bay, similar patterns occurred beneath Mount Fairweather: ice stood at the mouth of Lituya Bay a thousand years ago, when the Grand Plateau Glacier spilled into the Pacific (see Map 2).[26]

During the Little Ice Age, the ice-free foreshore between Yakutat Bay and Dry Bay was surrounded on three sides by glaciers, much as it is now encased by national parks and a World Heritage site. The Malaspina Glacier at the north end and the combined Grand Pacific and Grand Plateau glaciers further south must have settled like giant bookends enclosing this slim sixty-kilometre beach backed by the Hubbard, Tweedsmuir, and Melbern glaciers. But these bookends were far from stable during the seventeenth and eighteenth centuries and posed alarming risks for humans as we can see in just two examples, one from each end of this shoreline.

At the northern bookend, Malaspina Glacier, a series of observations over a two-hundred-year period trace massive glacial advance and retreat at Icy Bay. This bay, at the edge of the glacier and just northwest of Yakutat, is now six miles deep and five miles wide and is still considered a fine sealing camp by Yakutat hunters.[27] It has undergone dramatic changes since 1794, when Archibald Menzies, ship's surgeon and naturalist with George Vancouver's expedition, observed that it was "choaked with massy ice and frozen snow" flowing from the Malaspina Glacier.[28] By the time Edward Belcher arrived in 1837, the Malaspina had apparently advanced much further: he encountered a thirty-foot ice cliff and no evidence of the trees Vancouver had reported forty-three years earlier.[29] When British alpinist Harold Topham visited Icy Bay in 1888, he learned from local Tlingits that an ice dam had recently blocked the nearby Yahtse River, and that when it broke, massive chunks of ice carried downriver destroyed a village formerly at the bay's mouth.[30] Geologists Tarr and Martin later estimated that this flood must have occurred during the mid-nineteenth century and certainly before 1886, when prospective mountain climbers Heywood Seton-Karr, William Libbey, and Frederick Schwatka encountered a twenty-five-mile-wide glacier filling Icy Bay.[31] Sixty years after this, Frederica de Laguna heard an account of this outburst flood at Yahtse River attributed to flamboyant behaviour by some young Tlingit men who taunted the glacier, inciting it to surge. She also heard that the Malaspina Glacier began to melt rapidly in 1904, following the embalmment of a Tsimshian sea-otter hunter whose internal organs were left behind at Icy Bay so that his preserved body could be transported home.[32] By the time de Laguna first arrived in the 1940s, Icy Bay had grown to its present dimensions.

At the south end of this "bookended" beach, similar transformations were occurring. Lituya Bay was fully open by 1786 when La Pérouse arrived (his experiences there are discussed in Chapter 4). Initially hopeful that he had discovered the Northwest Passage to Hudson Bay, La Pérouse rapidly revised his expectations when he encountered glaciers sliding down from Mount Fairweather at the head of Lituya Bay, only eleven kilometres from its mouth. By the time Otto Klotz visited Lituya Bay with the Alaska Boundary Commission in 1894, glaciers had again advanced, altering the bay's contours from those La Pérouse mapped so carefully. Klotz further noted that a "deserted Indian village" George Vancouver had identified a century earlier in 1794, south of Lituya Bay and near what is now Brady Glacier, was by 1894 covered by three hundred metres of ice.[33] In 1904, ethnographer John Swanton recorded a narrative account, discussed later in this chapter, that may describe this same destructive event.[34]

During the warming that accompanied late stages of the Little Ice Age in the eighteenth century, wasting glaciers deposited debris that extended the ice-free foreshore between Yakutat Bay and Dry Bay, providing an especially attractive habitat for new populations. Geologist Israel Russell visited Icy Bay in 1893 and described the emerging land as "a natural garden" and as "one great strawberry meadow."[35] In 1905, Ralph Tarr marvelled at how land was actually growing seaward: offshore bars developed, creating lagoons behind them that subsequently filled with sand. "The coastline," Tarr wrote enthusiastically, "is characterized by features of youth," and "is rapidly growing outward, not as a fan does, by steady growth, but by successive steps or leaps, as offshore bars develop."[36]

The earliest known inhabitants on these shores were Eyak speakers, never a large nation, who were settled at Yakutat Bay when others arrived. Subsequent immigrants adopted the place name Yakutat from the Eyak word Ya.gada.at (a lagoon is forming), referring to open water that appeared as glaciers melted.[37] Eyak residents probably came originally from the interior, where they once shared a language with ancestors of Athapaskans, but Eyak prehistory and their long linguistic isolation, possibly for thousands of years, remains a mystery. Linguist Michael Krauss suggests that they may have been separated from Athapaskan speakers by glaciers during earlier glacier advances.[38] Sometime during the eighteenth century, Eyak were joined by newcomers: Athapaskans from both the Alsek and Copper rivers, Tlingit clans moving north from Prince of Wales Island,[39] and ultimately, in the 1780s and 1790s, by British, French, Russians, and Spaniards.

To summarize, in late-eighteenth-century Gulf of Alaska, tentacles of European exploration were matched by a different kind of international expansion. Eyak, Tlingit, and Athapaskan nations converged on the narrow coastal lands that were becoming accessible as glaciers receded during late stages of the Little Ice Age. Scientific exploration began on the Alaskan coast a full century earlier than in the Yukon interior, but at the time of the earliest voyages by Cook (1778), La Pérouse (1786), and Vancouver (1794), interior peoples were apparently crossing over glaciers much larger than those we see today. Simultaneously, Tlingit were pressing north from the Alaska archipelago by sea. Frederica de Laguna has described this foreshore extending from Yakutat Bay to Dry Bay as the only area extensive enough to support more than a sparse population, and as being, "with the possible exception of Greenland ... the most beautiful country in the world."[40]

The remainder of this chapter focuses on oral histories that trace three broad travel corridors across glaciers leading to this ice-free coast. One set of accounts documents migration south and east from Copper River (Alaska) to Icy Bay, then on to Yakutat Bay. A second traces travels of a Tlingit ancestor who journeyed north and west from Cross Sound to the Alsek River, where he "discovered" Athapaskans and incorporated them into coastal trade networks. A third group of narratives follows movements up and down the Alsek River through the mountains to the interior during a time when glaciers periodically blocked that river. The three travel routes can be followed, at least roughly, on Map 2.

These stories are about many things: historiography, experiential science, social history, and complex verbal traditions. They are not specifically "about" glaciers. Yet glaciers figure significantly in histories, which include close empirical observations about land and about humans inhabiting a rich but uncertain social and spiritual world that was changing dramatically in the late eighteenth century, just before the arrival of Europeans.

Stories recorded in different times and circumstances have their own social histories. I draw on oral accounts recorded by ethnographer John Swanton, a student of Franz Boas, at Sitka and Wrangell in 1904; by Walter Goldschmidt and Theodore Haas at Yakutat in 1946; and by Frederica de Laguna in Yakutat in 1949, 1952, and 1954. Other sources include ongoing work by Nora and Richard Dauenhauer in southeastern Alaska,[41] and Thomas Thornton's continuing work on the linguistic and social context of place naming.[42] In the Yukon interior, Catharine McClellan began recording accounts of travel between coast and interior in the late 1940s.[43] Yukon elders I worked with in the Yukon during the 1970s and 1980s – Kitty Smith, Annie Ned, and Angela Sidney – included stories about strong coastal connections in life histories they told.[44] I also draw on work by Gertie Tom with John Ritter at the Yukon Native Language Centre[45] and by Patrick Moore in collaboration with the Kaska Tribal Council during the 1990s.[46]

The significance of kinship is implicit in clan narratives. Tlingit and their Athapaskan neighbours all claim membership in one of two matrilineal exogamous moieties (translated as Raven and Eagle on the coast, and as Crow and Wolf in the interior) with marriages between opposite-moiety clans a foundational principle.[47] On the coast, primary units of national history and property ownership have long been matrilineal clans whose migration narratives are equivalent to national histories. Clan membership regulated access to resources as well as transmission of property, including historical narratives and associated rights to tell them. Oral traditions from this region also demonstrate the social nature of all relations between humans and non-humans, including animals and such landscape features as glaciers.[48] These narratives capture some of the accumulating, vanishing, and changing meanings associated with glaciers from the distant time of ice ages to the present era of parks – meanings that continue to be enmeshed in social worlds.

Moving South: From Copper River to Icy Bay and Yakutat Bay

In 1904 at Sitka, John Swanton recorded an account of an eighteenth-century migration from the upper Copper River to Yakutat.[49] K̲'áadasteen, the man who narrated this account to Swanton, descended from these travellers and had grown up at Yakutat. He spoke in the Tlingit language while another Tlingit man, Don Cameron, assisted Swanton with translation. Thirty-five years later, in 1939, John Harrington recorded accounts of the same journey with other clan members living at Yakutat, and a decade after that, in 1949 and in 1952, Frederica de Laguna worked with Harrington's notes and recorded what women as well as men living in Yakutat still remembered hearing about this migration. Narrators named below, all members of the Kwáashk'i K̲wáan clan, are in essential agreement about why clan members left their original inland home near the junction of the Chitina and Copper rivers and the various routes by which they reached first Icy Bay, then Yakutat Bay. They later intermarried with Eyak speakers already living at Yakutat Bay, and eventually adopted Tlingit language and customs.[50] Here, I am especially interested in how references to glacier travel enter the narratives.

K̲'áadasteen's account begins far inland with the death of a Raven moiety chief on the Copper River and internal dissent about disposition of his property, specifically a highly prized moose-horn dish. As conflict escalated, unsuccessful claimants chose to leave and headed south. They were speakers of Ahtna, an Athapaskan language spoken inland, and they had no previous experience of coastal regions. Pausing at the foot of Mount Saint Elias to select a route, they came upon a large population of ground squirrels and clubbed some. As a direct consequence of this act, fog rolled in, and some of their members became separated from the main group. The remaining men and women were unable to wait because of deteriorating weather and their own precarious situation, so they pressed on. They could see no easy route over the mountain but identified a glacier leading to the north side and ascended it. Fully expecting to perish, they dressed in their finest marten- and weasel-skin clothes, so that they would be properly attired if they did not survive, and set out to make what may have been one of the earliest partial ascents of Mount Saint Elias. Gaining altitude, they were astounded to look down and see an ocean for the first time, and they held a quick caucus to discuss what this might mean. "The Athapascans did not know about the sea, and they called one another together," K'áadasteen explained. Descending to the terminus of another glacier, they crossed the Yahtse River boiling out from underneath and followed this river to its mouth, near Icy Bay. Their first act was to claim Mount Saint Elias as their clan's crest, because that mountain had successfully guided them across the ice from Copper River, and they built a clan house to commemorate their successful arrival.[51] Their route from the Chitina River across the Tana Glacier and Bagley Icefield to the Gulf coast was an established pre-contact Ahtna trade route.[52]

In 1949, Frederica de Laguna heard an account of this same journey from Harry Bremner (b. 1893). He described how his ancestors had navigated across Saint Elias mountain, using nunataks and mountain peaks for orientation: "Our people kept walking over the glacier. There was only ice, no bushes, nothing ... They had nothing to eat. There was starvation out on the glacier. It was a long way for us to walk." At one point, they thought they spotted a wolverine in the distance and walked toward it, then recognized that it was only a nunatak, "a little island, a mountain with no trees on it, just a little hill." Desperately hungry, they made a small fire and when a wolverine wandered into their camp they fended off starvation by eating it. In the distance, they saw a rabbit and walked toward it for two days before they realized that it was actually Mount Saint Elias – Yaas'eita Shaa. "It was a compass for the people so they wouldn't get lost ... The mountain was so steep that they had to walk in zigzags up the snow ... Then they finally found that Icy Bay, Yahtse. The glacier was all over the bay, way out ... They built their camp on the west side at a place they named 'place of the yellow cedar bark.'"[53]

Songs, such as the Marching and Resting and Dancing songs that Copper River people composed during their migration toward the coast, play an important role in clan histories.[54] K'áadasteen spoke to Swanton in 1909 about the mourning songs his ancestors sang to commemorate companions lost in fog on this journey. Forty years later, in 1949, Sarah Williams sang the same songs for Frederica de Laguna, and she contrasted these dirges with the joyful songs clan members composed when they actually discovered Icy Bay: "They danced down from that mountain. They were happy when they were coming on this side. Lots of things happen[ed] there and there are songs [about those events]."[55]

Maggie Harry (b. 1892) told Harrington in 1939 and de Laguna in 1949 about an alternative sea route to Icy Bay. Her ancestor, one of the disinherited brothers, had travelled downriver to the mouth of the Copper River with his family and approached Icy Bay by sea. Just as overland migrants mistook Mount Saint Elias for a rabbit, the ocean travellers saw its snowy, white, triangular peak "looking like a seagull on the water" and used it to guide them to Yakutat. "Our tribe thought they saw a seagull far off when they first saw Mount Saint Elias. Every day it was getting higher."[56]

But Icy Bay was only a first step on their route southward, because they soon recognized that the Malaspina Glacier was fast advancing on that bay. K̲'áadasteen explained that one man began an experiment with his nephews, "living away from town in order to make the frame of a skin boat ... He told [his nephews] to travel along the shore in the canoe he had made, to search for people," and indeed they reached Yakutat Bay. Just as their predecessors had aroused bad weather by clubbing squirrels, these young men were the architects of their own difficulty. When they made the fatal mistake of laughing at eulachon they were cooking, they excited fierce south winds that drowned one and left the others stranded for weeks.[57] From this trip, though, they learned that prior residents already claimed Yakutat Bay. Other Athapaskans from the mouth of the Alsek had already taken up residence here and had intermarried with Eyak, becoming the founding clans Kosk!e'dî and L!uq!oe'dî, of Raven and Eagle moieties respectively.[58]

Recognizing the attractions of Yakutat Bay, where glaciers were receding as fast as they were advancing at Icy Bay, the enterprising uncle dispatched his nephews back to their original homeland near the Copper and Chitina rivers to retrieve a valuable copper plate buried there. The young men completed their return trip over the glaciers in record time, carrying a hammered copper plate that was reportedly worth ten slaves. They travelled directly to Yakutat Bay, where they emerged from behind the mountain onto a glacier with gravel-covered steps leading down to the ocean. At each platform, they composed a song and a ceremonial dance as they worked their way down to the beach. At Yakutat, a lagoon had already formed behind melting ice, reportedly because someone had killed a dog and thrown it into a glacier crevasse. "And that's why the glacier receded so far and left all the bay there. That's why they call it 'Yakutat' ... That's what it means – yakwdat means 'lagoon' in [Eyak] language up there," Katy Dixon Isaac told de Laguna in 1952.[59] The newcomers successfully used their copper to purchase rights that allowed them to share Yakutat Bay.

In K̲'áadasteen's version of this clan narrative, stories of travel shift back and forth between ocean and glacier, and clan ancestors prosper at Yakutat largely because they have acquired an array of skills – those crucial at sea as well as those needed to navigate glaciers on shore. One brother discovered a cottonwood tree at the head of a stream that reportedly provided useful weather predictions for glacier crossings. A prospective traveller could put his ear to the tree, and if a noise reverberated, this signalled a coming storm and a dangerous crossing.[60] De Laguna reported that even though the glacier in this story had melted by 1952, Yakutat residents still associated this tree with safe ice crossings.[61]

On another occasion, when these same brothers were seal hunting in Yakutat Bay, their canoe was carried off by the swell raised by a calving glacier, and they had to fall back on mountain- and glacier-climbing skills. It was winter, winds were blowing bitterly, and they ran out of food. "When they became discouraged they made steps across the glacier. In one place was a precipice and they had a hard struggle."[62] One brother was lost. A single sentence near the end of this story foreshadows some of the global complexity now reaching these coastal shores. "When they reached [Yakutat]," K̲'áadasteen reports, "there were other people in the town. These were the Teik̲weidí [clan] who had come up from Prince of Wales Island to the south."[63] Elsewhere, de Laguna suggests that Haida were displacing Tlingit residents from Prince of Wales Island by about 1750.[64] They pushed north, reached Yakutat rapidly by sea, and these Teik̲weidí clan members were established as a powerful clan by the time Russians met their leaders at Yakutat in the late 1780s.

Moving North: From Cross Sound to Alsek River

The majority of eighteenth-century migrants to the Gulf of Alaska were Tlingit, moving north under pressure from expanding Haida. Of seventy-four Tlingit clans de Laguna has enumerated, many no longer exist.[65] Their disappearance reflects both normal processes in Tlingit social organization and catastrophic consequences of epidemics. Over time, there was inevitably strategic expansion of some clans at the expense of others, fissioning of house groups to form new clans, and reversals of fortunes by clans who lost members. Trying to find chronology within oral tradition is probably fruitless, since that was seldom the teller's purpose. With epidemics, though, chronology is inescapable even though cursory names and dates of diseases reveal little of their horror. Smallpox in 1775, 1836, and 1862; measles in 1800; and typhoid in 1819, 1848, and 1855 all coincided with late stages of the Little Ice Age.[66]

Tlingit migrants moving north sometimes found the narrow foreshore of the Gulf of Alaska already occupied. On the alluvial fan of the Alsek River now known as Dry Bay, Athapaskan speakers from the interior were the earliest known residents, their prior occupation reflected in the Tlingit name for Dry Bay, Gunanaxoo (among the Athapaskans).[67] Swanton identified early residents at Dry Bay as descendants of interior Athapaskans, and de Laguna heard them described as "more of a river than a coastal people," who relied largely on land animals rather than sea mammals and who made regular trips up the Alsek River to hunt, fish, gather berries, and trade with interior people.[68] Incoming Tlingit intermarried with Athapaskans, and together they founded the village of Guseix̲, near Dry Bay.

At Sitka, in 1904, John Swanton also met Deikinaak'w, the Tlingit man whose words open this book. Swanton describes him only briefly as "an old man of the Box House [Kaagwaantaan or Eagle clan] people ... [whose] stories appear to be entirely after the ancient patterns."[69] One of the narratives Deikinaak'w told chronicles the journey of a Tlingit ancestor, K̲aakex'wtí, credited as the first Tlingit person to meet Athapaskans on the Alsek River. Swanton also recorded a second version of this narrative, in English, from K̲aadashaan, a headman of the opposite-moiety Kaasx̲'gweidí Raven clan.[70] We will meet this second narrator, K̲aadashaan, again in Chapter 5 as a much younger man when he accompanied John Muir to Glacier Bay in 1879.[71] More recently, Nora Marks Dauenhauer also recorded and transcribed this story as told by her father, Willie Marks, in 1972.[72]

Each narrator tells how a Tlingit man named K̲aakex'wtí, a member of the Chookaneidí clan[73] living somewhere between Mount Fairweather and Cross Sound, travelled inland and met, then "organized," Athapaskans living on the lower reaches of the Alsek River, and ultimately incorporated them into trading relationships with coastal Tlingit. K̲aakex'wtí's journey was prompted by distressing events, including an epidemic, that caused him to turn his back on the sea and head inland, fully prepared to die. He crossed a glacier that de Laguna suggests could refer to two probable routes. One route originates at Icy Point, just north of the entrance to Cross Sound, and leads across a glacier that has now receded; however, on that route he would have required someone to ferry him across Lituya Bay to connect with beach access to Dry Bay. The other route begins at the head of Glacier Bay and would have involved crossing the combined Melbern and Grand

Pacific "through glaciers" to the Alsek River. In either case, K̲aakex'wtí headed northwest, using Tsalx̲aan (Mount Fairweather) as both compass and weather vane. He reportedly wore snowshoes with claws that allowed him to scale cliffs and cross glaciers.[74]

Eventually, K̲aakex'wtí reached the Alsek River, where he encountered a party of Athapaskans. He studied them from a distance (just as they observed him), amazed to see that they had only the most rudimentary techniques for procuring food. Curiosity grew on both sides, and when they met he taught them how to make fish traps for eulachon and salmon, and deadfalls to catch small game; how to preserve and store meat, roots, and berries; and how to use a pit oven. There is a hint of noblesse oblige in Tlingit versions: "The Athapaskans were very wild and did not seem to have any sense ... [K̲aakex'wtí] was teaching the people there to live as do those down on the ocean" so that they could have "an easy time." These Athapaskans, in turn, arranged for him to marry "the daughter of a chief,"[75] and their wealth amazed K̲aakex'wtí: at his wedding he received moose skins, marten skins, beaver skins, and two copper spears valued at two slaves. The relationship strengthened, and other glacier crossings are reported during K̲aakex'wtí's residence on the Alsek, including the arrival of a slave from a Chilkat Tlingit community on the Lynn Canal via an interior route across a glacier to the Alsek.[76]

After some years – the number varies from version to version – K̲aakex'wtí proposed that his Athapaskan in-laws accompany him back to his coastal home to formalize more systematic trade. They gathered "small coppers" and set off.[77] At their first destination, they had a rude shock. Tlingit residents, ironically members of K̲aakex'wtí's own Chookaneidí clan, were so alarmed by the strangers that they insulted and dismissed them, forfeiting his gift of copper and their opportunity to participate in what would become a flourishing trade.[78] Persevering, the party crossed another glacier above Cross Sound and reached a Kaagwaantaan clan settlement called Sand Hill Town. Thomas Thornton identifies this as L'eiwshashakee Áan (town on the glacial sand cutbacks), located at Bartlett Cove near the site of the present-day Glacier Bay National Park Visitor Center.[79] These Kaagwaantaan clan hosts were more welcoming and ultimately profited so much from their subsequent trade with Athapaskans that they were able to build the enormous eight-beamed Shadow House that took a year to complete. "The house was so big that a person who walked in front of it always appeared small, and when he entered, one had to speak loudly to be heard across."[80]

Yet just a year later, Deikinaak'w continued, Shadow House was completely crushed by an advancing glacier when a young woman who was secluded at the onset of puberty angered it by speaking carelessly. "This girl said to the glacier, 'Would that that glacier were my father's,' and during that night it began to grow out over their new house. It extended itself far out over the town, and the people fled from it."[81] The story merges with those told more recently by two elders from the Chookaneidí clan, Susie James (in 1972) and Amy Marvin (in 1984), recorded in Tlingit and translated by Nora Dauenhauer.[82] All three versions are discussed in more detail in Chapter 5, and they bring us to the heart of questions regarding social consequences of moving glaciers, because they take as their central theme issues of social responsibility. In each version, a secluded young menstruant foolishly calls out to the glacier as though her words had no consequences, triggering an advance that destroys the village. The story's impact lies in the choices people are forced to make instantaneously as the glacier advances with alarming speed. In one version, the girl's grandmother insists that she will remain at the site so that her grandchild can leave and go on to bear children – crucial for the survival of the clan. In effect, she takes responsibility for her granddaughter's flippant words. In the other, the young woman insists on remaining behind, accepting full responsibility for her actions and being unwilling to face the shame of living with the consequences her actions have unleashed on others. Whatever the outcome, the image of the "woman in the glacier" remains the embodiment of the current Chookaneidí clan title to Glacier Bay, a claim clan members say is verified by the fact that they paid for this place with the blood of their ancestor, the woman in the glacier.

Geologist Ross Powell confirms that during the Little Ice Age, while glaciers in the rest of the world advanced only several hundred metres, those in the Glacier Bay Icefield system experienced at least eighty kilometres of terminus advance.[83] Glaciation here has erased most remains of ancient settlements, and isostatic rebound and tectonic uplift make other sites difficult to locate.[84]

The Alsek and Tatshenshini Rivers: "Highway" to the Interior

Beyond the mountains in the interior, Yukon elders report intense periods of cold, privation, and loss of life during late stages of the Little Ice Age. In 1975 two senior Yukon women, Rachel Dawson and Angela Sidney, each told harrowing accounts about a year when "two winters joined together" sometime during the 1800s, when even lakes failed to thaw, and starvation took the lives of young and elderly.[85] My initial guess was that this might refer to 1816, the reputed "year without a summer" following Tambora's eruption, but genealogies suggest that it happened more recently. Catharine McClellan heard these stories in the 1940s and estimated that they referred to the middle of the nineteenth century.[86] Older Tutchone men and women on the upper Yukon River and its tributaries, as well as Kaska elders living in southeastern Yukon, tell similar stories about events also recorded in Hudson's Bay Company journals from 1848 to 1852.[87] Tree-ring data for the nineteenth century from the northern Yukon show the lowest growth during the nineteenth century in 1845, 1849, and 1850, a period that coincides with other chronologies in the Canadian North.[88] Here, then, orally transmitted genealogies, scientific research, and archival accounts support one another and point to dates different from those one might at first expect.

Cutting through mountains and glaciers, the Alsek River axis between coast and interior was considered a highway by the late nineteenth century, despite its perils, with connecting glacier routes leading to Yakutat Bay, Lituya Bay, Glacier Bay, and Lynn Canal. As on the coast, travel through transforming landscapes is a recurring theme in inland glacier stories. Living with the risks associated with the behaviour of surging glaciers is another – unexpected advances, violent surges, catastrophic floods, and accompanying weather variations. Apprehension about the behaviour of surging glaciers was always balanced by concerns about how human behaviour magnifies or diminishes those risks.

Chronicles of river travel under ice bridges to the coast are reported along every major river leading from northern interior to coast. Deikinaak'w's observations about an ice bridge on the lower Alsek River opened this book, and they echo memories from the Copper, Stikine, and Taku rivers: "In one place Alsek River runs under a glacier," he reported. "People can pass beneath in their canoes, but, if anyone speaks while they are under it, the glacier comes down on them. They say that in those times this glacier was like an animal, and could hear what was said to it."[89] At Yakutat, Frederica de Laguna heard that when the Alsek was formerly blocked by ice, Tlingit travellers heading inland from Dry Bay made a portage on the west side of the river, and then later paddled back downstream through an ice tunnel.[90] Narratives from both the Taku and Stikine rivers dramatize how elderly men or women made subglacial journeys, prepared to sacrifice their lives for the benefit of their descendants. Like the Copper River migrants who ascended the glacier toward Mount Saint Elias, two men navigating under the Taku Glacier dressed in their finest clothing, painted their faces, and decorated their hair before undertaking the dangerous journey. Paddling toward the glacier, they composed songs for each stage of their journey. "This little child is going to take my place after I die," one sang. Remarkably, they arrived at the other side of the glacier tunnel unscathed. Next, "two young fellows" made the trip by boat and then crossed back *over* the glacier to report the good news. Then everyone walked across the glacier, collected fish, and returned on foot. The following year, people say, the glacier dam broke and salmon returned upriver.[91] Inland Tlingit elder Elizabeth Nyman explained the Taku Glacier's retreat as the result of blood left on the glacier following a violent death, an explanation similar to those cited earlier for other recessions at Icy Bay and at Yakutat Bay.[92] We will hear one such account told by Angela Sidney in Chapter 3.

As if to confirm old stories, the remains of a young male hunter were discovered melting from a glacier near the Tatshenshini River in August 1999. His identity is still unclear, but he seems to have been traversing one of the glacial routes between Lynn Canal on the coast and the Alsek River.[93] Among remnants of clothing preserved with him was a finely woven hat that resembles those that Tlingit residents at Lituya Bay were wearing when French navigator La Pérouse visited more than two centuries ago, in July 1786. "The head," he wrote, "they commonly cover with a little straw hat, curiously woven," adding later that "hats and baskets of rushes are no where woven with more skill."[94] Dates for the hat and fur garment obtained by several standard methods indicate that the young man was travelling through here between AD 1415 and 1445, suggesting that trade between coast and interior may have been under way by the fifteenth century.[95]

When La Pérouse sailed into Lituya Bay in 1786 as its first European visitor, he described it as a hub of human activity – a summer settlement occupied by experienced Tlingit marine navigators who were probably using it as a base for northward expansion. His descriptions of clothing also suggest a flourishing trade with interior Athapaskans by this time. "The common dress of the grand chief was a short tanned [moose] skin bordered with a fringe of deer hoofs and beaks of birds, the jingling of which when he danced was not unlike sheep's bells."[96] Moose were unknown on the coast until the mid-twentieth century, when they began to move down the Alsek valley,[97] so either hides or ready-made clothing must have come through trade. A drawing by the expedition's artist Gaspard Duché de Vancy in 1786 depicts a group of residents at Lituya Bay (see Figure 2). The man on the left is wearing interior Athapaskan-style tanned hide clothing with footwear incorporated into leggings. His tailored suit bears a striking resemblance to those Alexander Murray drew in his Yukon River journal six decades later, in 1847-48.[98]

Inland narratives about glaciers dramatize the dangers of travel between the interior and the coast. In Chapter 3, we will hear three differently

Figure 2 Costumes of the Inhabitants of Port des Français [Lituya Bay], 1786, a drawing by Gaspard Duché de Vancy, ship's artist with La Pérouse's expedition. The man sitting second from left wears a tailored costume resembling Athapaskan clothing then being worn inland, near the Yukon River. *Source:* Dunmore and de Brossard, *Le Voyage de Lapérouse, 1785-1788,* vol. 1 (Paris: Imprimerie Nationale), Plate 8. All rights reserved.

positioned accounts of a trip made by trading partners, one interior Athapaskan and one coastal Tlingit. The Tlingit man accidentally slips into a crevasse, and his Athapaskan trading partner, terrified of being blamed, nevertheless travels to the coast to report the tragedy. The grief-stricken relatives hold a potlatch and then journey back to recover the body, but rejoice to find their kinsman miraculously alive, sustained both by the provisions he was carrying and by food his relatives offered the fire at his potlatch. The story underscores the perils of glacier travel but also the responsibility of Athapaskan men to Tlingit trading partners and the shifting and uncertain ethnic boundaries differentiating them.

Behaviour – of both humans and glaciers – takes centre stage in many of these inland narratives. Like stories told on the coast, they are set in a dynamic landscape where named glaciers sometimes intrude unexpectedly on everyday life. In both locations, there are serious prohibitions about behaviour around glaciers. We have seen how an outburst flood at Icy Bay and a glacial advance at Glacier Bay were each attributed to excitable young men or women who joked conspicuously about glaciers. Inland, the Donjek, the Steele, the Lowell, the Fisher, the Tweedsmuir, and other glaciers have surged repeatedly in recent centuries and will do so again.

Figure 3 The Lowell Glacier, also known as Nàlùdi in Southern Tutchone, is about sixty-five kilometres long and five kilometres wide, and flows from the Saint Elias Icefields. It has surged across the Alsek River (shown here) several times during the last three thousand years, building a dam and creating Neoglacial Lake Alsek. *Photograph by Julie Cruikshank, 1999*

The Lowell Glacier, for instance, has crossed the Alsek River several times. Mrs. Kitty Smith, who was born approximately in 1890, spent her childhood near its upper drainage and identifies this glacier by name as Nàlùdi (fish stop) because it interrupted salmon migrations up that river to the interior, leaving land-locked salmon in Kathleen Lake (see Map 3). Her explanation of causes and consequences of the surge differs from one scientists would offer. A young Tlingit boy travelling with a party of coastal traders to the interior joked about a balding Athapaskan shaman. "Ah, that old man!" he reportedly said, "the top of his head is just like the place where gopher plays – a bare stump." To punish this insolence, the shaman summoned the glacier across the river, creating a dam and, behind it, a lake. When that ice dam burst, the resulting outburst flood scoured the landscape, drowning Tlingit families based at the Alsek-Tatshenshini junction and at Dry Bay. Nàlùdi has surged again, she says, most recently in her "Grandma's time," shortly after her own birth. That year, Nàlùdi blocked the river and flooded the upriver valley basin in just a few days, killing hundreds of ground squirrels before the lake drained.[99] Orally narrated accounts of this disaster appear in Chapter 3.

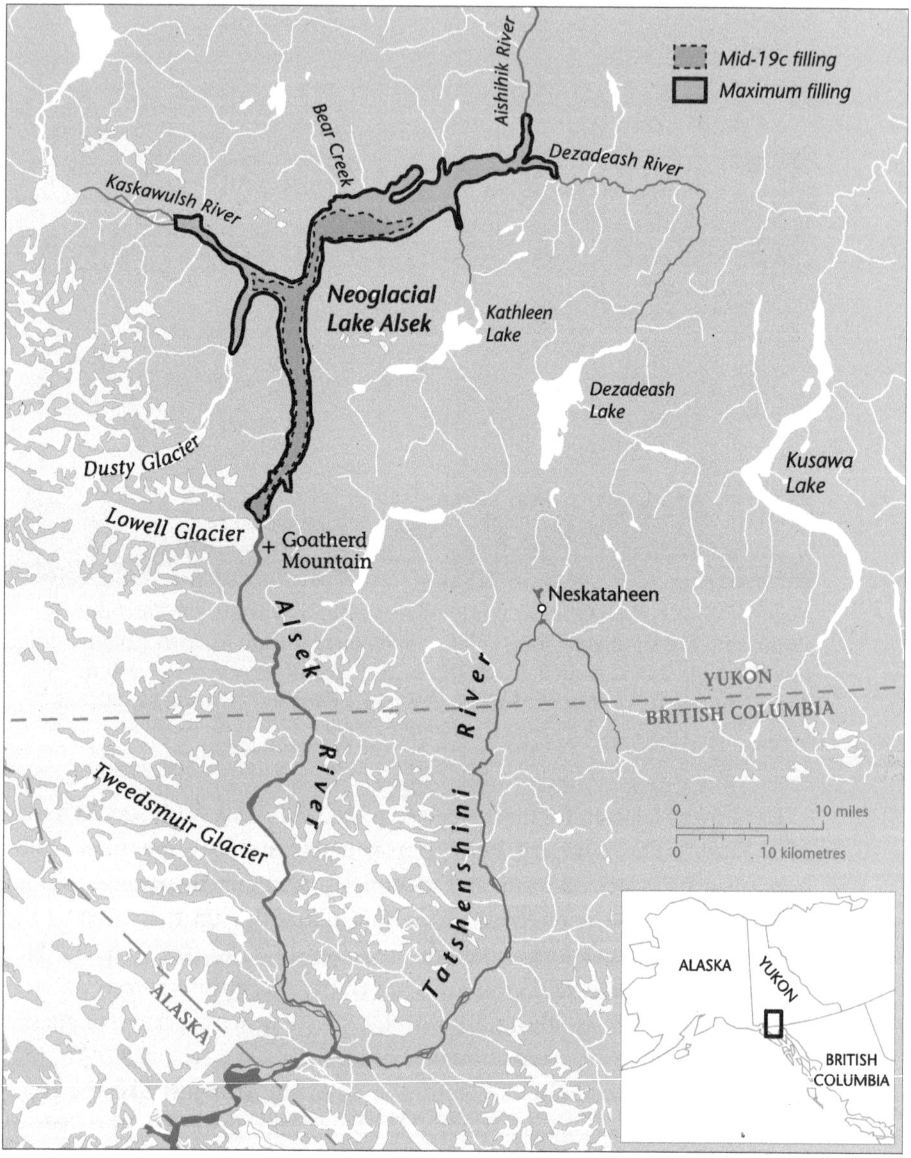

Map 3 Neoglacial Lake Alsek formed several times during the last three thousand years when Lowell Glacier crossed the Alsek River, built up against Goatherd Mountain, and created an ice dam. The map shows the approximate extent of a mid-nineteenth-century filling as well as shorelines of the maximum filling. Repeatedly, when the ice thinned and the dam broke, the lake emptied catastrophically into the Alsek River valley.

In the 1940s at Yakutat, Frederica de Laguna heard about a lake that built up behind this glacier's expanding flank sometime during the mid-nineteenth century, and then emptied with catastrophic consequences. On the basis of oral accounts, she estimated that this event had occurred in roughly 1852.[100] When Chief Albert Isaac told Catharine McClellan this same story inland at Aishihik in 1963, he drew a sketch of ice advancing on the Goatherd Mountain bluff and described how the shaman took to his bed and dreamed the powers he needed to move the ice across the Alsek River.[101]

These events are also preserved in the geoscience record, although scientists provide different causal explanations. Their data show that Lowell Glacier advanced across Alsek valley and blocked the south-flowing Alsek River several times during the last three thousand years, a period scientists refer to as the Neoglacial interval.[102] The Alsek is a powerful river, so Clague and Rampton estimate that for the Lowell Glacier to both cross the river and seal the flow, the advance would have had to have been rapid and could have occurred only during a strong glacier surge. In at least one of those fillings, the ice dam built up almost two hundred metres after it came to rest against Goatherd Mountain, and created spectacular Neoglacial Lake Alsek, more than one hundred kilometres long. Neoglacial Lake Alsek formed once or more between 800 and 2900 years ago, though evidence has been erased by subsequent ponding. Scientists can give more precise dates for subsequent lakes, estimating that Neoglacial Lake Alsek formed twice between 250 and 500 years ago, again between 1736 and 1832, and again sometime between 1848 and 1891, with a smaller lake after 1891 and before 1917. When the dam we hear about in these stories broke, possibly in the 1850s, the lake emptied very rapidly, discharging its enormous volume of water through the Alsek River valley. Giant ripple marks left in its wake are still visible from the air and on the ground. A carved wooden paddle was found in a driftwood layer at twenty-eight metres above the Alsek valley floor.[103]

Other narratives we will hear in Chapter 3 attribute surges to glaciers that are described as dens for giant animals – giant copper-clawed owls or giant worms easily provoked by human hubris. They can be rendered harmless, but this is more likely to be accomplished by quick-wittedness than by brute strength, as conveyed in the story of a grandmother and her young grandson who managed to destroy an owl inhabiting a glacier near the old village of Noogaayík on the Tatshenshini River. Similar narratives surround surges of the Donjek Glacier and the Steele Glacier (the latter named gyu shäw [giant worm]).[104]

Human populations along the Alsek-Tatshenshini river drainage were undoubtedly once substantial. Sockeye salmon ascending the relatively short distance from the coast to the upper Tatshenshini River made this river system a magnet for subsistence and trade, drawing people from Aishihik and Hutshi, as well as from Dry Bay and Lynn Canal. Elderly men and women who spoke with anthropologist Catharine McClellan in the late 1940s remembered the inland village of Neskataheen as a "big city ... thousands of years old."[105] Yet as we will see in Chapter 6, the first visitor to leave a written account of his journey down the Tatshenshini, Edward Glave, was struck by how few people seemed to be living there by 1890, despite evidence of large populations in the past.

When Catharine McClellan first came to the southwest Yukon in the late 1940s and early 1950s, she found it difficult to determine what proportion of the nineteenth-century population along the Alsek may have been Athapaskan, what proportion Tlingit, and the extent to which populations had merged. Those formerly headquartered at Neskataheen had adopted coastal Tlingit clan names during the nineteenth century but eventually incorporated clans into their moiety system rather than maintaining clan distinctions. By the mid-twentieth century, they expressed only "half-hearted interest" in questions McClellan asked about Tlingit clans.[106] She points to the 1836 and 1862 smallpox epidemics as being responsible for breaks in memory as well as devastating loss of life. Survivors either moved downriver to Guseix̱, near Dry Bay, or upriver to Neskataheen on the Tatshenshini River. A subsequent attack at Dezadeash Lake by Tanana from the northwest, reported by Glave in 1890 and remembered in the 1950s as "the war between Alaska and Canada," further reduced the number of people living between Kluane Lake and Dezadeash Lake.[107] As on the coast, impacts of disease and conflict may have been especially devastating because they coincided with late stages of the Little Ice Age.

Southern Tutchone elders Catharine McClellan met still vividly recalled stories we heard earlier in this chapter about how K̲aakex'wtí taught their ancestors to make fish traps.[108] But in narratives they told her in the 1950s, the point of view was inverted from coastal versions so that inland people were portrayed as the ones who prospered after they acquired the services of K̲aakex'wtí and "put him to work" by arranging his marriage to an interior woman.[109] Representations Swanton recorded on the coast of Athapaskans being "wild" and needing instruction by K̲aakex'wtí also contrast sharply with those presented by Annie Ned, a Southern Tutchone elder well into her nineties when we recorded her life story together. In Mrs. Ned's account, Tlingit traders first came inland, attracted by the wood chips they observed floating down the Alsek River, and found Athapaskans rich in resources and using ingenious technology. She describes coastal Tlingits, by contrast, as relatively impoverished "poor cousins" and suggests that Athapaskans taught them all the skills they needed to survive. "They've got *nothing*, those Tlingit people, just cloth clothes, groundhog clothes. Nothing! Goat and groundhog, that's all. But people here had lots of fur and they used it in everything themselves – ready-made moccasins, buckskin parky, silverfox, red fox, caribou-skin parky sewed up with porcupine quills ... So that's how they got it! Coast Indians got snowshoes and moose-skin clothes – all warm – parky, caribou parky, caribou blanket, caribou mattress. Anything like that they want to use. Those [Tlingit] people wanted clothes from here in Yukon ... so they traded. They did it for a purpose!"[110]

In the end, she says, Tlingit came to dominate trade with interior peoples only because of their greater access to consumer goods on the coast – sugar, tea, and tobacco – and the growing desire of inland people to acquire those goods. By 1950, the elders with whom Catharine McClellan spoke were making a clear distinction between themselves and "saltwater people" at Yakutat and Dry Bay.[111]

Intersecting Narratives?

Surging glaciers present some of the navigational, spiritual, and intellectual challenges of a sentient "land that listens." On the surface, narratives that geophysical scientists and Athapaskan/Tlingit elders tell about glaciers seem largely incompatible. Glaciers equipped with senses of smell and hearing, alert to the behaviour of humans and quick to respond to human indiscretion, sound wholly unlike glacier field sites where scientists can "sieve" for reductive moments that allow them to measure variables contributing to climate change. Environmental earth scientists – geophysicists, physical geographers, geologists – study processes that are thousands or even millions of years old, and this seems further to confound issues of commensurability. So what do overlapping accounts from passing historical observers, contemporary field scientists, and Tlingit and Athapaskan elders suggest about the porosity of approaches to knowledge? Are there ways of speaking about global issues such as climate change that accord weight to culturally specific understandings as well as to universalizing frameworks of science?

In June 2002, I attended the International Glaciological Society's conference on Fast Glacier Flow at Yakutat, Alaska. The timing seemed fortuitous. The enormous Hubbard Glacier at the head of Yakutat Bay, now the fastest growing glacier in Alaska, was advancing and seemed certain to close off nearby Russell Fiord as it had briefly in 1986, trapping tidal waters in an ice-dammed lake. The gap closed two weeks later, recreating Russell Lake, which rose this time 18.6 metres above sea level before it burst through the ice dam on 14 August. Each of these floods, in 1986 and again in 2002, exceeded in volume any other glacial lake outburst in historical times. It seems certain to re-form.

As part of the conference, the Yakutat Tlingit hosted a thoroughly successful cultural evening in their Alaska Native Brotherhood Hall. The dance group included some thirty adults, teenagers, and youngsters who wore elegant, handmade ceremonial regalia featuring the wearer's clan crests – Beaver, Eagle, Thunderbird, Brown Bear, and notably Mount Saint Elias, the mountain that we heard once guided their ancestors to Icy Bay and eventually to Yakutat Bay. They performed a series of songs and dances that traced webs of kinship and narratives of first arrival at Yakutat Bay. References to glaciers were embedded in larger stories about human migrations and connections among clans.

A "Copper River song" commemorated the history we heard in this chapter about how clan members originally travelled to Yakutat Bay and found it occupied, so retraced their route westward across the Bagley and Tana glaciers to retrieve a valuable ancient copper plate that allowed them to purchase living space at Yakutat. A second song told of travels inland to the Yukon across mountains that one of the performers, David Ramos, reminded the audience are "the children of Mount Saint Elias and Mount Fairweather," spread between the coast and interior. Yakutat people, he said, were attracted to trade with interior peoples whose hide and fringe clothing they admired and copied. Another song, about walking through those mountains, was composed by a Tlingit trader who fell in love with an interior woman and travelled east to the Alsek River to see her again – probably on the old route provided by the Nunatak Glacier, now greatly reduced in size. David Ramos also mentioned that glaciers dislike intensely the cooking smells of human food, echoing concerns of inland elders who speak in similar ways.

The audience of scientists was appreciative and enthusiastic. But the visual spectacle inevitably dominated, partly because Tlingit clan names were unfamiliar to most visitors, but also because of a now globally familiar tendency to privilege the visual in such performances.[112] Domains of knowledge now seem predetermined by all participants. Performers that evening in the Alaska Native Brotherhood Hall were Tlingit residents, and observers were visiting scientists. The following morning at the high school auditorium, the scientists performed (also using elaborate visual displays in PowerPoint presentations) and Tlingit residents politely observed from the audience. Boundaries distinguishing "science" from "culture" were maintained by familiar strategies of location, technology, and styles of formality that clearly differentiated them.

We can recall from this book's introduction how the flamboyant arctic traveller Frederick Schwatka responded to his guides' concerns about the consequences of cooking smells and loud noises near glaciers, and classified local glacier stories as "superstition." While none of these scientists would now be so dismissive, the trajectory connecting his remarks with contemporary practice is part of what anthropologists Jean and John Comaroff call "the long conversation" in which old meanings are set afloat and new meanings take root.[113] The ongoing intersection of such old and new meanings also tells a story. Local ideas about glaciers are now relegated to the domain of "culture," thoroughly distinct from scientific studies of "nature." Formal scientific papers presented during the conference were based on close observation (facilitated by magnificent instruments), followed by reduction of observations to key variables that can be configured as equations. For scientists, the creativity comes in the selection of variables and the skilful use of metaphor, rather than in composing a song, but the creative processes may not be so very different.[114]

In the following two chapters, I pursue in more detail the contributions that local voices from this region make to our understanding of glaciers and their role in human history. The overlap with documentary sources is consistent, as we will see, but the approaches and interpretations often differ.

2

Constructing Life Stories: Glaciers as Social Spaces

My introduction to glaciers and their stories came from elderly Aboriginal women who lived their entire lives inland from the Saint Elias Mountains in the southern Yukon Territory. During the 1970s and early 1980s, I was living in the Yukon Territory and had the good fortune to meet energetic senior women eager to record life stories for family members. From the outset, we framed this as collaborative research with the goal of documenting social histories largely absent from written records. Our conversations began with questions very different from those animating natural histories of glaciation or contemporary accounts of northern "wilderness."

It rapidly became clear that these women were working from a model of life history very different from my own. I had been attracted by social history movements then emerging in Europe and North America and was intrigued by connections between everyday experience and more public events that are transmitted in (or erased from) community memory. The women I came to know in the Yukon responded to my questions about the Klondike gold rush, the construction of the Alaska Highway, and the changes engulfing women's lives during the twentieth century by insisting that I first transcribe ancient and complex stories that initially seemed unrelated to what I perceived as our shared objective. As we continued to work together, it became clear that they were drawing on established local narrative conventions to reflect on complex life circumstances. I came to admire the ways they grounded precise social histories of twentieth-century life within a scaffolding of much older narratives. Good stories, like good theories, make connections that are not always straightforward. But I was *not* prepared for glaciers.

Kitty Smith, Annie Ned, and Angela Sidney were each born just before or shortly following the 1896-98 Klondike gold rush, often cited as a turning point in the modern cultural history of northwestern Canada. All three were raised by mothers or grandmothers born in the mid-1800s who, in turn, communicated accounts of nineteenth-century life to daughters and granddaughters born on the brink of a new century. A consistent feature of accounts these women told was their use of what might be called "traditional" stories, learned from parents and grandparents, to explain modernist changes that swept through their twentieth-century lives. By the 1970s and 1980s, the women I knew each brought close to a century of experience to this task. In the words of Angela Sidney, ancient narratives had helped her to "live life like a story."

Some stories, though, seemed to head in another direction. I heard narratives about glacial caves inhabited by intemperate beings that might emerge unexpectedly, and others that depicted glaciers as living and responsive themselves. Stories dramatized the filling and bursting of ice-dammed lakes into river valleys, and narrators weighed and evaluated possible explanations for these disasters. They told stories of travel between coast and interior, sometimes crossing crevasse-ridden glaciers on foot and sometimes piloting hand-hewn cottonwood boats beneath glacial bridges that periodically spanned rivers draining the interior plateau. They all talked about how strangers, *k'och'en* (the colourless "cloud people"), first began to arrive from the coast across glaciers, and the transformations their arrival heralded.[1] There was agreement about the troublesome consequences of cooking with grease near glaciers.

My fascination with glaciers grew from their persistent and puzzling appearance in life stories, and from my sense that these women were often actually talking about larger issues when they spoke about glaciers. Their descriptions of jarring life transitions from childhood to early adulthood and marriage, for instance, drew on icefield imagery of a "winter world" where whiteness – of landscape and animals – seemed to signify abrupt social adjustments. Economic transformations that were straining relationships with coastal Tlingit traders by the late nineteenth century reminded them of stories they had heard from their elders about the physical risks of crossing crevassed glaciers and the social responsibilities of trading partners to one another. Other more puzzling stories described glaciers as radiating blinding heat that drove people to cool themselves in nearby rivers.

To learn more about natural history and human ecology in this region, I turned to accounts written by biologists, geologists, and geophysicists, as well as to Tlingit oral narratives recorded during the early twentieth century. I read histories of North Pacific coastal navigation and notes made by pre-gold-rush travellers. I was struck by how often oral traditions from both coast and interior depict events that are also reflected in accounts penned by Jean-François de La Pérouse in 1786 (discussed in Chapter 4), by John Muir in 1879 and 1880 (discussed in Chapter 5), and by Edward

Glave in 1890 and 1891 (discussed in Chapter 6) – individuals who undoubtedly met or at least were contemporary with these women's immediate ancestors. Converging accounts helped me to appreciate how meanings of northern landscapes continue to be shaped by the culture, gender, age, and historical circumstances of the teller.

Coexisting with glaciers was risky during the Little Ice Age. Consequences flowed, as they still do, from the glaciers' immense physical energy, as well as from the vast imaginative possibilities surrounding what John Muir later referred to as the work of moving ice. But as we will see in subsequent chapters, geophysical changes coincided with equally fraught colonial transformations. Northrop Frye has defined imagination as "the power of constructing possible models of human experience," a process that he suggests works from established conventions, involves both intellect and emotion, and provides the basis for social life.[2] The enduring tradition of storytelling in the Yukon requires us to pay attention to how narrators draw on expressive conventions that graft colonial histories onto accounts of environmental change from the same period.

Because the work of Angela Sidney, Kitty Smith, and Annie Ned is central to the puzzle at the core of this book – the appearance of glaciers in life stories – I begin this chapter by summarizing life experiences they have elaborated elsewhere and at length in their own words in our co-authored book, *Life Lived Like a Story*.[3] I then turn briefly to three writers who have helped me to think about the broader work of oral storytelling, and I link their observations with an overview of historical forces that were bearing down on the Yukon Territory during the narrators' lifetimes. I then briefly summarize local narrative conventions and social principles governing place, kinship, and personhood that narrators would expect an informed listener already to know. I conclude with a summary of recurring themes in these glacier stories – origins and transformations, glacial travel, and the astonishing force exerted by surging glaciers, with an eye to their implications for understanding local knowledge in northern Canada. The significance of stories about glaciers, I suggest, centres on both the close empirical observations and the rich imaginative possibilities that glaciers provide for thinking about historical continuity and social change.

All the stories summarized or identified with an italicized title in this chapter appear in the narrator's own words in Chapter 3.[4] In structuring these chapters, I have concluded that presenting orally narrated glacier stories in a single chapter, with brief comments on their provenance, best preserves their integrity and the narrators' intentions. Readers can then approach them independently of any narrative that I might weave around them and make their own interpretations. These women expected listeners to reflect on and think about the stories, as I have done, but other readers will undoubtedly make different connections. No single interpretation can capture all their meanings, in any case. Keeping the stories together also lets readers discover how different narrators tell the "same" story from differing perspectives.

Life Stories from Glacial Places

Kitty Smith (Figure 4) was born in approximately 1890 near the mouth of the Alsek River and became familiar with its drainage as a child, growing up on its tributaries. Her coastal Tlingit father and her inland Tagish mother met in the course of trade, and by the time their daughter was born, they were spending most of the year on the headwaters of the upper Tatshenshini River, at the large fish camp, Neskataheen.[5] She recalls making a trip downriver to the coast, in a dugout canoe, when she was five or six years old and her family visited an important coastal shaman or "doctor" – this is the same route that Edward Glave describes vividly in Chapter 6. Her father died when she was an infant, and she was seven or eight when she

Figure 4 Mrs. Kitty Smith, photographed in Whitehorse, in the summer of 1988. *Photograph © 1988 by Jim Robb, Yukon*

last saw her mother, who from the child's perspective simply disappeared and then perished in an influenza epidemic that accompanied the Klondike gold rush. Orphaned as a youngster, she was raised by her father's mother, unusual in a society where obligations of clan and kinship are traced through one's maternal line.

Living in these glaciated valleys as a child, she became well acquainted with the unpredictable advances of surging glaciers. The interpretive challenges of living here must have been demanding. With curiosity, an attentive ear, and narrative talent that persisted throughout her life, she struggled to make sense of these events. Nàlùdi, the Lowell Glacier, was provoked to surge by a reckless child who teased a shaman about his balding head, she says, and then quotes the offending words: "Ah, that old man! The top of his head is just like the place where gopher plays – a bare stump."

This classic local story about the folly of hubris is well known in the southwest Yukon, as we heard in Chapter 1. It is incidentally very similar to a story we find in the Old Testament about Elisha, successor to the prophet Elijah. When Elijah chose Elisha for that role, the newly appointed man shaved the top of his head in a tonsure (characteristic of some religious orders) as a sign of his new prophetic status. He made a pilgrimage to Bethel, and on the way two young boys mocked his apparent baldness, calling out: "Go up, bald head; Go up, bald head." Elisha sent two she-bears to destroy them with forty of their friends.[6] In our conversations, Mrs. Smith used to ask me regularly to tell her "whiteman" stories, and once remarked that among white men she had met during her lifetime, missionaries seemed to be especially skilled in this art. Might she have heard someone tell the Old Testament story about Elisha, successor to Elijah? Whatever the source, the underlying message of her story remains consistent: hubris has consequences.

When I was able to visit the upper Alsek River, I was struck by giant ripple marks left behind when Neoglacial Lake Alsek drained in one or two days, discharging its waters down the valley in an enormous flow that rearranged glacial till in deep troughs. A glacial cave I visited on the Nadahini River in 1977 rose in a high vault that summer, but had collapsed when I returned two years later, so I was not surprised when she identified other glaciers as dens for giant animals easily antagonized by human arrogance and terrifying when they emerge. Such features must have fed memories for generations, and they animate her stories titled *Dadzik*, *Owl Story*, and *Woodpecker and Wolf*.

Much of her life story, though, revolves around her successful efforts as an adult to re-establish relations with her "mother's people" by reconnecting with her maternal grandmother who lived some two hundred kilometres further east at Marsh Lake.[7] This was a turning point in her life, highlighted in a context where significant kinship obligations follow matrilineal linkages. Speaking of these issues, and especially about the dangers of distance from one's maternal kin group, she drew on glacier stories that mirror social boundaries and transitions she experienced herself. When she spoke of the trials of vulnerable young women, she told stories like *The Stolen Woman* whose female protagonist travels beyond the horizon and acquires knowledge that hastens her maturity to adulthood. Her story *The First K'och'en*, about the white people who travelled toward this valley across glaciers, emphasizes their uncertain origins from beyond this same horizon. Her account *Falling through a Glacier* dramatizes the journey of two trading partners, one lost in a crevasse, and the expectations surrounding alliances between coastal and interior traders.

Annie Ned (Figure 5) was born a few years after Kitty Smith, also during the early 1890s, but further inland near the Hutshi Lakes.[8] Her mother had grown up near the Alsek-Tatshenshini drainage and her father was one of several sons of the man known as Hutshi Chief, a central figure in Athapaskan-Tlingit trade. Annie Ned also lost her mother when she was five or six years old and was raised by grandmothers who were probably born during the 1850s and who gave her a conservative education in the "old ways," convincing her, in her own words, that "old-style words are just like school."[9] Her maternal grandfather, Kàkhnokh, or Big Jim, was based in the Alsek-Tatshenshini valley, and it was he who told her much of what she knows about the Lowell Glacier (or Bear Creek Glacier, as she calls it) and its troublesome behaviour. In her *Bear Creek Glacier*, she recorded her grandfather's observations as she remembered them. As an adult, she travelled with her husband between Tatshenshini River and Kusawa Lake. One high, glaciated region where they hunted goats was a mountain pass leading from the head of Kusawa Lake to the coast, an old trade route between coast and interior. In *Lake Arkell Glacier*, titled after her name for the place, she reports her own experience here, describing her observations of a near surge after someone foolishly started to fry meat nearby. Catastrophe was averted only when the offender threw an old blanket into the fire to mask the smell.[10] She, too, tells a story about a Tlingit man who was returning home to the coast with his Athapaskan trading partner when he disappeared into a crevasse. Her version of *Falling through a Glacier* underscores the dangers of glacier travel but also social responsibilities surrounding trading partnerships.

Figure 5 Mrs. Annie Ned, photographed near her home in 1987. *Photograph by Norma McBean*

Throughout her long life, Mrs. Ned was a remarkably independent woman with a wry sense of humour. Of the elders with whom I worked, she was the most curious about archaeologists and biologists and what they were up to, and she was always glad to speak with them. When archaeologist Sheila Greer invited us to visit her field camp at Kusawa Lake in the summer of 1985, Mrs. Ned insisted that we begin at her old trapline at the lower end of the lake. She recalled memories of hunting caribou in this long valley where corrals could be built to snare caribou between the lake and surrounding mountains. She spoke of caribou "blackening the ice" on nearby lakes early in the century. Sheila, in turn, explained the archaeologists' work and showed Mrs. Ned some of the tools they had found as part of their survey. As we left, late in the afternoon, Mrs. Ned remarked to me, "Now I see what they are doing. They are looking for *things,* and you are looking for *words.* I'll tell you the words, and you can write them down for them." Sheila Greer subsequently arranged for us to prepare a report on the region's oral history for the Archaeological Survey of Canada. More than a decade later, when Annie Ned was no longer living, her words moved into a new context. Scientists reporting discoveries of ancient tools and caribou droppings melting from a high alpine ice patch above her trapline cited her oral account in their initial scientific paper on prehistoric caribou.[11] Chapter 8 discusses how recent discoveries and collaborations among scientists and First Nations investigating these melting ice patches are reinvigorating discourses surrounding memory, science, and politics, and how local knowledge is being produced in such encounters.

Angela Sidney was born in 1902 at Carcross, Yukon, to a Tlingit mother whose ancestors came from the coast and an inland Tagish father (Figure 6).[12] Her parents had already lost four children in epidemics brought when prospectors streamed through their territories to the Klondike after 1896, and Angela was the eldest daughter in their second family. She had many opportunities to hear about her bicultural Tagish and Tlingit ancestry when, as a young woman, she took on the responsibility of caring for her mother who was plagued by ill health following measles, the legacy of one of the epidemics. At our first meeting in the early 1970s, she was enthusiastic about working on the project of recording her life history for family members.[13]

A gifted storyteller, her great talent was to show the work that stories can do. She delighted, for instance, in showing how local stories provide a fresh perspective on global issues – the discovery of Klondike gold, for instance, or the experiences of the Second World War, reinterpreted from perspectives of Tagish participants.[14] In her role as social commentator, she showed that while oral tradition can indeed illuminate the past, its meanings are not exhausted with reference to the past. Orally narrated stories also provide an alternative set of principles for thinking about current events.

Early in our acquaintance, Angela Sidney spoke about the historical migration of her father's clan down the Stikine River to the coast during an earlier century, the perils they faced when they were forced to navigate beneath a glacier that was blocking that river, and their delight when everyone survived this ordeal. *My Father's Dak̲l'aweidí History* traces this journey. Her version of *Falling through a Glacier* is set in the recent past and also draws on her father's experience. Tagish John, or K̲aajinéek', once made a trip to the coast with his trading partner, and their route crossed a glacier. When his partner accidentally slipped into a crevasse, her father was able to rescue him by reacting instantly and efficiently.

Figure 6 Mrs. Angela Sidney, photographed in Whitehorse in July 1988. She is holding a replica of her Deisheetaan Beaver clan crest. *Photograph © 1988 by Jim Robb, Yukon*

Such stories are still part of everyday conversation. In Mrs. Sidney's version, her father carried out the successful rescue before she was born. In the summer of 2002, her daughter Ida Calmegane and I were visiting one evening at Ida's home in Tagish, and we began discussing her mother's stories, as we often do. Ida explained that she was well past childhood when she first heard that her grandfather Tagish John had successfully rescued his partner, Kodéinaahaa, from a crevasse. Her grandfather always carried a walking stick, and when the accident happened, he dug a hole to brace himself and attached babiche – cordage prepared by cutting and soaking strips of moose or caribou hide – then lowered his staff while shouting down instructions and was able to propel his partner to the surface. At the time, she queried her grandmother about this: "How come you never told us that story about when our grandfather saved his partner?" "Why would we talk about that?" her grandmother Maria Johns responded. "*That's* not a story ... the story would have been if he had *not* saved him. Then there would have been a *real* story to tell." Ida laughed as she explained the substantial payments, exchanges, and responsibilities that would have followed to repair the rupture in the social fabric had the rescue been unsuccessful, alluding to the more complicated outcomes in versions Mrs. Smith and Mrs. Ned also told, where rescue was delayed until after a funeral potlatch.

Storytelling and Social Imagination

In a recent article assessing the Boasian text tradition and its impacts on North American anthropology, Charles Briggs and Richard Bauman argue that Franz Boas created a rhetorical opposition between what he deemed to be "disappearing (oral) traditions" and a salvaging modernity. He then used this axis to construct transcribed spoken texts as scholarly artifacts that he insisted could be collected like museum objects to provide "the foundation of all future research."[15] That Boas ignored (and even erased) the sewing machines, the canneries, and the epidemics from his ethnographic project is now widely acknowledged, but Briggs and Bauman go further in their critique. In at least one instance, they note, he trained ethnographic fieldworkers to use the metaphorical incentive of the book as "storage-box" to elicit texts, a method that they argue gave him enormous power to regulate the production, circulation, and reception of those accounts. They assert that he then took an additional giant but problematic step by arguing that such text collections provided direct access to timeless cultural traditions – to "myth" rather than to history. Yet in the process of collecting and recontextualizing those texts in a form that he alone chose, Boas erased his own role and that of individual Native narrators, as well as the context from which each speaker spoke. He subsequently re-rooted them in a thoroughly modernist practice – preservation and protection – while continuing to burnish them as authentic replications of "the native point of view."

For someone so committed to historical specificity, Briggs and Bauman suggest, Boas foundered on a radically ahistorical paradox. His categorical distinction between "mythic time" and "historical time," his allocation of each narrative to either one category or the other, and his further insistence that these categories actually reflected ancient pan-Native North American categories ultimately denied Native Americans the historical authority that he appropriated for himself. What seems compelling in the stories Annie Ned, Kitty Smith, and Angela Sidney tell is the way they use the same method Boas advocated – making a written record of spoken words – in a way that dramatically subverts Boas's strategy. They have each authored their own books of narratives; however, instead of positioning their stories as curated artifacts extraneous to history, they consistently use timeless narratives in timely ways as valuable historical commentary.[16]

The place and meaning of stories and their contribution to how we think about the past is receiving fresh attention in the humanities and human sciences. Oral histories were once evaluated by historians and anthropologists primarily with reference to questions about accuracy, objectivity, reliability, and verifiability. A richer vein now examines storytelling as a practice that is part of everyday life and that provides a framework for understanding historical and contemporary issues. Viewed from this perspective, narrative helps us to take in and interpret the world. Oral transmission of stories is a panhuman activity, probably the oldest form of history-making, and in many parts of the world it has a continuing role in the production and reproduction of history.[17] The stories these women tell summon up a moral system that includes relationships with non-humans – animals and also features of landscape, like glaciers – that share characteristics of personhood.

Theoretical attention to the actual work accomplished by narrative destabilizes any simple idea that stories passed on as oral tradition transparently "speak for themselves," or that there is *a* prescriptive, cross-culturally valid method for assessing their historical value. Facts, as Eric Wolf points out, cannot find their voice without some assistance from a theoretical scheme.[18] The notion that oral traditions from North America can be viewed as broadly homogeneous data from which facts about "what really happened" can be extruded ignores substantial research on memory and forgetting now emerging from regions as diverse as post-Stalinist Russia, sub-Saharan Africa, Kentucky coal mining communities, post-Fascist Italy, and elsewhere.[19] If there are broad pan-North American similarities in storytelling traditions, they probably have more to do with epistemology than with content. Indigenous people who grow up immersed in oral tradition frequently suggest that their narratives are better understood by absorbing the successive personal messages revealed to listeners in repeated tellings than by trying to analyze and publicly explain their meanings – an approach that contrasts sharply with protocols in many academic disciplines.[20] My search for theoretical guidance grew as I came to see how Aboriginal elders in the Yukon Territory continue to tell stories that make meaningful connections between past and present.

In trying to understand issues surrounding the transmission of orally narrated histories in northwestern Canada, I have been drawn to questions raised decades ago by scholars working independently in very different parts of the world – Canadian economist Harold Innis, Russian theorist Mikhail Bakhtin, and German philosopher Walter Benjamin. Each was concerned about the diminishing role of oral storytelling in the world, and each deplored the consequences when this form of communication becomes marginalized by more powerful knowledge systems. Each insisted that narrative is grounded in material circumstances of everyday life and is capable of addressing large questions about human behaviour.

Two things especially strike me when I read their work. First, Angela Sidney, Kitty Smith, and Annie Ned seem to have exemplified the potential role each of these scholars envisioned for the storyteller, but second, they were all simultaneously thinking about these issues from very different social positions and physical locations. Kitty Smith (b. approximately 1890), Walter Benjamin (b. 1892), Annie Ned (b. approximately 1893), Harold Innis (b. 1894), and Mikhail Bakhtin (b. 1895) were almost exact contemporaries. Angela Sidney was born just a few years later, in 1902. These women long outlived those male peers, and their universes differed considerably, but they *did* share the same world. Coming from very different traditions – excelling in formal scholarship as compared to excelling in listening, watching, participating, and remembering experiences on the land – they all reached similar conclusions: the act of storytelling provides one crucial way of engaging directly with the contemporary world.

Approaches to analysis of oral narrative have become embroiled in broad methodological and theoretical debates in the social sciences that I merely flag here and will return to later. Timeworn arguments about the reliability of oral history are familiar enough, but there are deeper issues. To begin with, oral tradition is frequently situated at one pole of century-long discussions opposing universalist and particularist explanations, now usually framed in terms that oppose global with local concerns. While I would argue that we need to pay more attention to local consequences of global forces, relegating these stories only to the local and the particular oversimplifies the very real work they do.[21] Second, oral narrative has frequently been positioned on the "mentalist" side of a philosophical divide distinguishing materialist from idealist approaches to understanding power. Here, I agree with Innis, Bakhtin, and Benjamin that this binary distinction is never so straightforward and that oral narratives are often firmly rooted in the material circumstances of the teller. Third, approaches stressing narrative understanding may seem superficially to strand oral tradition on the shores of postmodern relativism when they actually confront hierarchies of power in very precise ways. Such troublesome dualisms have a long history, but insights from these authors may guide us through this thicket to a broader understanding of narrative's role in exploring intersections among knowledge, power, and ideology. Contemporary indigenous peoples are acutely aware of modernity's tenacious grip and regularly employ counter-narratives that address this.[22]

The shifting power relations described by Innis in Canada, by Bakhtin in Russia, and by Benjamin in Western Europe speak to modernist practices that were bearing down on the Yukon by the late nineteenth and early twentieth centuries. Late in life, Harold Innis, an economic historian, developed an enduring interest in oral tradition. Best known for his thesis that capitalism inevitably flourishes at the expense of regions it exploits, he attributed Canada's early existence to profits it offered imperial Britain, both as a source of unprocessed staples – furs, gold, cod, and timber – and as a market for commodities manufactured in distant industrial centres.[23] Investigating how empires manage the awkward problem of administering far-flung territories, Innis was drawn to the history of communications. He pointed out that imperial regimes conventionally assert power by monopolizing and categorizing information and by routinely silencing local traditions that don't fit official categories. A crucial feature of administration in the hinterland, he argued, is the classification and control of activities and the authorization of official observations, categories, and statistics in written texts. While this process is conventionally rationalized as both producing knowledge and serving the interests of those administered, it invariably occurs at the expense of existing regional traditions. Innis came to see colonialism as simultaneously economic and intellectual.[24]

Innis identified arctic and subarctic regions as furnishing a classic illustration of the modernist tendency to conceptualize time as spatially laid out, mechanically segmented, and linear. Colonial projects, he observed, move forward by devising and reinforcing categories – such as objectivity, subjectivity, space, and time. Once normalized as "common sense," such classifications provide a visual template for the annexation of territories and the subjugation of former inhabitants.[25] Gradually, those at the centre monopolize what comes to be considered rational discourse, and they marginalize those who speak in a different idiom. Innis admired the structural characteristics of oral tradition and saw it as having potential to counterbalance this mechanical segmentation of time and space by insisting on the importance of qualitative time in human affairs. Oral tradition, he argued, permits continuous revision of history by actively reinterpreting events and then incorporating such interpretations into the next generation of narrative. Its flexibility allows a gifted storyteller to adapt a given narrative to make sense of a confusing situation.[26]

Innis went on to investigate historical processes by which literacy has displaced the authority of the spoken word, tracing the demise of oral tradition in Egypt, Babylon, Greece, and Rome. He singled out Socrates as the last great exponent of oral tradition and his death at the beginning of the fourth century BC as coinciding with a shift from customary to codified law. Until then, he maintained, oral tradition had given vitality to the written word and had actively prevented the concentration of power, because a society retaining a central place for orality could not be disciplined to the point of political unity.[27] He was especially intrigued by the ways oral tradition worked in conjunction with writing to provide a kind of dialogue that he saw as a model for social action.[28] "My bias is with the oral tradition ... and with the necessity of capturing something of its spirit," he concluded. "The quantitative pressure of modern knowledge has been responsible for the decay of oral dialectic and conversation."[29]

Innis's views about the creative potential of oral tradition mirrored those of his contemporary, Mikhail Bakhtin, also writing during the 1930s and 1940s from more constrained circumstances in Stalinist Russia. They wrote in different languages, and neither ever encountered the other's work, yet their approaches were similarly eclectic. Bakhtin, like Innis, was drawn to the open-ended possibilities he saw in oral dialogue and the thoroughness with which totalitarian regimes work to suppress those possibilities. Observing the chilling transformations occurring in 1930s post-revolutionary Russia, Bakhtin concluded that there must be forms of resistance more effective than the violent replacement of one set of leaders by another, and he looked to everyday spoken language for inspiration. He sought out cases where narrative successfully resists such domestication, marginalization, and erasure and was eventually drawn to conversational forms from oral storytelling. He interpreted what he called its "dialogic," relational possibilities (especially when laced with disruptive humour) as a model inherently opposing authoritarian speech.[30]

Bakhtin, with his energetic appreciation of the destabilizing possibilities of folk humour, struggled in 1930s Russia to imagine subversion in totalitarian states. Any adequate reading of contemporary culture, in his view, required an understanding of how ordinary people have used oral communication strategies to resist arbitrary power. In terms applying equally to the capitalist frontier of subarctic Canada and the communist frontier of subarctic Russia, Bakhtin formulated the problem of history as its tendency to foster apparent randomness and for the order of events seemingly to disintegrate. And he saw narrative's role as a constraining, countervailing one of holding things together. The metaphor underlying his model of communication was that of a centrifuge with two countervailing forces –

authoritarian speech displacing local ideas to the margins, and irascible, irreverent, brash orality straining to hold a centre.[31] His larger point mirrors that made by Innis: narrative challenges hegemonic institutions.[32]

A decade later and in another country, Walter Benjamin grappled with similar issues engulfing Europe during the early years of Hitler's ascendancy. He, too, noted the insidious consequences of deteriorating dialogue in modern society, attributing this at least partly to the diminishing role of the storyteller. As communications technology proliferates, he argued, information becomes fragmented and detached from the moral philosophical guidance we think of as knowledge and might once even have called wisdom. Benjamin believed that orally transmitted narratives develop in their hearers a capacity to listen, a deteriorating skill in an age of ever-fragmenting information. The power of narrative storytelling, in his view, lies in its capacity to interweave drama and practical experience with moral content. Storytelling is open-ended rather than didactic and allows listeners to draw independent conclusions from what they hear. Medieval storytellers chronicled events without imposing their own interpretation, and their practice had equally important consequences for the arts of telling and the arts of listening. By telling stories, narrators explore how their meanings work; by listening, audiences can think about how those meanings apply to their own lives. Stories allow listeners to embellish events, to reinterpret them, to mull over what they hear, and to learn something new each time, providing raw material for developing philosophy.[33] Once interactive storytelling is replaced by mechanical communication, he alleged, human experience becomes devalued.

What relevance have these ideas to understanding Aboriginal North American oral histories from the northwestern part of the continent? Bakhtin's reference point was Russian peasant culture, and his target was the increasingly authoritarian Soviet state in which he lived. He drew his examples from how medieval French peasants used ribald, satirical humour to challenge authority through carnivals,[34] yet he never, in any of his translated writings, directly discusses everyday storytelling from his own times. Similarly, Innis carried out his economic studies in northern Canada and his historical investigation of classical oral tradition without ever seeming to connect the two. His prodigious appetite for labour-intensive research took him across northern Canada. He openly admired the work of his colleague, linguist Edward Sapir, on indigenous languages, yet he seems not to have encountered living oral traditions himself. In a book published near the end of his life, he reported regretfully that "We have no history of [oral tradition] except as ... revealed darkly through the written or printed word."[35] Had he been aware of the intensity with which indigenous residents were drawing on longstanding oral traditions to interpret the same events he was analyzing near the Klondike gold fields,[36] he might have observed dynamics similar to those that so intrigued him elsewhere – processes set in motion when writing first began to overwhelm narrative traditions and then actively to suppress them.

Historical Forces in Canada's Far Northwest

The economic and political forces bearing down on northwestern North America during the nineteenth and early twentieth centuries were precisely those discussed by Innis in his accounts of the fur trade and the Klondike gold rush, by Bakhtin as he observed the mechanics of aggressive state expansion, and by Benjamin, whose writings documented Europe between world wars. By the time Russians arrived in force on the North Pacific coast during the late eighteenth century, they found Tlingit traders already enmeshed in trading relationships with inland speakers of Athapaskan languages. Following the rapid slaughter of coastal sea otters, European traders redirected their efforts beyond the mountains to the fur-bearing animals on the upper Yukon River. Coastal Tlingit traders were able to position themselves as middlemen in this trade and effectively barred whites from crossing the mountain passes to the interior until nearly the end of the nineteenth century. Tlingit traders inevitably held the balance of power in arrangements with inland peoples, using their intermediary position to establish and formalize lifelong partnerships, often through marriages.[37] As interior neighbours adopted Tlingit-named clans and concepts of social ranking, they also incorporated Tlingit themes into their storytelling traditions. This Aboriginal trade network also had the unintended consequence of transporting epidemics, including smallpox, from the coast to the interior in the mid-nineteenth century, well before the first whites crossed the mountains.

On a global scale, the extreme northwest rapidly became embedded within layers of hierarchy centred in European fur markets. In 1825, powers centred in Moscow and London formalized the Anglo-Russian Treaty as a way of neatly dividing northwestern North America between Britain and Russia. It was another century before the Canada-United States border was actually surveyed and located, a story we return to in Chapter 7. Official records, though, remain largely silent on its implications for long-term inhabitants.

The local consequences of imperialism that so concerned Innis were much at work in northwestern Canada by the late nineteenth century. The British empire achieved its most northwesterly extension in the Yukon, where furs and gold coincided, but as Europe spiralled into a depression at the end of the century, the more lucrative and liquid commodity, gold, replaced furs as the staple of choice. News in 1896 that gold had been discovered on the Klondike River attracted some forty thousand prospectors and fellow travellers. Aboriginal people along the Yukon River became involved in packing, guiding, and providing food for prospectors, and a few years later served as deckhands on sternwheelers built to navigate the Yukon River from its headwaters down to Dawson City. Consequences of the gold rush included disruption of indigenous trade networks, further decimation of the health of Aboriginal families, expansion of missionary activity, and the establishment of a federal and territorial government infrastructure to administer this additional Yukon Territory from Ottawa, the new nation's capital.

What some older people still refer to as the "second rush" advanced during the Second World War. Hastily constructed in 1942-43, the Alaska Highway was built to deflect an anticipated invasion of North America by Japan. Again, more than thirty thousand men, this time US soldiers and Canadian civilians, arrived to participate in the construction phase, and then left as quickly as they had come. Again, epidemics tore through Yukon communities.[38] The new road replaced the Yukon River as the administrative axis of the territory, subjecting indigenous peoples to increasing bureaucratic surveillance as the "opening of the north" proceeded. The highway acted as a kind of gravel magnet attracting people from distant settlements to short-term jobs.[39] It also precipitated the establishment of a new Kluane Game Sanctuary (subsequently expanded to Kluane National Park) when federal government inspectors argued that overhunting by soldiers during the construction period had severely depleted wildlife in the region.[40] In 1942, an area stretching west from the new highway to the Icefield Ranges was closed to all hunting, including procurement of meat, hides, or furs by Aboriginal peoples who were relocated from lands they had long used to the less productive margins on the east side of the Alaska Highway.

Narrative Conventions and Social Principles

Storytelling may be a universal human activity, but understanding what one hears requires close attention to local metaphor and local narrative conventions. When speaking in story-like constructions, Yukon elders tend to make generous assumptions about their listeners' or readers' understandings of such precepts. Annie Ned, in particular, assumed that such knowledge is basic common sense, the kind of background that, in her words, "everybody knows." It is, of course, precisely the absence of such knowledge that often makes cross-cultural communication so fraught. Three concepts that carry particular significance – place, kinship, and ideas about personhood – deserve some discussion because they frame principles vital to understanding the stories about glaciers.

First, glacier stories seem to be closely linked with ideas about place, and by extension with space and with time. Philosopher Edward Casey's distinction between space and place is helpful here. Western modernity, Casey suggests, treats space – mappable, measurable, and easy to fix using Cartesian coordinates – as a universal category, and he identifies place as the more restricted notion. Casey challenges this hierarchy. Drawing on historical evidence from ancient Greece, he argues that place is actually the more universal concept. Space, he insists, is landscape one navigates in the course of travel; place-making occurs at locations where one chooses to stay or return.[41]

Jonathan Boyarin brings concerns about qualitative time to discussions of place. In the Yukon, for instance, narrators speaking about significant places do not make the analytical distinction between space and time that Isaac Newton took to be absolute. Glaciers in these stories are places where ideas about time seem more aligned with Einsteinian notions of relativity than with Euclidean geometry. The stories in the following chapter seem to conceptualize time *as* a place that provides "a sense of solidarity, of common human identification with those who lived and died in previous generations." Boyarin suggests that such places provide an "archive of endangered memories."[42]

Yukon elders address this conjunction of place, space, and time explicitly when they speak about where they have lived and travelled. Angela Sidney, for instance, documented more than two hundred Tagish and Tlingit place names for southern Yukon lakes, summarizing annual movements during her childhood years, naming places she stayed during the course of successive years, identifying extended family members who camped together on different occasions, and explaining routes that loop out from a central headquarters.[43] Kitty Smith announced, "My roots grow in jackpine roots! I'm born here. I branch here," when asserting her connections to place. When we visited old campsites, Annie Ned would comment, "You don't know this place, so I'm going to sing it for you." All these women took for granted that it is largely impossible to speak about past social relationships among people without reference to place, or to speak of place without explaining how people who lived there were connected. As they reached their mid-eighties, each expressed concerns about difficulty remembering the names of once-familiar places and the need to revisit them in order to recall names and associated stories and songs. When we were able to drive or travel by boat to these places, memories came flooding back. But memory proved more troublesome for inaccessible places they could no longer visit.

Second, these women use the language of kinship to speak about social relationships that bind humans despite distances that separate them physically. As noted in Chapter 1, two matrilineal kinship divisions or "moieties," the term anthropologists use to describe the widespread organizational principle of intermarrying kin groups, have long guided social organization. In the southern Yukon, these divisions are known as "Wolf" (Agunda) and "Crow" (Kajít), and membership is inherited from one's mother. Rules of exogamy were formerly strictly enforced: a Crow must marry a Wolf, Wolves could marry only Crows, and endogamy was deemed incestuous and was punishable. Alliances thus forged between moieties linked people from widely dispersed locations, such as in trading relationships among brothers-in-law. The social accomplishments of these arrangements for hunters and fishers during successive periods of summer aggregation and winter dispersal were enormous – widespread social networks, incorporation of strangers, and regular exchanges of labour, food, and other assistance.

Third, concepts of personhood and behavioural expectations surrounding kinship extend implicitly to animals on whom humans depend.[44] In stories, human and animal characters frequently address one another by kinship terms, like "brother-in-law" or "auntie," which convey clearly understood behavioural expectations. A common theme in stories told by Angela Sidney, Annie Ned, Kitty Smith, and their peers concerns alarming repercussions suffered by protagonists who exhibit casual arrogance in the face of other-than-human powers emanating from non-human persons. The unfolding drama often concerns a protagonist's ability (or inability) to re-evaluate behaviour and to chart a more socially responsible course.

Notably, these three concepts – place, personhood, and kinship – are deeply interconnected in stories, as we will hear in Chapter 3. If the boundary distinguishing humans and animals is fuzzy, the boundary distinguishing persons (whether human or non-human) and features of land is equally indistinct. Glaciers, for instance, sometimes appear in these stories as dens for ancient giant animals, and at other times as living sentient beings. In either case, glaciers or their subterranean inhabitants are alert to human behaviour. Glaciers are especially evocative in a geophysically active environment where human (mis)behaviour is often the chief suspect when a glacier surges. Recall from Chapter 1 what happened when reckless young men at Icy Bay, or a bored young woman secluded near Glacier Bay, called a glacier down to join them, with catastrophic consequences for both places. Like the landscape features in the American southwest that Keith Basso has described so closely, glaciers seem to be invested with moral dimensions that illuminate social values and consequences of breaching them.[45] Such landscape features, as Frances Pine argues from her research in mountainous rural Poland, are often as integral to the shaping of social worlds as is kinship.[46]

Glacier Stories

Glaciers, like stories told about them, are enigmatic. Surging glaciers, in particular, are sometimes solid, sometimes liquid, and always flowing. They are shape-shifters of magnificent power. Like tidal zones, they signify transitional spaces. Aboriginal elders who speak knowledgeably about such glaciers refer to observing, listening, and participating in ritualized respect relations with glaciers and go to great lengths not to disturb them.[47] In northern Athapaskan and Tlingit traditions, the line between human and non-human beings is less distinct than some might imagine.

Surging glaciers engage the senses. Visually, they are spectacular. Aurally, they are alarmingly noisy. Hunters, scientists, hikers, and Aboriginal elders all remark on the thunderous cracking and explosive noises they make. Tactile imagery is central to many stories that portray glaciers as bitterly cold but also, surprisingly, as emitting unbearable heat. Glaciers in these stories appear to be sentient themselves. They respond to humans and especially to smells when meat is fried nearby. They are also quick to hear and to take offence when humans demonstrate cockiness by making jokes at their expense. They are apparently equipped with vision when, for example, they are characterized as giant worms "with eyes as big as the moon." Ambiguous entities like glaciers call to mind other ambiguities. Stories told about glaciers slide into other stories.

Thematically, the thirteen stories we hear in Chapter 3 all seem to involve transformations of one kind or another. The first three, *How Animals Broke through the Sky*, *The Stolen Woman*, and *The First K'och'en*, come from a time when the world was just beginning to be formed. Originally, its axis was the horizon, where the immense icefields meet the vaulting sky. Beyond this horizon, the "other side" resembled a rather grim and colourless world perpetually locked in snow. The next four stories, *My Father's Dak̲l'aweidí History* and three versions of *Falling through a Glacier*, refer to travel between the interior plateau and the Pacific coast during late stages of the Little Ice Age. The final six stories, four about named glaciers (*Nàlùdi*, *Bear Creek Glacier*, *Lake Arkell Glacier*, and *Dadzik*) and two about inhabited glaciers (*Owl Story* and *Woodpecker and Wolf*) draw on imagery from surging glaciers to explore transforming landscapes and changing social worlds.

In the first story, *How Animals Broke through the Sky*, Angela Sidney tells how, at the beginning of time, animals and humans collaborated to

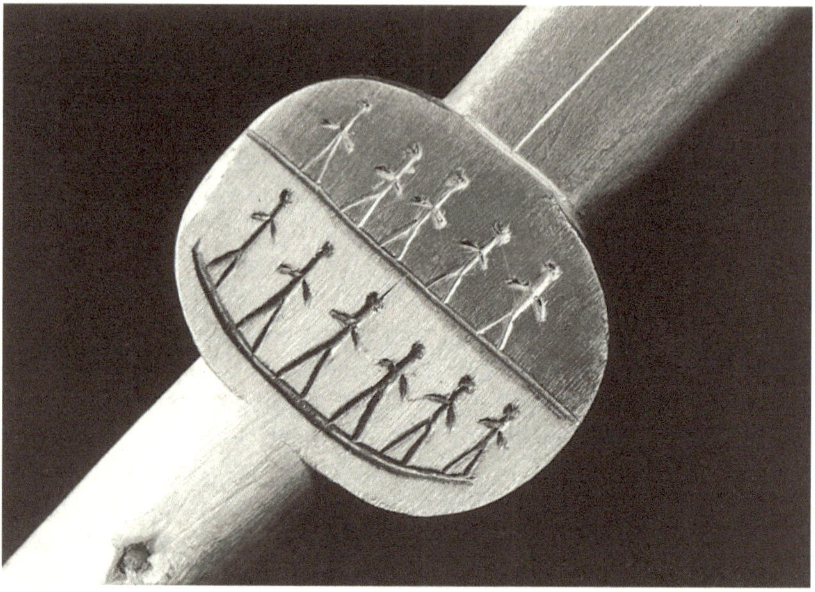

Figure 7 Medallion from speaker's staff from the central or southern Yukon. The face of the medallion is divided, as if into the red summer world and the white winter world. The figures in the winter world seem to be travelling in a boat. The theme of summer and winter worlds is reflected in several stories in Chapter 3. *MacBride Museum, Whitehorse, Yukon #1973.1.158*

inaugurate daily and seasonal cycles, an ancient theme that in Northrop Frye's words, "stretches like a backbone through the middle of human and natural life."[48] Such work, we learn, was accomplished by co-creation: human and non-human persons working together produce a moral framework and a physical order that mirror one another. Kitty Smith's *Stolen Woman* story addresses jarring transitions from childhood to early adulthood and marriage, tracing a young woman's journey to this wintry, white dimension beyond the horizon "where the clouds meet the ground." In *The First K'och'en,* Mrs. Smith uses this same imagery to reflect on social transformations and upheavals that accompanied the arrival of ambiguous strangers, their pale skins implying that they originated in the timeless dimension of this wintry world. Some people now link stories about k'och'en with reference to the whiteness of products that led to impaired health: salt, flour, and sugar.

The next four narratives address physical challenges of crossing over or under glacier passages between the interior and the coast – along the river and glacier "highways" mentioned in Chapter 1. Angela Sidney's account in *My Father's Dak̲l'aweidí History* highlights dangers posed by glaciers when ancestors migrated down the Stikine River, and their joy when they were able to navigate successfully beneath ice bridges and to reach the ocean. This story is told on every major river cutting from the interior through the icefields to the Gulf of Alaska coast – the Copper, the Alsek, the Taku, and the Stikine. I begin partway through her narrative in the selection presented here, and her full account appears in Chapter 3.

> They floated down the Stikine River to Wrangell.
> They were close to salt water when they saw a glacier coming down – just touching the creek, like this.
> You can't go across in front of it: that glacier always falls down, makes a noise.
>
> So they landed above it and started to talk about it:
> "How are we going to get further down?
> That glacier might fall down and get us all killed!"
> So they don't know what to do ...
>
> Finally, two old men decided to go – to try it. Two little old men, ready to die, I guess.
> "Send us through it. We're old now. We're no good to you people. If we die, you won't miss us much anyhow."
> That's what they told the rest of the younger people, the rest of the people.
> Those two little men had a boat of their own, so they must have gone under the glacier.
> I wish I could get up that way and find it!
>
> When they're ready to take off, they made a song:
> "Shove it out now!"
> This is the song they pushed them out with.
> They remember it [still] – that's the song they separated on.
> My father's people used to sing it if they're going to make a potlatch.
> I remember they sang it in 1912 when I was a little girl – I was ten years old that time. They sang it just before they're going to spend money at that potlatch ...

Annie Ned, Kitty Smith, and Angela Sidney each independently recount *Falling through a Glacier*, where trading partners, one Athapaskan and one Tlingit, travel across glaciers to reach the coast. The Tlingit trader disappears into a glacier crevasse, and the story is told from the perspective of his inland partner who in one case rescues the victim, but in two others continues on to the coast to report the loss, despite his conviction that he may be blamed for the tragedy. Each version has an unexpectedly fortunate outcome.

Finally, six stories about transforming landscapes often recruit surging glaciers as powerful symbols. Kitty Smith's account, *Nàlùdi,* about the Lowell Glacier and the lake it dammed, both overlaps with and diverges from scientists' explanations. So does Annie Ned's. Clague and Rampton report a clearly defined Neoglacial Lake Alsek beach ridge near Bear Creek, some 174 metres above the level of the Alsek valley floor at Lowell Glacier.[49] Annie Ned heard from her grandfather that this lake reached Bear Creek, and calls her story *Bear Creek Glacier.*[50] (See Map 3.) Both narrators also refer to the Lowell's more recent and less dramatic surge, in approximately 1890, within a few years of their own births. In *Lake Arkell Glacier,* set near Kusawa Lake, Annie Ned tells of a narrow escape when someone cooked carelessly there.

Chief Albert Isaac was living at Aishihik Lake in the 1960s when he told Catharine McClellan about a similar incident that occurred during his own lifetime downriver from the Donjek Glacier,[51] accounts that I heard repeated by elders at Kluane Lake in 2002. Two men were hunting sheep and returned to their camp at the end of a long day. As they were crossing the river, one at a time on a pole bridge they had built, the first man to cross was killed instantly by an explosion of ice from an outburst flood that erupted without warning. In Chief Isaac's account, the man who died had reportedly insisted on cooking bacon earlier that morning, after casually dismissing warnings by his partner and joking that "a glacier has no nose" (and hence no sense of smell). Chief Isaac attributed the tragedy at least in part to the victim's poor judgment, a theme we have heard several times already, specifically concerning the consequences of joking about glaciers within their hearing. Notably, scientists observing the Donjek Glacier reported an outburst flood during summer 2000 when an ice-dammed lake trapped *under* the Donjek Glacier broke through.[52] Enormous blocks of ice exploded down the Donjek River valley with no warning and at high velocity.

Kitty Smith attributes other characteristics to surging glaciers that are more challenging to understand. Her story, *Dadzik,* refers to a glacier near Dalton Post that began to advance when someone incautiously "cooked with grease." At first it emitted light and then intense heat, driving men, women, and children to abandon their camp and rush to submerge themselves in the Tatshenshini River. We know the terrible consequences of epidemics, particularly smallpox, that raged north up the Pacific coast, but less about those which travelled up the Alsek and Tatshenshini rivers. Smallpox victims resorted to a treatment of alternating sweating and cold baths that exacerbated their condition.[53] Is it possible that this story refers to this terrifying time when so few survived? Owls also seem to be associated with glaciers, and Mrs. Smith's *Owl Story* depicts a troublesome pair of giant owls that once inhabited a glacier cave until they were dispatched by a young boy and his grandmother, and the glacier/den melted. Her story *Woodpecker and Wolf*, more difficult to understand, certainly associates glaciers with transformations: throughout this narrative, things appear to represent one thing when they actually turn out to be something else. Glacier stories, in other words, may not always be "about" glaciers in any transparent way but may instead provide imaginative material for thinking about broad historical issues.

Repeatedly in these stories we encounter the issue of cooking near glaciers: the probability of triggering a glacier surge by cooking fat nearby; the subsequent transformation of liquid grease to solid form when it is cooked; the possibility that men who fall into crevasses can be saved by food cooked miles away at a potlatch fire; the transformative powers of fire and the association of glaciers with the "other side" of a wintry world where everything, including humans and animals, remains white. Narrators reaffirm the now-familiar prohibitions against "cooking with grease" and their concerns about frying bacon. They enumerate rules for cooking food near glaciers: it should be boiled and never fried, and none of the grease should spill from the soup. Circumspection defines appropriate behaviour.

What connects surging glaciers with grease? I asked this question often and was always met with puzzled responses suggesting that the answer is self-evident – "because cooking with grease causes the glacier to come out." Geophysicists tell me that when they cook bacon for breakfast on Trapridge Glacier, a surging glacier in the Icefield Ranges, they sometimes get grizzly bear visitors.[54] If these icefields have one of the world's largest concentrations of surging glaciers, the surrounding Kluane National Park has one of North America's largest concentrations of grizzly bears. Historically, Aboriginal peoples in the circumpolar north have demonstrated widespread ritualized respect for bears, and in some of these stories, at least, rules of behaviour for bears and for glaciers seem to merge, especially in stories where glaciers are cast as dens for giant animals.

One of the main shortcomings that pervades contemporary scholarship, and especially studies of local knowledge, is the idea that truthful knowledge can be somehow "captured." Increasingly, studies of "traditional knowledge" seem to do damage to northern visions when statements by knowledgeable people are stripped from their evocative contexts and evaluated as data.[55] I can perhaps illustrate some of the problems from my own rationalist tendency to try to "figure things out." The grease that narrators refer to was formerly rendered by boiling fat from moose, bear, or sheep in birch bark containers. A mixture of water and fat was heated by adding fire-heated stones. Once the water boiled away and the grease cooled, it hardened. The refined grease was then remelted and stored in moose-stomach containers as a solid white product that looks like blocks of cooking lard. One good-sized moose reportedly provides about forty pounds of tallow.[56] Grease preserved in this way takes the form of a solid white mass, but tallow liquefies into a puddle when heated – when someone is cooking with grease. In their way, surging glaciers seem to behave rather like grease rendered in this way – solid one moment and swept along in a flood the next. Furthermore, frying grease crackles noisily, almost a micro-scale version of a surging glacier that cracks explosively as it moves.

Possibly, then, "cooking with grease" near a glacier is equivalent to taunting the glacier by mimesis or mimicry – the kind of hubris that so many animal-human stories dramatize as the offensive mocking or "playing with" an animate world that can evoke catastrophic responses. In Chapter 1 we heard about Raven's response when he thought Echo was mimicking him: he identified Mount Fairweather as the source of the problem and ripped away part of its face. We saw in Mrs. Smith's account of Nàlùdi what happened when a boy likened the head of a respected shaman to a gopher stump. The consequences of joking about glaciers are also exemplified by the unfortunate comment made near Donjek Glacier that "a glacier has no nose." Maybe, though, efforts to capture particular meanings invest too much in a rationalist tradition and miss more evocative meanings alluded to in Lévi-Strauss's apt reference to phenomena that seem "good to think with."[57]

Listening for Different Stories?

Oral tradition is capable of performing many tasks simultaneously. In Chapter 1, I argued that Tlingit and Athapaskan oral traditions undoubtedly incorporate empirical knowledge about geophysical changes. Stories about glaciers are indeed referential; that is, they refer to an external, empirical world that includes transforming landscapes. On the other hand, narratives about glaciers are also constitutive: they are about how humans are responsible for making and maintaining the places where people dwell. In thinking about such issues, Kitty Smith, Annie Ned, and Angela Sidney convey a stubborn faith in a world beyond mere ordinary experience.[58]

In this chapter, I have suggested that narrators tend to use glacier stories to comment on broad human issues and the process of history-making. In subsequent chapters, I make a similar argument about the role glaciers played in written accounts left by Euro-American visitors, even though their depictions differ radically from those we hear in Chapter 3. If Aboriginal stories from these borderlands draw on mountains and glaciers to narrate complexities in local economic and social life, accounts by visiting strangers in the eighteenth and nineteenth centuries enlisted such features in the name of other social forms – imperial expansion, science, religion, and nationhood.

A region like the Saint Elias Mountains provides an ideal location to think about these issues. Scientists have been able to map and to measure its dimensions, to extract ice cores from beneath its highest summit, Mount Logan, and to use satellite imagery to determine the depths of its frozen rivers. Environmentalists and eco-tourists reconstruct it as one of the world's few remaining "natural" spaces – their imagery more likely to stress "fragile" than "harsh" environments. International parks increasingly resemble artistic productions, with photographs of indigenous peoples contributing an aesthetic veneer.

What is usually missing from this picture is the story of radical "purification" of nature, assisted by the physical eviction of indigenous inhabitants from these foothills and valleys. At roughly the same time that Harold Innis was analyzing how modern classification schemes assist annexation of territories, indigenous northerners were experiencing the effects first hand. In the 1940s, their former territories were added to the Kluane Game Sanctuary, the Yukon Territory's first Protected Area. This is a subject we will return to in Chapter 8.

3
Listening for Different Stories

In autumn 1982, a one-day conference was held in southern Yukon. Sponsored by the Yukon Historical and Museums Association, this meeting had the laudable goal of bringing together scientists and First Nations elders in a setting where exchanges about regional history could occur. The day's events were held in the community hall at Haines Junction, headquarters for the Champagne-Aishihik First Nation, rather than in Whitehorse where conferences were customarily held. More than a hundred people – adults and children – attended. Elders from First Nation communities filled the front row, and the program unfolded with interesting papers and thoughtful questions from engaged audiences.

Memorably for everyone who attended, Mrs. Annie Ned, then in her late eighties, unexpectedly rose from her seat late in the afternoon to interject: "Where do these people come from?" she asked us all. "Outside?[1] You people talk from paper. I want to talk from Grandpa." She then proceeded to speak about human and environmental history from her own experience of hunting, trapping, and living there for almost a century. Her advice to "listen for different stories" has stayed with me and prompts the title for this chapter. Eudora Welty, an American writer who, like Annie Ned, lived well into her nineties, also maintained that there is a distinction between listening *to* stories and listening *for* stories. "Long before I wrote stories," she reflected in her autobiography, "I listened for stories. Listening *for* them is something more acute than listening *to* them."[2]

This chapter provides a counterpoint to the previous one, an opportunity to listen for stories that different readers and listeners will undoubtedly interpret in various ways. They appear in the words of Kitty Smith, Annie Ned, and Angela Sidney and were recorded in the 1970s and early 1980s as part of the oral history work that engaged us at the time. All have been previously published, most in booklets authored by the narrators, and distributed within the Yukon soon after they were recorded. These transcribed texts, like all documents, come from a particular historical period, and it is worthwhile outlining editorial decisions we made at the time. Reviewed almost three decades later, our methods of transcription reflect concerns that may now seem quite distant. One controversial issue in the 1970s, for instance, was that editors too often erased names and voices of narrators and reframed them in standard English as "children's stories," a choice we were determined to avoid.

When we began working, several senior women responded to the idea of recording life stories with considerable enthusiasm, but since our initial objective was to produce booklets for families, they specified that their narratives be recorded and transcribed in their own spoken English so that they would be accessible for young people who spoke only that language. The Yukon Territory has a multilingual history that includes eight spoken languages representing two distinct language families, Athapaskan and Tlingit.[3] Remarkably, Angela Sidney, Kitty Smith, and Annie Ned each spoke languages from three different language *families:* an Athapaskan language (Southern Tutchone or Tagish), Tlingit, and English. Most individuals born after the construction of the Alaska Highway in 1943, though, attended residential schools where English was compulsory. In the mid-1970s, when we began this work, there were no Native language programs in place, nor had orthographies been developed for indigenous languages. That has all changed since the Yukon Native Language Centre came into being, but during the years we worked together, these women had specific goals they wanted to accomplish. They saw themselves as recording narratives directly for young people for whom English, in many ways, had become an indigenous language. In the 1970s, as well, Aboriginal young people were beginning to develop organizations that would eventually lead to detailed negotiations crucial for land claims settlements, and they viewed the documentation of social history in English as an appropriate task for an outsider willing to take direction from elders and their families. At the turn of the twenty-first century, young men and women are doing this kind of work with elders from their own communities, and there is much more attention paid to indigenous languages. In many ways, the purposes for recording oral tradition may have changed.

At the time, I had no difficulty with the idea of recording in English (a language in which all three women were comfortable) as long as we were documenting what might be called "secular history" – the narratives associated with the Klondike gold rush, the early-twentieth-century fur trade, the construction of the Alaska Highway, the changes brought to women's lives by increasing governmental control during the 1950s when the highway made it easier for the state to intrude directly into family life. But I *was* troubled when women expected me to record more foundational narratives in English, again because of what seemed to be the inevitable loss in content that occurs when narratives learned in one language are told in another. When I later came to see how they were using these complex narratives as reference points to talk *about* their life experiences, we continued to have long discussions about whether or how to turn these stories into written texts.

The following texts are distilled from many hours of discussions. I recorded, transcribed, and lightly edited the transcripts, after careful review with each narrator (and in some cases daughters, nieces, or granddaughters) about how that text should appear. We settled on a form that tries to retain as much of each woman's voice as possible, and a detailed discussion of the process and choices we made appears in our co-authored volume, *Life Lived Like a Story*.[4] One consistent editorial change involved personal pronouns. Gender distinctions are not marked in Athapaskan languages, so "he" and "she" are often used interchangeably in English. This is sometimes confusing for listeners steeped in English, and I have substituted a referent for a third-person pronoun if that is unclear, quite often the case in narratives with several active characters. Speakers of Athapaskan languages often remark that English language structure is "backwards" because in Athapaskan languages, object precedes subject, whereas in English it follows. I have reordered the sentence if this clarifies the meaning, just as I have standardized subject-verb agreement when there is ambiguity. When it seemed helpful to add words for clarity, I have placed them in brackets. I have further changed verb tense to make it consistent with English when stories cross several time periods.

Converting spoken words to written texts also raises questions about the "texture" of oral narrative. Breaking lines to correspond with a pause by the narrator, and indicating longer pauses by inserting a blank line seems to reproduce the emphasis and cadence of the spoken word more accurately than does conventional paragraphing. Family members who knew the narrators and read various versions of our texts at the time said that they found it easier to "hear" the speaker's voice when reading this form. Throughout, I sometimes use a dash (–) to punctuate a phrase when a period seems too abrupt; ellipses (...) may indicate a longer pause or an incomplete thought. I am acutely aware that editorial decisions we made in the early 1980s might not be the same as those we might make now, but I would be more uncomfortable reversing decisions we made together years ago, now that the narrators are no longer able to participate in the process.

All of us who do this kind of work have questions concerning what happens to oral traditions when they are written down. On one hand, we all acknowledge that writing down spoken language has the potential to freeze or arrest speech. In the words of linguists Nora and Richard Dauenhauer, who have done so much fine work in Alaska, "The writing down of oral literature, no matter how well intentioned or how well carried out, petrifies it. It is like a molecule by molecule replacement of an organic plant by stone. A petrified log may look like wood, but it is actually stone."[5] On the other hand, during my years of living in and now regularly visiting the Yukon, I continue to marvel at the social life that transcribed texts gain in the communities where they originate and continue to be told. I am especially intrigued by the ways Yukon elder storytellers point to writing as just one more way to tell their stories and to make them part of larger social processes that continue to be embedded in clan and community. They use written versions of their stories as points of reference to demonstrate to family members, to other members of their community, and to the larger world the potential of stories to make us re-evaluate situations we think we understand.[6]

During their lifetimes, the women with whom I worked specifically demonstrated their willingness to tell stories in whatever ways "worked" to translate messages they considered important – on radio or video, in public presentations, in visits to school classrooms, by carving, or by authoring their own books. They drew on narratives told and recorded in English to demonstrate how stories inform us about larger processes. From this perspective, writing becomes just one more way of familiarizing readers with narratives so elder storytellers can do the real shaping of narrative when they tell the story to a responsive audience. Viewed in this way, reading is the handmaiden of listening.

Thirteen stories that directly or indirectly concern glaciers follow. I include a short introduction to each story that reflects discussion with the narrator. Annotations are minimal, placed in endnotes, and provide information that narrators would expect an informed listener to understand – the kind of background that Annie Ned insisted, "everybody knows."

Though not directly about glaciers, the first three stories refer to the imaginative force that nearby icefields provide for thinking about origins and transformations of the world and its inhabitants. Icefields appear both as horizons to be breached and as boundaries crossed by strangers who arrive or depart unexpectedly. Angela Sidney's initial narrative follows a classic narrative journey. At the beginning of time and before they acquired their respective forms, humans and animals shared a dark and exclusively winter world, perpetually freezing and helplessly watching their offspring die. Still more troubling, they knew that a parallel "summer world" existed adjacent to the one they inhabited, sealed off from them by the horizon. Eventually, these beings came together and resolved to rupture this boundary in order to steal summer and distribute it more equitably. They conscripted bloodsucker to make the initial puncture and wolverine to push through after the first small opening appeared. Then they dragged a moose hide behind them to enlarge the breach. Beyond this skyline, they were able to escape their perpetual misery by capturing summer in a gigantic bag, stealing it from the powerful but ungenerous controller of weather, and releasing it to establish a seasonal cycle that more fairly distributed access to warmth and vegetation. In this way, a "winter" world with its perpetual whiteness and a brighter "summer" world were brought into alternation by the efforts of humans and animals who jointly made the world as we know it now. Her story frames the setting for two that follow.

Angela Sidney, *How Animals Broke through the Sky*[7]

One time the sky used to come right down to salt water.
Here the animals lived on the winter side. It was cold!
Squirrel always came amongst other animals, crying all the time.

One time they asked her,
"What are you crying for?"

"My kids all froze up again."
Every now and then her children, her babies, all froze up.

So they went to a meeting, all the animals: they are going to try to
poke a hole through the sky.
They are on the winter side and they are going to poke a hole through
the sky so they can have summertime too.
Summer is on the other side.

So they gathered together with all kinds of people –
they're animals though –
Bloodsucker is the one they picked to go through that hole.
He poked that hole and then different animals went through.
Wolverine is the one who made that hole bigger –
He went through pulling a dry moose skin – made that hole bigger.
That's how they all got through.

Now they are going to steal good weather.
They went to a high person[8] – he's got all the weather –
the hot air, cold air,
He's got flowers and leaves.
So they took all that – they stole it when people weren't home.

But there was one old man there.
He went outside – took his blanket outside and waved it around his head.

"Get wintertime over there and summer over here.
Don't go away for good," he told them.
He kept them from taking summer completely away.

That's how, when winter goes for good that's the time we get summer.
Then when summer goes back to the south side, that's the time we get winter.

He waved his blanket and said,
"Don't go away for good," he told the weather.
"Go back and forth."

Those two worlds were side by side – winter on one side, summer on the other.
On one side were winter animals – on the other, summer animals.
They broke the sky down, and after, it went up.

After they got it across, they bust it – the summer bag.
Pretty soon, snow melted – they got leaves,
They had all the leaves tied up in a balloon.
Then they bust the balloon and all the summer things came out.

HUMAN LIFE CYCLES are also about transformation. When Kitty Smith describes jarring transitions from childhood to early adulthood and marriage, she frequently draws on icefields imagery about a colourless winter world where whiteness – of landscape and animals – signifies abrupt social adjustments. Her story *The Stolen Woman* traces the journey of a young woman who is moving on from the safety of childhood to a new stage of life. She has passed puberty and is already married when she is kidnapped and spirited beyond the immense snowy horizon, "[where] daylight broke, the time the sky lifted from salt water ... the other side." Relying on a range of practical skills she has learned during her training at puberty, she manages to outwit her captors, assist her rescuers, and even engineer her own escape. The successful rescue party retreats from the "winter side" by reversing direction and returning to the horizon where they "wait for the sky to lift up" and return to the "summer side."

Kitty Smith, *The Stolen Woman*[9]

A man and a woman had a bark boat.
They make dry meat.

One day he said, "Look. Our boat is cracked.
We'll have to fix another one."

Somebody did that to their boat.
"Looks like somebody cut it, see?" that woman said.

They had a camp on shore.
The husband kept hunting; all the time he hunts.
She fixed a skin, tanned a skin.

Boat is coming.
They see her – two men.
"You've got a husband?"

"Yes, I've got a husband."

"We're going to take you for our wife."

"What are you talking about?
I don't want to leave my husband!"

Two men.
She tried to stop them. No.

"We're going to kill you if you don't go with us.
Get in our boat!"

She took her sewing bag.
Puts away her husband's moccasins, tied up his blanket.
Everything – put some kind of light there, matches, I guess.

They wait for that husband to come back.

"What are you doing with my wife?"

"We're taking her. We're taking your wife."

Bad people, eh?

"Where do you come from? I want to know." he tells them.

"You know that sky?
You see that sky?
We're going through that way, the way daylight broke, the time the sky lifted from salt water.
We go the other way: other-side people are us," they say.
"Your wife we pay for," they say.
They shoot squirrel tail to him on bow and arrow.
Then they shoot owl foot to him.

He called to his wife:
"Don't be too sorry.
Used to be I got lots of people, you know.[10]
Don't be sorry too much, but think about me sometimes."
Gone now.

From there, he went to his country.
He has lots of people, that man.
They make ready for war. They are going to take back that woman.
They fix everything, that way, war stuff.
Bow and arrow, horn, sharp stick for spear, club.
They go now.

Those men told them where they come from.
They keep going, keep going.
They see an island – round island.

"I guess that's the place," that man said.
Soon, daylight.
That sky lifts and they go in [beyond the horizon].

The other side is winter: this side is summer.
They are lucky they took their snowshoes. Ice here.
They see just where the boat landed there, so they put away their boat.

There is an old trail up there.
They keep going on that trail, big trail – snow on top.
They keep going, keep going.
Big lake in there, though.
On the other side is a camp – brush camp.
At night they are going to sneak down there.

They see two old ladies. They've got fish there, hanging up.
They're sitting outdoors.
One tells her partner,
"Bring that wood so we can cook that fish quick."
She pulls and pulls ... Gee, what's the matter ...
Those men push that lady and she falls down.
The other one laughs.

The other one [who fell] whispers,
"Don't say anything. Somebody did that to me."

Those war people are coming.[11]
Gee, those women get scared.

"You know my wife they took this way?" the man asked.

"Yes, we know," they said.
"They went to summer side and took a woman.
This place, though, is all the time winter: no summer here.
As many years old as I am, I don't know that summer place.
I don't know where that place is they got that woman.
Summer place, that place.
No snow." That's what they said.
"She's got two husbands here," those women said.
"We're going to tell you how to get there.

You're going to go this way.
Trail is going to split here: one is going to be a-big trail; other trail same, too.
You fellows got to go this trail [to the right].
All the time they do that way, hunt."

They see that trail now, and they follow this one [on the right].
They see some people watching from the top of the hill:
See fire ... See Indians' camp ... That camp is full.
They are going to sneak there.

That lady's husbands are gone.[12]
It's dark – no daytime there either, I guess.
Somebody cut wood.
That lady camps behind all the time with her husbands.
People camp on ahead – she doesn't want to get mixed up with those people.
Just all the time [lags] behind.

Somebody cut wood.
They sneak up ...[13]
That's his wife, that man. That's the one they take away.
They are coming to her. They help her cut wood.

"Where's your husbands?"

"They hunt, all the men. Just women here."

"We're starved," they tell her.
"You got meat?"

"Yes."

She broke her stone axe: her husbands' mother is in there.

"This axe broke. Look," she tells that mother-in-law.

"Oh, my," she said. "I'm going to tie it up."

While her mother-in-law is fixing that axe
That girl put fat, grub, under her clothes.
She kept walking around, packing wood.
She packs wood in, and she packs food out to the men.
I don't know how many times.

She came back: "That stone axe is broken again."

That time she cleaned off all that skin sleigh of dry meat.
She feeds them lots.
"I'm packing my wood," she says to that mother-in-law, "Packing wood."

It's getting darker.
That night is going to be war, now, going to fight.

They tell her, "You try to get away."

"I'm going to run this road."

Her husbands come back with skin sleigh.
Another one comes back. He's got wolf-skin blanket.

All night she said, "Too hot this wolf-skin blanket.
Too hot, I can't breathe.
That's why I feel sick all the time."[14]

"All right."
They give her marten-skin robe, her husbands.

Her husbands sleep right there, another one right there,
One on each side of her.
Soon she has a stick right ready – club, you know.
Puts it beside her, listens all the time.

They start to fight now.

Her husbands, she clubs them right away.
Pretty soon, she gets up. She runs out the door, sees people going that way.
She goes on that road, her.
All those people get killed. Nothing left.

Those people come back. Going home now.
Those two old ladies are sleeping.
They are frozen there – I guess they gave up.

They all got in the boat again.
They waited for the sky to lift up.
I don't know what place that is ... I guess that moon is on the other side.

IF PROTAGONISTS ARE sometimes transported to an unfamiliar dimension characterized by "whiteness," the colourless strangers who crossed the glaciers were assumed to have come from this winter world. In Kitty Smith's account, a young man, scarcely more than a child, is led away by an invisible helper. This journey, expected of a young person seeking special knowledge, is conventionally marked by a sharp transition beyond the horizon or perhaps under a point of land; in this case, a rainbow marks the boundary. He finds himself in a disorienting world where rules of social behaviour are unclear, food is unfamiliar, and appropriate behaviour must be learned from scratch. Rather than encountering the anticipated spirit helper, he meets pale visitors who give him a clear set of rules and instruct him to convey them to others when he returns home. They give him a sack of unfamiliar food as tangible evidence of his experience and then order him to eat that food exclusively and to instruct his family to sleep on raised beds. Instead of acquiring a shaman's song, he is given a song that predicts the coming of k'och'en and their power to absorb his people. When he returns home, uncles and brothers who anticipate that he is returning with profound new knowledge from this vision quest greet him. In lieu of new insights, he delivers disciplinary rules from his encounter with white strangers. Only his grandmother understands how profoundly troubling, if prescient, his messages are.

Kitty Smith, *The First K'och'en*[15]

You know my grandson, Kenneth?
He looks after me, takes care of me.
They're that way, Indians, long time ago, I guess.

One Indian boy got meat for his grandma.
All the time he does that, that boy.
No white man that time – they don't know about white man!

I'm going to tell you a story about this one, that boy.
He looked after his grandma – he took care.
Where they kill meat, he goes, that boy.
He gets meat. They've got two dogs –
No dogs long time ago, they say; just a little while ago, that dog.

They kill two caribou – his uncle killed them.
"You get meat: your uncle killed caribou.
Are you going to go?"

He says, "Yes."

They say, "You take your dog."
He took his dog. Goes.
He told his grandma, "Don't get wood, Grandma.
I'll come back. I'm going to get you wood.
My uncle killed caribou."

People go to get meat.
Everybody packed it: everybody went to that meat place.
That boy, he looked for bones some place, after people go –
Looks around to see if he finds something: he takes them.
He's got two dogs to pack them, too.

People are gone already.
He goes back. He's as big as my grandchild Kenneth.
This is a story, you know, not a "story." It's a true story.

He sees a rainbow, about as big as this tent.
He stood up about this far from it, and somebody talked to him.

"Go through." He doesn't see who said that.
"Go through."

He comes, his dogs behind. Goes through.
Other side, little bit long way, he stands back.
A big sack falls down there.

"Don't eat that meat any more!
You're going to eat this grub – this one in the sack.
Don't drink water from this ground for one week!
That many days, don't take water from this ground.
You're going to use this [water], from inside your grub bag here,
Or else we're going to come, going to get you."

He took that sack, put it on top of his pack.
He doesn't see that man who talks to him, but he sees that rainbow.
But he talked to him.

His grandma cooked already –
That's what I do with Kenneth here – cook soup, everything.

So when he comes back, he runs here,
"What you cooking, Grandma, soup?"

"Yes."

Last night [that person] cooked, him. Fed me there.

"I cook some gopher. I killed two, grandchild," she said, that old lady,
"I'll cook that one."

"No Grandma, I'm not going to eat it.
I've got something to eat," he said.

She looked.
Something's wrong, she thinks.

"I'm not going to eat [your food] any more, Grandma.
I've got my grub here, my sack."

That one who talked to him told him,
"Tell those people to fix some things for you."

He told his grandma,
"Tell those boys they got to come,
Their uncle, too, has got to come here."

Grandma goes to tell them,
"He wants you ... Don't know what's the matter.
That's what he told me."[16]

They come there and the boys sit down.

"I want you to fix that high bed for me," he said.
"I want to lay down on top."
Just quick they fixed it.
"And two bridges, I want you to fix this way."
Bridge goes right there, right here, that far.
"Well, thank you," he said.
"Somebody talked to me; that's why I say that.
You come tonight before you eat: you come to this bridge.
Then I'm going to tell you.

You hold your wife's hand when you come on that bridge.
I'm going to tell you."

His Grandma got scared, you know.

"Don't think about it, Grandma. Eat. You eat good."

They fix already that bed for him. On top.
He opens his sack – he doesn't know this kind of grub.
He eats something from there.
Water in there, too. He drinks water.

And he said,
"They're coming now."
He sings some kind of song,

"Come on, come on my friends."

"You hold your wife's hand.
Go down, turn that way."
He tells them, "I'm going to be white man."
Nobody knows K'och'en that time. That boy called them K'och'en.
Right today they use it.
He said, "K'och'en you, K'och'en that one."
Turn that way, turn that way – everyone does that.

"You fellows are going to be white." That's what he said.
They don't know what he means.

"I'm not going to eat any more for seven days," he said.
"One day, this ground going to be full of K'och'en.
You're going to be K'och'en, you people."
Nobody knows.
"Going to turn white man."
How many white man grandchild have I got now?
That time, look!
I talk white man way, too, now.
He's honest, that boy, isn't he?

Seven days he stayed there.
And he told his Grandma.

He gave her a big sack, that big one – don't know where it came from –

"Right here your grub is going to stay, Grandma.
Anything you want stays there.
It's not gone 'til you're gone.
That sack is all full of grease, everything.
No more you're going to look for grub.
Anything – fresh meat, you want it –
It's going to stay there – inside.

You want ribs? It's there.
What you wish for before you open, you say you want that one –
Right there it is.
Until you're gone, I leave this sack for you.
I'm going to stay here two days more, Grandma," he told her.
"Then gone. Don't be sorry, nothing."

Him, he called them K'och'en.
That's why this time Indians, nothing.[17]
Right today, everybody calls them K'och'en.

That time he gave them bread, nobody knows that.
"This kind of grub you fellows are going to eat."

It's true, this one.
That boy, he's gone – nobody knows where.
Now I sit down on top of that bed [like the one he had them make].
You sit on bed.
Before that, bed was on ground.

"You're going to be that way and you're going to turn to white man."
What white man?
That time nobody knows it.

The next four stories address the challenges glaciers posed to travel between coast and interior in the eighteenth and nineteenth centuries. In the first story, Angela Sidney is speaking about her father's Da<u>k</u>l'aweidí clan history, and orally notes her source, Mrs. Bert Dennis, a member of that same clan. In Chapter 1, we heard evidence from oral tradition about migrations to the Gulf of Alaska during late stages of the Little Ice Age, both southward from the Copper River and northward along the Pacific coast. But inland peoples were also migrating coastward down major rivers flowing from the interior. Dak̲l'aweidí is now an important Tlingit-named clan both in southeast Alaska, where it is part of the Eagle moiety, and in the southern interior Yukon, where it is grouped within the equivalent Wolf moiety. Her father's Dak̲l'aweidí clan crest, Angela Sidney explains, is Killer Whale. Mrs. Sidney traces that clan's early migration from the interior downriver to the coast and under the Stikine Glacier, once much larger than it is now. She discusses their dispersal and their eventual return to Tagish, where she was living when we recorded this account.

Angela Sidney, *My Father's Dak̲l'aweidí History*[18]

Now I'll tell about my Dad's side.

My Dad is Dak̲l'aweidí: Dak̲l'aweidí owns Killer Whale and is Wolf.
Tagish Dak̲l'aweidí came from Telegraph Creek – that's where they were staying – at Taltan.
Tal means a platter, Indian way, [in] Den k'e; Tan means "it's laying there."[19]
Taltan – "tal" laying there – "it's all flat."
That's where my father's people were.
That's their Shagoon, they call it, their history.

They had some trouble down there over a woman – that's why they parted, why they moved away.
They floated down the Stikine River to Wrangell.
They were close to salt water when they saw a glacier coming down – just touching the creek, like this.
You can't go across in front of it: that glacier always falls down, makes a noise.

So they landed above it and started to talk about it:
"How are we going to get further down?
That glacier might fall down and get us all killed!"
So they don't know what to do.
They didn't want to go back to Taltan because they made trouble with each other.
That's why they're moving out.

Finally, two old men decided to go – to try it. Two little old men, ready to die, I guess.[20]

"Send us through it. We're old now. We're no good to you people. If we die, you won't miss us much anyhow."

That's what they told the rest of the younger people, the rest of the people.

Those two little men had a boat of their own, so they must have gone under the glacier.

I wish I could get up that way and find it!

When they're ready to take off, they made a song:

"Shove it out now!"

This is the song they pushed them out with.

They remember it [still] – that's the song they separated on.

My father's people used to sing it if they're going to make a potlatch.

I remember they sang it in 1912 when I was a little girl – I was ten years old that time. They sang it just before they're going to spend money at that potlatch.

Those two men were going to make a sign if they got through safely.

Here, they made it through!

So they made a sign – what kind of sign I don't know – they made a sign when they landed safely on the other side of the glacier!

So the rest went through, too.

When they reached Wrangell they camped on a gravel beach.

That's where they got their name – Dak̲l'aweidí.

That's what they called themselves now – I don't know what their name was before.

Before they started out again, they made another song:

"Way out to the sky I aim my boat."

Then that group split three ways: some went out to deep water, and some went to Yakutat.

[The third group] came up the coast and went up Chilkat River.

They landed up there, and then they cut across country by Bear Creek Pass, and they landed in Tagish.

That's where they made their home.

That's how my father's people landed in Tagish: therefore they have got people in Telegraph Creek, too.

It's Dak̲l'aweidí who own Tagish: they were the first to make their village here.
That name passes through women, but the woman stays in the husband's ground.

My aunt, Mrs. Bert Dennis, told me about this.

IF TRAVELLING UNDER glacier bridges could be perilous, crossing over glaciers promised other risks. All three women tell the story *Falling through a Glacier*, about a coastal Tlingit man who disappeared into a crevasse on the way back home following a trading trip to the interior. In Mrs. Ned's version, the setting is a glacier at the head of Kusawa Lake. This is the same glacier that Edward Glave crossed with Chilkat Tlingit guides in 1890, and their route is traced in Chapter 6. It also appears as "Great Glacier" on a 1901 map published by American scientist George Davidson (see Figure 19). Davidson, in turn, drew much of his information from an earlier map drawn by the well-travelled Tlingit chief Kohklux, whose work will be discussed in Chapter 7.[21]

In Annie Ned's and Kitty Smith's versions, the Tlingit man slips into a crevasse and his Athapaskan trading partner, knowing he will be held accountable, nevertheless travels on to the coast to report the tragedy. Distraught kinsmen hold a funeral feast and then accompany the inland partner back to the site to recover the body. They are astonished to discover their kinsman alive, sustained both by the "lunch" his inland partner's wife prepared for him prior to their departure and by the food his relatives offered the fire at his funeral potlatch. Fire, like ice, has transformative force. The relationship between trading partners, frequently reinforced by marriage ties making them brothers-in-law, was especially sensitive and laden with responsibilities during the acceleration of nineteenth-century trade.[22] Kitty Smith reminds us that because the preferred trading partnership was between brothers-in-law, the woman who prepared the victim's lunch was probably his own sister, married to his inland trading partner. In Angela Sidney's version, her father is able to save his partner by quick thinking and skilful technical work.

Annie Ned, *Falling through a Glacier*[23]

At the head of Lake Arkell[24] [Kusawa] they've got that ice – glacier, you know.
That's the place that Coast Indian fell in, when he's going back to Haines.

They should do it the same time; they should get him!
But they didn't.
They went on.

He fell through to a little island there – a dry place – and he stayed.
He's got lunch in his pack, some grease.
They've got no rope, I guess; that's why they go.
Well, he's gone already, I guess they think – he went through a crack.
He should holler there!

So, they went back now.
They put up potlatch in Klukwan.
Everybody cried.
He hears them ... he's cold![25]
They should have tried to get him!
Ah, people are crazy!

Just pretty soon, now, he's feeling cold.
Don't know how many days it is now.
He's got moose skin in his pack and he put it on.
When it gets wet, he gets another one.
He put beaver skin – you know how it can't get wet through –
He put it on.
Big place, they say that is: more water than sand.
He sleeps and eats. He's cold though.

Oh he's strong.
He eats his last grease now.

So then they came back with that rope and they put it down.
They send one [person] in – they had to get that body, I guess.
So that man slid in that way, too.

Pretty soon something came down.
Ice. A big chunk of ice.
Something is coming down – he touched it.
"Ahhhh. Oh my!"

Well, that man is just about all in!
He moved his head.
Over ten days by now.

He [the man who went down the crevasse] told them,
"If I've got his pack, got his body, I'll do this," he said [pulling the rope].
Everybody cried.
They should have done that the same time [that he fell in],
Cut up moose skin [to make a rope to rescue him].
They've got lots of moose skin.
But they just let him go.
But that man saved himself, wrapped himself in moose skin, in gopher robe.

They pulled him out.
His head went just like that [limp].
They make fire already.
They covered him up.
They gave him something hot.
They took off his wet clothes.

They put up camp there.
He ate lots of grease, started to get stronger.
He moved.

Already they had the potlatch!
He told them that he saw that potlatch.

> Why? Did they see the body? What for they want a potlatch!
> They should have taken the body out first!
> Awful, eh?

They stayed there maybe two days; they fed him.
So, he started to go, he started to get strong and go.
They carried him half way there in a moose skin.
About half way there, he got strong and he started to walk.

People were coming.
They were coming to help, I guess.
Here that man is walking around. Goodness!

This happened at the other end of Lake Arkell.
I've been there, but I've never seen that glacier.

Figure 8 A "glacier highway." Kaskawulsh Glacier provides one contemporary example of what glacier travel routes described in these stories might have looked like. *Photograph by Julie Cruikshank, 1999*

Kitty Smith, *Falling through a Glacier*[26]

Two men went from Klukwan to get freight – fox, lynx – skins.
They got ready, took guns – there were guns that time I guess.
This is a true story!

One of those men told his wife,
"We're going to stay a long time up there, Yukon.
We'll come back, August. We're going to stay there all summer."
That's what they say. They got fur all the time then, Indians – there's no store that time.

And so they're gone, two people.
That's a man and his brother-in-law – they each married the other one's sister.

And they stay, stay in the Yukon.
Oh, they buy fur ... they trade, you know.
That one man has got lynx skin blankets – he buys them, he trades them.

They're going back now, to Klukwan. Now they've started.
They've got lunch, I guess. One woman tells them,
"I'm going to fix lunch for you. You gave me that chew [chewing tobacco] for nothing."
They chew, chew – you know that snuff – yeah, they chew ... used to be a long time ago it looked just like a dry leaf.
That's the time he's going back and she told him, "I'm going to fix lunch for you."

She smashed dry meat and she made grease – put in grease.
That big bag is just full – lots of meat just smashed like flour mixed up with grease.

That man said, "When I come back to Klukwan, me and my wife are going to eat this, you know."
They've got dry meat and they've got fat, too.

They go back now. They follow a foot trail, used to go that way.
There used to be a glacier down that way.
They go as far as the top – that glacier goes across to the mountain.
They eat lunch there, then they start to go now.

The first one starts across – walk, walk, walk.
Just in the middle, he falls down, that man's partn.er – down the crack in that ice.

The other one is scared now – his partner is gone!
I guess he hollered – I don't know. I guess he was scared, he cried someplace –
He poked his stick – his walking stick that way [into the crevasse].

When that man falls down, he's got his pack on.
He cracked this way, that ice, and from there, this way [indicating that the crack went straight down and then there was a ledge].
Right there, that's where he landed. He's not hurt, nothing.
That man is not dead. He landed there – long way down, you know.

I guess he hollered.
But his partner got scared and ran away.

He stays there ... takes off his backpack ... puts those furs, skins underneath him.
He sleeps ...
Then he eats his lunch, I guess.
When he wants a drink of water, I guess he melts ice in his mouth.
He does it that way.

It's tough for that other man, his partner.
That man made it to Klukwan.
"My partner fell in the ice, through a crack."
And they know he died.

Big potlatch is started.
They made a big table [of food]. That man was a good man.
Pretty near one month they stayed there.

Then those people took a slave, took him.
His [the lost man's] nephew said,
"Where my uncle is dead, that same place we're going to put him [the slave] down [on a rope].
They're going to hang that slave down there, he's going to look around.
He's going to look for that body.
If he doesn't find the body – if my uncle is dead – we're going to kill him so that slave will be his partner."

They go now.
Just those who are going to carry the body go.

Over that month, sometimes he sleeps, that man – he sleeps, I guess.
He's got fur blankets.
Sometimes they bring him dish [food transformed from the potlatch feast].
When down there they make potlatch at Klukwan, they call out the names – "you, that one too ..." and they put food in the fire, throw grub, more grub ...
I guess that's what it means. It comes to that man down there,
So he eats. He stays there.

Well, people go to that place now.
They're going to find him now.
That man's partner put a post there, a marker: he put his walking stick to mark that place.
"Right there, right there he fell down."
His brother is an old man, too. He cries
"Ayyyy! ..." he said. "You died right there, my brother."
He hollered, you know.

That man down there, he heard ...

"Ayyyy ..." somebody hollered back.

"Somebody hollered down there!"

"Who hears him?"

"I hear too!"

"Who hears him?"

"I hear him." Somebody hollers!

"Aye ... Aye ..." they holler.

"Aye, Aye ... I'm living yet." He says that there.
Oh my!

"They're going to put a string down there. Look for it." They tell him.
Put a little rock on that.

"I got him," he hollered. He ties up his stuff, all tight.
They pull up.
His stuff comes up!
His pack, fur, everything comes out of there.
Now his body is going to come.

They send down a wide belt.
They're going to tie him up (around his waist).
He ties up ... strong rope.

Now they pull him ...
He comes out ...
He's fat!
He's alright!
One month he stays in that ice.

"You're alright? You starve?"
"No, I'm alright. I've got lots of things."
That woman who fixed him lunch, she smashed that grease in that meat.
He eats that good. He eats that.
And that slave is saved. They give him to that man.
"This is going to be your own. I give him to you uncle.
He's going to take care of you.
I was going to kill him right there and he was going to be dead and he was going to stay in there with you.
'You're saved.'
He's your slave now."

They walk now.
From there they make the boat – they've got a boat there, used to be.
They go down the creek.

Two men got in one boat – they go fast to tell the people down there the story.

Down there, those people are talking.
Then those two man came to tell them, holler
"Ayyy ... Kanakh comes back! He's not dead! He's coming down!"

My goodness, his wife jumped in the water – he's got two wives.
Boat is coming now.
He's wearing clothes he brought down from the Yukon.
Ah, fancy clothes!
Everybody comes.

"Kanakh, is that you?"

"Yes, I'm living."

Oh, my. Everyone's surprised.
Big potlatch they paid for him – but he comes back anyway.

Angela Sidney, *Falling through a Glacier*[27]

You know how people used to go down to sell their furs on the coast?
One time my father was going back home.
His trading partner, the one who buys furs from him all the time was going with him.

Here, they started from Lkoot Lake, between Haines and Skagway.
At the end of Lkoot, they started coming back that way.
They came out at Robinson, or someplace like that.
And here there was a glacier they had to cross.

My Daddy got across,
But there was a crack in the glacier
And that man fell in!
I don't know how he did it.

My Daddy didn't know what to do.
If he dies there, he thought, they're going to blame him for it,
Think he killed him or something.
So he hollered at him, and here he answered!

"Are you okay?"

"Yes, I'm okay."

"I'm going to try to get you out.
I'm going to untie my pack,
And I am going to send the string of my pack rope down to you.
You tie it around your waist and climb up."

So he did.
He untied his pack, my Daddy
And he tied a string around a stick and let it down to him.

"You jerk it when you got it," he said.
He felt a jerk.
"Put your elbows against the glacier and try to pull yourself up.
I'm going to keep pulling you too."

He kept doing it, and finally he got himself out of the glacier.
Finally, he came out.

Then they came out of the pass around Robinson or someplace around there.
And they went over the mountains this way to Tagish.
That place is between Robinson and Lkoot.
There's a valley in there, I heard them talking about it.

That man's wife said that her husband talked about it all the time.
Kodéinaahaa is his name.
That man stayed with my father quite a while and then he went to Dyea.

The final six accounts refer directly to surging glaciers. The first two, *Nàlùdi* and *Bear Creek Glacier,* concern the Lowell Glacier and its dramatic consequences. In the past, as we've seen, it has crossed the Alsek more than once, building up an ice wall against Goatherd Mountain on the opposite side of the river. When this happens, a lake – Neoglacial Lake Alsek – fills behind an ice dam that eventually bursts with catastrophic downstream consequences. Mrs. Smith's name for her story, *Nàlùdi* (fish stop), refers to the salmon run halted by its advance. Mrs. Ned's name for her story, *Bear Creek Glacier,* comes from a creek of that name that flows into the Dezadeash River, which in turn flows into the Alsek, and may refer to one of the levels Neoglacial Lake Alsek reached (see Map 3).

In a third story, *Lake Arkell Glacier,* Mrs. Ned refers to a glacier at the head of Kusawa Lake where she hunted with her first husband. While scientists do not classify this as a surging glacier, people living near icefields would have no way of judging which glaciers were risky in this way, so precautions about "cooking with grease," central to this story, were applied broadly.

A fourth story, *Dadzik,* refers to a glacier that apparently once flowed to the Tatshenshini River near Dalton Post, though its location is uncertain and it may no longer exist. Mrs. Smith says that people once camped near here after shooting some goats, and cooked the meat. An old man warned them to be cautious about the grease, but someone was careless. Later that night, they heard alarming sounds and then saw a bright light on the glacier shining through the darkness. The intense heat caused people to flee, and they rushed to the river leaving behind meat and possessions. When they returned, they found all their meat cooked.

Kitty Smith, *The Lowell Glacier, Nàlùdi*[28]

One man lived down there, at Yaakwdáat,
"Yakutat" they call it, way down there: people lived at that place, near salt water.
Klukshu River goes down to that place.
From there, people came up to this Yukon.
One old man is coming and a little boy about so big.
When they got there, they met an old man, a Yukon Indian.
That old man has no hair on his head, nothing.
The little boy who came from Yaakwdáat told him,

"Ah, that old man!
The top of his head is just like the place where gopher plays –
A bare stump."
That kid laughed at him.

One old man who was with him said,
"Don't say that.
You don't know that old man!
Why do you say that?
That old man is your grandpa. When you're old, your hair is going to be that way, too!"

Well, that old man is from Yukon, you know.

After that, they went back.

Summertime, that old man went to Nàlùdi.
He's medicine man, you know, a big doctor.

That ice was coming right down from the mountain.
At the end of the ice, a creek came down.
Right there, he sat down.

He said to himself,
"What am I going to do?"
His doctor[29] talks to him.

"You think I'm going to bring that glacier to this mountain?
It's going to be flooded, that side."

His doctor told him,
"You try it. It's going to come."

That old man lay down, right there.
His doctor's working now on that glacier.
It comes down, comes down ...
Glacier ... glacier ... comes down ... comes down.
Until it's all level with this mountain.

That's the first time it [Lowell Glacier] crossed.
That Indian doctor did that.

After he did that, it crossed another time.
My grandma told me it was like that one time, in her time.
All flooded again, that 1016, Haines Junction, that way.[30]
Talk about gophers die! she said.
Before, that glacier didn't do that.
But after he did that, first time, from there it started.

That man stayed there on top of that glacier until that water is filled up.
Champagne Landing, everywhere is all full with that water.
There's a water place shows that yet.[31]
"All full now," his doctor said.
"You know how far I'm going to clean them?
Pretty near to the middle of the mountain all I'm going to wash down."

"All right. Break it now," he said.
It broke down, that ice.
Water goes now.

People were staying at a flat place where Champagne Creek [Alsek
River] and Klukshu River [Tatshenshini River] meet[32] –
Some kind of Coast Indian people.
They all died there people – all washed down to salt water.
Just that one man was saved, that one who told the boy not to make fun.
That's the one he saved, that's all.
All cleaned right out.
They say they saw water coming half way up the mountain.

That happened before my grandmother's time,
But in her time, that ice still goes, touches that mountain.
That time the water was still full.

I've been there, Nàlùdi.
That's the one that broke.
It's a long time since that ice met that mountain.

When my grandmother was a little girl, she stayed at Dalton Post all the time.
That's the time she said all the time when they cook they don't use cooking stick.
They boil food.
They don't let that soup run over, too, because there is danger in that ice.
If that ice smells grease, he doesn't like it.
Should be people just boil meat.
If he smells grease, that's the time he starts.

Just goats and sheep there, no caribou, no moose.

There was a flood in my grandmother's time, though,
But not as big as when that man did that: it's after him.
In his time, that ice came right up to that mountain –
That's why they call it Nàlùdi, "fish stop."
Right there, there is a big creek coming [Alsek River]
Bigger than the Klukshu [Tatshenshini] River.
That creek came from the mountain.

That was before me, in my grandmother's time –
Maybe I was just born then.
August, they go to Kluane. Indians used to walk around like that.
Kluane people, Big Lake people – they're friends together.
They're going to Kluane, I guess.
They stay there, come back.
Flooded! Bear Creek is full of water! So they stayed on the other side.
No trees, I guess, just gravel, willows.
Just a little while, that flood: that flood was just a little while, just to Bear Creek.
Then he broke down again – and then it's dry.

That's when one old lady told me,
"Talk about gophers!" she said, that flood.
Lots of gophers there. Dead ones. Just full of gophers!
They packed them in:
"Talk about gophers! I wish you were coming that time," she told me.
"That water dropped down in the morning when the glacier broke.
My husband packed in a big bag of gophers.
Then we started, dogs, everything, lots of gophers."

Since the doctor did that the first time, it happens again.
Some young people don't believe me when I say that.
But I don't say that: *people* say that.[33]

Figure 9 View from Goatherd Mountain. Jack Schick is sitting at or near the spot where the shaman made his decision to call Nàlùdi across the Alsek River. *Photograph by Julie Cruikshank, 1982*

Annie Ned, *Bear Creek Glacier*[34]

This is the story about that Bear Creek –
My grandpa – Frankie Jim's namesake – he told me this story.
Lots of people tell it, too.

That time, they say, the water raised in this Yukon, long time ago.
You heard about it?
That time, the water raised, they say.

He said this happened at Bear Creek, when my grandpa is young.
They put up gophers for wintertime.
Meat, too, they dried.
He's pretty old, that time he died, Grandpa.

So, him, his wife, and lots of people hunt –
You know, put up food for winter, everything.
That time they worked, water's getting high!
They didn't know about it until that water came to the meadow where
they stayed.

So he said to his wife,
"We've got to pull out those snares."
And they went half way up that hill – it's high, there, [above] Bear Creek.

Then what are they going to do after?
Well, glacier, he opened, I guess.
Then, they went on top of there, half way up that hill, above that lake.
Just like a wave, half way, that water.

Well, they thought about believing that:
That's Coast Indian, he told them that, long-time people.[35]

Well, they stayed there.
As soon as it comes up half way,
It's just like a wave, they say.
Everybody feels bad:
They don't know what they're going to do.

In the morning, Grandpa got up, measured that water:
They're going to go to the mountain if that animal comes out.[36]

But that water doesn't come out quick.
You can see waves on the hill, this time still.

So he tells his wife,
"That water's going down!"
He measures that water with a stick.
"It goes two sticks down," he said, where he measured.

Gee! Then they stay, they stay.
Someone got raft – they want to go to the mountain.
But then it went down quick, that water.
Then, meadow again! Oh gosh!
He goes down to that meadow: talk about gophers!
Dead gophers!

He was packing dog pack, him.
Now people don't go [anywhere]! Got to stay one place.
But Grandpa, he walked around.
Bunch of gophers; everybody is just packing gophers.

From then on, those gophers are gone.
How many years it took those gophers to come back!
That's what they say.[37]

Annie Ned, *Lake Arkell Glacier*[38]

When you fry grease by fire,
That's the time it cracks, that glacier.
Then lots of water comes – that's what they say.
Then the water is all full.

One man did not believe that – Frank Stick, his name.
He didn't believe it.[39]
He put goat grease, thick like that.
He burned it.
Then that glacier started.
When he threw a blanket in the fire, that made it stop again.
Well, there's something inside that glacier: he smells it.
Then it quiets down.
I don't know myself what is going on that time.

That one story my grandpa tells me, Bear Creek glacier.[40]
But this time, myself, this one I'm telling you the story.

We had it, one time, head of Lake Arkell with my first husband.[41]
Old man tells me,
"Don't put grease. It spoils everything," he tells me. "It's no good."

We wanted to meet my husband's mother from Dalton Post.
We've got kids that time.
That glacier, that head of Lake Arkell,
We got njäl there, his daddy.
Njäl, long-time-people.[42]
[Near] where they dry meat is njäl.
Inside, it's good: you dry your meat there.

He says he killed three caribou there close to that glacier, that mountain,
Close to that place that man fell through the ice.[43]

We got in there – just small kids with us,
Johnny is with us, too: he's a man though, that time.[44]
We got to those caribou, three bulls. Fat.
We got little tent.

I don't know what for he wants to hunt, hunt, hunt, Old Man.[45]
My old man, I tell him not to go that way [toward the glacier].
"Around here, lots of caribou," I tell him.
Just willows, no trees there; just little trees on top of the mountain, that's the ones we burn.

Then *he's* the one put grease [another hunter, she identifies as Jack Smith].
He's Indian! He knows!
I don't know what for he did that!

We just came out from down there.
Then Old Man, he wants to go hunt.
I don't know, me too: pretty dangerous, that way.

So pretty soon, we brought in meat.
Johnny wants to take meat down where boat is.
Pretty steep hill down.

I tell him, "Don't go that way!
You come where your brother is going to come this way.
You go down and look for him."

He goes that way.
Gee! Well, we start to eat now.
Ha! Big wind!
Just first time he[46] comes out, that rain put the fire out.
All wet.

It gets dark.
Johnny, he cut those little trees on the mountain.
They made fire.
Then we tried to put strong way that tent.

Just like that! Rain.
Gee, I worry about Old Man.
"Shoot!" I tell Johnny. "Shoot!"[47]

It's alongside that glacier, it happened.
He's got slicker coat, though.
Gosh, nothing.

Then I heard something break.
You know he carries around blanket in bush.
I smell something burning: that man burned up his blanket.
He stopped that rain!
But it's dark, though.

Gee, we holler, we holler.
How come my husband goes that long way, near that glacier?
He doesn't know where to go:
He started fire under that kind of bushy little tree in mountain.
He put light there, but it's raining.
He goes there under that little tree.
Thick.
He stays there, underneath.

Then pretty soon that rain stops.
He knows, he says, which way that rain goes.
Gee, that glacier is close!

That time he brought that, Johnny,
He talked.[48]
"He's going to come back," he tells me.

Then he heard that gun. Right!
Goes right through.
"Shoot some more."
Little longer he shoots.
Then he found out his way.
Pretty soon we hear shot – then we shot.
Just soaking wet!
Hole in his blanket he threw in the fire.

Jack Smith is pretty old; just the same he burned grease.
When Old Man came back, he said,
"There's no kids here! Who did that?" he said to us.
Well, we don't know, us, he did that.
Gee, Jack Smith got mad at himself.
"That's me," I did that, he say after he burns that grease, fat.

There used to be lots more thunder than now:
Thunder comes from cracking glaciers.
That glacier makes big noise when he wants to do something.

Kitty Smith, *Dadzik*[49]

Dadzik –
Yeah, that's a bad place, that place, they say.
One time when Mary Kane's father was a little boy, he went hunting with his Daddy.[50]
Later, when they told that story, he said, "Yes, I was there."

Lots of people were hunting that time.
It was just goats they were hunting – they shot lots of things.
No caribou or moose there, though.[51]

One old man said, "Take good care of that grease.
The wind is blowing that way, toward the ice.
I smelled grease when I was walking around.
Ah! Right there! Look at that grease! Be careful of the grease."

And he took off from that ground.
"The grease smell is strong down there where I was walking around."
He said that, that old man.

The creek went down that way to Dalton Post River.[52]
My, some people were getting excited – it was getting dark already.
Somebody went outside for a few minutes, and when he came back, he said,
"Gee, I heard a groundhog whistle up there.
It's funny how game talks that way at nighttime – gopher, geese – they just talk for nothing!"

Then it started to get light – just like there was a light on top of the ice.
It starts getting warm. People start to sweat.
"Well," that man said, "we've got to get away."
They're close to that glacier.

They started.
That little kid, his dad held him.
Meat, blankets, everything they left behind – just to get away.
When they began to move down they could see eyes, just like the sun, on top of the ice.
Two eyes came out when they were going down.
It's getting hotter and hotter – too much heat, just like a stove.
So they went into the water – first just shallow and then deeper.
They were about five miles from that ice by now. That's where they camped.

Gee whiz, daytime now!
Sun all came out, now everyplace, so they went back again.
That meat is pretty near cooked, they say.
I don't know what did that.
They told Jack Dalton about that story.
He married an Indian woman, used to be, at Dalton Post.
He went down there and he took a horse, but it was too hot – too much.
The horse fell down just like he was sleeping.
[Dalton] went into the water – he just let the horse go, dead. Too much heat.
They say he came back without his horse, nothing.

Dadzik, they call that place – it's a big glacier, that one, below Dalton Post, on Dalton Post Creek.
Everybody saw that. I guess my grandma saw it too, ran away, when my Daddy was a baby.
That place they made grease was bad.

GLACIERS ARE SOMETIMES depicted as dens for giant animals. Mrs. Smith says that if the animal inhabiting the glacier is killed, the glacier melts. There is also a tradition from the Tatshenshini River drainage of a giant copper-clawed owl that terrorized and consumed people until a resourceful old woman managed to destroy it at Noogaayík, a major fish camp downriver from Neskataheen. A mountain near here is named mA'dzi^{n} k'EzUnlÀt[53] meaning "Owl Burned Up" in Southern Tutchone language. As in several other stories she tells, Mrs. Smith emphasizes the bond between a grandmother and her grandchild who together save the community.

Kitty Smith, *Owl Story*[54]

This is a story about that owl they burned.
It happened down at Noogaayík.

Lots of people were staying down there.
They dance, sometimes; Indians dance just for fun.
They were doing that.

One lady said, "Where's my kid?"

One kid missing. They run around – nothing.

That time one man said,
"What is that track I see down there?
It looks just like one big grouse track on the sand.
Big," he said. People went there.

Yes, they saw them.
Big tracks there – like grouse tracks.
Ah, well.
Something came and took that little kid, little girl.
They don't know what.

Well, they are coming now – two owls.
They talk just like people. They come in here.

"One little kid.
Give me one little kid or I'm going to eat you all," he said.

"Where do you come from?"

"We come from that place," they said.
There used to be a glacier there, in that place.
That owl came from a little glacier in there.
That glacier hasn't melted yet ...
I guess Owl lived inside there – he melted it down a little bit.

They gave him dog:
They can't kill owl, can't kill him anyway. Too big, you know.

One old lady couldn't walk around.
She crawled around, but her hands are strong.
She got paralyzed, I guess.

"What are we going to do now?
We gave them all our dogs."
Nobody's got dogs that time, just a few men.

They got one slave – somebody had him.
They gave that one to the owls:
Those owls didn't come back for four days.

People say: "Maybe they're not going to come back.
They're gone. They took that slave.
We can't do anything now."
Well, that old lady, she can't walk.
"We might as well throw her away," they think.

Her grandchild is just a little boy.
He doesn't want to let his grandma go.

"Just as well I die if my grandma dies."
No, his daddy doesn't want it; his mamma cries.

"No." He won't leave his Grandma.
"Just as well you kill me right there," he said.

They let him go now, that kid.
Well, they built a brush camp that way –
I guess it was her own brush camp, I don't know –
It was big.
I guess she can still make good brush camps.
His grandmother brought him those things.
Then she dug a hole [tunnel], that lady, out the back way –
I guess they crawled around that way – a long way.

That ground was frozen now, on top.
Her grandchild packed that grub.
Then they packed in branches and filled that brush camp up.
They got ready now:
They fixed some kind of grease, gopher grease.
They put on rags, anything.
Then they tied it up, wrapped it around sticks.
They gathered up pitch – her son-in-law had brought it to them to start fire.

He's coming now, one Owl Man.
His wife is not with him.
"Where have these people gone?" he asked.

I wonder how he can talk that way?

"Well, they've gone to another city," that old lady told him.
"They threw us away so you can eat us.
That's why they threw us away."

"Heh. You're an old lady. I guess your heart is good."
He doesn't know that little grandchild is in the ground, that way.
She's got something she is going to close off that tunnel with, too.

"Gee, I'm an old lady.
If you eat me, you're going to be sick.
Where's your wife?"

"She ate a dog bone.
She got choked," he said. "She died."

"All right. You might as well get warm, dry yourself.
I'm just an old lady.
Not good to eat."

"All right."

That old lady made a dry fire.

"Gee, your back is wet."

He turned around that way. His back to her.

That old lady put grease on the fire.
It started to burn.
She threw on pitch.
Everything she threw on. Wood, too.
Then she rolled down that big rock, rolled it away from the mouth of the tunnel.
She closed it right back.

She's gone with her grandchild out there.
I guess there's fresh air in there – that ground is not thick.

They hear him ... That house started to burn.
"Hunh. My eyes start to burn.
What's the matter with that old lady?
She talks too much.
Should be I killed her already."

He starts to burn.
Then it's quiet. Quiet now.
They guess they can get away now.
But they stay there, stay there.

Well, it's a long time now.
That's when the old lady pushed away the rock.
She came up. That big owl is all burned.
He lies on his side, all burned.

That boy told his grandmother,
"We killed him already.
Where's your house?" No house there.

They made a fire.
I guess they put away their own grub.
That owl is pretty near half cooked. They eat now.

Then – it's funny, you know – that old lady got up!
She got up with two walking sticks!
Hey! She just walks that far [twenty feet].
She doesn't feel anything – just goes that way.

"What's the matter, grandma? You walk!"

"Well, I don't know, my grandchild."

Yes, those claws are long.
They chop them, tie them up that way in a little sack.
That owl is dead, now.
Her grandchild is going to pack it – they have skin sled, too.
She walked that way.
The little boy is strong now, I guess. He went.

They go, go, go.
Someplace he pulls his grandma, you know – does that.

Gee, they see that open space – fire, smoke.
People living there right in that open place.
They're coming there. That's her daughter.

"What's the matter. They're coming, them.
My mamma looks like she is in skin sleigh."

"Run there," she tells her husband.

Yes, he pulled his grandma. I guess he's big.

"Where's your owl?"

"We killed him."

"How did you fellows kill that owl?"

"We killed him anyway."

"They say they killed owl!" [people say]

"No! Which way?"

"We burned him."

"My goodness," say lots of people.

Same time they started to go back with that old lady.
Gee, right there, owl is burned.
They explain that owl's wife got choked – she's dead.
They look around that way. He's dead, anyway. Burned.

I saw that place.
It's a rock now.
It looks just like burned bones right there at Noogaayík.

WOODPECKER AND WOLF are key protagonists in the following story. It centres on successive hunting episodes at a glacier den that swells overnight when cooked fat is incautiously left behind at the hunting site. The plot hovers on a series of contradictions that perplex the protagonist, Wolf, whose confusion sweeps up the audience.

Wolf marries Woodpecker's daughter and is transported to the winter world, where he struggles with the inexplicable paradoxes. His father-in-law urges him to hunt a moose that turns out to be an owl. Unable to challenge his father-in-law directly, Wolf kills the owl and hauls it back, but is disoriented when everyone else, including his wife, behaves as though this owl really is a moose. His brothers-in-law even offer him the owl's beak to eat, insisting that it is the prized moose nose. Reversal follows reversal. By remaining calm and reflecting seriously on each about-turn, Wolf is able to normalize this disturbing situation. Much of the dramatic action takes place on a glacier that Woodpecker insists is a bear den but that, to Wolf, appears to house a giant snake. Further drama comes from "cooking with grease" that is subsequently transformed to ice.

The confusion between moose and owl here may involve a play on words: in Inland Tlingit, moose and owl have the same name, *tsísk'w;*[55] however, this may not be an adequate explanation, because Mrs. Smith also uses the Southern Tutchone name for owl, Mädzi. The analogy of a bear den with a glacier "den" inhabited by a snake is consistent with other stories about giant snakes burrowing in glaciers in the Saint Elias ranges. Catharine McClellan heard stories of giant worms living on the flanks of the Saint Elias Mountains from elders in the 1960s but says that only people living near glaciers claimed to have any direct experience with them.[56]

Kitty Smith, *Woodpecker and Wolf* [57]

This is story from a long time ago, I guess,
From the time when Crow made people, that's the time.

This is a story about Woodpecker.
Wolf, he's married to Woodpecker's daughter.
One time Woodpecker said, "My, I see moose tracks.
I guess fresh moose is going that way."

"Where?" asks his son-in-law.

"Up there. You see that tree? That's cow moose."

Wolf knows it's not cow moose, but he goes there.
Gee, he sees no track, no track, just owl.
And that owl flies away.
Finally, he looks around all over and he comes back.

"Where does your daddy see moose track?" he asks his wife.

She asks her daddy, "Where do you see moose track?"

"That place."

"Well, nothing there.
My husband has been there and he saw nothing.
Just owl, too – Mädzi – that's all he sees.
It flies away, too."

That Wolf is mad about that – just Mädzi there.

"No," says Woodpecker. "That's a cow moose and a calf over there."
So he went again, that son-in-law, and he killed that Mädzi,
Brought it back.

"Daddy," that daughter called, "he got all two."
She carried that owl around – not heavy, you know.
She put it there, woodpile place.

"My goodness, she pack around cow moose," her father says.
"That's heavy!"

Well, they start now. Woodpecker kids [his sons], too.
They cut up the owl, hang up the head, just like cooking moose head.

"Give the best part to your brother-in-law," Woodpecker tells his sons.

They cut off the nose and give it.
He laughed, I guess, that Wolf. Just like he eat for nothing.
They all eat, but they say they gave the best part to Wolf.
I guess he threw it away, pretended to eat.

Then, after, he hunted.
That Wolf got cow moose – real moose.
He brought in the fat, told his wife.

"Ahh ... it's heavy," he told his wife.
"Hey, I got in a glacier and my snowshoe froze, see?"

"Bring them here."

He brought them.
She put them near the fire to make them dry.
That old man, her father, Woodpecker, is watching.

"Ahh ... my daughter, that's bear den.
Bear owns that glacier ice, that ice frozen on those snowshoes."

She doesn't know what he's going to say, that Wolf.
That Wolf said, "What does your Daddy mean?
I got in water! That's what's on my snowshoe.
What kind of bear stays in that kind of place?"

"Well, I don't know that," said his wife.

In the morning, that Woodpecker tied up everything, sharpened weapons for his kids.
They're going to go there.
They're going to try that bear den
But he doesn't see bear den, that Wolf man.
He just sees a glacier going that way.

"My son-in-law, you come too," Woodpecker tells him.

He comes, looks around.

"Yes, he's sitting there, [that bear]," Woodpecker says.

That man [Wolf] doesn't know what he means.
Woodpecker bangs his stick on the top of that ice ...
Bang ... bang ... bang.
"I don't know why he won't come out."
Bang ... bang ... bang.

Woodpecker does that.
Wolf man, though he just stands there.
Woodpecker stopped.

"My packsack. There is something inside will bring that bear on top this way.
Get your husband, my daughter.
Send him to your Mamma. She knows that sack.
Tell your husband to get away from my packsack, my daughter.
Your Mamma knows my sack."

Wolf ran back:
"Bear doesn't come. Get that sack your husband wants."

"Oh," that lady looks around ... she gets some kind of thing, gives it to him.
He takes off, that Wolf.

"This one?"

"Yes, that's the one," said Woodpecker.

That Woodpecker tied it in a stick and put it on top of ice.
I don't know what it is – he sent for his doctor [medicine] I guess.

Crack! He bust that ice. Something came out of that ice – big snake.
They poke it, Woodpecker's kids and Wolf man.
They kill him.

My, lots of fat – they cut it up. Pack it home.
Wolf doesn't eat, though, just his wife eats.
"I don't want it," he said.

Woodpecker said, "Don't you kids leave any cooking stuff [cooked food].
Don't save any cooked food. Eat it *all.*"

Wolf thinks, "I don't know what he means."
He takes a little piece of cooked fat.
It froze there, I guess.
They left the rest of the raw fat to lie around 'til tomorrow, fix it up tomorrow.

Next day, they wake up.
"Ahh." All that [cooked] fat turned to ice.
Just from that little piece of meat he saved, that's all.
They should not have saved that little piece of cooked one.
That's why it turned that way.

That old Woodpecker got mad:
"Who did that!
We wanted to eat that good bear meat!"

Wolf went hunting.
He got bear, killed it, brought in the fat.
He brought it to his father-in-law:
"This is bear! You just say bear for nothing."

That Woodpecker wants to even up.
He saved a little bit of that cooked bear fat.
They ate that fat and tomorrow they go to get that meat, bear meat.

But the next day, nothing wrong.
He didn't even up, that Woodpecker.

Èchù chìa gyu inshana, they call it
From Dalton Post way down, a little way.
"Woodpecker he got snake."

Longtime ago, it's like that, I guess, when Crow turned animals to people.

That's the time.

PART 2

Practices of Exploration

4

Two Centuries of Stories from Lituya Bay: Nature, Culture, and La Pérouse

Practices of exploration were becoming visibly entangled with matters of locality by the late eighteenth century. Exploration and science proceeded hand in hand in northwestern North America, conveying to the Gulf of Alaska ideas framed rather differently from those we have just heard. The concept of "the field" as a space of scientific exploration emerged in places that were simultaneously constructed as peripheral – distant from European centres, "at the verge of the world" – and as central, crucial to the mercantilism fuelling European cities.[1] We saw in Chapter 1 that scientific expeditions, arguably driven by European commercial interests, were matched by a different kind of international expansion as Eyak, Tlingit, and Athapaskan peoples converged on coastal lands reappearing when glaciers receded during late stages of the Little Ice Age. Well before expeditions headed by Cook in 1778, by La Pérouse in 1786, and by Vancouver in 1794 reached the Gulf of Alaska, indigenous peoples were travelling and trading between the high-country interior and the Pacific coast.

Stories drawn from Lituya Bay, an ice-scoured tidal inlet on the Gulf of Alaska, draw attention to cross-cultural encounters in 1786. Some are transmitted through Tlingit oral tradition, visual imagery, and song. But members of a French expedition commanded by Jean-François de La Pérouse, who visited Lituya Bay that year, also documented them. La Pérouse's journals were published in France in 1798, and then subsequently in two English translations – one appearing within a year and another almost two hundred years later.[2] Oral traditions were recorded a century after the events in 1886 and 1888 by George Thornton Emmons, in the late 1940s and early 1950s by Frederica de Laguna, and by Richard and Nora Dauenhauer in the 1960s and 1980s.[3] Significantly, both the written records and Tlingit traditions refer to separate but sequential tragedies that occurred in the summer of 1786 at Lituya Bay.

Figure 10 View of La Pérouse's two ships entering Lituya Bay, 1786. Drawing attributed to Gaspard Duché de Vancy, ship's artist with the expedition. *Source:* Dunmore and de Brossard, *Le Voyage de Lapérouse, 1785-1788*, vol. 2 (Paris: Imprimerie Nationale), Plate 45. All rights reserved.

In this chapter, I look at a range of accounts – oral and written, sung and visual. Together, these accounts document how new concepts of nature and culture were emerging in the late 1700s. While the surviving accounts may tell us about the "facts" of events and encounters, they also evoke a defining moment in which Tlingit practices that relied on a notion of geography as socially active and sentient were confronted by French Enlightenment conceptions of an inanimate nature subject to empirical investigation and measurement. The French exploration narratives document the invention of categories and practices that divide nature from culture. Longstanding Tlingit and Athapaskan oral traditions, on the other hand, rely on their inseparability. The encounter provides an opportunity to follow the travel of concepts and the transformations they bring about, and to see how they find their way into oral and written narratives that persist to the present.

The chapter addresses a number of questions that also run through subsequent chapters. What do participants' narratives tell us about the epistemological consequences of such encounters? Can the encounter between members of two distinct cultural groups in Lituya Bay in 1786 be understood as a transformative moment in which concepts, knowledge, and objects were transferred with significant consequences for *both* parties? Does the contribution from Tlingit stories, sung, carved, and told for two centuries, add to our understanding of the science that emerged in this period? What do the stories themselves accomplish – where do they go and what are *their* effects? What can intersections of local knowledge that occurred two hundred years ago contribute to contemporary discussions about connections between local and scientific knowledge?

Narrative and History: Accounts from Lituya Bay

Both French and Tlingit stories fall within the category of "local knowledge," but they develop from different premises. Treating them as symmetrical approaches may clarify some of the exchanges of ideas that were occurring. Such stories document the encounter between Tlingit and Europeans, but they also signal a series of other encounters whose implications will be addressed in this and the following chapters: between both groups and ecological risk; between various accounts of events and their subsequent readers and listeners; and between old concerns and contemporary interests.

The Gulf of Alaska extends for almost five hundred kilometres between Cross Sound and Controller Bay (see Map 4). An anomalous shallow beach stretches the entire distance, interrupted by only two possible harbours, one at Yakutat Bay and the other at Lituya Bay. Lituya Bay is eleven kilometres long and less than three kilometres wide. Its steeply sloping sides rise dramatically to eighteen hundred metres at its head, where two arms extend, giving the bay a "T" shape. When La Pérouse first mapped this bay in 1786, the glaciers descending to it had receded further than today, making the bar of the "T" almost fifteen kilometres long. A century later, Otto Klotz visited with the International Boundary Commission and found that glaciers had re-advanced, reducing the arm-span to five kilometres, as it has remained since then.[4] The bay is deep, but its mouth is both narrow and shallow, creating a bottleneck through which notorious tides race at velocities of up to twelve knots.[5] The navigable portion of the mouth is only forty-five metres wide, and slack water lasts from ten to twenty minutes at the turn of the tide.

I visited Lituya Bay in July 2001, in a boat named *Yakobi* skilfully piloted by Paul Johnson from Gull Cove, on Icy Strait. Our departure was governed by weather and tides, and we were fortunate. We left Icy Strait heading north early on 12 July and caught the flood tide into Lituya Bay some four hours later, anchoring in a sheltered cove northeast of the entrance and spending the rest of the day exploring the bay's contours in a small gas-powered boat we had towed. At dawn the following morning, the fiord

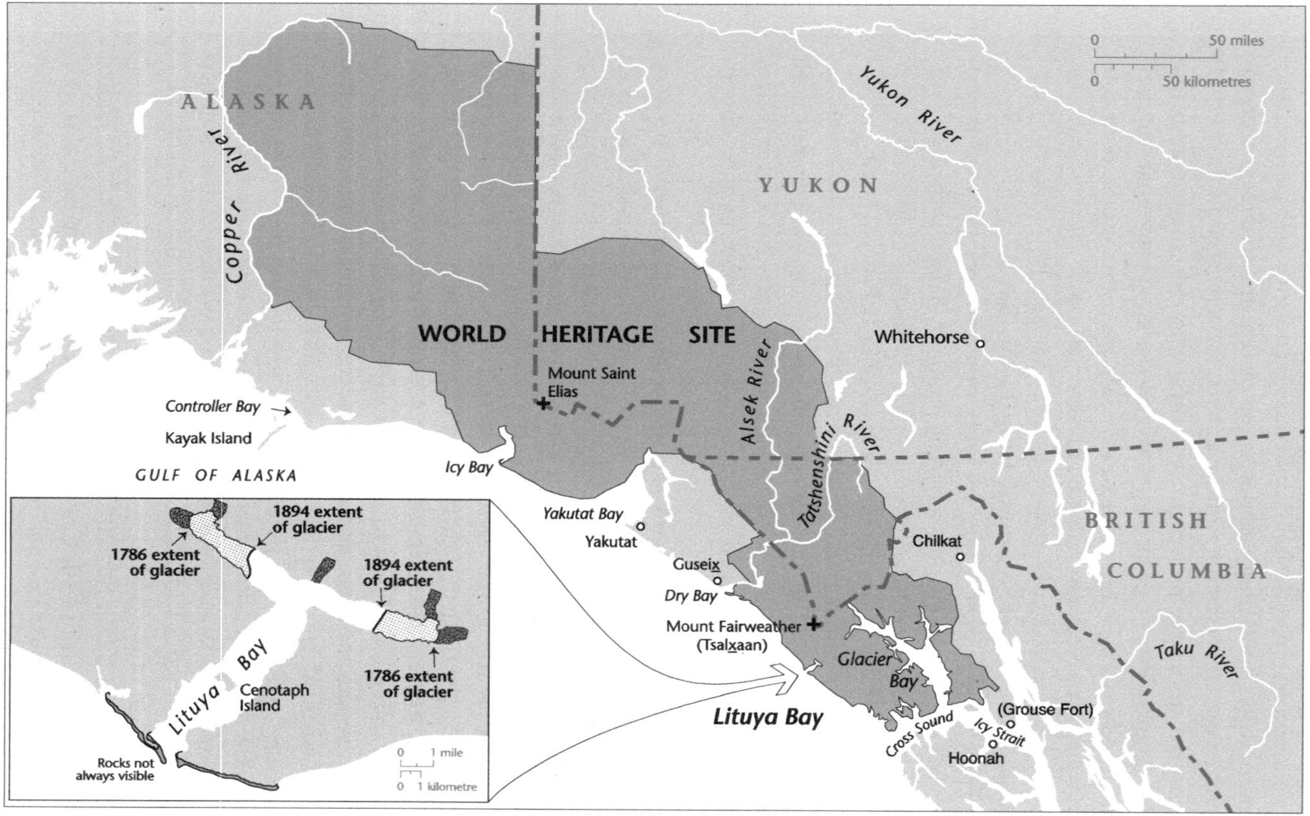

Map 4 Lituya Bay, today. This map shows the Gulf of Alaska and the boundaries of the contemporary World Heritage site, with an inset of Lituya Bay, identifying the extent of glaciation in 1786 and 1894.

mirrored mountains and glaciers, and silence was broken only by a colony of kittiwakes, creating an impression of tranquility interrupted by the unsettling observation that small icebergs were drifting smoothly but rapidly toward the mouth of the bay on an ebb tide. They were then swept out of sight and into the open Pacific by crested waves crashing across the entire entrance to an otherwise glassy bay. It was only then that I recalled that this date, 13 July, marked the anniversary of the morning that La Pérouse lost twenty-one crewmembers in the same place two hundred and fifteen years earlier.

George Emmons learned from Tlingit residents in 1886 that their name for the bay, Ltu'a, is a compound word meaning "lake within the point" and he referred to it as the most feared harbour on the North Pacific coast.[6] The arms of the "T" lie directly along the Fairweather fault, where two enormous continental plates meet in constant tension and periodically shift. Because of its contours, this bay has been repeatedly subjected to giant and devastating waves generated when huge portions of the mountain, possibly dislodged by earthquakes, fall into the head of the bay. La Pérouse reported no recent evidence of such disasters during his extensive mapping of the bay in 1786, but scientists using dates from forest regrowth have dated catastrophic giant waves that occurred in 1853, 1879, 1899, and 1936. The most destructive wave accompanied a 1958 earthquake, sweeping down the bay to maximum heights of 525 metres, destroying ten square kilometres of ancient forest, and erasing any archaeological evidence of human habitation. "All the inhabitable area around the shoreline of the bay has been swept clean as if by a giant hand," archaeologist Robert Ackerman reported a decade later.[7] The contours of that flood are still distinctly visible today, as new growth takes hold on the steeply sloping sides of the bay.

The entire region remains geologically active and risky terrain. Partly because of such risks, Lituya Bay is no longer inhabited, but it was once a summer village occupied seasonally by coastal travellers throughout the nineteenth century, and it retains significance in Tlingit oral history and memory as a place of intense sociability.[8] Its features are embedded both in physical processes and in memories passed on in Tlingit oral traditions, like those we will hear in this chapter. Tlingit place names, for example, encapsulate ecological knowledge that is often rendered invisible by contemporary cartography and English toponyms.[9] Tlingit mariners accumulated geological and social knowledge simultaneously and passed it on in stories that graft social relationships onto place. Several ethnographers have documented this confluence of ecological knowledge and social history in Tlingit oral tradition. Thomas Thornton discusses how such knowledge is embedded in named places that act as "mnemonic pegs" or (following Bakhtin) "chronotopes" that fuse time and space and provide symbolic linkages between physical and social landscapes.[10] Orally transmitted names and narratives remind residents of how physical landmarks came to be where they are, how people came to be where they are, and how named places provide points of reference for clan histories. Narratives set on this part of the coast indicate familiarity with earthquakes, giant waves, floods, and exceptional tides. They attribute these forces to the activities of Raven, who made the earth at the beginning of time. Raven established geological features and the orientations of freshwater lakes and streams, but he also set in motion processes that put humans at risk.[11]

Lituya Bay is also one of the places where La Pérouse's expedition came ashore, bringing their own local North Atlantic knowledge and finding opportunities to put into practice concepts that were developing in Europe at the time. In eighteenth-century France, science still fell within the broader rubric of natural philosophy. The *philosophes,* La Pérouse's contemporaries and countrymen, showed a growing appreciation for empirical methods involving the collection of observable facts that could be subjected to rational scrutiny. La Pérouse's expedition, sponsored by Louis XVI, included "Engineers, Men of Science and Artists" who shared a commitment to the idea that improvement of the human condition and human knowledge depended on the steady improvement of technology. Influenced by Montesquieu's *De l'esprit des lois,* written in the 1740s, La Pérouse also brought specific questions about the "laws of nature" governing the manners and customs of non-European peoples he encountered.

With these themes in mind, I sketch the outlines of the stories, and then turn to a discussion of the circumstances leading up to and following the events the stories represent. I go on to argue that the meeting between French and Tlingit can be framed as a transformative moment composed of a series of encounters and transfers that continue to resonate in both Europe and the Gulf of Alaska. Parenthetically, by the mid-twentieth century, the name Lituya Bay is most commonly associated with US Geological Survey reports concerning earthquakes and seismic activity. More recently, the bay has been included in Glacier Bay National Park and Preserve, now incorporated within the larger area designated from Geneva as a World Heritage site, and unleashing new metaphors of "pristine wilderness."

Accounts from Tlingit Oral Tradition

Overlooking the Gulf of Alaska, Mount Fairweather rises 4,663 metres above sea level and now anchors one corner of the mountainous border separating Canada from Alaska, as shown on Map 4. Tlingit mariners knew it as Tsalxaan, and considered it a navigational guide that also provided warning of volatile weather conditions. By the time Europeans first reached the Gulf of Alaska, Lituya Bay was providing Tlingit people secure anchorage during long coastal marine journeys as well as reliable summer hunting and fishing. Shortly before La Pérouse arrived in 1786, several large canoes or frame boats carrying Tlingit traders, reportedly all members of the L'uknax.ádi clan, capsized at the mouth of the bay. Either Tsalxaan had failed to give a sign, or the travellers had failed to heed it – interpretations are ambiguous in oral accounts that have been passed down. One boat escaped, and its members survived. Because of their devastating losses, this clan claimed Tsalxaan as a crest that they say was paid for by the lives of their ancestors. The clan, dramatically reduced in numbers by the loss of its ablest men, eventually dispersed to other villages, where they continue to live today. The narrative remains crucial to L'uknax.ádi clan history.

The earliest written account of this tragedy was taken down by George Thornton Emmons, a lieutenant in the US Navy, stationed in Alaska in the 1880s and 1890s. Cowee, a Tlingit clan leader, informed him in 1886 that "a large party" of L'uknax.ádi clansmen from Grouse Fort on Icy Strait had been travelling north to trade at Yakutat when they entered Lituya Bay. Four canoes capsized, drowning all aboard.[12] Subsequent accounts report eight or sometimes ten canoes, each carrying eight men; they generally agree that in their haste the party failed to pay attention to the guidance provided by the mountain Tsalxaan and capsized.[13]

Contemporary narrators agree that the first European ships were attracted to Lituya Bay by furs spilling from the capsized Tlingit boats. Jack Ellis, from Yakutat, reported that the Tlingit canoes had been carrying large hand-sewn bags made of halibut skins.[14] Charlie White, a member of the L'uknax.ádi clan, reported that the ten canoes were actually travelling south, from Yakutat, when the "tides turned to rapids on them" at Lituya Bay and the canoes capsized. The telltale bundles of fur that attracted Europeans were "in a halibut skin bag ... like rubber bags."[15] Charlie White's wife, Jenny, spoke of furs in bags made of bear intestines that "resembled a plastic bag." As the bags floated "to the face of the cloud at the edge of the earth," they attracted the white "cloud people" from beyond the horizon.[16]

The story is documented in memorial songs composed by Tlingit mourners. In 1952, Frank Italio sang for Frederica de Laguna the songs associated with L'uknax.ádi losses, including one composed by a woman named Wooshkika, whose eight brothers perished in the tragedy. De Laguna's translator, a member of the same clan, began: "Mount Fairweather gives a

Figure 11 Kah Lituya (left) guarding the mouth of Lituya Bay and raising waves to capsize a canoe with two occupants. George Thornton Emmons acquired this wooden pipe in 1888. (Courtesy National Museum of the American Indian, Smithsonian Institution, N31531.)

sign if something terrible is going to happen. They knew it before they started ... [Wooshkika] used to sit on the sand dunes and cry and sing, especially when the tide was smooth. The song composed by the woman belongs to Mount Fairweather. That's why we [L'uknax̲.ádi clan members] claim the song." As Frank Italio continued to sing, the translator was so overcome by grief that she was unable to continue speaking.[17] Later, another woman translated: "Your grandfathers were watching the paddler's mountain [Tsalx̲aan]. Close by, your hands missed it. [The canoe was overturned and they tried to grab it.]"[18]

The story of Lituya Bay is told visually in the striking carved wooden ceremonial pipe that Emmons obtained from a Hoonah clan leader in 1888 (Figure 11). Unlike the oral stories, it left the community when Emmons collected and then sold it, eventually reaching its current home at the Museum of the American Indian in Washington, DC. Emmons learned that it was used in clan ceremonies to honour the dead, or when important policy issues were being deliberated. The carving depicts a monster guarding the bay's entrance and posing a threat to anyone who tries to enter. At one end of this pipe sits a frog-like figure with eyes of abalone shell, representing Kah Lituya, the "Spirit of Lituya." Facing him is a bear, sitting on his haunches. Between them they hold the entrance to Lituya Bay, and two brass-covered ridges represent the wave they have raised to submerge a brass canoe with two occupants. Humans drowned in this manner are enslaved by Kah Lituya, who transforms them into bears and sends them to watchtowers on Mount Fairweather to look for approaching canoes. Then, "with their master they grasp the surface water and shake it as if it were a sheet, causing the tidal waves to rise and engulf the unwary."[19]

Notably, Emmons's account elaborates the familiar theme of "first contact." While Western historical narratives frequently make this theme central, it is usually muted in Tlingit accounts. The latter more often identify such meetings as a secondary *consequence* of the main story about Tlingit mariners and their catastrophic losses, or they omit it entirely. According to the story that Emmons was told, the few survivors from the accident made camp at Lituya Bay and were mourning their lost companions when they observed two ships entering the bay. Tlingit reportedly interpreted these first European ships to arrive at Lituya Bay as the return of White Raven, Yéil, the world-maker who had promised to be reborn.[20] In the version Emmons recorded, the Tlingit initially fled to the woods, fearing that they might be turned to stone if they observed Raven directly, and later cautiously re-emerged and rolled tubes or "telescopes" from skunk cabbage so that they could regard him more circumspectly. Eventually one old man advanced, boarded the ship, and was fed rice (which he initially interpreted as maggots), sugar (which he took to be sand), and alcohol (which caused him feelings of "strangeness"), and received gifts that he carried back to shore.[21] Shortly after this, Emmons heard, two smaller boats from these ships were lost in the same place and the white men aboard all drowned.

The Journals of Jean-François de La Pérouse

On an unusually clear spring morning in May 1778, Captain James Cook caught sight of the mountain Tsalx̲aan and bestowed on this peak the English name "Fair Weather." Eight years later, in July 1786, French crewmen on two ships under the command of Jean-François de La Pérouse spotted the same mountain but also identified a nearby bay that did not appear on Cook's charts. Stopping offshore on the evening of 2 July 1786, La Pérouse noted in his journal that "this port was never seen by any navigator" and followed the European custom of claiming it as a national possession, naming it "Port des Français." Entering the bay the following morning, he was deeply shaken by the navigational challenges: "During the thirty years that I have followed the sea," he wrote, "I never saw two vessels so nearly being lost," and he expressed relief at their safe arrival "at the verge of the world."[22]

La Pérouse found the bay far from deserted and later reported that throughout his stay there were never fewer than three or four hundred residents. Arrivals and departures were constant. Almost immediately, Tlingit men in formal attire approached the ships; then trading commenced so briskly that La Pérouse interpreted some behaviours of their Tlingit hosts as "theft."[23] Already familiar with rare drift iron from shipwrecks, which they worked like native copper into tools, the Tlingit initially showed interest only in iron. Once initial trading formalities were accomplished, La Pérouse anchored his ships in the lee of the bay's only island, adding substantially to the population as his crew of almost two hundred spilled ashore.

Turning promptly to the work of science, he ordered the observatory prepared and instruments set out, including a chronometer (an instrument for determining longitude at sea, designed to remain accurate in extreme conditions) and two "dipping needles compasses" used by Cook on his final journey and contributed to the expedition by the British government.[24] He assigned to crews tasks of collecting wood, fresh water, fish, and edible birds. He was shocked when the Tlingit, whom he took to be separately camped on the mainland, converged on the island, expressing intense interest in the observatory and was even more troubled when they helped themselves to some items of clothing and took the record book filled with "all our astronomical observations since our arrival at Port des Français."[25]

Once settled, he made an exploratory trip with several crewmembers to the head of the bay, where they found ice so thick that they had to push away chunks in order to proceed. His description of the bay blends notions of the sublime with hints of trepidation:

> perhaps the most extraordinary place in the world. To form an idea of it, it is necessary to conceive a basin of water, unfathomable in the middle, bordered by peaked mountains, of great height, covered by snow, and without one blade of grass to decorate the vast heap of rocks, condemned by nature to eternal sterility. I never beheld the surface of the water ruffled by a single breath of wind. Nothing disturbs it but the fall of enormous masses of ice which frequently separate from five different glaciers, while the sound is re-echoed by the distant mountains ... It was at the head of this bay that we hoped to find channels, by which we might penetrate into the interior of America.[26]

Beaching the small craft to investigate, three crewmembers clambered up glaciers leading toward Mount Fair Weather (now Fairweather) but only "advanced two leagues, being obliged at extreme risk to leap over clefts of great depth ... [returning] ... with unspeakable fatigue." A calving glacier nearly capsized their boat, hurling it onto the rocks. After a hasty inspection of the eastern terminus, they returned to the main part of the bay, completing what must have been the earliest European observations of Pacific tidewater glaciers. So ended their attempt to find a Northwest Passage, and they returned to camp, "having finished our voyage into the interior of America in a few hours."[27]

The following day, a Tlingit spokesman arrived in formal attire offering to "sell" them the island on which the observatory was erected. Noting misgivings about the legality of the transaction, La Pérouse nevertheless proceeded. In exchange, he offered "several yards of red cloth, hatchets, adzes, bar iron, nails, presents." Concluding that the necessary payments had been made, he set out in his words "to take possession of the island *with the usual formalities*" (my emphasis) and buried at the foot of a rock "several bronze medals which had been struck before our departure from France with a bottle containing an inscription recording our claim."[28] Strikingly, his assumptions about which conventions were "usual" at Lituya Bay differed from expectations that Tlingit brought to the encounter and contribute to the argument I make later about how the encounter produces transformation on both sides.

Their survey completed, the men loaded additional wood and fresh water onto their ships and were preparing to depart on 13 July when disaster struck. Twenty-one men took two smaller boats to record some final soundings of the bay, planning a recreational day, described as "a party of pleasure" with plans "to shoot, and breakfast under the trees."[29] Despite precautions, their boats were swept into a strong riptide and capsized, drowning all aboard within minutes (Figure 12). Devastated by the loss of his men, La Pérouse built a monument on the island he then named Cenotaph Island, and, at the foot of this memorial, he buried a written account, this time telling the story of their loss and noting as part of his inscription that "the Indians appeared to participate in our grief which is extreme ... Reader, Whoever thou Art, Mingle thy Tears with Ours."[30]

The Tlingit assisted with the search for survivors, and during the following days La Pérouse learned of their own prior losses at the same location – "seven very large canoes ... lost in this passage while an eighth escaped." He was shown the surviving frame boat and described it in detail – thirty-four feet long, four feet wide, six feet deep, and fit for long voyages.[31] As he watched visitors arrive and leave by boat during the remainder of his stay, he further observed, "The Indians seemed to have considerable dread of the passage."[32]

They delayed for eighteen more days, partly with the faint hope of finding survivors, partly to reassign responsibilities following their losses.

Figure 12 La Pérouse's boats lost at the mouth of Lituya Bay, 13 July 1786, with twenty-one crewmembers aboard. Drawing by Gaspard Duché de Vancy. *Source:* Dunmore and de Brossard, *Le Voyage de Lapérouse, 1785-1788*, vol. 2 (Paris: Imprimerie Nationale), Plate 55. All rights reserved.

Deteriorating weather delayed them further. La Pérouse spent this time recording observations and "visiting the Indians daily," but it was a liminal period and he was restless. He commented on the scale of human traffic in the settlement: "every day we saw fresh canoes enter the bay; and every day whole villages departed and gave place to others ... It is probable that we saw but a very small part of these people, who in all likelihood occupy a considerable space along the seashore." La Pérouse concluded that this was a summer settlement.[33] His observations shifted from landscape to people and back again, but his descriptions became increasingly strained.

Tlingit customs largely distressed him, especially the wearing of labrets by high-status women. His journal entries shift from sympathetic reflections concerning the Tlingit losses to cranky soliloquies about the advantages of agriculture. As the days wore on, he began to rail against followers of Rousseau whom he decided were seriously misguided. Showing the same impatience he would later display in the South Pacific,[34] he asserted his own views about the relationship between nature and culture: "For a country so frightful, nature provides inhabitants differing as widely from civilized nations, as the land I have described from our cultivated plains. Rude and barbarous, their soil is wild and rugged, they inhabit the country only to extirpate every thing that lives and moves upon it. At war with every animal, they despise the vegetables that spring up around them."[35] Here, then, the connection between civilization and environment begins to be articulated. Culture and nature emerge as conceptually separate entities, with nature determining what culture is destined to become. This is a theme we hear again in Chapter 6.

Eighteen days after their disaster, and twenty-six days following their arrival, La Pérouse's party finally departed on 30 July, travelling south to Nootka, then on to California. In Petropavlovsk, the following year, La Pérouse entrusted a logbook and drawings to his Russian interpreter, Barthelemy de Lesseps, who carried them across Siberia and to the king in Versailles by October 1788.[36] By this time, his two ships had mysteriously disappeared without a trace one night in a South Pacific cyclone off the island of Vanikoro in the Solomon Islands. As the French Revolution escalated into the Terror, an official editor was chosen to compile the journals. Louis XVI went to the guillotine in 1793, still a fervent supporter of the expedition, despite his other distractions. When La Pérouse's edited journals were first published in France in 1798, his fate and that of his crew were still unconfirmed, and apocryphal reports continued to circulate, like one from a Dutch captain who claimed to have seen in the South Pacific a canoe "manned by the natives, who appeared to him to be dressed in the uniform of the French navy."[37] Only forty years later were the deaths finally verified, and it took an additional century before aqua-lung diving technology, developed after the Second World War, made it possible to determine where the ships actually sank.[38] Most records of the voyage were lost, but together with La Pérouse's journals, a series of drawings by the ship's artist, Gaspard Duché de Vancy, reached France. Among Duché de Vancy's surviving drawings, one depicts events similar to those represented in the Tlingit carving of Kah Lituya – the final moments of La Pérouse's crewmembers at Lituya Bay.

Local Knowledge Practices: Tlingit and French Encounters at Lituya Bay

In the two previous sections of this chapter, Tlingit traditions told, sung, and carved in wood, and French journals, notations, and drawings are framed as counterparts that provide us with different perspectives on very similar events. The notion that the land listens and responds, so central to Tlingit epistemology, now appears quite distinct from the ideas that French voyagers brought to the North Pacific in the late eighteenth century. Yet, viewed as coexisting practices, they may not have been so divergent.

The two sections that follow also point to Tlingit and French knowledge practices as counterparts. The goal is to show how knowledge took shape during an initial encounter that was unexpectedly extended by disasters, and how that knowledge has continued to be circulated and interpreted. La Pérouse's initial few days at Lituya Bay were consumed almost entirely by intensive exchanges with Tlingit residents. Then, disaster forced the French to delay and regroup. During this period of prolonged encounter, transfers of technology framed by the French as "gifts" and "collections" continued. In La Pérouse's journals, we can trace how knowledge acquired a more definite shape. Immediately following the disaster, he described moments of connection when Tlingit men helped search for the lost French crewmembers. Then he began to distance himself from the Tlingit in his journal, as notions of "the primitive" came into play. In rapid succession, then, the encounter produced two opposite assessments.

We also see knowledge taking shape in Tlingit narratives that have been circulating now for more than two centuries and come to us in the form of nineteenth-century carvings, in songs like the ones Wooshkika composed for her uncles and brothers, and in twentieth-century books – ethnographies, popular histories, scientific papers, and translations of orally narrated stories. Oral traditions have their own social lives, and it would be naive to treat these interpretations merely as static remnants from the past. Accounts narrated to George Emmons in 1888, to John Swanton in 1904, to Frederica de Laguna in the late 1940s, and those now transcribed in Tlingit by Nora and Richard Dauenhauer all represent struggles surrounding knowledge and the shapes it has taken in this century.[39]

Sociality and Sentience in 1786: Tlingit Knowledge Practices

In Chapter 1, we saw how glacial activity in the Gulf of Alaska has repeatedly scoured the coastline and how this has affected the archaeological record. To review, human habitation was possible nine thousand years ago, but glaciers re-advancing some five thousand years ago erased prior material evidence of human history. A general retreat began again about two thousand years ago. More recent local fluctuations are documented in carbon-dated shards from ancient forests embedded in glacier moraines. This evidence indicates independent local advances at Icy Bay and Yakutat Bay roughly a thousand years ago, followed by a retreat behind the present limits from AD 1200 to 1700. Then a series of advances occurred in the late seventeenth century, culminating at Yakutat Bay in the eighteenth century and at Icy Bay more recently, in 1904. At Lituya Bay, regular human use and occupancy may have begun in the fifteenth or sixteenth centuries when ice was in retreat, but successive earthquakes and giant waves have destroyed all evidence.[40]

The first geologists who worked in this area were immediately struck by the contrast between the deeply chiselled coasts of the Alaska panhandle and Prince William Sound and the straight, shallow beaches stretching along the arc of the Gulf of Alaska.[41] Changes in sea level have continued to accompany earthquakes, glacial advances and retreats, and winter storms. The mountains in this region are also rising two centimetres each year, with additional uplift added by seismic activity.

Oral traditions maintain that Tlingit origins lie in the interior. In the distant past, as we heard from Angela Sidney, their ancestors travelled to the coast down the Alsek, Taku, and Stikine rivers, navigating beneath ice barriers to join clans who were moving north under pressure from expanding Haida populations.[42] Documentary and linguistic evidence indicates that by the eighteenth century, Ahtna were also moving south from the Copper River delta. For at least a century before the earliest Europeans arrived, then, populations were converging on this new land that was emerging at the end of the Little Ice Age, even though new settlements remained at risk from advancing ice. The first European ships arrived at around the same time that indigenous populations were expanding purposefully to repopulate a "land reborn."[43]

For Tlingit, memories are part of the record etched on the landscape. But Tlingit records are narratives about how Lingít aaní, the land of Tlingit people, took its present shape. Features of the land were moulded by the world-maker, Raven, who left evidence of his travels as he worked his way along the coast, transforming geographical features. We have already heard earlier how Raven strategically disappeared down the blowhole of a whale and spent the winter inside feasting in comfort on rich whale blubber. Eventually, he steered his dying host ashore at Dry Bay, the mouth of the Alsek River, fifty miles northwest of Lituya Bay. It was also at Dry Bay that Raven opened his Box of Daylight, so alarming people that they turned into the various land and sea animals depending on the furs they were wearing at the time. We also heard earlier how Raven slashed one side of the mountain Tsal<u>x</u>aan, or Mount Fairweather, when Echo offended him by imitating sounds Raven makes when he is slurping sea urchins.[44] This same Tsal<u>x</u>aan both failed to forewarn the L'ukna<u>x</u>.ádi travellers about treacherous sea conditions at Lituya Bay and guided La Pérouse there.

Like the Russian, French, Spanish, and British histories from this period that come down to us in published journals, Tlingit oral traditions are national histories. In these histories, the primary units are intermarrying matrilineal clans, rather than artificially bounded states, and they regulate cooperation as well as the exchange of ritual services that accompany life's transitions. Clans owned territories, controlled the use of resources on those territories, and claimed harvesting rights that were shared with non-clan members according to specified rules. A clan might be part of one local group (called a *kwaan*) or (if it were expanding) might initiate new relationships through marriage, thereby gaining rights of ownership in several different territories. The number of clans has always fluctuated, as some died out and others grew, expanded, and subdivided. De Laguna identifies more than seventy named clans – thirty-eight Raven and thirty-six Eagle – that were part of this intensely social world at the time when La Pérouse arrived.[45] Kinship was *the* idiom of social relations and was so foundational that immigrant Native Americans – Athapaskans and others – generally adopted Tlingit-style clans in order to function more comfortably.[46] Early European visitors had more difficulty comprehending the rules.

We saw in Chapter 2 that conventions associated with kinship and personhood extended to relations with non-human entities, including a sentient landscape that listens and responds to human indiscretion. This concept does not translate well into European languages, especially not in English where any word that may be used to capture Tlingit views is heavily laden with connotations of science and religion. Words like natural, supernatural, spiritual, animate, or inanimate all carry specific connotations that their Tlingit counterparts do not. As anthropologists have noted, Tlingit language draws some lines very differently, and blurs other distinctions that are embedded in English. Instead Tlingit language reflects subtle differences between ordinary and extraordinary, commonplace and mysterious, safe and dangerous.[47] Moreover, the language is rich in verbs and emphasizes activity and motion, making no sharp distinction between animate and inanimate. Hence mountains, glaciers, bodies of water, rocks, and manufactured objects all have qualities of sentience. Landscape is defined by actions attributed to animate entities, like mountains or glaciers.[48]

Instructions and Instruments: The French Scientific Exercise

Different though they may at first seem from Tlingit ideas, conceptualizations of nature in Europe at the very time that scientific expeditions were setting out were in some ways similar. Writing about the Little Ice Age in France, the French historian Emmanuel LeRoy Ladurie documents that tithes went unpaid and lawsuits were launched as glaciers advanced at Chamonix, crushing and burying hamlets, farms, and gold mines. Desperate citizens approached glaciers in procession, lighting candles and placing crosses at the edge of terminal moraines in efforts to stop the onslaught of ice.[49] Recall that Mary Shelley drew on these images in 1816, often remembered as the "year without a summer,"[50] when she chose the expanding *Mer de Glace* as the setting for Chapter 10 of *Frankenstein*.

Anthropologist Elizabeth Povinelli traces how conceptions of sentience persisting from Medieval Europe were suppressed during subsequent centuries. A "country that listens" had to be rejected as concerns about manufacturing and imperialism took hold. Industrialists, Povinelli points out, were not about to stand for objects that act wilfully, for how could manufacturing proceed under such circumstances? The new sciences came to see alchemy as too animistic and wilful objects as too troublesome, and they opted instead for mechanical models.[51] Such models became current during the Enlightenment and posited a "natural" mechanical order, liable to human manipulation. Inevitably there emerged the archetypal construction of the hunter-gatherer, a category of human that merely responds to, rather than acts upon, nature, whose knowledge was redefined as superstition.[52] In late-twentieth-century science studies, Robert Boyles's development of the air-pump three hundred years earlier became a metaphor for this transition by establishing the conception of a laboratory behind closed doors where nature could be experimentally manipulated.[53] It is probably not accidental that an air-pump was among the prestigious instruments that La Pérouse later brought to the Gulf of Alaska.[54]

Departing France in 1785, La Pérouse received from King Louis XVI instructions to match in the North Pacific the scientific and cartographic achievements that Cook had accomplished for England in the South Pacific. Scientific expeditions derived prestige from their instruments. For their times, La Pérouse's ships were fitted out with cutting-edge accoutrements that we might comparatively now associate with space shuttles. His ships were even named after instruments – *L'Astrolabe* (a precursor of the quadrant and sextant that was used to measure latitude and local time, by gauging the altitude of the sun or a given star)[55] and *La Boussole* (the magnetic compass).[56] He was issued a prototype of the "field methods handbook," now quite conventional for students in social and natural sciences. His directions included "Private Instructions from the King" and research questions from the Academy of Sciences (Académie Royale des Sciences) and the Society of Medicine (Société Royale de Médecine).[57] The king outlined a voyage plan, a program for "politics and commerce," and advice about emerging sciences deemed relevant to the business of imperial expansion – astronomy, geography, navigation, physics, and natural history. His instructions were clear. First, chart "parts not yet known" and look specifically for "some river, or some narrow gulph [sic], forming a communication, by means of the interior lakes, with some parts of Hudson's Bay." Second, determine the whereabouts of Spaniards, British, and other colonial expeditions, taking care not to offend them. Third, assess opportunities for trade: latitudes at which furs are found; quantities in which they appear; and commodities that might attract Native traders.[58]

La Pérouse's crew included two astronomers, two botanists (one a gardener), two engineers, two naturalists, one geographer, one "natural philosopher, mineralogist and meteorologist," and three draughtsmen – two specializing in botanical drawings and one in "landscapes and figures."[59] The king's advice for administering scientists was equally precise. Upon arrival at any port, they were to set up the portable observatory, including instruments furnished for the expedition, and "set a guard over them." Then they should take all possible measurements of temperature, air pressure, magnetic field, etc., ensuring that two copies were made of all notes and that they were filed separately, collected periodically, and forwarded to His Majesty. Each scientist should be assigned to a specific project "that his knowledge and zeal may have their full effect."[60] That notions of intellectual property rights might accompany such zeal even during the eighteenth century is suggested in introductory comments by La Pérouse's editor, Milet-Mureau, criticizing unnamed scientists who were "prevented by self love" from turning in notes that were subsequently lost.[61]

The king also provided advice concerning "Conduct to be Observed toward Natives" – what might now be called ethical guidelines – that urged none of the restraint that was suggested for encounters with other European powers. Initially, La Pérouse was to identify "Chiefs" and give them gifts. Then, he was to supply the vessels with food and fresh water, assess the available resources, and begin trading. Crews were never to sleep ashore, and someone should always remain armed and vigilant. If relationships with Natives deteriorate, "endeavor to keep them in awe by threats."[62] The gifts the expedition carried included a heady inventory: fifty-two dragoon helmets of copper with plumes of feathers and horses' tails; a hundred silver and bronze medals with an effigy of the king and an inscription; and six hundred additional medals of silver and copper.[63] The ships were also supplied with seeds and vegetables, and the official ship's gardener (enumerated among the scientists) was assigned the role of distributing "through royal munificence ... the pulse [edible seeds], fruits and useful trees of Europe" and teaching the useful arts of cultivation.[64]

The distribution of such gifts was to be balanced with the acquisition of collections, and the king provided meticulous directions for their preparation and documentation. "Natural curiosities of land and sea" were to be "collected, arranged in order, and a descriptive catalogue of each to be drawn up." "Cultural curiosities" were also solicited, and La Pérouse was instructed to provide "garments, arms, ornaments, utensils, tools, musical instruments and everything used by the people ... collected, classed ... ticketed, and marked with a number corresponding to that assigned it in the catalogue ... in the collection intended for His Majesty."[65] Ethnobotanical collections were to offset plant distribution, and the gardener was given guidelines for transporting them back to Europe.

The importance of written instructions was already developing a role in scientific research. Just as the king documented his instructions to the expedition, La Pérouse, in turn, issued written instructions to senior crewmembers, a precaution highlighted during the loss of his two boats at Lituya Bay. Concerned about his own culpability, La Pérouse included in the notes and journals he sent by courier to France the written instructions he had issued to his first lieutenant (who perished), spelling out the dangers of currents at the mouth of the bay and warning him to take extra precautions to avoid the alarming tides. His written instructions, like those he received from Academy and king, were published as part of the text of *Voyage Round the World*, along with an eyewitness account that his second lieutenant provided as documentary evidence that, as ship's commander, La Pérouse had taken all reasonable care.[66]

The Academy of Sciences assigned specific research questions to each discipline. Disciplinary boundaries were being invented at this time, defined sometimes with reference to research questions and sometimes with reference to distinguishing instruments. Questions were directed to "Geometry, Astronomy and Mechanics," for example, concerning the measurement of gravity as demonstrated "by the length of the pendulum in different latitudes." But elsewhere "Astronomy" was coupled with "Navigation," a classification based on their special instruments, which included the two famous dipping needle compasses previously used by Cook, as well as a graphometer (theodolite) "for measuring angles on shore and taking plans."[67]

"Natural philosophy" was assigned questions concerning the comparability of phenomena in different places and at different latitudes. "Is it true, as some have imagined they have observed," queried the Academy, "that the mercury in the barometer is an inch higher on the western coast of America than on the eastern?" Other questions concerned "the intensity of magnetic power," "the oscillations of the dipping needle," "characteristics of ocean currents," and "the causes that produce water spouts." Characteristics of arctic ice intrigued the Academy, as did causes of phosphorescence "which sometimes shines on the surface of the sea [and] has been ascribed to the presence of a multitude of little luminous animals."[68]

In the area of "instruments," natural philosophy was twinned with chemistry and assigned a large balloon, twenty-six feet high and twenty-two feet in diameter, lined with gauze paper. More prestigious was the "double-barreled air pump with its apparatus complete," a symbol of laboratory science that was now brought to the field to measure "the specific gravity of air at different latitudes." Chemistry was asked to determine whether air is "more vital" at the sea's surface, whether such vitality might throw light on "the theory of gases," and how the air's vitality might be affected by seaweed. Botany and natural history were assigned less prestigious instruments: nets for catching insects; boxes for collecting them; scalpels for dissection.[69]

When the Academy turned its attention to human residents, its questions explicitly addressed distinctions between natural and cultural phenomena. Scientists were asked vaguely to undertake human anatomical investigations by scrutinizing the number of thoracic vertebrae as well as "the structure, texture and make of the head" of peoples they met.[70] Questions about bodily disfigurement especially excited the Society of Medicine. What might be observed about tattooing? What about the "different parts islanders are accustomed to disfigure ... by holes, incisions, extraneous substances introduced into them?" More specific were inquiries about the use of labrets by high-status Tlingit women, described as the "two mouths ... observed by Captain Cook ... produced by a transverse incision made through the lower lip ... Are these owing to nature?" the Society queried,[71] undoubtedly contributing to La Pérouse's growing determination to categorize his observations about Tlingit customs in terms of "the natural" and "the Other."

In La Pérouse's journals, we see a commitment to engage with the philosophical questions that were being asked in France by his display of empirical methods and observable facts. Before *Astrolabe* and *Boussole* vanished with no trace in 1788, he managed to send back charts, journals, and notebooks – documenting latitudes and longitudes, observations about tides, temperature records, and comments on forests detailing heights and diameters of trees. He admired the "vigorous vegetation," listing the berries, fish, and animals that contributed to the crew's varied diet and commenting on the excellence of salads, evidently an asset in keeping scurvy at bay.[72] He spoke of the mountains as "ardent and indefatigable," but ensured that they were "measured trigonometrically."[73] He remained deeply troubled by the lost astronomical observations taken by the Tlingit on the day of his arrival.

Where the guidelines for "conduct toward natives" fail, they do so in much the same way that prescriptive ethical guidelines often fail today.

They begin with authoritative assumptions about appropriate questions, reasonable choices, and rules for proper conduct that often *invert* local ethical codes and understandings. In this case, imperial instructions universalize local French conceptions of leadership and of property that clashed with highly developed concepts of rank and ownership in eighteenth-century Tlingit society. The problematic idea of locating "chiefs" and dispensing "gifts" has been discussed by both Frederica de Laguna and Sergei Kan, who point out that Europeans frequently mistook feted visitors for local leaders, and set out to negotiate with the wrong individuals.[74] La Pérouse, for instance, was puzzled when a man he describes as "ornamented" and "a chief" offered to sell them the island where his men were encamped. De Laguna suggests that this was probably a clan headman who was trying to avert a dangerous situation as crewmembers liberally helped themselves to resources they took to be free – water, wood, and fish – but that were subject to precise rules of clan ownership.[75] La Pérouse speculated briefly in his journal about the validity of the sale, but then proceeded "with the usual formalities." Tlingit, of course, had their own "usual formalities" and were adamant that visitors acknowledge their customs and were perturbed when they did not.

A template of a coherent, crushing colonialism leaves no room for unexpected surprises. Even though he embraced the principles laid out in the directives from Academy and king, La Pérouse was prepared to make his own decisions. Despite his instructions, he encountered unusual circumstances where the "usual formalities" collapsed, and where he could not simply distance himself from his social context. There is a brief period, following the loss of his men and his discovery of similar Tlingit losses, where his journal hints that his awareness of shared experiences influenced his decisions. At two critical junctures, La Pérouse apparently considered and then chose to ignore official instructions. First, he ignored orders to collect and classify material objects when he came across the sole Tlingit frame boat that survived their disaster. He briefly considered taking the boat back to Europe, but then noted that "a religious respect for the asylums of the dead is universal, and I was willing that this should remain inviolate."[76] Second, the Academy of Sciences specified interest in the "bones of the head," urging the collection of skeletal remains.[77] Again, La Pérouse declined. When some of the crewmembers came upon a tomb, they initially opened a package wrapped in several layers of hide. Learning from the Tlingit that bodies were customarily cremated but that heads were preserved and wrapped, they "replaced everything with scrupulous exactness, adding presents of iron instruments and beads."[78] This choice differs notably from those made a century later by museum collectors like George

Thornton Emmons, who procured and then sold the Kah Lituya feast pipe, but who also had no reservations about plundering shamans' graves. By the late nineteenth century, science had more firmly established its authority.[79]

Delayed further by poor weather, La Pérouse grew increasingly impatient. His inability to grasp the complexities of Tlingit social organization led him to speculate on agricultural remedies that might "soften [Tlingit] manners and render him a social being."[80] He drew on a trope still conventional for invoking ethnographic authority – that of "being there." "Philosophers," he fumed, "may exclaim against this picture if they please. They may write books by their fire-sides, while I have been voyaging for thirty years." Frustrated by his inability to grasp the intense clan-based sociality in which he had been immersed for some weeks, he began to universalize his conception of "the usual formalities" to lament that he had failed to communicate to the Tlingit "a law of nations, which is never to be violated with impunity."[81]

Two years after the French left Lituya Bay, Tlingit life there was briefly interrupted once again by Russian ships under the direction of Izmailov and Bocharov.[82] They arrived on 3 July 1788, traded briefly, and then departed on 9 July. One hundred years after La Pérouse's departure "to parts not known" on the verge of *their* world, the Tlingit only vaguely recalled his visit and often referred to his boats and their crews as "the first Russians."[83] La Pérouse becomes a footnote in their history, just as they become data in his chronicle.

Transformative Encounters and Knowledge Transfers: "The Fury of the Waves and the Rage of Cannibals"

Stories from Lituya Bay, then, document an experimental moment in the history of ideas, arising from a particular time and place when European expansion was erupting into regions that were rich with their own complex histories. Here, two distinct bodies of knowledge about the physical environment met – one rooted in an emerging French natural philosophy, the other in Tlingit concepts of sociality and sentience. I suggest that their encounter provides not merely a story from the past, but one whose consequences continue to cascade through twenty-first-century debates, such as those now framing environmentalism, biodiversity, and global warming.

If we view these accounts as documenting a series of four encounters, we can see moments when knowledge and technology were transferred and ultimately transformed, but also when new tensions around property and property relations emerged and escalated. The meeting between Tlingit residents and French visitors at Lituya Bay constitutes one such encounter.

The confrontation between each group and marine disaster is a second encounter. A third follows ongoing exchanges among various stories and their readers and listeners, as those stories are subsequently taken up in different knowledge traditions. A fourth concerns the current meeting between age-old concerns and contemporary struggles surrounding knowledge and power.

Oral and written accounts all conjoin the first two encounters: the meeting of Tlingit and French marine traders with distinct traditions of knowledge and experience, and the encounter between human activity and ecological risk. French and Tlingit mariners were aware of the hazards posed by the geological activity in Lituya Bay, and they were independently acquiring and creating critical knowledge about the dangers lurking in geological formations like the mouth of this recently glaciated bay. Both sets of narratives also suggest that human encounters were ultimately brought about, or at least enabled, by the sequential drownings that are attributable to a changing landscape shaped by glacial erosion. The calamity prolonged the encounter and made space for shifting judgments on both sides. If the primary story that is reported in Western texts selects the *meeting* between Tlingit and French as the main story, with ecological disaster playing a secondary role, the emphasis is reversed in Tlingit accounts. There, *clan losses* arising from ecological disaster are the main story, and the French connection is a secondary consequence – French ships attracted by debris scattered by capsized Tlingit boats.

Together, French visitors and Tlingit hosts created a space constituting eighteenth-century notions of the field, an idea that has its roots in shifting philosophical debates about rationality, knowledge, and experience. As questions emerged that seemed answerable only by leaving the library or laboratory, expeditions of discovery set out from Europe to measure the world and enumerate its contents. No sooner had La Pérouse arrived and his crews disembarked at Lituya Bay than he installed the ubiquitous observatory with its chronometers and dipping needles, signifying that the work of science was beginning. Historians of science have argued persuasively that the field, where boundaries and statuses are inherently ambiguous, can never be so clearly policed as a laboratory, where doors can be closed, precisely because it is inhabited by other interested observers.[84] At Lituya Bay, La Pérouse encountered Tlingit people whose knowledge practices were shaped by convictions that relations among humans and features of landscape – including mountains, bays, and glaciers – were mutually constitutive. This idea that human and non-human forces collectively "make" the world was an idea once transparent in Europe, but it was already becoming opaque to eighteenth-century scientists. As indigenous constituents of what was rapidly becoming "the field," Tlingit people and their practices came to be viewed by their visitors as irremediably "other" during the weeks they spent together. Rousseau's celebration of nature only deepened La Pérouse's own hostility to what he perceived as Arcadian nostalgia. Yet those two men shared their own local concept of nature, embedded in a specific cultural order laden with symbolism and underlain by subterranean faults – faults that, incidentally, would soon be cracking under the pressures of the French Revolution.

Ideas about exchange rapidly became situated within the realm of fundamental property concepts. Specific transfers began with objects that the French defined as "gifts" (cloth, bronzes, dragoon helmets, medals, and the especially prized iron) traded for Tlingit "collections" (handmade clothing, carvings, and basketry). As Marcel Mauss was later to point out in his formative statement about exchange, giving and taking are always interrelated in complex and often opportunistic ways.[85] The radically different expectations about "the usual formalities" surrounding ownership became clear when the French casually took supplies they assumed were freely available – wood, fish, wildlife, and fresh water – that were actually all subject to strict rules of clan ownership. When Tlingits took his notebooks, La Pérouse labelled their behaviour as "theft," but he never for a moment regarded his own practices in the same vein.

A third set of encounters, between stories and their readers or listeners, concerns how knowledge continues to be transferred and transformed. La Pérouse's final letter to reach France was written from Botany Bay in February 1788.[86] Three years later, in May 1791, the French National Assembly agreed to sponsor a search for the missing ships and to publish La Pérouse's surviving journals, those sent overland by courier before the vessels disappeared. The Revolution, the fall of the Bastille, the demotion of Louis XVI to a constitutional monarch, and the subsequent political and economic collapse complicated the process. Louis Antoine Milet-Mureau, a former military commander, began to edit the journals in 1793, aiming to represent La Pérouse's interests and to expedite a search (delayed by domestic turmoil) that would "cherish the hope we have of saving those of our brethren who have escaped the fury of the waves or the rage of cannibals."[87]

Under Milet-Mureau's editorship, *A Voyage Round the World, Performed in the Years 1785, 1786, 1787 and 1788 by the Boussole and Astrolabe under the Command of J.F.G. de La Pérouse* was published in 1798 and then translated into English in 1799. Almost two hundred years later, John Dunmore, a New Zealander who had already published a biography of La Pérouse, located the original journals in a Paris archive. Working with La Pérouse's marginal notations, he prepared an updated and meticulously footnoted translation of the journals.[88] Dunmore's annotations, though, strengthen the scientific detail at the expense of ethnohistorical scholarship by Frederica de Laguna, Sergei Kan, and others, that was widely available when his translation was published in 1994. Dunmore's footnotes provide Latin names for every plant, animal, and fish mentioned by La Pérouse, and he is attentive to shifts in scientific language occurring even as La Pérouse wrote.[89] Yet he replicates errors made by all early European visitors, conveying La Pérouse's eighteenth-century misunderstandings into late-twentieth-century commonsense truths. He sympathizes with La Pérouse's complaints about "theft," and details Captain Cook's "unavoidable" resort to arms in similar circumstances. When La Pérouse expresses concern about the "chief's" right to sell the island in Lituya Bay, Dunmore concurs, in a footnote, that, indeed, any Tlingit claim to the island was dubious because the bay was used only as a summer village. When La Pérouse laments that Tlingit society is in its "infancy" and would undoubtedly benefit from the civilizing influence of agriculture, Dunmore sympathizes, citing "the apparent absence of local rulers and formal enforceable laws" and La Pérouse's "difficulty in identifying chiefs and heads of families among his visitors." In Dunmore's analysis, once again, La Pérouse has become the host and the Tlingit the "visitors." Responding to La Pérouse's own concluding statement that "we found no case of anthropophagy," Dunmore quite inexplicably notes that "the practice [of cannibalism] seemed to have been linked to warfare and only prisoners taken in battle were eaten."[90]

Michel Callon writes about how certain frameworks of translation acquire durability and robustness during complex processes of social and technical change. He suggests that they achieve this by attachment to and circulation within prestigious networks, thereby contributing to the "hardening" of facts. Each subsequent interpretation becomes increasingly dependent on previous translations, and a process of normalization accompanies and ensures the irreversibility of widely disseminated accounts.[91] In effect, Dunmore's translation and lengthy annotations, published by the prestigious Hakluyt Society, reinforces La Pérouse's interpretation of the events, updating scientific details in his journal while allowing his eighteenth-century prejudices to remain unchallenged "facts." The resulting authoritative translation reinforces arguments about the sedimentation of colonialist categories in much contemporary scholarship: what sinks into history and what floats away is not random. Dunmore's annotations reiterate rather than question two-hundred-year-old clichés, referring to La Pérouse as "the first visitor to this lonely part of the world,"[92] and echoing

Milet-Mureau's anxieties about "the fury of the waves and the rage of cannibals."

But oral traditions from Lituya Bay have also continued to circulate through two centuries and to be transferred and transformed, most recently in published books that now move beyond the originating communities. Transmission of these histories requires mastery of specific fields of local knowledge – genealogy, kinship, visual art and iconography, songs, stories, and specific rules of protocol. In June 1993, the Tlingit Naa Kahídi theatre group travelled from southeastern Alaska to Whitehorse, Canada, to perform a memorable dramatization of the L'uknax̱.ádi encounter with Raven Boat at the Yukon International Storytelling Festival. Clan histories endure and their performance engages contemporary readers and listeners because they continue to be rooted in general social concerns and dramatize areas of social life that seem problematic. Nora and Richard Dauenhauer, who have been recording oral narratives in the Tlingit language since the 1970s, identify *at.óow* as a key concept of ownership framing contemporary Tlingit historical consciousness.[93] The Dauenhauers build their argument about the crucial importance of at.óow in three volumes that demonstrate how this concept underlies narrative, visual imagery, oratory, and social life.[94] At.óow, they argue, refers to both tangible and incorporeal "things owned." It can be a geographical feature (like the mountain Tsalx̱aan), a place (like Lituya Bay), a spirit (like Kah Lituya, represented in the carved wooden pipe), or even a glacier. It may be a song, like the one Wooshkika made for her lost brothers and uncles. The concept of at.óow unifies social humans with sentient places.

Fourth and finally, transfers of knowledge percolating to the present confirm that ideas have material consequences. Two hundred years later, issues raised at Lituya Bay continue to reverberate in debates about how transfers of indigenous or "traditional" knowledge might contribute to scientific research, a topic to which we return in Chapter 8. Anthropological perspectives on the ways that indigenous knowledge and science have been compared and differentiated remind us that scientific knowledge is also indigenous, local, and bound to idiosyncratic practices.[95] Pressures that Tlingit people experienced at Lituya Bay in 1786 have only intensified for their descendants, especially as resources once considered renewable, like forestry and fisheries, come under increasing threat. In agreements driven by global capital, clan protocols and sentient landscapes carry little weight. Not surprisingly, when oral histories are told now, they often address tensions surrounding longstanding concepts of ownership. The narrative of L'uknax̱.ádi clan losses, emphasizing Tlingit ideas about ownership, is more difficult for outsiders to understand than familiar genres of first contact narrative. Consequently, it is more likely to disappear in conventional Western histories. In the next two chapters, we shift to encounters a century later, where similar issues arise, but where the fulcrum of significance shifts from issues of science to those of spirit (Chapter 5) and economics (Chapter 6).

5
Bringing Icy Regions Home: John Muir in Alaska

A century after La Pérouse's 1786 visit to the Gulf of Alaska, the Little Ice Age was still producing fresh surprises. Stories told by glaciers and the work of moving ice are nowhere more dramatic than at Glacier Bay, Alaska (see Map 5). Ten thousand years ago, at the end of the last ice age, a receding ice sheet exposed long-submerged lands that initially invited tenacious growth of vegetation along the Gulf of Alaska's coastal rim. Forests grew and matured, only to be churned up several millennia later as glaciers expanded again during the Little Ice Age. Oral traditions report that prior to this recent advance, a rich salmon river flowed through the valley now filled by Glacier Bay. Two rows of clan houses stood at S'é Shúyi (the edge of clay), so-named for its clay-filled basin bristling with sharp grasses.[1] Then, perhaps five centuries ago, a glacier trunk fed by numerous ice streams poured back into the deep fiord, filling it and continuing to swell into the strait beyond. By the time George Vancouver passed through Icy Strait in 1794, the ice was again receding, but he reported only "compact and solid mountains of ice, rising perpendicularly from the water's edge"[2] at the mouth of what is now Glacier Bay. Vancouver's observations continue to be cited by visitors as a benchmark attesting to startling ecological transformation.

The next published description appeared almost a century after Vancouver's visit. Charles Erskine Scott Wood stopped at Icy Strait in 1877 and described an ice-scoured, glacier-fed inlet that must have appeared within decades. He reported that Huna Tlingit were hunting seals and procuring salmon and seagull eggs nearby, and he spoke with a thirty-year-old man, "Coon-nah-nah-thklé [who] told me that within his own lifetime this place where we now sit had been solid ice."[3] Two years later, John Muir visited Icy Strait where Huna residents told him their name for the bay, Sit-a-da-kay (Icy Bay), and described rich sealing grounds at its head.[4] Muir's travelling companion, Samuel Hall Young, wrote enthusiastically, "where Vancouver saw only one great crystal wall across the sea, we were to paddle for days up a long and sinuous fiord, and where he saw one glacier, we were to find a dozen."[5] As the bay continued to enlarge, Huna Tlingit were once again able to support themselves almost entirely on its rich marine resources, and it became their "breadbasket."[6] Its deepest arm, Tarr Inlet, now extends inland ninety kilometres from the bay's mouth, almost to the Canadian border.[7] Released from its massive burden of ice, Glacier Bay is rebounding some two to three centimetres a year, further transforming landmarks Muir described more than a century ago.

Narratives told from this bay entwine accounts about the unpredictable nature of the cryosphere with reports of startling changes wrought by colonial histories. By the late nineteenth century, encounters could no longer be detached from imperial designs or from successive regime changes in the North Pacific overseen by Russia, Spain, Britain, and the United States. Sea otters had been decimated by the mid-nineteenth century. Epidemics had torn through Tlingit communities: the 1836 smallpox epidemic, alone, had taken the lives of half the Tlingit population, and more diseases followed. The American purchase of Alaska from the Russians in 1867 brought a shift in colonial practices, as Russian Orthodoxy gave way to evangelical Presbyterianism and US martial law. Discovery of placer gold in British Columbia in 1873 meant that by the time John Muir arrived at the mouth of the Stikine River in 1879, Fort Wrangell was a busy supply town for prospectors heading inland to Dease Lake. Tlingits were converging on Fort Wrangell and were taking up employment in canneries, on riverboats, and as packers.[8] Alcohol was becoming readily available. The new nation of Canada with its uncertain boundary, meanwhile, was becoming Alaska's eastern frontier.

We have seen how La Pérouse's entourage of scientists, officers, and crewmembers arrived at Lituya Bay with visions of mapping, measuring, and classifying the natural world, and how environmental risk provided a crucial axis for encounters. A century later, in 1879 and 1880, two visitors linked by their shared commitment to a purposive world rather than to Enlightenment science reached nearby Glacier Bay: naturalist John Muir and Presbyterian missionary Samuel Hall Young.[9] By now, concepts like nature, society, and culture had taken on commonsense meanings that provided scaffolding for heated debates about progress, race, gender, social inequality, and the relative contributions of nature and nurture to each. Anthropology was inventing itself as a discipline that claimed authority to disentangle social and cultural phenomena from those deemed to be natural. Even as these definitional firewalls revealed their inadequacies, both Muir and Young steadfastly clung to the concept of a self-evident Great Divide. Muir took the study of nature as his project and considered

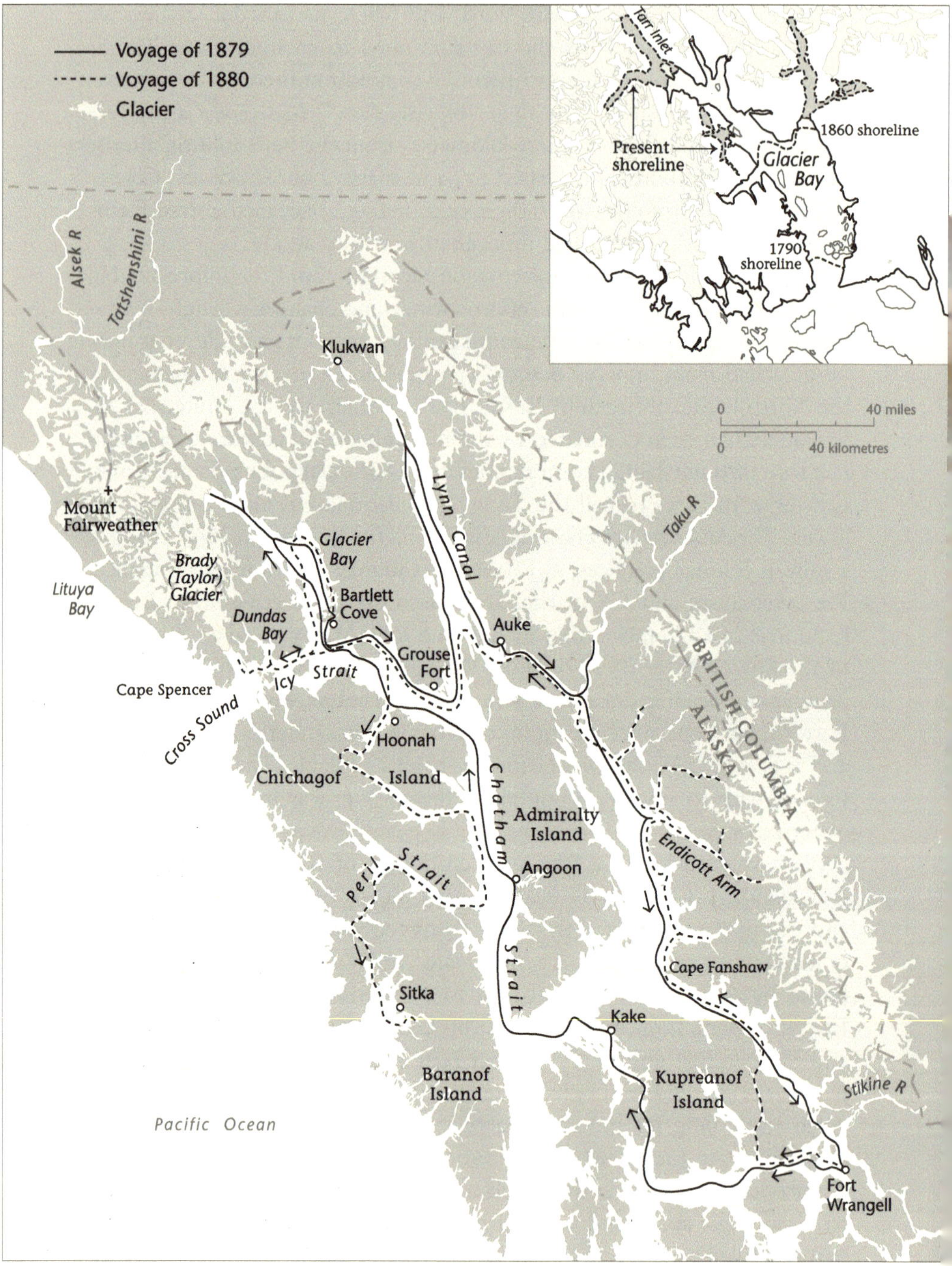

Map 5 Routes followed by Tlingit mariners who transported John Muir and S. Hall Young in southeastern Alaska, 1879 and 1880. Inset shows 1790, 1860, and present (2004) shorelines of Glacier Bay.

humans largely irrelevant to its workings and of little general interest. Young later described his and Muir's partnership as reflecting a harmonious division of labour that perfectly mirrored this nature/culture divide – his own interest in people as he scouted mission sites and promulgated "civilization," and Muir's interest in the world of nature as mirrored in forests, mountains, and glacial action. Their interpreter in 1879 soon chose to introduce them in Tlingit communities as "the preacher chief" and "the ice chief."[10]

This chapter, like the previous one, centres on a glacier-fed inlet and returns to questions about encounters and their consequences. Again, I draw on oral accounts passed on in Tlingit tradition, as well as on journals recorded by the two late-nineteenth-century visitors, Muir and Young. Oral accounts recorded by John Swanton in 1904 and by Nora Marks Dauenhauer in 1972 and in 1984 provide Tlingit perspectives.[11] For visitors' views, we turn to Muir, who published numerous short pieces during the next few decades, and to Young. Both Muir and Young produced books about their Alaska travels thirty-five years after the events.[12]

I begin with an oral account from Huna Tlingit historiography. I then outline the circumstances that brought Alaska Tlingit into close contact with two Midwestern Americans on two long canoe voyages in the late nineteenth century, and I provide a short summary of their travel routes in 1879 and again in 1880. As in the previous chapter, I go on to consider exchanges that occurred on both trips and some of their long-term consequences. First, encounters involved daily interactions that included struggles over ideas among Tlingit mariners and the two passengers they transported. By now, both Tlingits and their American interlocutors appreciated that local knowledge had significant consequences, so there were questions on all sides. Second, the parties stopped at most camps and villages they encountered. Matters of social etiquette in Tlingit Aaní had become contentious, and Tlingit leaders were increasingly assertive about defining "the usual formalities" that La Pérouse had universalized so confidently a century earlier. Third, encounters between humans and ecological risk in these changing northern waters focused and sharpened points of difference. As the travellers explored Glacier Bay, their experiences with transformed ecology were disconcerting for everyone, especially for the Tlingits who best grasped the dangers and took Muir's reckless enthusiasm about glaciers as evidence of witchcraft or even of madness. Finally, encounters among various iterations of the oral and written stories and their subsequent listeners, editors, and readers continue to have further consequences now that Glacier Bay is part of a national park and is incorporated into a World Heritage site.

My questions remain the same. What can these narratives contribute to our understandings of local knowledge? Which ones persist and which ones become submerged? Where do the stories travel, what do they accomplish, and how do they contribute to current discussions about environment, history, and harvesting rights?

My argument builds on principles set out in previous chapters. We have seen that Tlingit oral narratives make no sharp distinction between natural and social spaces, but rather explore their underlying unity. Local understandings of ecology incorporate glaciers as part of a responsive social world. In Muir's nature writings and Young's evangelism, on the other hand, the separation of natural from social worlds is more foundational; for both men, glaciers epitomize natural spaces beyond human influence. Muir struggled with this issue as his interest in matters of "spirit" grew. A passionate naturalist, he spoke a language of sentience that must have surprised his Tlingit hosts because he drew on metaphors that overlapped with their own without ever tapping into a common well of experience. He described glaciers as "traveling animals that make their own tracks," and as "crawling through gorge and valley like monster glittering serpents." He spoke of glaciers "in labor" giving birth to mountains, and of falling icebergs emitting "the outcry of a newborn berg."[13] Yet he failed to grasp local social conventions associated with glaciers and distressed his crewmembers by disappearing for hours into "ice-mountains" with no apparent purpose or concern for his fellow travellers. Categorical distinctions between nature and culture became one point of tension in these encounters, and distinctive notions of "spirit" straddled this axis as awkwardly as "science" had a century earlier.

As encounters moved from utilitarian exchanges to philosophical questions – about whether wolves have souls or whether glaciers respond to humans – struggles over meanings became intense. What distinguished these encounters from other contemporaneous meetings were the attempts the parties made to find common ground, specifically through the telling of stories, a mode much admired by all participants. Other forces operating on the coast by now preferred military action to dialogue; the US Army destroyed Kake in 1869 and the US Navy shelled Angoon in 1882 – each following a disagreement between Tlingit leaders and US military officers deputized to maintain "order."[14]

Narratives of Little Ice Age Advance: Oral Accounts from Glacier Bay

If physical evidence of human occupation prior to the Little Ice Age advance has been erased at Glacier Bay, traces remain in named places and stories. The main settlement where people were living when the glaciers re-advanced is remembered by a Tlingit name, L'eiwshashakee Áan (town on the glacial sand cutbacks), and was situated at Bartlett Cove near the present-day Glacier Bay National Park Visitor Center.[15] Ecological transformations are also documented in place names – Sít Eeti G̲eey (the bay where the glacier was), and also the name Xaatl Tú (among the icebergs).[16] Glacial events that scientists and historians now study are memorialized in stories Huna elders tell about being driven from their homes by a glacier advance. Recall from Chapter 1 that Deikinaak'w, the Tlingit elder who narrated most of the stories in John Swanton's volume *Tlingit Myths and Texts,* described a clan house built from the successes of Tlingit trade, and so grand that a speaker had to shout from one end to be heard at the other. That house, as we saw in Chapter 1, was reportedly crushed like kindling by a glacier that responded when a young woman flippantly joked in its presence.[17] The story has passed through generations of descendants, two of whom worked with Tlingit linguist Nora Dauenhauer to record accounts they had learned – Susie James in June 1972, when she was eighty-two years old, and Amy Marvin, more than a decade later in May 1984.[18] Like Deikinaak'w, they each tell the wrenching story of a young woman, Kaasteen, who was nearing the end of her puberty confinement, secluded comfortably enough in an extension to the main house walled off with a cedar-bark curtain, but undoubtedly bored. Her family home was one of several clan houses that stood along the salmon river, Gathéeni.

One evening, Kaasteen's mother brought her daughter dried salmon strips. After eating them, Kaasteen unaccountably pulled up the cedar-bark curtain and then began waving the remnant bones, calling the glacier just as though she were summoning a dog: "Hey, Glacier, here, here, here. Glacier, here, here, here."[19] Remarkably, she did this in full view of her younger sister who, even at the age of eight, recognized aberrant behaviour when she saw it and rushed off to inform their mother. But it was already too late. Villagers at a feast sensed some trembling, but put it down to an ordinary earthquake, probably a common enough event, because they paid no attention. But then they began to feel the ground churning beneath their feet as ice began to advance, not on the surface of the land but underground, "pushing the village along ... like a whirlpool."[20]

Word spread about Kaasteen's double violation. To begin with, she had casually joked with the glacier, although both narrators stress this was spontaneous rather than premeditated, and the Dauenhauers refer to it as "an unconscious act of whimsy." But she had also summoned the glacier directly by name, "sit'," rather than referring to it indirectly, the convention for addressing spirits expected of a young woman learning self-restraint as part of her seclusion.[21] In diverging versions of this story, each narrator goes on to dramatize the terrible choices residents had to make instantly, as the glacier bore down, "growing like a running dog."[22] Everyone knew that someone had to remain behind to pay for this infraction. The girl's maternal grandmother, Shaawatséek', ordered Kaasteen to flee with everyone else and insisted that she would stand in for her because of the young woman's potential to bear children, crucial to the continuity of their Chookaneidí lineage. In one version, Kaasteen accepts this duty to bear children as her obligation and leaves. In another she refuses: "No! I won't go aboard. What I said will stain my face forever."[23]

Departing members of both the Chookaneidí Eagle and the T'akdeintaan Raven houses, now refugees, left behind food and warm clothing. As the canoes moved away from shore, two men each composed a song to ensure that future generations would remember that people "didn't just abandon her carelessly," songs that are now among the most cherished Chookaneidí clan possessions because they demonstrate that members "paid for this land with their blood." As they drifted away, the Chookaneidí house – now a giant coffin bearing grandmother in one version and granddaughter in the other – slid into the sea. Refugees dispersed and became separate Eagle clans – Wooshkeetaan lineage travelling to Excursion Inlet, Kaagwaantaan to Grouse Fort at Ground Hog Bay, and Chookaneidí to the north shore of Chichagof Island – a diaspora subsequently reconstituted at the present-day village of Hoonah, their main settlement by the time the first European visitors arrived.

Narratives of Glacier Retreat at Glacier Bay: The Journeys and the Journals

If oral traditions about Glacier Bay begin with spectacular glacier inundation, the earliest published accounts begin with glacial retreat – the fastest on record.[24] Best known are observations recorded by John Muir, with his uncommon passion for glaciers. Muir is conventionally portrayed as a prototypical nineteenth-century individualist, but in Alaska he is more accurately described as enmeshed in relationships with Tlingits on whom he depended entirely for local knowledge and for mobility through unfamiliar territories. The participants met through a convention familiar on this northerly coast: an "explorer" might represent himself as independent, but inevitably needed "guides." Muir's encounters with Tlingit people, and his reflections about what he learned, like those of La Pérouse, reveal more than initially appears on the surface.

A transplanted Scot born in 1838 to parents who emigrated to Wisconsin a decade later, Muir headed west as a young man to California's Sierra

Nevada and Yosemite Valley where his best-known writings are set. He brought to his travels an intense interest in landscape origins. Largely self-taught, his ideas emerged as a creative blend of science, religion, and literature. Lyell's radical ideas about gradual geological change rather than instantaneous creation, Darwin's hypotheses about evolution, Agassiz's theory that much of the earth had once been covered by ice, and the nature writings of Wordsworth, Keats, and Emerson all fed his imagination. A lapsed Calvinist, he nevertheless came to interpret the North American landscape as shaped both by glacial action and by God's master plan – a source of religious revelation he referred to as his "glacial gospel."[25] This precept centred on his idea that immersion in wilderness and the study of nature, specifically glaciers, could transform humans. Images of Alaska representing nature in its most essential form drew him north in 1879, and he arrived eager to study the stories told by glaciers and the work of moving ice.

The initial crevasses he observed in Alaska, though, resulted not from straining glaciers but from advancing missionaries. The same boat that brought Muir to Fort Wrangell in July 1879 also transported three missionary couples travelling to dedicate Alaska's first Presbyterian church. A few days after their arrival, Muir accepted an invitation to join an excursion to a deserted village, where he uses the term "sacrilege" to describe what transpired. He was recording descriptions of totem poles when he heard the sound of an axe and reported that the missionary in charge (Sheldon Jackson)[26] had ordered a pole chopped down and transported to the boat with a view to "taking it on east to enrich some museum or another." The measured response of their Tlingit guide, Kadachan, was undoubtedly muted by his recent conversion to Christianity: "How would you like to have an Indian go to a graveyard and break down and carry away a monument belonging to your family?"[27] An embarrassed exchange of gifts paved over the rupture, but a comparison with La Pérouse a century earlier reveals directions of colonial transformation. As we saw, La Pérouse considered, and then rejected, his instructions from the Academy to collect funerary objects in 1786. A century later, Presbyterian missionaries had no such qualms.

After a full century of Russian rule, Tlingit leaders fully grasped the linkages between church and state, and following the sale of Alaska to the United States, they were cautiously interested in acquiring new missionaries with presumed links to Washington.[28] Stikine chiefs welcomed this missionary delegation to Fort Wrangell with a feast (from which local foods were carefully edited) followed by a dance performance with an elaborate apology to the missionaries, assuring them that such dances came from a time "when we were blind" and were performed only to illustrate the benighted past. All sensibilities accounted for, senior men made speeches and singled out Muir to receive a Tlingit name, "Ancoutahan." Muir subsequently came to appreciate its value – protection while he travelled and insurance that if he were harmed, the offender would be called to account.

During that first summer, Muir travelled up the Stikine River to Telegraph Creek by steamer and then overland as far as Dease Lake. On the Stikine, he was thrilled to see glaciers in action, as well as extensive evidence of outburst floods.[29] He fashioned hieroglyphic metaphors, recasting Saint Augustine's Book of Nature on his own terms as "Nature's Bible," with its pages the "icy cañons ... opened to view and closed again in regular succession, like the leaves of a book," and with messages "inscribed on the sides of the walls and over the tops of the rocks."[30] His appetite was whetted by stories of even more dramatic glaciers further north. Young, the resident Presbyterian missionary at Fort Wrangell, accompanied Muir upriver on this Stikine trip and developed increasing admiration for Muir's knowledge, enthusiasm, and conversation, but he stuck to his own orthodox Bible. He found Muir infinitely more interesting than his fellow missionaries, "those well-meaning DDs and their motherly wives."[31] When Muir insisted late that autumn that he simply *must* travel further north, Young hastily assembled a crew from recent converts – Toyatte, Kadachan, John, and Charley – and then joined himself, eager to scout out future mission sites.

A decade younger than Muir, Young passed his childhood and youth in poor health, but eventually followed in his father's footsteps and attended theological seminary.[32] Against all expectations, he announced his decision to go to Alaska. If glaciers and their stories attracted Muir, Young was drawn there by Sheldon Jackson's enthusiastic reports about the "heathen multitudes" and grew eager to impart his own stories, the better "to direct the battle of Christian civilization against heathenism."[33] He arrived in 1878, a year earlier than Muir. Despite the superficial differences between the evangelical Christian and the obsessively energetic Muir (who preferred to sleep only a few hours a night, and whose climbing skills Young once described admiringly as including the ability to "slide uphill"), their partnership provided a firm foundation for travels during the two summers they spent together, and gave much puzzlement to their Tlingit hosts.

The Journeys

On 14 October 1879, almost a century after La Pérouse's visit to nearby Lituya Bay, four Tlingit men transporting two American passengers in a red-cedar canoe began travelling north from Fort Wrangell. The canoe was owned by the experienced mariner Toyatte, whose crew included Kadachan, a powerful orator with valuable kinship ties to Chief Shotridge at Klukwan; John, a multilingual man from the Stikine River; and Sitka Charley, the youngest but also the only member of the party with personal experience of the northerly glaciers that galvanized Muir's attention.[34] Their voyage was a last-minute affair, and their destination was unclear when they left Fort Wrangell. At their departure, Toyatte's wife and Kadachan's mother were visibly distressed, less about the lateness of the season than about lingering hostilities the travellers might encounter among Chilkat Tlingits further north.[35] Both Kadachan and his mother would work with John Swanton twenty-five years later to record many of the stories in *Tlingit Myths and Texts*.[36]

Their routes followed overlapping circuits, one in 1879, and a second in 1880, traversed in the opposite direction (see Map 5).[37] That first year, they headed westward and stopped at the village of Kake,[38] then turned north up Chatham Strait, visiting Hootsenoo[39] (now Angoon). By now, Charley was coming to appreciate Muir's determination to find glaciers, and he recalled a trip he had made as a boy to hunt seals with his father in a "large bay full of ice." At Icy Strait they stopped at a third village, Hoonah, and met with the chief, Kashoto. Muir recorded that they departed for "Charley's ice-mountains" on 24 October, but remained skeptical about Charley's description of this northern bay as "woodless" as they paddled past dense forest and took on firewood.[40]

At the mouth of the promised bay, the disorienting changes so thoroughly perplexed Charley that his memories were of little help. Muir and Young, whose only map, "Vancouver's chart, hitherto a faithful guide, here failed us altogether," were also stymied. Relieved to see smoke from a Huna sealer's camp, they made their way there, and Charley flatly insisted that they engage a local Huna hunter familiar with the bay's current shorelines before proceeding further. They spent the next six days exploring this bay, to Muir's enormous delight and the Tlingit crew's increasing dismay about the apparent absurdity and visible dangers of their mission. Muir spent his days clambering over glaciers in states of high excitement, while the Tlingit seamen contended with drifting ice jams and took only minor consolation from the rich seal-hunting possibilities at the head of the bay.

After navigating the bay's margins, they exited on 30 October and revisited the Huna sealing camp overnight. From there they made formal preparations to visit the powerful Chilkat Tlingit at the head of the nearby Lynn Canal, where they spent five days being generously received but also vigorously cross-examined. Toyatte's discomfort now deepened because of lingering enmities between his own Stikine ancestors and Chilkats, rather than because of mere ecological dangers. When an invitation to the main village at Klukwan arrived expressly stating that Toyatte would be unwelcome, the travellers concluded unanimously that lateness of season made it expedient to move, and did so on Saturday, 7 November 1879.

From there they travelled south, making brief stops at Auke village and then at Endicott Arm, where they met a party of white miners. After a passing encounter with Taku Tlingit travellers also en route to Wrangell by boat, they returned to Fort Wrangell safely on 22 November, five weeks after their departure. Muir had just missed the steamer south by a few days and took the next boat a month later.

The following summer, 1880, Muir returned to Fort Wrangell where he and Young resumed their journey, this time leaving in August and with a different crew. Their former helmsman, Toyatte, had died tragically that winter when he tried unsuccessfully to intervene in a fight between Stikines and Taku visitors and was shot on 10 January 1880.[41] They engaged new guides: men named Lot Tyeen,[42] Joe, and a young interpreter named Billy, and they departed in a twenty-five-foot canoe equipped with two sails. They retraced their former route, travelling back up the coast to Endicott Arm, where they had abandoned investigations the previous summer, then north across Taku Inlet, and across Lynn Canal. From there they followed the north wall of Cross Sound almost to Cape Spencer, where they had a view of open ocean. Here, they were startled to discover that Taylor (now Brady) Glacier was advancing at the same time that those in nearby Glacier Bay were retreating. Unbeknownst to Muir (and as we saw in Chapter 1) the Taylor Glacier had by now buried a "deserted Indian village," identified by Vancouver a century earlier, beneath three hundred metres of ice.[43] Muir spent a long and ultimately harrowing day exploring this glacier, became lost in a maze of crevasses, and barely managed to return to camp that night.[44] As they retraced their route to Glacier Bay, they encountered Huna families at both Taylor Bay and Dundas Bay.

During this second trip, Young remained in camp with the Tlingit guides while Muir often spent entire days and evenings hiking by himself. While Young undoubtedly spent more time talking with (or preaching to) local people that year, he was always less inclined than Muir to admire Tlingit accomplishments, given his commitment to civilize, and was more inclined to count. He made the first census in the region, instructing residents to use beans as counters: brown beans indicating men; white beans designating women; and Boston beans for children.[45] Young grew progressively impatient to tell his own narratives of Christianity. He was frequently shocked by customs such as the "strange law of matriliny" and by outbursts of violence.[46] Returning south, they crossed Icy Strait, then navigated the circuitous Peril Strait to Sitka where Muir paid and discharged the crew, compensating them for their return to Wrangell while he caught the southbound steamer.

Encounters and Knowledge Transfers

What can we infer about the nature of exchanges among these canoe-borne visitors, their guides, and various Tlingit communities they visited in 1879 and 1880? A century earlier, La Pérouse and his crew had arrived at nearby Lituya Bay in self-contained ships bearing vast stores of trade items. Muir and Young, by contrast, approached Glacier Bay in a canoe piloted by skilled Tlingit seamen and negotiated their way through the archipelago with stories and modest gifts of tobacco and rice, rather than with prestigious material goods.

By 1879, the United States had governed Alaska for only twelve years, and political outcomes were still unclear. These journeys provide a snapshot of one critical moment when choices still seemed possible. Tlingit participants still anticipated that changes could occur at least partly on their terms, and they seem to have welcomed and interrogated Muir and Young in this spirit. In written accounts, one theme that stands out is how stories, the medium through which exchanges with strangers occurred, contributed to struggles over ideas. Muir and Young each recognized the importance of oratory and increasingly reported their successes in competitive terms.

If the veil of exploration science limited the communications between Tlingit leaders and La Pérouse a century earlier, the shoal on which Muir and Young more often foundered concerned matters of "spirit." Young saw himself as the bearer of civilizing forces and worked from a presupposition that Tlingit were "naturally religious."[47] Muir likewise came to view their hosts as possessing "natural reason," which he described as an "immanent living principle"[48] and attributed to their close association with nature. Immersed in monotheism, both the visitors focused on otherworldly, transcendental notions of spirit. Tlingit, on the other hand, rejected any view of desocialized spirit – the idea simply made no sense. Anthropologist Mary Douglas has argued in her book *Natural Symbols* that this association of the secular with "modernity" and of religion with "tradition" is both nonsensical and deeply damaging to understandings of human history.[49] Here, indeed, is the impasse where conversations often stalled.

Do Wolves Have Souls?

As the six travellers left Fort Wrangell on 14 October 1879, they initially framed their transaction in pragmatic terms. Tlingit residents at Fort

Wrangell were engulfed by a money economy by 1879, so they enjoyed financial benefits from guiding as well as opportunities for travel. Muir paid his crew sixty dollars per month in 1880, though his published accounts mention no specific rate for the previous year.[50] He considered humans of little relevance to his larger puzzle of deciphering landscape origins, but he appreciated the need for local guides to navigate the island-studded coastal waters and to locate rainforest campsites. His rural Calvinist upbringing had infused the virtues of work (which he applied rigorously to himself) and conventional Victorian hierarchies equating cultural development with subsistence modes and levels of technology (which he steadfastly applied to others). He soon came to admire Tlingit technological accomplishments – seaworthy canoes, immense totem poles, and solid log and plank buildings – which he deemed especially impressive in the absence of agriculture.[51] He also recorded his deepening appreciation for the expertise of the seamen who transported them, at the same time that he rather too quickly came to take both the guides and their abilities for granted.

Exchanges rapidly shifted from utilitarian transactions to the realm of ideas. Muir was much intrigued by matters of "spirit," and he came to recognize that his travelling companions had thoughtful ideas on this subject. They were equally impressed by his evocative use of glacial metaphor – his crawling and procreating glaciers. He seemed to share the language of sentience, and his imagery initially intrigued his Tlingit hosts.

It was during long evenings around fires as they camped that more reflexive exchanges occurred. Muir was a better listener than Young, judging by accounts each wrote later: "I greatly enjoyed the Indians' camp-fire talk this evening on their ancient customs, how they were taught by their parents ere the whites came among them, their religion, ideas connected with the next world, the stars, plants, the behavior and language of animals under different circumstances, manner of getting a living, etc. When our talk was interrupted by the howling of a wolf on the opposite side of the strait, Kadachan puzzled the minister with the question, 'Have wolves souls?' The Indians believe that they have."[52]

Even if Muir tended to translate what he heard into his own emerging environmentalist framework, he still approached the task of trying to understand Tlingit concepts with a kind of reflexivity uncommon for his time. He noted approvingly that "before whites came, most Thlinkits held, with Aggasiz, that animals had souls, and that it was wrong to speak disrespectfully of the fishes or any of the animals that supplied them with food."[53] To illustrate, he related an account he had heard in Fort Wrangell of a boy whose soul was snatched by a crawfish after the child made fun of its crooked legs and awkward gait. The child weakened and became little more than a hollow shell, no longer really alive. Muir's careful recording of such conversations, and the choice of his editor at *The Century Magazine,* Robert Underwood Johnson, to delete this and similar passages from articles later published in that magazine will be discussed below with reference to Muir's ongoing legacy.

If Tlingit stories stressed reciprocity between humans and animals, Muir continued to focus on their separability, giving preference to animals. Famously, he insisted on rocking the boat when they hunted seals. The incredulous crew came to refer to him, perhaps ironically, as "duck's friend," because "when we want to shoot, Mr. Muir always shakes the canoe."[54] An interpretation that they almost surely made among themselves was that Muir was offending animals who were offering themselves to hunters. Already we see hints of the conceptual differences that would pit environmentalists and Native North Americans against one another in subsequent debates about hunting a century later.[55]

Once, during their second trip in 1880, Muir became outraged when Joe, the crewmember primarily responsible for hunting, casually shot and killed a seagull. Muir accepted Joe's explanation that he had learned such irresponsible behaviour from whites, and interpreted this behaviour nostalgically as a manifestation of culture loss rather than as possible resistance to colonial practices. He also recorded without comment a statement by the captain of his crew that year, Tyeen, who "denounced the deed as likely to bring bad luck."[56] Frederica de Laguna summarizes two accounts of glacier-related outburst floods attributed to disrespectful treatment of seagulls, one at the mouth of the Alsek River and another at Point Latouche on Yakutat Bay.[57] Tyeen was undoubtedly referring to broadly shared understandings that eluded Muir because they were so incongruent with his conservationist commitment to a Nature detached from human affairs.

Although these shared ruminations were sometimes a point of genuine exchange among the travellers, differences seemed to sharpen precisely at such junctures. Again, we see how encounters produce two different assessments. While Tlingits were curious about the visitors' ideas, they held to their own view that knowledge was unified and not divisible into separate social, ecological, and spiritual components. They came to recognize that Muir's appreciation of glaciers still failed to disrupt his own firm categories that made no space for reciprocity between humans and nature. Points of tension seem to have arisen largely because of the visitors' insistence on abstracting knowledge from local contexts. These were experimental moments where ideas sometimes facilitated exchanges, sometimes provoked disagreements, and inevitably had consequences that participants could not foresee at the time. Tlingit uneasiness seems prescient, given the subsequent impact of Muir's ideas on their lives, once his conservation movement took root.

Local Etiquette and "the Usual Formalities"

When La Pérouse began trading with Tlingit at Lituya Bay on terms laid out by the Académie des Sciences he felt confident enough to speak of "the usual formalities" as though they were universal. A century later, despite serious encroachments on their autonomy, senior Tlingit heads of clans were much more assertive in establishing what those formalities were, and what indeed was "usual."

Young retrospectively described the formalized protocols, noting that travellers were expected to begin any visit by giving meat, rice, and tobacco to the senior man. Muir added that a chief never spoke first, "it being considered impolite to look at visitors or speak to them before time had been allowed them to collect their thoughts and prepare any message they might have to deliver." Following introductions, Young would request that members of the camp or village be called together, and once they were assembled, he would address the gathering. Then Muir would speak, and finally the chiefs would speak. If problems arose, Toyatte or Kadachan would intervene.[58]

Muir described these meetings from his perspective: "Every Indian party we met, we interviewed, and visited every village we came to."[59] It appears, though, that the Tlingits were doing just as much of the interviewing. In October of 1879, as the canoeists approached a Huna encampment near Glacier Bay, shots were fired and their greetings were met with counter-questions. When they arrived at the Chilkat village at the head of Lynn Canal, Muir and Young each reported that they were welcomed rather too warmly by "a swarm of musket bullets, flying scarce high enough for comfort" and a messenger shouting, "Who are you? What are your names? What do you want? What have you come for?"[60] The "usual formalities" were no longer at the whim of visitors, and Tlingits were not shy to ask strangers to account for themselves.

Tlingit residents were by now familiar with missionaries and recognized Young as one more category of collector – an accumulator of "souls" rather than of fish, furs, or minerals. Muir's behaviour, though, increasingly puzzled them and provided fertile ground for conversation. Frequently, they asked Young to account for his colleague's behaviour: "Why does this strange man go into the wet woods and up the mountain on stormy nights? Why does he walk along on barren peaks or on dangerous mountains?" When Young replied that Muir was only seeking knowledge, Toyatte scoffed that Muir must be a witch to seek such knowledge in such weather. In Muir's company, they found even Young puzzling, and one Huna chief inquired whether he intended to preach to seagulls or to the ice mountains when he reached Glacier Bay.[61]

Young portrays himself as dispensing spiritual salvation, pure "spirit" in his terms, but Tlingits perhaps had a sharper appreciation of the situation. Whenever Young proposed to establish a mission, he met counter-offers: requests for teachers in exchange for mission sites, and for technology rather than mere clergy. The Stikine chief Shakes summed up the equation early on: "The white man ... makes great ships ... that go with the wind and go with fire and they have better axes."[62] At Kake, the chief assured them, "You know about God, and ships and guns and the growing of things to eat. We will sit and listen to the words of any teacher you send us."[63] Repeatedly, Young heard this preference for teachers. At Admiralty Island, at Chilkat, at Huna camps near Glacier Bay, at Hoonah, they heard one chorus, and this continued when they returned a year later in 1880: "Give us a teacher ... a school for the children."[64]

Tlingits seemed as eager to discuss technology and geomorphology as Muir and Young were to address matters of spirit, and their questions came swiftly. Why, they inquired, had Professor Davidson come to a mountain behind Chilkat village some years earlier and used instruments to look at the sun when it grew dark in mid-day?[65] Muir responded with a lecture about the nature of eclipses and the working of the tides. When discussions turned to geomorphology, it was Muir's turn to quiz his hosts:

> When I asked them ... how they thought this gorge was made, they gave up the question, but offered an opinion as to the formation of rain and soil. The rain, they said, was produced by the rapid whirling of the earth by a stout mythical being called Yek. The water of the ocean was thus thrown up, to descend again in showers, just as it is thrown off a grindstone ... The soil, they said, for the plants to grow on is formed by the washing of rain on the rocks and gradually accumulating. The grindstone action of ice in this connection they had not recognized.[66]

In matters of social etiquette, Muir seemed to grasp selectively some principles and to ignore others. He spent the first part of the trip avoiding Tlingit foods "even for manner's sake," and surviving on beans and hardtack, but when he and Young insisted at Hoonah on pitching their tent instead of staying in the chief's house, Toyatte and Kadachan exploded at their bad manners. Toyatte informed them that if they continued to behave this way when the group reached the Chilkat village, he and Kadachan would be shamed (and, he might have added, endangered, given historical tensions between these neighbours). Muir hastily promised to amend his behaviour and to eat and sleep "like good Chilkats."[67] At the home of the Chilkat chief Don-na-wuk, Young described a meal of four courses: fish, deer, potatoes, and berries, all lavishly served with seal oil, "a feast of fat things," followed by oratory with both clan headmen and visitors expected to speak. Muir's comfort level seems to have risen, as he proved himself an outstanding orator, winning praise from the assembly. While their interpreter John translated, Don-na-wuk passed over Young and offered Muir the job of teacher: "He knows how to talk and beats the preacher far." An aged man stood to praise Muir's speech: "It has always seemed to me that while trying to speak to traders and those seeking gold mines that it was like speaking to a person across a broad stream that was running fast over stones and making so loud a noise that scarce a single word could be heard. But now, for the first time, the Indian and the white man are on the same side of the river."[68] Oratory and storytelling were clearly emerging as a highly valued medium of exchange with non-Tlingit strangers.

Muir's effusive praise for Chilkat hospitality coincided with his crew's escalating discomfort about awkward moments. When Kadachan presented Chilkat chiefs with a gift of two white blankets on his and Toyatte's behalf, their offering was barely acknowledged, and this deliberate coolness contributed to the visitors' collective decision to move on rather than to extend their visit. As they took leave of their hosts, the Chilkat chief requested that Muir leave behind a written certificate verifying that neither he nor Young had been harmed, lest the party come to some grief on the return voyage. Extended reciprocity that incorporated temporary strangers also brought potential burdens to hosts.

Environmental Risk

Environmental risks accompanying late stages of the Little Ice Age sometimes drove further wedges in human encounters. All the travellers recognized that the area around Glacier Bay was changing, but their interpretations diverged in ways that affected their responses. Muir and Young saw this as evidence of God's handiwork: Muir's "glacial gospel" was saturated with Romanticism about the educational potential of glaciers and the passivity of humans.[69] The Tlingits who transported them interpreted the dangers as requiring circumspect behaviour and restraint that were part of careful negotiations with the landscape they were entering.

As the canoes advanced on Glacier Bay, their evening discussions shifted to potential hazards well known to crewmembers who exchanged their own stories. One arm of the bay, they maintained, was guarded by Devilfish (octopus) waiting to snatch, submerge, and ingest travellers. Another bay was the home of Kooshda Kah (land otter), much feared on both coast and interior because it preyed on camping travellers or drowned humans, stealing their forms. Still another bay submerged Killer Whale, known to devour passing canoes along with their occupants.[70] Young, who was spending more time in camp with Tlingit guides than the peripatetic Muir sensed the incredible fortitude it took the Tlingit guides even to enter those bays, and their increasing resentment of the seeming pointlessness of "this aimless journey" to a place where there was little to hunt, no wood, and no gold, where Muir's goals seemed so unfathomable. "Our Indians were sullen and silent, their scowling looks resenting our relentless purpose to attain the head of the bay," he wrote, also observing that "all night long the ice guns had bombarded us from five directions, when great masses of ice from living glaciers toppled into the sea, crashing and grinding with the noise of thunder. The granite walls hurled back the reiterated peals, multiplying its volume a hundredfold."[71]

Muir remained largely impervious to the sensitivities of his own crew, and they came to find his references to sentient glaciers disturbing, not least because of his curious mix of idiom. He seemed willing to risk their lives to satisfy his own zeal for adventure, and eventually they came to refer to the man who so dismissively rocked the canoe when they were trying to procure food as "always hungry for ice."[72] In his eagerness to add more hours of airy mountain exploration to each day, Muir often returned far too late at night for the travellers to move on safely. This especially distressed Toyatte, who considered himself personally responsible for his charges' safety. When Muir had behaved in this fashion earlier in the summer on the Stikine River, riverboat captains had simply abandoned him and departed, leaving behind astonished deckhands to guide the eccentric traveller overland back to Fort Wrangell. At Glacier Bay, Toyatte had no such option.

During lengthening winter evenings, Muir consistently tried to push the Tlingit crew past the best campsites, often leaving Toyatte struggling to pilot the boat in darkness with no safe place to land. Once, after Muir had rejected Toyatte's choice, it began to snow and Muir quickly changed his mind and decided they should indeed stop and camp. Toyatte, by then furious, refused to stop and deliberately steered away from shore. He announced that the tide was good but that if they were so eager to complete their journey they should leave early in the day rather than travel during the night like thieves. On another occasion, Toyatte selected a safe harbour one afternoon as a violent wind was building, but again Muir refused to stop so early. At dusk, Toyatte was still indignant, and this time even Muir conceded that he had grounds, since, as captain, Toyatte had the right to make such decisions. "He seemed determined to give us enough of night sailing as a punishment to last us for the rest of the voyage. Accordingly, though the night was dark and rainy and the bay full of icebergs, he grimly pushed on ... We made slow, weary, anxious progress while Toyatte, who was well acquainted with every feature of this part of the coast and could find his way in the dark, only laughed at our misery."[73]

Each visitor reported one final confrontation, Young more graphically than Muir. Rounding Cape Fanshaw in an icy gale near the end of their 1879 trip, Toyatte decided that it was too dangerous to continue and that they must camp. Muir demurred, insisting that they go on, and he slyly accused Toyatte of cowardice. Toyatte responded, "Very well, if we die you die too" and smashed into white water where they struggled to avoid jagged rocks, so shocking Muir and Young that they stopped paddling. "Paddle you fools," Toyatte shouted as they made a narrow escape. Young, perhaps editorializing slightly, almost fifty years later, reconstructs Toyatte's blistering reprimand to Muir as they reached shore:

> You know many things I do not. You tell us about the sun and the stars and the great world outside; you have traveled on the steam horse to many lands, but you do *not* know Alaska and her waters. Many times on this trip you acted like a silly child. If we had listened to you, we would not be alive now. You forced us to cross that reef when we were taking our lives in our hands. Perhaps you, Charlie and Kadishan [sic] might have swum ashore if our canoe had been smashed, but Mr. Young and I are not strong, and I am old, and we would have drowned. Would you be happy on the shore now with us lying among the breakers? Hereafter, let me manage this canoe. Don't act like a fool any more.[74]

Young depicts Muir as "meek as a child, a rare sight," after this speech.

Changing landscapes continued to produce surprises. The following year, 1880, at Taylor (now Brady) Glacier, just west of Glacier Bay, the party stumbled on "the great exception," a glacier that was advancing rather than retreating, "ploughing up and shoving forward moraine soil that had been deposited long ago ... overwhelming and grinding and carrying away forests on the sides and front of the glacier." Even Young was excited this time, calling it "one of the most tremendous examples of glacial power that I have ever seen," and seizing the opportunity to record an agro-biblical metaphor in his notes: "See the mighty ploughshare and its furrows."[75] While Muir was exploring the glacier, Young met a Huna family with salmon weirs at a nearby fish camp. The senior man told Young that this had once been an important salmon stream, but that now the glacier was advancing a mile a year and the fishing habitat was very nearly destroyed. Salmon still approached the stream but were turning back to sea, bewildered. He knew that he must have inadvertently offended the glacier, the man went on, and had already sacrificed two slaves in an effort to atone, but with no result. When Young expressed horror, the man responded with bewilderment, protesting that the slaves were, after all, his property, legitimate gifts to animate glaciers. He then proposed that Young try to achieve a better result by asking *his* God to intervene. Eight years later, Young reports, the Brady Glacier finally began to recede and the man came to congratulate Young and converted to Christianity.[76] As balanced reciprocity, Tlingits may have perceived this intercession as one of the missionary's more successful accomplishments.

The Separate Lines of Stories

What do we know about how these stories move to later audiences? Where do they travel, what do they accomplish, and what drifts away? Encounters among stories, told or published, and their ongoing listeners, editors, and readers have new consequences now that Glacier Bay is both a national park and part of a World Heritage site.

Tales of these summer encounters with Muir and Young seem not to have passed into twenty-first-century Tlingit oral traditions. The untimely death of Toyatte, probably the person best positioned to relay observations, may have played a role. Ultimately, though, the escalating pace of change must have been crucial. By 1879, two travellers in a canoe were curiosities, but no longer especially noteworthy. Mostly, the oral and written accounts from these years seem to drift apart – Muir's accounts taken up by environmental historians[77] and Young's by students of church and school,[78] while Tlingit orators have continued to tell, record, and enact their narratives about Glacier Bay in ever-expanding contexts.

Muir's Alaska writings make up only a small part of his opus, but they have generated diverging interpretations, especially concerning his relationships with Tlingit people. Within a few years of his first visit, Glacier Bay had become a destination stopover for boatloads of tourists, many of them drawn by Muir's writings, and by 1890, five thousand visitors were reaching Glacier Bay each summer, transported by train and by steamship.[79] His work also attracted scientists: wildlife biologist George Bird amplified his preservationist values, and ecologist William Cooper furthered Muir's conception of Glacier Bay as a giant scientific laboratory for research on vegetative succession.[80] Theodore Roosevelt admired Muir's contribution to the conservation movement and once referred to him as a "perfectly natural man," further consolidating his status as a national environmental figure.[81] On one hand, then, Muir is extolled as a visionary architect of protected lands and credited with the environmental ethic underlying Glacier Bay National Park. On the other hand, he is faulted for constructing an artifice of wilderness that eventually excluded Huna Tlingit from a bay he claimed to have "discovered" after they guided him there.[82]

Historian Ronald Limbaugh has worked extensively with John Muir's voluminous correspondence, manuscripts, journals, and notes.[83] He is particularly interested in discrepancies between Muir's unpublished and published writings and in how editorial interventions by Robert Underwood Johnson, Muir's influential editor at *The Century Magazine* in the 1890s, shaped versions widely disseminated during Muir's lifetime.[84]

More than an editor, Johnson became Muir's partner in efforts to establish protected status for Yosemite, and he choreographed much of this as the golden hand behind Muir's popular writings in that magazine. It is well known that Johnson made additions to Muir's writings, but Limbaugh is interested in the deletions. One thread that he follows, as he traces the movement of ideas from Muir's written submissions to polished and published products, is relevant to Muir's encounters with Alaska Tlingits.

In the space between nature and culture, Limbaugh observes, Muir was also attracted to the animal-rights movement emerging in the late nineteenth century. He became preoccupied by questions about animal sentience and whether animals had souls, suggesting that those conversations he had with Tlingits in 1879 were more than idle chatter. He questioned them about the transmigrations of souls, specifically the souls of wolves, and he reported their observations. Reading Darwin had convinced Muir that animals and humans were related, and he struggled with questions about the equivalence of species and the implications for what he perceived as the near-human, moral, and intellectual qualities of animals.[85] If animal sentience could be demonstrated, Muir pondered, should human rights be extended to animals, and perhaps even to women and children? Johnson apparently deemed such ideas too radical for readers of *The Century Magazine* and expurgated such passages from Muir's submissions.

Limbaugh's meticulous record of how some of Muir's ideas were massaged provides perspective on how Tlingit world views also became an editorial casualty once Johnson identified them as "philosophical digressions" and purged them from published versions.[86] Muir was committed to Victorian notions of social hierarchy, but he concluded that religions could not be hierarchically ordered: "We throw our heaven open to every vertical mammal but close it against all the horizontal ones. Indians are more charitable. They allow their dogs to follow them," Muir wrote in one draft of his Alaska story.[87] This passage, Limbaugh notes, was too bold for Johnson, who excised it.

Johnson undoubtedly found even more inflammatory Muir's account of the meeting with the Huna chief who sacrificed slaves in an effort to halt the advance of Brady/Taylor Glacier as it blocked off a salmon stream:

> The Indians regard glaciers as living creatures, & are careful not to offend them as they crawl on their way devouring the woods & rocks. The Hoona tribe, as we afterwards learned, know very well that this one had recently advanced about a mile, for it flows across the mouth of a stream from which for time immemorial a branch of the tribe had obtained their yearly supplies of salmon. This disastrous advance was supposed to be a punishment & being anxious to appease the wrath of the gods & get them to withdraw the damming glacier, they consulted their Shamans, who advised them to kill and offer in sacrifice a number of their best slaves. This was done; but the precious salmon-stream is still dammed, & the sacrificial blood was shed in vain.[88]

Johnson evidently judged this likely to offend *Century*'s nineteenth-century readership and deleted it. Muir was by now being groomed for iconic national status and agreed to temper his public views.[89] As Muir's streamlined and sanitized nature stories gradually became reworked as "America's story," both the specificity of Tlingit local ecological knowledge and Muir's attention to Tlingit perspectives slid from the published record of those encounters. His posthumously published *Travels in Alaska,* compiled from multiple versions of that manuscript, appeared a year after his death with some of the passages reinserted, but not the one cited above.

Muir returned twice to Glacier Bay, once in 1890 and again in 1899. On that first trip his health was poor and he suffered from snow blindness. He expressed irritation with the stream of tourists habitually snapping their Kodaks and asking naive questions, and at the haste with which they ceased gazing at glaciers whenever a dinner bell sounded.[90] Railway-sponsored packaged tours were already shifting the focus from Muir's educational vision to a more marketable "experience" in which Tlingit people and glaciers came to share the role of commoditized backdrop, part of the scenery.

In 1899, Muir returned to Glacier Bay as part of the Harriman Expedition. Edward H. Harriman, president of Union Pacific Railroad, leased a steamship and launched a late-nineteenth-century equivalent of La Pérouse's northwesterly voyage, studded with prestigious scientists, writers, and photographers, and accompanying support staff. An incident during this expedition echoed Muir's experience two decades earlier. At Cape Fox, near Ketchikan, the party descended at a "deserted" Indian village where the railway baron removed two carved wooden bears, and other participants helped themselves to "souvenirs" including nineteen totem poles. Twenty years earlier, at Fort Wrangell, we saw how Muir railed against such behaviour, referring to it as "sacrilege," but this time he merely absented himself from the activities and from the photographs of expedition members with their trophies.[91] An earthquake at Yakutat Bay that same year put a moratorium on tourism for several decades, and Tlingit subsistence activities briefly gained ground.

By 1927, more than a decade after Muir's death and five decades after their voyages, Young completed a book in which he assumed the role of sole survivor and finally told his own story. *Hall Young of Alaska: "The Mushing Parson"* has a ponderous tone that demonstrates apparent stiffening of ideas that regrettably sometimes accompanies aging. No hint remains of his youthful curiosity. Michael Krauss, pre-eminent Alaska linguist, cites passages from this book to argue that while Sheldon Jackson may have been the architect of "English-only" school policies that so seriously undermined Alaska Native languages, Young was probably the first to enforce this practice.[92]

If written documents can have their meanings reshaped by a firm editorial hand or by cranky revisionism, oral accounts also take on new layers of meaning as past events are reshaped to frame current issues. The recent history of Glacier Bay National Park and Preserve includes the establishment of a National Monument in 1925; the expansion of boundaries to include more territory in 1939; the reclassification in 1980 as a national park and preserve (where Muir's writings are highlighted in visitor programs); and the inclusion of that park in a UNESCO-designated World Heritage site in 1993 (see Map 1). Over time, a growing preservationist philosophy has contributed directly to marginalization of Native residents.[93] Prohibitions on hunting in the park were officially instituted early on, but enforcement increased in the 1960s. In 1992, the US Congress outlawed both subsistence and commercial hunting and fishing in Glacier Bay; the law forbidding Tlingit harvesting activities was reconfirmed in 1994.[94] Kaasteen's story is now sometimes told as a "cultural" component of the public education programs run from the Visitor Center, but its current performative context conveys an underlying message that Park policies, like the glaciers before them, have displaced the original residents. New clashes, the Dauenhauers point out, reflect the complex confrontations surrounding subsistence patterns, traditional land use areas, new laws, and new borders.[95]

Tlingit stories also travel. In June 1993, Austin Hammond, a Tlingit elder from Haines, Alaska, then in his eighties, with close connections to the Yukon Territory, Canada, attended the Yukon International Storytelling Festival at Whitehorse, Yukon. He spoke there about the work of his ancestor Daanawáak – the same Chilkat chief "Don-na-wuk" who hosted Muir and Young in 1879 and offered Muir a job as a teacher, on the basis of his accomplished oratory. From 1879 to 1884, the US Navy administered martial law in Alaska, the period now remembered as Navy Rule.[96] In 1885, as tensions between the US Navy and Tlingit chiefs threatened to lead to more attacks on Tlingit settlements, Daanawáak negotiated an agreement with Henry Nichols, a senior officer with the US Navy. Austin Hammond inherited Daanawáak's name and brought to the Storytelling Festival a coastal copper etched with the inscription, "Donawock, Chief of the Chilkats, Died Feb 12, 1904." This copper, like those from neighbouring coastal communities in the Pacific Northwest, was made from a flat sheet of beaten metal cut in the shape of a flared shield. Historically, such coppers have symbolized wealth and power. Mr. Hammond spoke about how he drew inspiration from his ancestor's role as a mediator and pointed out that Daanawáak's copper was "not going to tear down, like that paper you have. My father told me, 'Pass that story on. Everyone will need it. Don't die with that story ... It's got to be up to you.'"[97]

Other stories that Muir and Young heard travel even further. Recall that, in 1879, as they approached Glacier Bay in Toyatte's canoe, one of the Tlingit members warned of the devilfish (octopus) with arms as long as tree-limbs that lurked in one arm of Glacier Bay. Almost a century later, anthropologist James Clifford heard the same story told in Portland, Oregon, and later recounted it in an interview.[98] The Portland Museum of Art houses a series of masks, headdresses, and ceremonial objects collected from southeastern Alaska during the 1920s. The museum decided to reinstall the collection in the late 1980s and invited Tlingit elders representing clans that originally owned the objects to travel to the museum as consultants. As the ceremonial objects were brought out, Clifford reports, elders responded by telling stories and singing songs, rather than "explaining" the meanings, and these stories and songs took on additional meanings as they were performed. An octopus headdress, for instance, evoked memories about a devilfish that once blocked Glacier Bay. By the end of the story, Clifford concludes, the octopus had become the state and federal agencies regulating the rights of Tlingits to use that bay. This ancient story takes on precise political meanings in terms of contemporary struggles.

In the late 1990s, park personnel at Glacier Bay National Park and Preserve invited Huna Tlingit residents to a workshop to document their "traditional ecological knowledge" about an area from which they had been excluded for decades. Not surprisingly, the Huna delegation initially objected that this proposed "exchange" offered them nothing. They agreed to proceed only if the park restored limited harvest for seals and for eggs of glaucous-winged gulls that nest on the islands within the bay. A compromise of a kind was reached when the US National Park Service agreed to fund an independent study by an academic research team working in collaboration with both Huna residents and park personnel. Results published in the journal *Current Anthropology* in 2003 demonstrate that Huna subsistence strategies are indeed sophisticated, and participants hope that this study may generate new subsistence policies at Glacier Bay. But here, the jury is still out.[99] Now that tourists are again an important part of the equation, national parks must balance visitor expectations about "pristine wilderness" with Tlingit harvesting rights. Again, we encounter William Cronon's concerns about "the trouble with wilderness" as a concept that erases human history from culturally managed parks.[100]

The next chapter takes us inland, across mountains and glaciers into the interior plateau, where practices of exploration were shaping up rather differently. Edward James Glave came to glacier country in 1890 with a different passion – a budding concern for what would now be called human rights, mixed with nineteenth-century faith in the transformative power of economic development. Already saturated with narratives of river argosy, he hoped to find a river that might provide an economic corridor to the northwest interior. Glave eventually came to conclusions about glaciers quite opposite from Muir's – that they created a space of geographical misery[101] – but for him, too, they played a role in how he came to view this place and the people who lived there.

6

Edward James Glave, the Alsek, and the Congo

Early one evening in July 1890, four paddlers in a twenty-foot cottonwood dugout canoe shot into a coastal fish camp at the mouth of the turbulent Alsek River. Two were descendants of upriver Nua Qua Tlingit, whose ancestors had been attracted inland some generations earlier by sources of furs and flint.[1] The others were visitors, one British and one a seasoned Alaska woodsman, who had engaged these guides to transport them to the coast from the upper Tatshenshini River (see Map 6). Shank, the Tlingit steersman, had experience navigating the Tatshenshini-Alsek, remembered as a "highway" for travel between coast and interior despite its challenges.[2] Slicing through the Saint Elias Mountains, it drops more than six hundred metres between Neskataheen, where they began their journey, and the Pacific Ocean. "This stream is the wildest I have ever seen," wrote twenty-seven-year-old British passenger Edward James Glave, "running with an eight to ten knot current, and aggravated by rocky points, sharp bends, and immense bowlders [sic] ... the river becomes a writhing mass ... the hissing and roaring are deafening." Periodically they passed active glaciers, where "huge blocks snap off and tumble with a thundering crash into the river."[3] Everyone on board was relieved to reach the Pacific.

At Dry Bay, they attracted the immediate attention of resident Tlingits, one of whom extended an open invitation to his nearby cabin. Some thirty women, men, and children squeezed in and listened in rapt attention and without interruption until well after midnight as Shank spoke. Glave later described how Shank's presence and oratory expanded to fill the space, and how flickering light illuminated this bard bringing recent news of inland kinsmen and details of the turbulent journey.[4] While Glave's account conveys the ambience and intensity of Shank's performance, it leaves us wondering what Shank actually told his listeners that night. Glave was already composing his own version of their travels featuring himself and his companion, Jack Dalton, as "the first white men to navigate [these]

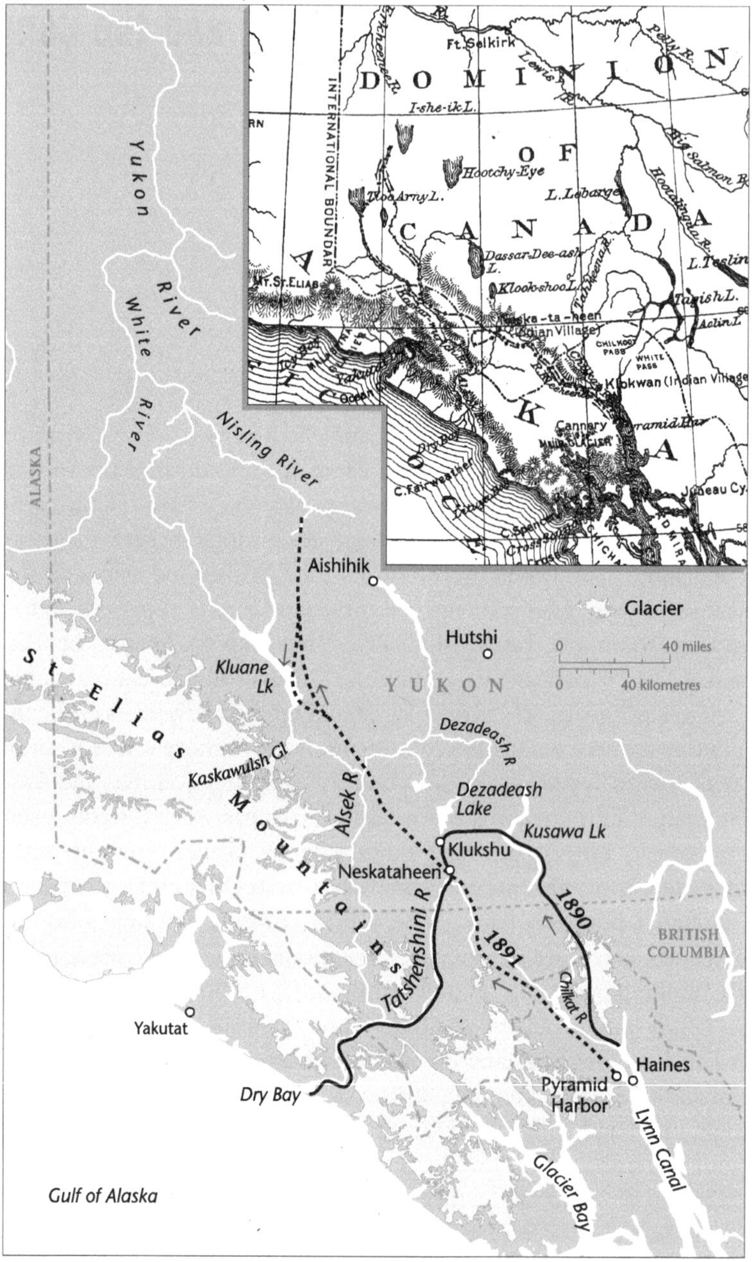

Map 6 Edward Glave's two routes in Alaska/Yukon with Jack Dalton, taken in 1890 and 1891. The 1890 route is quite clear from his description. The 1891 route is described less precisely. He complains that his instruments, jolted by travel, "enabled me to record only a crude idea of the lay of the land." The inset shows part of the map originally published with Glave's articles in *The Century Magazine* in 1892.

dangerous waters to the sea."[5] A few days later, Glave caught a schooner south from nearby Yakutat and then returned to New York to write his account, serialized in *Frank Leslie's Illustrated Newspaper*. Regrettably, Shank's version is not available for comparison.

Shank's and Glave's versions of this journey were directed to different audiences, but they echo thousands of small individual struggles over meanings everywhere on the frontiers of empire and the dynamics of who, in the end, gets to shape and tell the story. Postcolonial histories often provide compelling analyses of imperial institutions and their contradictions but less space for narratives of individual participants. Anthropologists Jean and John Comaroff tackle this issue in their study of South African colonial experience, and their point is equally applicable to northwestern North America: "Once the motives, intentions, and imaginings of persons living or dead are allowed to speak from the historical record, it becomes impossible to see them as mere reflections of monolithic cultural structures or social forces. This is especially true of the colonial encounter and of the civilizing mission in particular. And yet historians and anthropologists can be accused of not having paid sufficient heed to those voices – of not having done justice to the complexities and contradictions on either side of the encounter."[6] Anthropologists have become more careful about rendering colonial histories too simply as uncomplicated narratives of domination and resistance. Yet representations of such encounters still often float between indigenous oral traditions deemed to be "timeless" or "mythical" and postcolonial metanarratives that homogenize colonizers' activities. The actual records are usually more ambiguous.

This chapter evaluates Edward Glave's ambiguous role in exploration practices that reached northwestern America in the late nineteenth century. I originally became interested in his writings from the summers of 1890 and 1891 because they provide the earliest documented observations and reflections about indigenous economies inland from the Saint Elias Mountains. Glave left published and unpublished accounts, as well as sketches and photographs from what is now the southwest corner of Canada's Yukon Territory.[7] But he wrote even more extensive accounts from Africa, where he lived prior to and following his North American travels, so his own story highlights parallel transnational colonial processes that often remain invisible in regional studies. While his work on both continents has received minor attention, no one has considered his Alaskan and African writings together. By framing these stories as counterparts and as reflecting coexisting nineteenth-century practices, I try to determine how Glave's experiences in each location influenced his observations in the other. His records seem especially valuable when his interpretations are confused or contradictory because he was so clearly preoccupied with what he later called "matters of locality."[8]

As in previous chapters, I ask what diverse narratives passed on orally or in writing can tell us about moments of encounter among travellers and residents, but also about encounters between humans and landscapes where ecological risks were significant. How, for instance, did experiences of subarctic glaciers and equatorial jungles affect the observations of Edward Glave and the experiences of those who met him? Where did his stories travel and to what audiences? How do his accounts percolate through layers of history to current struggles surrounding knowledge and the shape it takes – concerning land claims in the Yukon or human rights in Africa? And can narratives like those in Chapter 3 told by Kitty Smith and Annie Ned, whose ancestors undoubtedly met him, illuminate some of Shank's preoccupations and Glave's observations?

In 1890, the popular illustrated American weekly, *Frank Leslie's Illustrated Newspaper*, sponsored a small expedition to explore what it called "unknown lands" in northwestern North America. Promotional notices published in the newspaper trumpeted "the result will be second only to that of Stanley's explorations in Africa."[9] Glave's primary credentials for membership seem, in fact, to have been his prior service on the Congo River as one of Stanley's "junior officers," and his extraordinary facility with pen and sketchpad. His reports were serialized weekly between May 1890 and January 1891. The following year, 1891, he convinced the prestigious New York-based *Century Magazine* to publish articles that resulted from a second, more precisely targeted, journey that he made with Jack Dalton, who had also been a member of the 1890 expedition. This time they took four horses they acquired in Seattle and announced their objective as opening up "the far interior" to commerce. Glave published two lengthy articles about this trip in *The Century Magazine* in 1892, the same periodical in which John Muir would publish his influential articles a few years later.

Glave's accounts of those two trips to northwestern North America are interesting, both for what they accomplish and for the puzzle they provide. The narratives could have been written by two different authors, so contradictory is their tone. His 1890 writings distinguish him from his contemporaries. From the first correspondence he sent to the newspaper, it is clear that he sought out the company of local inhabitants, did his best to learn local languages, recorded the names of those he interviewed, and included their names in his reports. When his colleagues casually renamed mountains and valleys after themselves, their sponsors, and their friends, he insisted that if visitors ever hoped to find their bearings, they must retain place names in local languages. He had a sharp eye for registers of experience differentiated by gender and age and expressed particular appreciation for the intellectual abilities of elderly women and the cheerfulness of children. While his companions peppered their reports with complaints about Chilkat etiquette, he would describe how risible they must all appear to their Chilkat guides. Glave is hardly free of the ideological values of his time, but his 1890 "reports from the field" stand out in a sea of nineteenth-century rhetoric. Compared with his peers, he sometimes appears to be a Victorian traveller with postmodern sensibilities.

It comes as a surprise, then, to encounter his articles in *The Century Magazine* following a second visit in 1891. By comparison, these accounts seem singularly unreflexive. They promulgate values of "whiteness" and "civilization" as though these were synonyms, stiffened by a mantra of progress. His assertive tone conveys a self-absorbed and cranky edge. Initially, I wondered whether inconsistencies might reflect differing editorial policies by different publishers. *Century*'s readership had reached two hundred thousand by 1890, and its editor-in-chief at the time, Richard Watson Gilder, was an influential and occasionally intrusive editor.[10] Another clue, though, comes from a byline that Glave began to add to his articles midway through his 1890 series, "E.J. Glave, One of Stanley's Pioneer Congo Officers." That reference led me on a trail to the Rare Books Room in the Cambridge University Library and to microfiche copies of Glave's personal journals from 1890 and 1891 in the Yukon Archives.[11] As I became familiar with Glave's African writings and then with some of his unpublished diaries written from northwestern Canada, a more complicated story began to emerge.

Edward Glave was born on 13 September 1862. After completing school at nineteen, he worked briefly at a London counting house, an experience he later described tersely as "distasteful."[12] For young Englishmen of his generation and with modest means, the category of Explorer seemed to offer one possible trap door exit from the constraints of Victorian Britain. He focused his efforts on the Brussels-based Association Internationale Africaine, bombarding them with letters until they finally assigned him to his childhood hero Henry Morton Stanley. Glave reached Léopoldville in spring 1883, and under Stanley's peculiar mentorship spent three years in charge of an isolated post, then three more years working on a riverboat for an ivory trading company on the upper Congo River. When his second contract expired in 1889, he went to New York on a "lecturing tour."[13] The chance to join the *Frank Leslie's Illustrated Newspaper* Expedition in 1890 must have seemed an ideal opportunity to broaden his experience.

By the time he made his second trip in 1891, Glave's motives seem to have become entangled with a different project. Shortly before he left Africa in 1889, Glave had become distressed by growing evidence of a flourishing slave trade on the upper Congo River, and by the winter of 1890-91, between his two Yukon summers, he was giving public lectures in New York on this subject. Privately, he was developing a plan to expose "Arab" slave traders, whom he believed were operating between the Congo River and the Indian Ocean. He became convinced that if he could travel from the east coast of Africa to the upper Congo River, disguised as a hunter, he would be able to document and eventually help to stop this systematic traffic in human lives. He tried to interest *The Century Magazine* in his plan, but they judged it too dangerous and urged him to return instead to Alaska.[14] Glave must have seen this second trip north as his final opportunity to convince potential sponsors of his capabilities. In 1891, then, Glave was not simply revisiting the Yukon interior, but also practising the idea of "solitary exploration" so that *Century*'s editor would advance him the necessary resources to embark on this African project. Glave understood neither the sources of the slave trade he aspired to dismantle, nor the forces driving it by 1890, but this nevertheless seems to have been the matter of locality on his mind when he returned in 1891 to what is now the Yukon Territory. His 1892 publication in *The Century Magazine,* then, can be read as a strategy for a very different project than appears on the surface.

A chronological account would start with Glave's years in Africa, but I will begin instead with an overview of his writings from the two Alaska-Yukon trips to highlight their distinctiveness for their time, but also their puzzling shift in tone. I then look at the larger context provided by Glave's African experiences and suggest how they frame his two Yukon summers. Glave's writings provide a window on how exploration practices and imperial designs were changing internationally at the end of the nineteenth century, with consequences for both Africa and northwestern North America.

"Our Alaska Expedition," 1890: Approaching Local Knowledge

In May 1890, members of the *Frank Leslie's Illustrated Newspaper* Expedition – Edward Glave, Alfred Shanz, and two men with previous Alaska experience, Frank Price and Jack Dalton – met at the head of Lynn Canal. The expedition leader, E.H. Wells, had preceded them to Pyramid Harbor, across the Chilkat River from what is now Haines, Alaska, to make arrangements for guides over the pass to the interior, a task that proved more daunting than they had anticipated (see Map 6).

Resident Chilkat traders were by now very familiar with exploration parties. Their longstanding role as middlemen in a lucrative fur trade with inland hunters made them understandably reluctant to lead aspirants across the coveted access route, especially ones so transparently bent on a mission "to traverse, and, as far as possible, map the interior of Alaska."[15] Three canneries were operating at the head of the Lynn Canal in 1890, and Chilkat fishermen could earn up to ten dollars a day selling fish, considerably more than the daily rate of "two dollars and board" offered by expedition parties.[16] Eventually an experienced senior man, Indiank, who had guided Frederick Schwatka down the Yukon River in 1883, agreed to take them and brought nephews to assist. While negotiations proceeded, Glave spent his spare moments visiting the Chilkat village. His earliest notes are filled with descriptions and sketches of house construction, artistic production, and cottonwood canoe manufacture.

Early progress reports submitted by Shanz and Wells are characterized by two established practices of exploration: naming (every mountain and glacier they passed), and complaint (about their guides). From the moment they left Pyramid Harbor, they began self-referential renaming: "Knapp Glacier," "Leslie Glacier," "Lake Maud," "Lake Arkell," the conventional detritus of exploration.[17] Glave, on the other hand, insisted on recording Tlingit place names and cited their crucial value as directionals and as sources of historical knowledge. In an era where geographical confusion soon resulted from competitive naming practices, Glave's choice was unconventional:

> The Indian names of mountains, lakes and rivers are natural landmarks for the traveler whoever he may be; to destroy these by substituting words of a foreign language is to destroy the natural guides ... Traveling in Alaska has already sufficient difficulties, and they ought not to be increased by changing all the picturesque Indian names. Another very good reason why these native names should be preserved is that some tradition of tribal importance is always connected with them. These people have no written language, but the retention of their native names is an excellent medium through which to learn their history.[18]

Complaints indicate just how tenuous the travellers' control really was, despite their proud self-identification as "the first party of white men from a civilized country to reach this region."[19] Shanz initially objected that the guides were tricking them into carrying most of their own provisions and slowing the party down, "refusing to move while the weather was bad and the sheep [hunting] held out."[20] Glave, on the other hand, was amused that their guides travelled light and refused to act as porters, while he and his companions "sounded like a band of the Salvation Army" with their gold pans, sauce pans, bread pans, and kettles clanging on their backs as they climbed.[21] When the guides moved off to hunt, Glave and Dalton joined them and enthusiastically documented the wild meat they procured. After eight days of travel, they reached the pass, and at three o'clock in the morning of 20 May, they began a harrowing sixteen-hour glacier crossing to avoid morning melt, their guides navigating around "great splits in the glacier, those dead-falls for Alpine explorers." [22] Exhausted party members now complained that the guides were moving too quickly and "gave us no rest at camp 9, and by six o'clock in the morning ... camp had been broken and we were limping over the trail." Glave, on the other hand, concludes, "Having climbed these rocky mountains, waded the cold streams, stamped through the rocky quagmires and broken through the prickly devil's club and stinging willow, I can conscientiously sympathize with the native trader who travels this same road to get the furs for which his price is considered so exorbitant, and I forgive him most heartily for demanding big pay for his services."[23] Once safely over the pass, all the Tlingit guides except Indiank returned to the coast, carrying with them these first "reports from the field" with instructions to forward them to *Frank Leslie's Illustrated Newspaper* in New York.

At Kusawa Lake, the party divided in order to maximize their exploratory outreach, with Wells, Shanz, and Price heading north with Indiank to the Yukon River, and Glave and Dalton travelling west with plans to "descend some stream" to the Pacific coast.[24] From here, we follow their progress through Glave's reports, written as nine additional instalments after he returned to New York and published weekly from 15 November 1890 until 10 January 1891.

Glave's initial euphoria about their new project soon was tempered by surroundings he described as "desolate" and "cheerless."[25] His relief when they encountered a family – Koona Ack Sal, his wife Koon Tcha, and their three small boys Tsook, Goo Cheeny, and Enock Doo Een – and his delight when they agreed to take him and Dalton to the upper Alsek is palpable. He recognized that the woman, Koon Tcha, shared his linguistic interests and praised her "quick intelligence," her "air of command," and her ability to decode his own and Dalton's "gibberish and sign." She became his language coach, and they practised as they travelled to Dassar-Dee-ash (Dezadeash Lake) and then on to Neskataheen (see Map 6).[26]

Glave's comments on "vacant space" are perceptive. The country may look empty, he mused, but he identified signs of old trails everywhere – blazed on large trees and knotted in the limbs of saplings.[27] He was struck by evidence of demographic decline, "whole forests felled" and "undoubted evidences of former occupation by great numbers of people."[28]

He repeatedly contrasts the scarcity of meat in this region with the abundance of salmon, referring to the meals Koona Ack Sal provides as "a salmon festival."[29] His praise for their hosts' local knowledge is unequivocal: "Had we not been able to avail ourselves of local knowledge and capable guidance we should have had great difficulty in discovering this stretch of rough country. Koona Ack Sal could generally ferret out a suitable trail. He gave what information he could concerning the geography and the country and tried to help us as much as possible. They even lightened our loads by carrying a little of our stuff."[30]

Neskataheen, near the head of what is now called the Tatshenshini River, was an inland trading centre where coastal Chilkat Tlingit travelled to meet Athapaskans. The latter were all downriver fishing at the time, and resident Chilkats were deeply displeased to see strangers in territory where they claimed exclusive trading rights. They castigated Koona Ack Sal for guiding strangers there, and Glave observed how tactfully Koona Ack Sal "feign[ed] repentance" and then discreetly acquired a new guide named Shank, skilled in river travel, to transport them to the coast by canoe. Below Neskataheen they spent the first five days on foot because the Tatshenshini, with its long canyon, was too fast and too shallow to navigate by canoe. Shank had cached a cottonwood canoe near present-day Silver Creek, Yukon, just north of the present British Columbia-Yukon border (see Map 9). As they moved downriver, Glave saw families converging to fish for sockeye salmon and estimated that even at the height of fishing season, there were only about two hundred people on the river that year.[31]

Each camp of people impressed him, and he mentions by name the generosity of specific leaders on the river, Ick Ars and War Seine, whose families "displayed all the hospitality that lay within their power."[32] Glave refers to his hosts as "people of magnificent physique," "scrupulously honest," and as "without exception the most peaceful people I have ever met in my life," adding "they appear to be living on the best of terms together ... lively and genial and full of fun ... they display affection and consideration for their wives and families." He notes approvingly that both Ick Ars and War Seine wanted their country "opened up so that they can earn more money by trade and labour."[33] Here, as in Africa, he never doubts the civilizing moral economy of imperial trade.

Glave's sketches and photos of people from these fishing camps, together with his written descriptions, have contemporary resonance. Local people were amused by his talents and even volunteered to sit while he sketched their portraits (see Figure 14). When Catharine McClellan took copies to the settlement of Champagne in 1948, people readily identified War Seine

Figure 13 Walking the upper Tatshenshini. In 1890, Glave, Dalton, the guide Shank, and Koona Ack Sal with his wife Koon Tcha and three children, had to walk downriver for five days because that part of the river was too fast, too shallow, and too rocky for a canoe to navigate safely. An artist in New York later made this drawing, which appeared in *Frank Leslie's Illustrated Newspaper* 20 December 1890, 374-75. *Newberry Library, Chicago*

as the former "Crow chief" and Ick Ars as former "Wolf chief," and recognized individuals in several of Glave's other sketches.[34]

If Glave's 1890 reports exhibit a peculiar weakness (or perhaps this was already his strategy) it is his insistence for his New York readership that he and Dalton were travelling "unguided," when it is clear that they were never able to accomplish this – not this year and not in 1891. For Glave to claim retrospectively that "we were unaccompanied by any Indian guide and had to rely solely on our own efforts to make a success of the undertaking" [35] dramatically overextends a narrative trope, given the successive guidance of Indiank, Koona Ack Sal's family, Shank, and an additional guide that Shank insisted they add as a matter of courtesy when they stopped at a downriver Nua Qua camp. Glave's praise for Shank is fulsome as they speed downriver, and he describes him as "full of pluck and dash, and possessed of a keen and rapid judgment, qualities which, combined with his strength of limb and great river experience, fitted him admirably for the dangerous

WAR SAINE, CHIEF OF STICK TRIBE.

SHANK, STEERSMAN DOWN THE ALSECK RIVER.

KOOSENEY, WIFE OF THE SECOND CHIEF, ICK ARS.

Figure 14 Glave's sketches of people on the Tatshenshini River. These appeared in *Frank Leslie's Illustrated Newspaper* 6 December 1890, 332; and 13 December 1890, 352. *Newberry Library, Chicago*

duty of steering a canoe down the Alseck River."[36] Under pressure, Shank "remains silent as death, grimly scanning the points of danger, and guiding the little craft as she leaps along the whirling current toward the narrow pass ahead."[37] As they hurtle into Dry Bay, then, Shank is the first to tell the story of their travels.

"Pioneer Packhorses in Alaska," 1891: The Counter-Narrative

After this introduction to Glave, it is somewhat startling to read his account of a visit the following summer. Published by *The Century Magazine* in two segments, "Pioneer Packhorses in Alaska" documents a return trip that Glave, Dalton, and four horses they transported by boat from Seattle made to the southwest Yukon in 1891.[38] They had even greater difficulty finding guides from the coast this time, but finally engaged three Chilkat men willing to lead them to Neskataheen.[39] Again, they travelled overland from Lynn Canal, but this time they followed the west bank of the Chilkat River to a pass that brought them directly to Neskataheen from the south. From Neskataheen, they appear to have travelled northwest through a valley past what is now Mush Lake, over the high pass behind that lake, and down into the Alsek valley. From there, they continued north for some twenty-five miles, crossed a major river, then trudged north as far as the Nisling River, returning via Kluane Lake and retracing their route back to the coast (see Map 6). Glave unabashedly cast himself as the hero of this account, with Dalton in the role of ingenious companion. He framed their journey both as a mapping project and as an experiment designed to open up commerce with the interior by travelling "without having to depend on Indian carriers."

The language he now was using to refer to Chilkat otherness begins to sound suspiciously similar to descriptions of "Arab traders" in a manuscript that, as we shall see, he was writing simultaneously about his African experiences. Glave now characterizes Chilkats as "arrogant, inconsistent, cunning and unreliable," as "buccaneers and pirates," and as "unemotional, morose, unsympathetic, superstitious, [and] indifferent to death ... They have no word for goodbye," he fumed in his diary.[40] References to slavery in Central Africa slide into his account, hinting broadly at parallels with Tlingit practices and tying both to warfare, human sacrifice, and serfdom.[41] Former friends come in for abuse: a year earlier he described Indiank as an expedition participant rather than as a guide, but he now speaks of him dismissively.[42] War Seine's warm hospitality, praised in 1890 writings, is now framed as "feigned geniality."[43] He admits that the Chilkats find his project of equestrian travel preposterous and are making fun of him. A year earlier, he would have turned this into an ironic and self-critical story, but no longer. In his unpublished diaries, he consistently records misgivings about both this mission and the drawbacks of his itinerant life and his desire to do "important work,"[44] but none of this goes into his published reports. Arguably, his mind is elsewhere.

The entire trip begins to sound more like a rehearsal for his anticipated return to Africa, or at least an opportunity to convince potential sponsors of his competence. He cites unsuccessful applications for assistance to Canadian and American governments for this Yukon trip, and his decision nevertheless "to go at my own expense."[45] He insists on the importance of a small party "so as not to arouse suspicions," precisely the language he had been using in New York to frame his proposed return to Africa.[46]

Glave's and Dalton's chief innovation this time was to make snowshoes from spruce saplings lashed to hoops fourteen inches in diameter and to train the horses to use them, an unnecessary precaution, as it turned out, because the snow on the pass had a solid crust by the time they arrived in late May.[47] His claim that "the bolted gate hitherto guarded by [Chilkats] to the exclusion of enterprise and progress has swung back at the approach of the packhorse,"[48] and his prediction that their accomplishment would someday receive recognition, was thwarted when the nearby Chilkoot Pass, more arduous but shorter, became the preferred route for prospectors heading to the Klondike gold rush and for a railway. A brief reference to this 1891 trip in Glave's obituary, four years later, mentions only their invention of "novel footwear" for the horses.[49] Accounts passed on in oral tradition include stories about their arrival at Neskataheen with what people then took to be "big dogs," and how one woman rushed out to remove her drying meat from racks lest the fearsome animals eat it.[50] At Kluane Lake, further north, people mistook the two riders for the colourless k'och'en (cloud people) that Mrs. Smith speaks of in Chapter 3, each having four legs and a long tail.[51]

Their initial attempts to locate guides at Neskataheen who might lead them further north were utterly unsuccessful. People were gathering for salmon fishing season, and no one would forgo the prospect of a full winter larder for the two dollars a day on offer by the visitors. Furthermore, local people warned them about "hideous obstacles" ahead of them – swamps, canyons, glaciers, and torrents. The outburst flood caused by the damming and breaking of the Lowell Glacier had occurred forty years earlier, as we heard from Kitty Smith and Annie Ned in Chapter 3, and the lake partially refilled sometime around 1890. Glave and Dalton must have travelled through parts of the old lakebed but apparently didn't recognize this (see Map 3). Glave comments on the luxuriant grasslands, the sticky quagmires, and the miles of blackened stumps marking the ravages of forest fires.

Despite bravado, once on their own, Glave and Dalton simply could not navigate. They would hunt, sometimes for hours, for signs of a trail. At one point, men and horses tumbled into a swamp they mistook for grassland, "a treacherous crust of floating meadow rocked into slimy grassy waves [that] gaped with a hideous opening before we could escape."[52] Management of the horses consumed more and more of their energy, and Glave depicts their days as a series of relentless verbs: packing up, striking camp, loading pack bags, saddling up, searching for or cutting a trail, pitching tent, cooking, watching out for the horses who by this time were being driven mad by mosquitoes, "in greater numbers and more ravenous than we had ever previously experienced them."[53] Desperate to procure guides, they devised a plan whereby Dalton would return by horse to Neskataheen, pretend to have forgotten something, and then casually raise their offer to two dollars and fifty cents a day. When this gambit failed, they were on their own again. Miraculously, just as a family had rescued them a year earlier, a hunter named Nanchay, and his son, Tsook, walked into their camp and struck an arrangement to guide the strangers north to their camp if the horses would carry their heavy packs. Once again, they had patrons, and Glave's tone warmed.[54]

Twenty-five miles later, they built a raft to cross a broad river a quarter of a mile wide that Glave identifies as the Kaskarwurlsh River (more probably the Dezadeash River).[55] From there, they continued north to Nanchay's camp where families from Hootchy-Eye (Hutshi) and I-she-ik (Aishihik) were putting up more fresh meat than they had seen all summer. "Already their roofed platform sagged and creaked and threatened to topple over with its weight of caribou, moose, mountain sheep, rabbits, squirrels and fish."[56] As his good humour returned, Glave spoke warmly of the hospitality and described this camp as "the lightest-hearted [people] we met during the whole season." He made detailed comments on children's games. He admired the efficiency of women hunting the noisy ground squirrels that perforate and tunnel the land in all directions: "The expert efforts of a band of Indian women with their snares will hush a whole colony of these little animals in one day. The women leave camp about five o'clock in the morning, and return home at night with several hundred squirrels, the skins of which are patched into robes, and the meat is one of their favourite luxuries."[57] Recall Kitty Smith's description in Chapter 3 of aunties swooping down on the ground squirrels after the outburst flood emptied Neoglacial Lake Alsek around the time of her birth, approximately 1890.

A few days later, they joined a small group heading west to hunt sheep on the mountains above Lake Tloo Arny (Kluane) who agreed to guide them if the horses carried their loads. On this leg of their journey, two incidents occurred that Glave records in his personal journals but in one case omits and in another alters in his published report. On 8 August 1891, they left Nanĉhay's camp and travelled first to "Naleheeni" (Nisling River) and then down to a small lake where they were shocked to see the unmistakable imprint of leather boots. Their guides confirmed that a stranger, "a creature like ourselves who 'loved' Indian legend," made the tracks. Glave recorded in his diary, then struck out the words, "probably Schwatka," as though he could not bear the sight of what he had just written. A few days later he grudgingly acknowledged, "We can be nearly certain that Lieutenant Schwatka has visited this lake. They are undoubtedly his tracks we saw at the small lake. He has gone a very long way around to reach here and we have made a short-cut." He went on to argue for the superiority of his and Dalton's route, "making our success a signal one."[58] All this, though, went unmentioned in his published article. Glave's secret remained safe, because Frederick Schwatka died shortly after returning from this trip, and his report faded into obscurity until it was located and published more than a century later, in 1996. Schwatka's maps and log are more precise than Glave's. Schwatka stopped at this lake, his "camp 40" (probably Serpenthead Lake, at 61°40', 138°45') on 18 July 1891, and Glave arrived just three weeks later on 8 August. Schwatka's glacier crossing and his jokes about his guides' concerns about "cooking with grease" near glaciers, noted in this book's introduction, occurred on 27 July, the same day that Dalton began his unsuccessful trip back to Neskataheen to try to enlist guides.[59] The few strangers mapping and measuring this landscape as part of a colonial vanguard seem to have crossed paths without ever directly encountering one another.

The second story is partially told in the published account. When the party now guiding Glave and Dalton reached Kluane Lake, they refused to lead their charges further toward the Kaskawulsh Glacier. Glave was outraged and took their dugout canoe hostage, presumably to detain them, but they simply vanished and went their way, leaving him to puzzle out his own route. Significantly, Glave had complained in his journals only days earlier about the unrelenting tedium of "bacon and bean breakfasts."[60] Assuming that his guides had opportunities to observe this reckless behaviour as they made their way toward Kluane Lake, it is hardly surprising that they refused to guide him into the nearby heart of glacier country. The taboos about cooking with grease near glaciers that Schwatka was simultaneously reporting in his own journal[61] indicate the extent to which local people viewed this as ecologically risky behaviour. Alone with the cottonwood boat, Glave and Dalton decided to use it to explore Kluane Lake.[62] Dalton fitted oarlocks and rigged a mast, and Glave gives a harrowing account of how a freak storm cost them most of their gear – and very nearly their lives – after the boat capsized, dumping them into the glacial lake waters three hundred metres from shore. Only Glave's camera, notebooks, and their blankets, sealed in an oil sack, were saved.[63] Glave again alluded to Africa as soon as he was sufficiently recovered to write: "I have had the contents of a flint-lock musket emptied at me at short range, and have experienced the satisfaction of stopping a charging buffalo; but I don't think I ever felt such heartfelt thankfulness as when I was out of reach of the angry waves on the rocky shores of Lake Tloo Arny."[64]

The narrative collapses as they beat a hasty retreat to the coast. The published account provides almost no discussion of their return trip, but in his journal, Glave describes a two-week delay at Neskataheen where they waited for enough snow to make it easier for the horses to return to the coast. At one point (his frustration echoing that of La Pérouse in similar circumstances), he notes that "the confounded dogs" at Neskataheen had stolen a notebook containing his sextant observations, barometer readings, camera notes, and part of his diary, but that he was able to retrieve and recopy some pages.[65] We turn now to the larger context that might illuminate Glave's divergent accounts.

E.J. Glave on the Congo River

Glave's writings from Africa provide perspective on his life both prior to and following these two Yukon summers. His autobiographical account, entitled *Six Years of Adventure in Congo-Land* and signed "E.J. Glave" like his other writings, takes us back to 1883 and the years he spent on the Congo River before coming to the Alsek in 1890. Illustrated with his own sketches, this book was published in New York in 1892, the same year that his articles about his packhorse trip appeared in *The Century Magazine,* so their preparation must have overlapped. The British edition appeared a year later, in 1893, with an introduction by Henry Morton Stanley, and it reads with an unmistakable whiff of "Boy's Own Adventure."[66] In spring 1883, after his application to the Association Internationale Africaine in Brussels finally succeeded, twenty-year-old Edward Glave travelled for almost two months by boat from London to the head of navigation on the Congo River, and then nine more days on foot to Stanley Pool. He was thrilled to meet his childhood idol, Stanley, and recorded a promise, which, regrettably, he keeps: "I felt, from the first moment I saw him, such confidence in his judgment that I never should have criticized anything he did."[67]

Following a summer's probation, Stanley offered him a choice of two outposts to manage, one already established and the other merely imagined in a dense forest some five hundred kilometres upriver in the district of Lukolela. He expressed hearty approval when Glave chose the more challenging option, and they set off together by riverboat on 22 August 1883. Stanley's first act at Lukolela was to summon principal chiefs to sign agreements giving the Association Internationale Africaine exclusive rights to trade at the post, a pattern he had already instituted elsewhere.[68] Some upriver chiefs initially viewed direct trade with Europeans as a way to circumvent established downriver African middlemen, but the latter showed their displeasure by twice burning an inland post at Bolobo in 1883, when an inland chief signed such a treaty (see Map 7).[69] Anthropologist Robert Harms suggests that the Lukolela post Stanley assigned to Glave was less controversial than Bolobo because Glave did not try to control or buy ivory there. Stanley dropped Glave off at the site, dispatched some crewmembers to remain and help him clear the forest, and moved on upriver by steamboat (that symbol of nineteenth-century imperial technology) with a "shrill whistle, the hissing of the safety valve, the sputter of the paddle wheel."[70] Glave had just turned twenty-one. He subsequently learned that Stanley had left explicit instructions about measures to be taken in case of his death.

When Stanley reappeared in January 1894, half expecting Glave to have decamped, he was impressed by the large clearing carved from jungle and the neat row of huts. Glave's writings indicate that he took "civilizing" as his organizing principle and "order" as its primary manifestation, a quality he consistently admired whether he encountered it at Belgian stations on the Congo River or in Nua Qua camps on the Tatshenshini-Alsek river system.[71] Glave basked in Stanley's brief praise: "To know that Stanley was satisfied with the way I had executed my duties was to me the greatest satisfaction I have ever experienced in my life."[72] Stanley continued downriver by steamboat, this time leaving Glave for two years.

Here, as in the Yukon, it is sometimes easy to caricature Glave, but what is more interesting is to identify where he diverges from his contemporaries. No one at Lukolela spoke English, so Glave set out to learn both Bobangi and Swahili, a skill that later enabled him to converse and collect testimonies when he traversed the breadth of the continent.[73] He was impressed by how important events were retained in memory and passed on in oral tradition, just as he later concluded in Alaska that totem poles were a Tlingit medium of recording historical memories "chiseled upon a wooden pillar."[74] Here, as later in the Yukon, he enjoyed language lessons enormously:

> When the [Lukolela] natives saw that I was anxious to learn their language, they evidently turned over in their minds the fact that I was from a new country, and would have some strange tales to tell when I was able to make myself understood. They, therefore, took the greatest interest in teaching me the words they thought would be most useful to me ... After a while, my friends discovering that when I heard a new word I immediately made a note of it ... would come into my room when they had any information to give, pick up my notebook, and handing me my pencil, insist on my writing down in their presence all that they told me. If the suspicion was aroused that I was trying to shirk my duty in this matter, they would request me to read aloud the different words with which they had furnished me.[75]

He good-naturedly describes being shaken unceremoniously from sleep one night by a man who insisted that he observe a mosquito and transcribe its name, "ngoong." Glave's friend Herbert Ward later commented on his "extraordinary powers of mimicry" and his close attention to sound that made it almost impossible to distinguish his voice from that of local people.[76]

For the next two years, Glave rarely spoke English. He transcribed names of villages, chiefs, and his daily companions, a pattern he was to repeat in the Yukon. He translated long explanations about customs, but also narratives about relationships between humans and animals, especially leopards, crocodiles, and hippopotamuses.[77] He was disturbed by evidence of indigenous African slavery, but illustrated its apparent flexibility with a story. One rich slave owner named Ndobo rashly became involved in a gambling game, *lobesi,* wagering all his possessions and finally his freedom, losing to a man who had formerly been his slave and now became his master.[78] Glave hunted large mammals in his spare time and always distributed the meat. Lukolela residents had initially nicknamed him Mwana Tendélé (son of Stanley), but they now renamed him Makula (arrows), even though his successes surely had more to do with his guns than with arrows.[79] When the Congo Free State was proclaimed in May 1885, securing King Leopold's hold on the Congo basin, the Lukolela post became redundant and was closed. Glave was reassigned for two short postings, one at Bolobo, another at Equatorville, returning to England in June 1886 at the conclusion of his three-year contract.

Ten weeks later, he was back in a different capacity as a member of the Sanford Exploring Expedition, a trading company subsequently absorbed by the Société Anonyme Belge. Travelling upriver on the Ubangi and Lulonga rivers, he became increasingly disturbed by a kind of slavery that seemed different from any he had observed downriver. Certain tribal groups

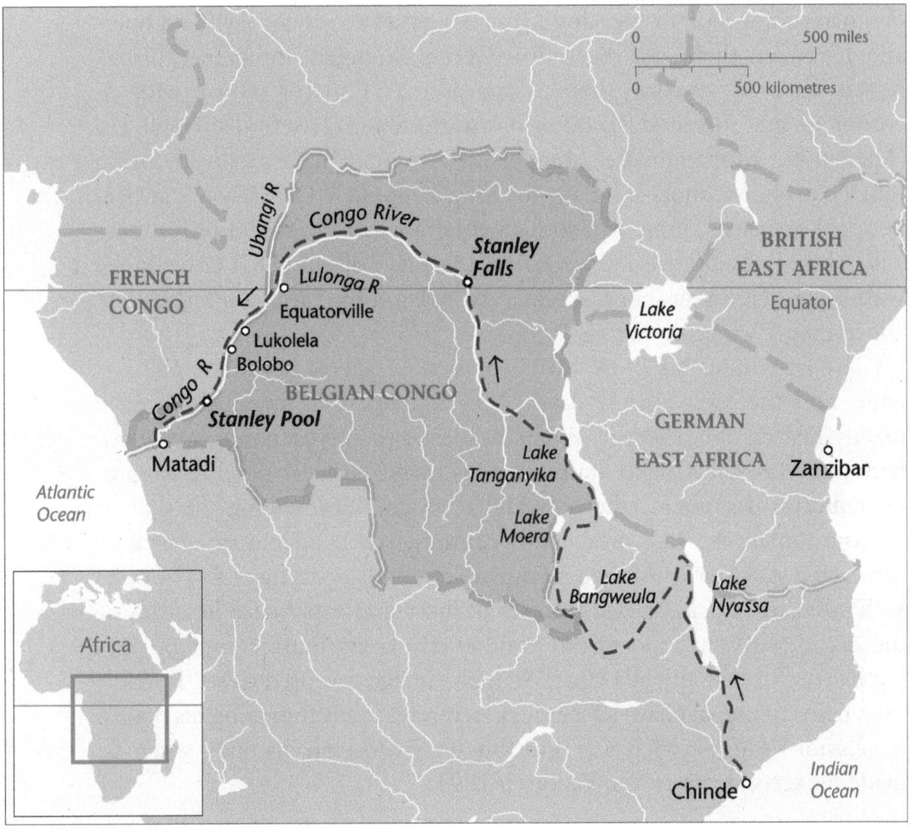

Map 7 Glave in Africa. The map, redrawn from one Edward James Glave left in his notes, shows the locations where he worked on the Congo River between 1883 and 1889, before he travelled to Alaska and the Yukon. It also traces his journey from the Indian Ocean to the mouth of the Congo River between July 1893 and May 1895.

seemed to be preying consistently on others. Glave began to record testimonies like one from a woman at Basankuso,[80] which he determined was a slave market: "I was living with my husband in an inland village, not many miles from here. My husband was a hunter. Ten days ago the Lufembé raiders attacked our settlement; my husband defended himself, but was overpowered and speared to death. I was brought here with my three children, two of whom have already been purchased by the slave traders. I shall never see them anymore."[81]

Her story deeply unsettled Glave, who began purchasing the redemption of slaves.[82] He also began to connect slavery with the ivory trade, but invariably attributed abuses to "Arab traders" (then a conventional designation for Swahili-speaking Muslims) based at Stanley Falls and operating between there and the Indian Ocean. Strangely, he seemed unsurprised when his mentor, Stanley, appeared at Equator station with an entourage that included the notorious warlord and slave trader Tippu Tip (Hamed bin Muhammed el Murjebi), whose influence had already made him a convenient short-term ally for King Leopold.[83] On Stanley's advice, Leopold installed Tippu Tip, so-named because of the sound of his musket, as his representative and governor at Stanley Falls in 1887. Glave spoke with Tippu Tip in Swahili and remarked only on his "accurate knowledge concerning European matters."[84]

Glave concludes his book with a passionate appeal about "Arab" enemies and the "war against slavery" in language that foreshadows early twenty-first-century rhetoric. When his second three-year contract expired, he travelled to the United States with his friend Herbert Ward to lecture. Riffenburgh documents the powerful iconographies fuelling the cult of exploration in the late nineteenth century, when adventure travellers achieved a status now usurped by movie stars and sports figures. The public flocked to hear illustrated lectures of first-hand experience in Africa or the Arctic, with one report from London estimating fourteen million paying patrons in that city in 1892.[85] Stanley's image was used to sell Bovril.[86] Fragments of one of Glave's New York lectures (closely mirroring his book's conclusion) suggest what was probably uppermost on his mind when he made his second trip to the Yukon in 1891:

> The cry for justice uttered by the poor African has already remained too long unanswered. No time should be lost in eradicating the existing bloodshed west of Stanley Falls. It is big work but it is a duty which the civilized world owes to the helpless slave. It should always be remembered that the suppression of slavery in Africa does not mean merely striking the fetters from the limbs of the slave; the end is not only substitution of paid for forced labor, but also the relief of enslaved humanity throughout all these regions from a life of unspeakable horror ... All of these atrocities are committed to enrich the white-robed Arab of Stanley Falls.[87]

Like almost everyone else in Europe and North America in 1890, Glave believed that Belgian king Leopold's "philanthropic" mission was poised to destroy traders responsible for this misery, and he wanted to be involved. If he initially used his Congo credentials to join *Frank Leslie's Illustrated Newspaper* Expedition to Alaska-Yukon, he now drew on his experience in northwestern North America as one qualification to return to Africa. His 1892 *Century Magazine* articles undoubtedly contributed to that magazine's ultimate decision to provide Glave with "such aid as he deemed adequate to the undertaking."[88]

Glave in the Heart of Africa

Edward Glave returned to Africa from New York in June 1893, this time disembarking at Zanzibar. His notes, an early genre of investigative journalism, chronicle the twenty-two-month period from 18 July 1893 until 2 May 1895 when he reached Matadi at the mouth of the Congo River. His route took him from the Indian Ocean via Lakes Nyassa, Bangweula, and Moera, to Lake Tanganyika, then to the head of the Congo River, and from there downriver to the Atlantic coast (see Map 7). He travelled initially on foot with a dozen African assistants and sent his "reports from the field" to *The Century Magazine* via couriers who carried them back to the Indian Ocean, just as his Tlingit guides, returning from Kusawa Lake to coastal Alaska in 1890, had forwarded his submissions to *Frank Leslie's Illustrated Newspaper*. Later journals, photographs, and sketches were sent, as he instructed, by missionaries at Matadi who gave him shelter just before his death on 12 May 1895.[89]

Glave's reports were published posthumously by *The Century Magazine* in five instalments, three in 1896 and two in 1897. Dated entries provide unfiltered impressions, so it should not be surprising that they are often contradictory.[90] Reading them is like following Joseph Conrad's character Marlow as he makes his way up the Congo River in *Heart of Darkness*, except that this time Glave is travelling in the opposite direction, downriver through familiar places changed irrevocably since his last visit. By 1894, rubber was replacing ivory as the Congo's prime export, and Belgian wars against Indian Ocean traders had eliminated competition. The lines distinguishing slave traders from philanthropists were becoming decidedly blurred. Glave was out of date with developments in colonial Africa after his four-year absence.

His notes for the first eight months cover travels from Zanzibar to Lake Nyassa, and his tone is optimistic.[91] His expectation that "officers" can be trusted and that Belgian officers are spearheading an anti-slavery movement proves profoundly misplaced. He is effusive, for instance, in his praise for Jules Jacques, a district commissioner, "and his good work done in destroying the power of the Arab slavers."[92] Jacques's own diaries confirm that he was implicated in some of the most brutal reprisals against villages that failed to meet imposed rubber quotas.[93] Glave is still very much working at surfaces.

From Lake Nyassa, he spent two and a half months travelling to Lake Bangweula.[94] If his weakness on this journey remains his blind spot about "the kindness of officers" and his maddening concern about gentlemanly debts, his strength remains his close attention to detail, and he never flinches from documenting suffering he encounters. Everywhere he hears reports about the misery caused by relentless raiding. At each settlement he interviews the chief – including one woman chief named Chikwa, who provided one of the many testimonies about raiding parties.[95] He travels north to Lake Tanganyika, visiting settlements he identifies by the names of their chiefs – Kalasa, Kinsunka, Kasembi – recording testimonies and taking photographs.[96] He has been travelling for more than a year now, and his own health is deteriorating, but his determination continues, even when huge blisters prevent him from walking: "Illness to me in Africa is as the bubble in a spirit-level; it moves and changes its position, but never ceases."[97] He has not yet reached the Congo River.

By mid-August 1894, he sees inescapable evidence that local people are fleeing east from the Congo and is astonished: "The natives are, strange to say, leaving Belgian territory and coming to settle about the B.C.A. [British Central Africa] stations ... The Belgians are undoubtedly friends of the natives ... The Belgian policy is liberal and thoroughly anti-slavery ... so why the natives should leave Belgian territory and come to the British I cannot say."[98] As he heads west from Lake Tanganyika toward the Congo River, a Belgian officer named Hambrusin welcomes him and confides that while he has orders not to let strangers proceed beyond this point, such a regulation surely cannot apply to Glave, a former employee of the Congo Free State.[99]

Now, finally back in King Leopold's Congo, five years after he first left for North America, Glave hears ever more violent reports as he comes closer to Kabambarré station. He learns, for instance, that slaves supposedly "liberated" by the Belgian Antislavery Society have been conscripted as labourers for seven years and that women and children are being flogged. He hears that tribes that formerly raided for the Arabs are now working for the Belgians.[100] On a short walk one day, he passes ten skeletons. His fevers worsen. He still cannot believe what he is hearing but methodically takes down mind-numbing testimony: December 8: "Sungula says the reason [that men refuse to hunt elephants for ivory] is that when the hunters are absent the Mynyema soldiers take their wives ... a heinous offense in the eyes of the natives."[101] December 29: "Kinteté's people have been most unmercifully persecuted by state soldiers." Glave, utterly conflicted, notes, "I must not forget the kindness of the Belgians" but continues to document his observations.

Glave's final report, the most frequently cited, records his journey from Stanley Falls to the mouth of the Congo.[102] From mid-January until the beginning of May 1895, he reports burned villages, chain gangs, beatings, child slavery, and this time he names the Belgian officers committing these acts: Lemery's acts of violence,[103] "Mr. Laschet's ... fits of rage."[104] His reports shift from the humanity of natives (which he never doubted) to the inhumanity of whites (which he still has trouble believing). "The state has not suppressed slavery but established a monopoly."[105] He still hopes that this is all a mistake: "Does the philanthropic king of Belgium know about this? If not, he ought to." "Everywhere I hear the same news of the doings of the Congo Free State ... rubber and murder, slavery in its worst form," he wrote in one of his final entries.[106]

Glave's most infamous entry refers to a Captain Rom who was the Belgian commanding officer at Stanley Falls when Glave arrived there in 1895. Rom, he learned, had ordered a village destroyed, and afterward "twenty-one heads were brought to the falls, and have been used by Captain Rom round a flower bed in front of his house."[107] Of all the abuses that Glave witnessed and documented, this image most electrified readers when it was published in September 1897, two years after his death. It was cited immediately in a published address about unmonitored Belgian practices on the Congo delivered to the Royal Statistical Society in Britain.[108] Edward Morel, architect of the Congo Reform Movement, and by then campaigner against Belgian abuses, cited Glave's journal entries as evidence in his influential book *Red Rubber,* where he argued that Free State practices were much more brutal than those of "Arab" traders.[109] Historian S.J.S. Cookey called Glave's "among the most sensational first-hand reports to emerge" and pointed to its immediate significance.[110] The brutality did not diminish for another decade, but it was no longer happening in secret. Glave's eyewitness accounts leave tangible historical traces.

Indirect Traces: Conrad's *Heart of Darkness*

There is another intriguing thread. Recently, three writers examining violence in late-nineteenth-century African history have speculated that Glave's image of Rom and his macabre collection of skulls may have inspired Joseph Conrad's novella *Heart of Darkness,* and specifically his portrayal of Kurtz, the ivory trader.[111] Conrad's enigmatic character Kurtz is depicted in part through his display of human heads mounted on palisades around his house. "Inner Station" is based on Stanley Falls, which Conrad visited in 1890, before Rom was assigned there, so he could not have observed this himself. Conrad began writing *Heart of Darkness* after Glave's article was published, although the actual date when he began this project is disputed.

Peter Firchow, a close student of Conrad's work, follows additional lines of evidence.[112] He suggests that Conrad was living in England by 1897 and was more likely to have been influenced by Glave's autobiographical account of six years on the Congo, published in London in 1893, than by an article published in a New York periodical. Firchow draws convincing similarities between Conrad's and Glave's biographies. Both fantasized about going to Africa (or the Arctic) as children. Both men worked on Belgian riverboats on the upper Congo River, Glave in 1888-89, and Conrad during the following summer of 1890, when Glave was on the Alsek River. Both men were deeply affected by their time there. Conrad's six months marked him permanently, and in trying to come to terms with the human corruptibility he had witnessed on the Congo River, he read widely about Africa during the next decade. He chose an aesthetic form to deal with the horror, transforming and extending his experiences through literature.

Firchow suggests that Glave's autobiography is more likely to have served as a model for Conrad's character Marlow than for Kurtz. The fictive Marlow, like Glave, has an early obsession with Africa, goes to considerable lengths to find work there, spends time assembling a steamboat and then travelling on it upriver, and encounters evidence of slavery – all themes in Glave's autobiographical account. Glave does bear a superficial similarity to Kurtz, Firchow agrees, especially in the two years he spent managing an isolated post, but the connection is tenuous because Glave was dedicated to exposing a system in which the fictional Kurtz was complicit. Firchow argues that Glave's horror arises from what he has seen others do rather than from what he has done himself, and that Glave would have felt a sense of accomplishment rather than Kurtz's dark terror.[113]

I wonder, though, whether this oversimplifies Glave. Of the authors now speculating about Glave's African years, only Firchow refers to more than one of his articles, and none refer to his North American experiences. We know from his Yukon writings that even when he was there, Africa was much on his mind. While Glave may well have felt some sense of achievement, even as his health deteriorated, part of his encounter with horror must surely have been his understanding that he had got this all wrong – that the premise motivating his passion for a decade had been flawed and that he was implicated, however unwittingly, in the system he now exposed. Glave saw evidence of unimaginable atrocities perpetrated by the agents he had always seen as philanthropists. Vacillating between praising Belgians and documenting testimonies of Africans, Glave remains conflicted; yet his conclusions were inescapable. In the end, I suspect, he was faced with what he called simply "rubber and murder,"[114] and in the brief interval when he knew he was dying, he ensured that his unedited notes, inconsistencies and all, were sent on to his patron and editor, Richard Watson Gilder, at *The Century Magazine*.

Glave died of fever, like Conrad's character Kurtz, ten days after his last journal entry and just as he was about to leave by boat from Matadi on 12 May 1895. He was thirty-two years old. *Heart of Darkness* was published in 1902.

Glacier and Jungle in the Work of E.J. Glave

These stories from the nineteenth century and from two continents initially sound dissimilar – observations about colonialism framed in one case as ruminations of a summer traveller and in the other as testimonies to the banality of terror. Viewed as counterparts, though, they provide snapshots from a historical moment when practices of colonialism were shifting from individualized exploration to what historian Jan Vansina has called "the structural realisation of European hegemony on the ground."[115]

When nineteen-year-old Edward Glave began writing to the innocuously named Association Internationale Africaine in 1882, he could not have known that this organization was an intricate smokescreen designed by King Leopold to establish a personal empire in Central Africa. Estimated death counts from Leopold's Congo now run to ten million, a holocaust of staggering proportions largely forgotten or ignored by the world until recently.[116] Its dimensions began to emerge publicly only in the late 1890s, after Glave's death, but Glave's painful role in helping to expose its arbitrary evil is part of the larger story about exploration and its practices. By 1889, after six years on the Congo River, Glave still understood little of slavery's complex history in Africa, but he accepted without question a phobia that had been spreading throughout Europe since the 1860s, framed as a crusade against "Arab" slave raiders, but fanned by European perceptions of threats to their own aspirations in Africa. When he returned to Africa from America in 1893, he was ill-equipped to grasp how fundamentally things had changed since his departure, so effectively had Leopold sealed off his Congo enterprises from international scrutiny.

Jan Vansina's work in Africa spans more than fifty years, and he identifies the years between 1890 and 1892 as the turning point in Congo history, more significant even than the founding of the Congo Free State. This was the period when a system of exploitation based on forced labour was established, a feudal serfdom that began to raise profits to record levels.[117] Then, between 1892 and January 1894, Belgian forces launched a final war on Indian Ocean traders with losses of seventy thousand Swahili-Arab fighters and unknown numbers of Congo soldiers.[118] During those same years, Glave was in America, giving lectures, composing his book, practising exploration in Alaska-Yukon, and planning his assault on a slave trade he believed could be banished by the "civilizing" influences of Europe. By the time

Glave returned to Africa, Indian Ocean traders were no longer a significant force in Central Africa, but he knew nothing of this. It was toward this murky new stage of colonialism transformed by rubber that he made his way from the coast of eastern Africa in late 1893.

While histories on the Congo and Alsek rivers may sound incommensurable, there are similarities. Prior to 1890, dynamic regional indigenous trading economies were oriented around river axes flowing to an ocean coast in each region. Both locations were experiencing commercial incursions from European competitors – for furs on the upper Alsek River and for ivory on the upper Congo, but local regional trade networks were still largely able to control the flow and distribution of goods and to force foreign traders to work through established channels. In the Pacific Northwest, Chilkat Tlingit control over access routes to the interior for some time prevented commercial penetration from the Pacific. In 1852, they destroyed a Hudson's Bay Company trading post that Robert Campbell had established on the Yukon River to lure trade away from Tlingit brokers, just as African entrepreneurs burned a British post at Bolobo in 1883. In 1890, Glave reported that Chilkat traders at Neskataheen were furious to see him and Dalton visiting camps on the Alsek, and furthermore that the two inland leaders, War Seine and Ick Ars, wanted their country "opened up for trade."[119]

Both subarctic northwestern America and equatorial Africa were about to erupt over competition for new resources just as Glave arrived in each place. His observations document the rapid hegemonic expansion of nation states in places formerly deemed "out of the way" following discovery of resources that would soon transform local economies. Invention of the rubber tire in 1890, a year after Glave travelled to America, and discovery of gold on the Klondike in 1896, fifteen months after his death, displaced ivory and furs as key commodities and provided almost simultaneous opportunities for imperial expansion on the ground. The differences in extractive processes enabled vastly dissimilar colonial projects in the two different regions. Wild rubber alerted King Leopold to the potentially enormous profits that could be achieved by enslaving local labour to extract it. The Klondike gold rush, remembered as a "poor man's" gold rush, brought some forty thousand goldseekers to the Yukon, each with the belief that human labour could be a passport to personal wealth. Railways and steamboats provided crucial technological underpinnings for the advancement of both projects. Globalizing forces were about to dismantle local economies in both places and permit the entrenchment of two very different forms of bureaucratic state.

The reign of terror that Glave helped to expose on the Congo was mirrored by a very different kind of terror on the Alsek River. While Glave never fully grasped this, his enumeration of absences – "whole forests felled" and "undoubted evidence of former occupation by great numbers of people"[120] – is one of the only documentary sources to hint at the experience of epidemics on the inland side of the Saint Elias Mountains. Robert Fortuine identifies the smallpox epidemic that occurred on the Pacific coast between 1835 and 1840 as one of the most significant events in Alaska history. Starting at Sitka in 1836, it spread from Tongass to the Lynn Canal.[121] Catharine McClellan estimates that smallpox swept up the Alsek in 1838. A century later, she learned from elderly residents that population along the Alsek had been heavy until this scourge raced upriver killing "thousands and thousands," an English translation that hints at its remembered impacts. Another smallpox epidemic followed in 1862.[122] Glave was troubled by sparse populations along the Alsek in 1890, given the many indications of former denser settlement. He tried unsuccessfully to establish a chronology for the death of a former Nua Qua chief, Tenasarti, who may have succumbed to an epidemic.[123] In the mid-twentieth century, McClellan learned that some smallpox survivors from Noogaayík went downriver to the village of Guseix̲ at Dry Bay, that others went to Neskataheen, and that Shank, who transported Glave and Dalton downriver to the Pacific, and whose story opened this chapter, was one of those who recovered.[124] Glave also heard accounts of a mid-nineteenth-century raid at Dezadeash Lake by White River people (probably Upper Tanana) that had reduced the population substantially.[125] We know from early chapters of this book that an enormous outburst flood from Neoglacial Lake Alsek destroyed at least one village in 1852. Epidemics, punitive raids by northern neighbours, and a natural disaster must have coincided within one generation. While both intentionality and causality differed markedly in such different settings, these terrifying times in both "Alaska" and Africa coincided with the expansion of empire in both locations.

Historians and anthropologists writing about histories of terror identify remarkable silences in oral tradition for unremarkable reasons. The scale of human losses and the dispersal of survivors contribute to the erasure of memory. Historian Mike Davis traces synchronous and devastating droughts between 1876 and 1899 in India, China, Russia, the Middle East, Brazil, and elsewhere, and proposes a "fatal meshing of extreme events between the world climate system and the late Victorian world economy ... malign interaction between climatic and economic processes."[126] Simultaneous drought, famine, and epidemics in these regions paved the way for imperial expansion, he insists. In the Pacific Northwest, natural phenomena (like the Little Ice Age) were also socially enhanced when glacier oscillations overlapped with the relentless arrival of European powers.

In the southwest Yukon, erasure of memory was further accomplished by bureaucratic means following the Klondike gold rush. The discovery of gold accelerated international boundary issues long simmering between the United States and Britain (with Canada being a minor inconvenience). Following the partitioning of the Alsek River across two countries and three jurisdictions (Yukon Territory, Province of British Columbia, State of Alaska), residents on the Alsek-Tatshenshini drainage were dispersed to either coastal Alaska or interior Canada. Jurisdictional boundaries fractured local and regional indigenous alliances, just as the Little Ice Age was ending.

Michael Taussig has written about rubber regimes in the Amazon during the early twentieth century and the ongoing challenge of comprehending the dynamics of terror and how to write effectively against it.[127] He argues that cultures of terror are based on and nourished by silence and myth, and that in such instances the question is not simply who has the power to speak and write, but also what form counter-discourses should take – what kinds of narrative might challenge terror in the first place. Social sciences, he argues, talk a great deal about ideology, but in the end it is really narratives that sustain cultures of terror. He singles out narratives about dark jungles and savagery as significant in shaping human fears complicit in terror.[128] What is needed to counter such narratives, he suggests, is attention to local indigenous narrative modes that de-sensationalize terror by conveying some of the impenetrability of everyday life.

The problem of how to write against terror is one that both Joseph Conrad and Edward Glave tried independently to confront in different ways more than a century ago. Roger Casement, a contemporary of both Conrad and Glave who knew both of them, also struggled with these issues. Casement, like Glave, worked for both the Association Internationale Africaine and the Sanford Exploring Expedition,[129] and he met Conrad in the Congo in 1890.[130] Casement later became a British consul and authored both the 1903 report on Congo atrocities for Britain and the 1912-13 Putumayo report on rubber crimes in the Amazon. Conrad may have drawn on Glave's writings to capture human vulnerability and corruptibility, but Casement also cited Glave's reports as evidence and considered him a friend.[131] Taussig is uncomfortable with aestheticizing terror, and suggests that Joseph Conrad flirts with this border. But he is also critical of Casement's measured realism, while acknowledging that Casement's reports did much to stop the violence. His objection to documentary realism is that it borrows the same metaphors used by those who perpetrate terror (substituting noble for ignoble savagery, or romantic for terrifying jungles) and hence may reinforce established patterns.

Glave's narratives, by contrast, convey no seamless whole, and his inconsistencies remain raw. In the end, perhaps they make their real contribution in their discontinuous, conflicted, contradictory, and unedited form. By the twenty-first century, Glave's accounts have seeped indirectly into debates about human rights in Africa, colonial accountability in Belgium, and land claims documents prepared by Champagne-Aishihik First Nation in their negotiations with the federal government of Canada. Glave also leaves a record of named local people in both places, documenting what they had to say about their experiences.

Taussig eloquently describes the role of jungles in feeding terror. Glave, though, much preferred the African jungle to glacier-scoured landscapes, and from his earliest years in Africa referred to its "undisturbed solitudes and its dark green recesses [which] always brought such restfulness to me, when wearied."[132] In Alaska-Yukon he came to intensely dislike glacier landscapes, and their role in his imaginative musings may have been to contribute to his comparatively crankier views of people he met near the Saint Elias Mountains on his second journey: "All this part of the country is suggestive of violence: these colossal heaps of rock crudely hurled from the mountain heights, the roaring and thundering of the internal forces of the glacier and moraine, whole forests laid low by the fury of the tempest, the wild and angry torrent of the Alseck River, roaring as it sweeps past the desolate scene – *a combination framed by nature to be inimical to life.*"[133]

Even at night he could get no real rest because of the "ominous grating of the rolling rocks, the roar of the angry torrent and the sullen growl from the workings of some adjacent ice field"[134] – images of sentience differently refracted in Southern Tutchone traditions. The Alsek he found too wild for his taste, and his assessment eventually leaked into his description of the people who lived there.[135]

Back at the mouth of the Congo in May 1895, Glave's possessions were already loaded onto a boat leaving Matadi for England when he realized that he was ill and retrieved them. Returning to the mission station, he gave the missionary, Mr. Forfeitt, instructions about disposition of his effects. Forfeitt later described (in print, and in both British and American sources) how Glave had dictated instructions about the disposal of his papers that Forfeitt copied in front of a witness before hastily drawing up a will.[136] Glave, by then delirious, died almost immediately and before he could sign. Forfeitt's sharp letter to the *The Times* (London) some months later suggests that British officials may have tried to dispute his decision to

Figure 15 This sketch, entitled *Colliding Icebergs at the Foot of a Glacier*, appeared as a frontispiece in *Frank Leslie's Illustrated Newspaper* 26 July 1890, in an issue that carried details of the expedition's progress. It was probably sketched in New York, based on reports Glave was sending. *Newberry Library, Chicago*

Figure 16 Glave's sketch of icefields, entitled *Active Inland Glacier on the Alsek River,* appeared in *Frank Leslie's Illustrated Newspaper* 27 December 1890. *Newberry Library, Chicago*

send the reports to *The Century Magazine*. Certainly, Glave's notes seem to have discomfited imperial powers.

If Glave's writings capture contradictions in the moment, oral traditions perhaps grasp those in historical processes. Glave leaves us with his image of Shank, whose story began this chapter, and his own insight, from watching storyteller and audience, that there were indeed stories told from this place that he could not grasp. We cannot now know the stories Shank told, but we can guess that they might address Taussig's concerns about the kinds of narrative that de-sensationalize. A survivor of epidemics and outburst floods, Shank surely must have reported to his listeners on the state of the glacier arch that British alpinist Harold Topham described bridging the shores of the lower Alsek River near Gateway Knob in 1888.[137] Glave did not mention this arch, so Frederica de Laguna infers that it must have collapsed between 1888 and summer 1890. Had it remained, Shank would have known that it was his responsibility to ensure that everyone in the boat dress in his finest clothes in case of imminent death, just as we heard from accounts in earlier chapters. As oarsman, he would have stood in the front of the boat, singing as they passed through the tunnel, prepared to shout with joy once safely through.[138] Perhaps Shank commented on their experiences as they passed by Gateway Knob, known as "Raven's work," where rocks fall continuously, but where Raven promised that they would strike the boat only if one of the occupants were destined to die. Probably Shank's stories echoed themes we have heard in earlier chapters about the "cloud people" he had just transported down the river, and the stories that were already being told about them inland.

Glacier stories we hear from Tlingit and Southern Tutchone oral traditions may, then, provide the kinds of responses to colonial narratives that Taussig insists are necessary. They neither aestheticize terror nor borrow from metaphors corrupted by colonialism. They are never easy for outsiders to understand. They merge ecological knowledge with social history by grafting historical events and human relationships onto place. A few years later, the region would come under very different shaping forces with the imposition of new kinds of boundaries, the subject of the next chapter.

PART 3

Scientific Research in Sentient Places

7

Mapping Boundaries: From Stories to Borders

Boundaries now stitch together a patchwork of colliding narratives in the Saint Elias Mountains. Canada and the United States intersect along its vertiginous crest, with the State of Alaska clasped to the Yukon Territory and the Province of British Columbia at curious angles. The recently appliquéd UNESCO World Heritage site adds a visual impression of postmodern design. Yet this seemingly whimsical geometry was actually fashioned by the most conventional practices of modernity – the dividing, mapping, and measuring of territories once claimed as "empty spaces," and now depicted as "pristine landscapes."

From their earliest meetings, Tlingit and Athapaskan residents on opposite sides of these mountains appreciated the ecological contrast between their habitats, and they entered into economic exchanges. We have no real way of knowing how long regional Aboriginal trade networks flourished before Europeans arrived on the scene because so much trade was in perishables – coastal marine products bartered for interior furs and tanned skins.[1] Mountains undeniably formed physical obstacles to travel, but the social meanings of such barriers seem to have varied regionally along the coast. Coastal Tlingit traders on the Lynn Canal, like Daanawáak and Shotridge, appropriated the role of middlemen in the nineteenth century, blockaded the few accessible passes to the interior, and compelled both their Athapaskan trading partners and Euro-Americans to deal through them. Yet not far to the west, at Yakutat, glacier throughways served as routes to the interior for trade, travel, and access to resources, and boundaries seem to have been more permeable.

By the early nineteenth century, the Saint Elias ranges began to provide imaginative possibilities for a new kind of boundary with distant roots. Models emerging in European nationalist traditions envisioned firm partitions along clearly marked lines that would confer jurisdictional authority. As we will see in this chapter, competing ideas about borders – some flexible and others straining toward certainty – demonstrate how physical landscapes came to furnish clues for thinking about social order. For indigenous peoples, values inhering in landscape features provided ways of imagining reciprocal relationships among humans and with an ever-responding land. For the vanguard of explorers, notions of a primordial natural world were drafted to provide the glue for unstable national social formations – first "Russian" America and "British" North America, and later Canada and the United States.[2] Politicians who masterminded the global positioning of an international boundary through these mountains, their deputized surveyors, and indigenous residents rarely met, but their intersecting narratives tell a larger story.

We can follow these narrative threads from transactions that begin in 1825, when distant powers centred in Moscow and London imagined a line of demarcation separating Russian from British North America and formalized this border in the Anglo-Russian Treaty. Imperial claimants had only the vaguest idea of where that line might be physically located, but they confidently used their treaty to detach a Russian coastal panhandle from the interior drainage claimed by Britain. When the United States purchased Alaska in 1867, Washington replaced Moscow at the negotiating table. Canada, a mere fledgling among nations, was eventually given token representation. "Indians" remained both absent and invisible. The international boundary was almost a century in the mapping, adjudication, and production. Like layers of an onion, the successive tribunals and commissions struck to resolve the thorny issue of why, how, and where it would be located demonstrate how an imagined "Nature" can become swept into the formation of nations, and how dreams of nationhood become embedded in a border.

This chapter traces boundary stories and their legacies. Because oral narratives from earlier chapters provide key points of reference, I will begin by reviewing briefly how glaciers enter indigenous oral traditions about boundaries. I then follow steps by which boundary making was visualized from distant capitals like Moscow, London, Washington, and Ottawa. Surveyors subsequently mapped those lines onto place, often at great personal risk, and glaciers influenced the ways they experienced their surroundings. Bureaucratic boundary making presents a kind of encounter distinctly different from any discussed so far. If indigenous residents experienced awkward intimacies with the likes of La Pérouse, Muir, or Glave, or violent confrontations with US naval officers, boundary surveys through the Saint Elias Mountains were conducted as though local inhabitants didn't exist. This bureaucratic approach to human encounters was later reinforced in contemporary constructions of "wilderness" parks.

Notably, both oral and written accounts are filtered by the time they reach us. Boundary survey reports appear through layers of official records and are laden with silences. They are rich in measurements and records of instrumentation, but thin on observations about human experience. Tlingit and Athapaskan memories of glacial landscapes are now filtered through a generation of women and men who heard about them only second-hand from elders born in the nineteenth century, the last to inhabit this place. Contemporary First Nation elders are more likely to have experienced the resulting regulations that divided them into "American" and "Canadian" residents. They especially recall restrictions on hunting, trading, and travel that followed the establishment of game sanctuaries and parks where all hunting, including Aboriginal subsistence hunting, was prohibited.

Boundaries and Passages: Early Maps

In 1867, and then again in 1869, an American scientist, George Davidson, led a United States Coast and Geodetic Survey party on what was then called "a geographical reconnaissance" of their country's newly acquired territory, Alaska. Davidson's second trip coincided with a long-awaited total eclipse of the sun. He had already determined on the earlier journey that the village of Klukwan would provide the ideal location to view this spectacle and was delighted when newly assigned US naval authorities prearranged a meeting in Sitka with Klukwan's Chilkat chief, whose name Davidson recorded as Kohklux (see Map 5). Arriving in Sitka, Davidson was startled to discover that Kohklux had been imprisoned there by authorities for "some petty offense," and he arranged for his release. In return, Kohklux graciously hosted the expedition back in Klukwan where they positioned their instruments to observe the eclipse. Their attention to visual instrumentation left memorable ripples. When John Muir arrived at the head of the Lynn Canal a decade later, as we saw, he was vigorously questioned about what Davidson had been up to "on a mountain-top back of the village, with many strange things looking at the sun when it grew dark in the daytime."[3]

During that visit, Kohklux, apparently on his own initiative, drew a map on a small sheet of paper and presented it to Davidson (see Figures 17 and 18). The map traces his own travel route through mountain passes inland as far as the Yukon River. As a young man in 1852, Kohklux (also known as Shotridge) had led a Tlingit party inland to launch a pre-emptive strike on the new Hudson's Bay Company trading post on the Yukon River, Fort Selkirk, which Chilkats saw as interfering with their trade monopoly.[4] Davidson was eager for more detail and provided Kohklux with a larger piece of paper, the back of a chart, which he describes as measuring

Figure 17 Kohklux's original map. Kohklux drew two maps in 1869 for George Davidson, an American scientist, showing the route he and others had taken inland to Fort Selkirk in 1852. This was the first of the two maps, which he drew himself, and onto which George Davidson then recorded the place names Kohklux provided. The second, more linear, map was drawn with the aid of Kohklux's wives. *Bancroft Library, University of California*

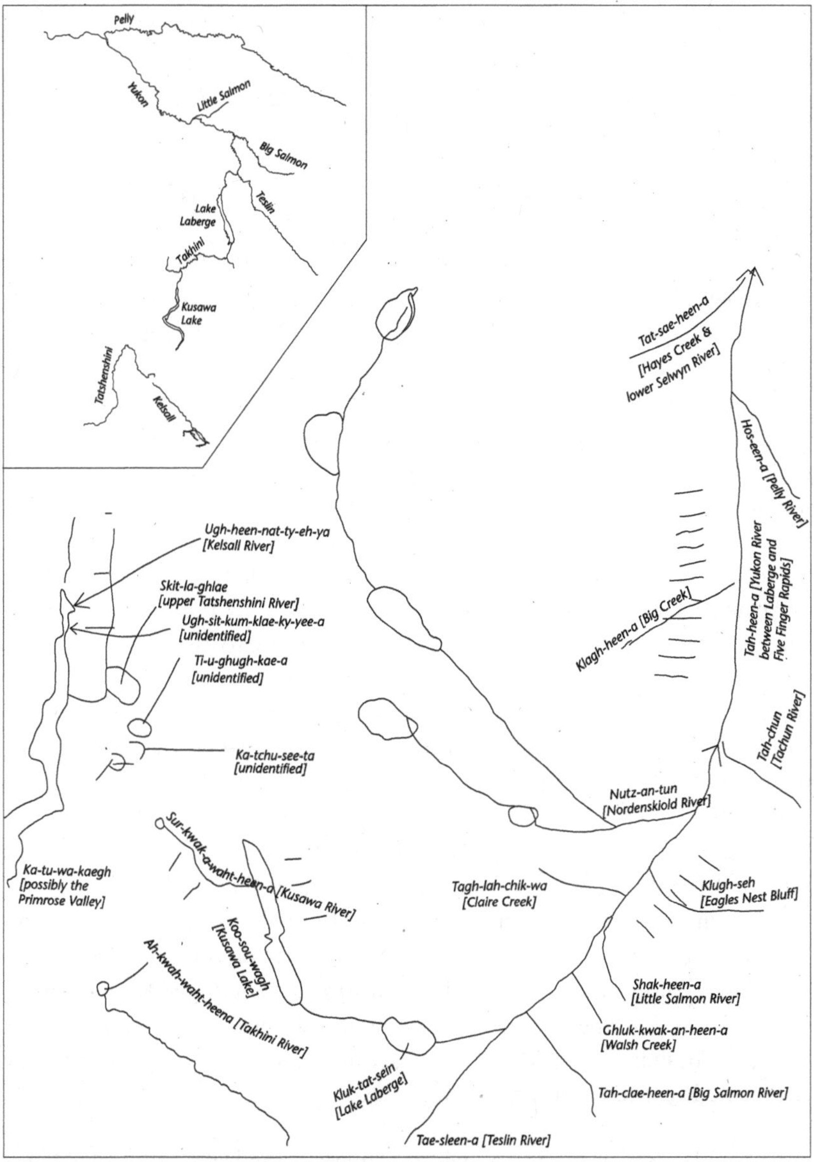

Figure 18 Kohklux's map, showing both his names and contemporary names for places. The small map in the top left corner shows where they would be located on a current map of the Yukon. *Map prepared by Eric Leinberger*

forty-three by twenty-seven inches. Kohklux was using a pencil for the first time and, this time with the help of his two wives (one of whom may well have been from the interior), he produced a more extensive and more linear depiction that also included the Tlingit party's return route to the coast down the Tatshenshini and Alsek rivers. Kohklux then dictated names that Davidson copied onto both maps, initially in pencil and later in black ink.

The larger map is certainly more extensive, but the smaller one reproduced here, which Kohklux made on his own and apparently without coaching, interests me more (see Figures 17 and 18). It fills the paper in a circle – almost a corkscrew spiral – rather than following a north-south grid, so his inland destinations are represented near the journey's starting point. The map clearly troubled Davidson enough to prompt the second, better-provisioned attempt at cartography. We can't be sure how much Davidson influenced the style of this second map, because he does not tell us whether he gave Kohklux any guidelines for its preparation. Evidently he found it more satisfactory and this is the one he chose to redraw in his 1901 article, "Explanation of an Indian Map"[5] (see Figure 19). By then he was able to situate and supplement Kohklux's map with reference to cartographic knowledge coming from international boundary surveys as well as from other travellers' notes, including Edward Glave's, and so he standardized Kohklux's map to meet conventions of the day. In 1984, the two original maps eventually found their way to the Bancroft Library in Berkeley, where Davidson's papers are held.[6]

Kohklux's maps of routes across mountain passages may be the earliest recorded graphic representations of what is now the Yukon, but in style they are similar to the sand maps drawn by Indiank, the Tlingit guide who led Frederick Schwatka inland and down the Yukon River in 1883, and then later guided the *Frank Leslie's Illustrated Newspaper* Expedition in 1890. Glave described Indiank's maps enthusiastically, but with some of the same hesitation Davidson may have felt about maps that in no way conformed to Mercator's projection.

> [Indiank] ... is proud of his geographical knowledge and takes great delight in imparting to us items of information. He selects a patch of fine sand on which he traces with his fingers the rivers and the lakes and places up stones to represent the mountains. When describing any extent of territory, he requires the whole sandbank for his operations. We, his audience, close around him to receive his geographical instruction, are being continually moved away in a larger circle to enable him to extend the area of his descriptions. His directions generally are fairly accurate, but his distances decidedly erratic. In the same

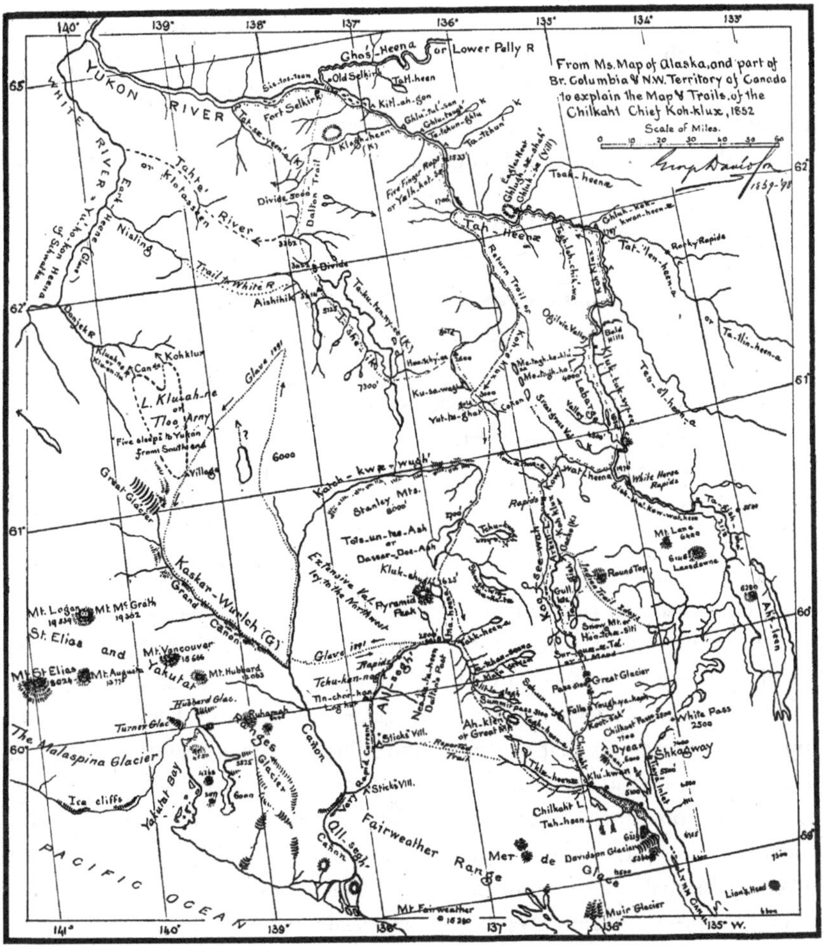

Figure 19 George Davidson's revision of the Kohklux maps, 1901. He had this map redrawn to fit modern rules of cartography and supplemented it with information by then available from Glave's two journeys, as well as from international boundary surveys. *Source:* Davidson, "Explanation of an Indian Map," *Mazama* (April 1901).

> drawing, he will represent a stretch of 100 miles by a mark in the sand six inches in length and again a line a yard and a half long would be but an hour's paddling in a canoe. His map, when complete, generally covers a space five or six yards square.[7]

What we can't now know, as Catharine McClellan observes, is whether such two-dimensional graphics were a purely historical development resulting from the interests of fur traders and explorers for whom they were drawn. It is likely, she suggests, that indigenous travellers learned landscape by constant travel, by repeatedly telling and hearing about these experiences and using the names, and that maps were rooted in internalized oral traditions rather than configured as external graphic representations. Her observations accord with much recent place-name research conducted in indigenous languages in the Yukon.[8]

Glaciers and Boundary Crossings

Women with whom I worked during the 1970s and 1980s, Kitty Smith and Annie Ned and Angela Sidney, were youngsters when the Alaska boundary surveys were being completed, but they probably never encountered surveyors directly. Life stories these three women recorded initially unbalanced my understanding of physical space, historical time, and social history in ways that are relevant to a comparative discussion of boundary concepts.

Their narratives in Chapter 3 depict permeable boundaries – among humans connected by relationships of kinship and trade; among human and non-human persons whose forms were interchangeable before animals and humans became so clearly differentiated; and among all those beings and the mountains, rivers, valleys, and glaciers. Like maps, they chart shifting social boundaries that preceded and followed the arrival of Europeans. They portray a land that was physically changing as glaciers advanced, receded, and sometimes surged. In such landscapes, humans learned to watch for subtle clues, to anticipate changes, and to acquire skills associated with dwelling in challenging ecosystems. Personal experience provided one set of clues, stories another. Stories were especially helpful in dealing with surprises, and surprises were certainly abundant during late stages of the Little Ice Age. One of the many lessons I learned from their insistent instruction is that while these stories may seem distant from the business of daily life, they do specific kinds of practical work in a profoundly material world.

Surging glaciers blur firm boundaries between sacred and secular, space and time, ice and land. Their characteristics – unexpected advances, catastrophic outbursts, looming crevasses, and colourless whiteness – suggest transitional spaces. Such glaciers are literal shape-shifters involved in ever-changing relationships with land, an imaginative force but also a physical presence that transforms the earth. Glaciers replenish the Alsek River, constrain human movements along its length, defy human control, and resist fixed boundaries. Their behaviour is reminiscent of coastal tidal zones. On the icefield margins, everything can change instantly, as we see in accounts about travellers who tumble into glacier crevasses.

Other glacier stories dramatize the powers that broken taboos unleash and how they upset clear notions of social boundary. We have seen that when young men at Icy Bay jokingly invited a glacier to join them in a salmon feast, an outburst flood followed, sweeping them away. When a young woman secluded near Glacier Bay wished out loud that a glacier could belong to her father, she instigated a glacier surge that ultimately forced permanent relocation by the entire village. When a Tlingit boy mocked an Athapaskan shaman on the Alsek River, the offended man "called" the Lowell Glacier across to Goatherd Mountain, building up a dam that ultimately broke, drowning downriver inhabitants. Protagonists who cook with grease experience similar catastrophic consequences: not only does ice begin to advance, it may emit blinding heat – precisely the kind of dramatic outcome one might expect in a story where bewildering upending of norms is never wholly unexpected. Surging glaciers seem to be wildly inconstant places where men and women can actually learn more about themselves and their world than might be possible in everyday life.

Before turning to boundaries of a different kind, it is worth briefly referring back to Harold Innis's trenchant observations about oral tradition, communication, and empire discussed in Chapter 2, because they resonate so clearly with processes surrounding the establishment of the international boundary. Innis was initially interested in the process whereby empires acquire and enforce economic power by establishing physical boundaries. Standard imperial practice, he argued, involved mapping, measuring, and surveying, a classificatory exercise that enhanced control over profitable hinterlands. In trying to understand how empires enforced boundaries, he began to analyze the role of writing and the uses of official observations, categories, and statistics in this process. Inevitably, he argued, empires achieve control by monopolizing information and by routinely silencing local traditions that seem not to fit. In oral traditions, he saw other possibilities, including the potential to subvert imposed boundaries. Oral tradition, he argued, can work against the enforcement of official accounts because it allows participants to engage in ongoing reassessment and revision of history by actively reinterpreting events and then weaving those interpretations into subsequent generations of narrative. Good oral storytelling is flexible, and this allows a gifted storyteller to bring insights from a rich narrative to the interpretation of new or disorienting situations. Glaciers and their stories, then, enliven debate about the place of humans in nature and speak to a legacy of discourses – of discovery, of nation, of nature – that have cascaded through these mountains for two centuries and still speak to contemporary debates.

Boundaries Imagined, Boundaries Emplaced

We turn now to a different boundary narrative that had enduring effects for the far northwest. During the nineteenth century, Russia, Britain, Spain, and France gained ground in the heady business of mercantile expansion, and each country independently identified America's far northwest as a potential source of raw materials that could be turned to profit. Western European nationalism was propagating boundaries both at home and away. A breathtaking example occurred in 1821. Tsar Alexander of Russia formally "closed" the North Pacific, declared an imaginary arc from 51° north latitude in America across the Bering Sea almost to Japan, and claimed all territories inland from this boundary as an exclusive possession of Russia. He specified that henceforth ships found within one hundred nautical miles of the coast anywhere along this line would be seized, taken to Petropavlovsk, relieved of their cargo, and their crews sent home. Yet, unable to ignore the imperial advance of Great Britain westward across North America, Russia was brought to the treaty table four years later at St. Petersburg.[9]

The 1825 Anglo-Russian Treaty specified a boundary that was precise in areas where the claimants had concrete economic interests, specifically Russia's concern to protect its Alaskan coast settlements and Britain's determination to retain the Mackenzie Delta. The treaty fixed a southern boundary at 54°40' N, then traced the shape of an irregular panhandle that included a maze of islands and channels. This line followed the Portland Canal to its head, and from there connected "the summit of the mountains situated parallel to the coast as far as the point of intersection of the 141st degree of west longitude." From here, it followed the line of longitude north "as far as the Frozen Ocean"[10] (see Map 8). The topographical vagueness attributed to these "mountain summits" snaking northwest indicates how little political consequence the location of this border really had in 1825. In an effort to forestall later controversies, signatories added a proviso to their imagined boundary: should "the summit of the mountains" prove to be further than ten marine leagues inland from the sea (55.6 kilometres or 34.5 miles in today's measures), the boundary "shall be formed by a line parallel to the windings of the coast ... which shall never exceed the distance of ten marine leagues therefrom."[11] In other words, the boundary should follow the mountain divide unless those mountains turned out to be located more than ten leagues inland, in which case Russia's claim would still be limited to that coastal corridor. When the United States purchased Russian America in 1867, this description of the boundary between the United States and Britain was copied word for word, unchanged from the Anglo-Russian Treaty,[12] as it was again when Canada took over British territories in 1871. Conflicting interpretations of key phrases stretched on for decades until the imagined locations of "the summits" were finally surveyed.

By the late nineteenth century, Canada and the United States were plotting their own expansionist national narratives closer to home, with Canada at a distinct disadvantage. Following Confederation, Canada was still required to route dealings with the United States through the British Foreign Office, so Britain acted on Canada's behalf in boundary negotiations. Neither Canada nor the United States gave any more thought to the indigenous inhabitants of this region than had Russia and Britain before them, except for periodic typifications of "tribes" as "hostile," "difficult," or "treacherous" whenever they tried to defend their own boundaries. Aboriginal peoples would wait another century to assert successfully the legality of their own territorial land claims.

Locating boundaries captured attention at specific historical moments. On the North Pacific coast, furs, gold, fisheries, and ultimately access to coastal ports all incited passions about the need for more precise lines of demarcation. On the Yukon River, for instance, the Hudson's Bay Company encouraged Alexander Murray to establish his Fort Yukon fur trading post in 1847 well within Russian territory, presumably calculating that the Russians would never get close enough to challenge them. But Britain lost this gamble following the Alaska Purchase when they faced expropriation by American authorities who evicted them in 1869. This was the same year that George Davidson learned from Chief Kohklux the inland route Tlingit traders had taken to drive the Hudson's Bay Company from their upriver post at Fort Selkirk in 1852.

Concerns about legal jurisdiction raised additional issues. Gold rapidly displaced furs as the commodity of fashion when workable amounts were discovered up the Stikine on Cassiar creeks in 1873, making jurisdiction an issue once again. Canada hastily established a customs post on the Stikine, facing immediate charges that it was on American territory. The United States launched a clandestine exploratory party into Canada – Frederick Schwatka's poorly kept secret military expedition down the Yukon River in 1883 to ferret out "hostile Indians" (and he met none).[13] Canada responded by sending a government astronomer, Otto Klotz, to Alaska to ascertain whether Americans were surreptitiously making surveys of the coast (and he learned that they were).[14] These junkets were followed by official expeditions led by more orthodox agents. Canada sponsored the Yukon Expedition in 1887-88, headed by George Dawson and R.G. McConnell, both from the Geological Survey of Canada, who coordinated their work with government surveyor William Ogilvie.[15] The US Coast and Geodetic Survey sponsored a parallel mapping exercise in 1889-91, led by men identified

Map 8 Locating boundaries. Demarcation guidelines for an international boundary were spelled out in detail in the Anglo-Russian Treaty of 1825. It took almost a century to physically locate the specified "mountain summits" that mark the international border. Boundaries propagate: international, territorial, provincial, state, park, and World Heritage site borders (the latter two identified in the inset) now overlap at irregular angles on northwestern North America's towering ridge.

only by their initials as J.E. McGrath and J.H. Turner, who cooperated with geologist Israel Russell of the US Geological Survey. By the time of the 1896-98 Klondike gold rush, the Yukon River had been carefully charted from both ends, and the location of the 141st meridian unarguably located the Klondike within Canadian territory.[16]

Fisheries negotiations between Britain and the United States were under way by the 1880s, bringing into sharp focus the thorny issue of a coastal boundary that denied Canada a seaport and highlighted conflicting interpretations of the 1825 treaty. William Dall, representing the US Coast and Geodetic Survey, and his Canadian counterpart, George Dawson, from the Geological Survey of Canada, began meeting in 1884. Both agreed about the need for more certainty in case of an international incident, but Dall airily dismissed as "impractical" the idea of tracing a line over the "sea of mountains ... shown on Vancouver's charts like a long caterpillar."[17] He suggested that a better "natural boundary" would be the bottom of the nearest inland *valley* parallel to the coast (and east of the troublesome summits), citing the greater ease of conducting a survey there. Such a strategy would have given the United States the entire Saint Elias Mountain range, as well as a large section of British Columbia's Coast Range. Unsurprisingly, Canada demurred.

Eventually, three successive commissions were struck to delineate once and for all this elusive "natural" boundary, each adjudicating body with its own cultural pitfalls: first, the Alaska Boundary Commission (1892), second, the Alaska Boundary Tribunal (1903), and third, the International Boundary Commission (1904). The stumbling block for the first two remained interpretations of those key phrases referring to "marine leagues" and "mountain summits." Canadians were understandably eager to demonstrate that a "summit of mountains parallel to the coast" lay close to that coast. Americans were equally determined to secure the full ten-marine-league limit wherever possible. Britain, acting on Canada's behalf, was anxious to maintain good relations with the United States, already frayed by the Venezuela-British Guiana boundary dispute. Only after these transactions were settled, not without acrimony, was the third commission assigned the project of actually surveying, mapping, and placing monuments along its length from the mouth of the Portland Canal to the Arctic Ocean.

The Alaska Boundary Commission, 1892

The Alaska Boundary Commission was a rather non-combative affair during which the United States and Canada conducted joint surveys over a two-year period, mapping independently but sharing information. The division of labour seemed to fall conveniently, so that US parties with their better boats mapped the river valleys and Canadians with their sturdy packhorses mapped the intervening topography, carefully marking off contour lines every 250 feet. They prepared separate maps drawn at a scale of roughly 1 mile per centimetre (1:160,000), Canadian maps marking contour lines and American maps documenting the highest peaks. Reviewing these survey maps many decades later, Lewis Green observed that they reflected predictable national orientations and interpretations of the 1825 treaty – Canadian maps depicting a neat row of mountains parallel to the coast, and American maps showing "a random distribution of mountains, resembling an attack of measles."[18]

The Alaska Boundary Tribunal, 1903

In 1903, the United States and Britain signed a treaty that required each country to appoint three "impartial jurists" to an Alaska Boundary Tribunal.[19] The six commissioners were instructed to answer specific questions about the location of the boundary line and to submit all written arguments within six months. Britain selected Lord Chief Justice Alverstone and two Canadians, Sir Louis Jetté from Quebec and Allen B. Aylesworth, a Toronto lawyer. Theodore Roosevelt, newly elected as US president in 1901, selected the three Americans: Henry Cabot Lodge, an outspoken opponent of Canada's claim; George Turner, a former senator from the state of Washington; and Elihu Root, Roosevelt's own Secretary of War. When challenged about his nominees' possible biases, Roosevelt reacted not by defending their objectivity but by asserting their partiality as a prime qualification: "No man in public life in any position of prominence could have possibly avoided committing himself on the proposition." Roosevelt then relayed to Britain's Colonial Secretary, Lord Chamberlain, his view that Canada's claims had the "scantiest possible warrant in justice." He warned that his sole objective in even making appointments to this commission was to sustain good relations with Britain, that he regarded Canada's claim to a seaport on the territory to be "indefensible" and "preposterous," and furthermore, that he doubted a chain of mountains within the ten-marine-league limit even existed. His message concluded with the threat that if the commissioners failed to reach quick agreement, he would arrange for Congress "to render me the authority to run the line as we claim it by our own people, without any further regard to England and Canada."[20] In a fine example of rhetoric for a boundary still only imagined, Roosevelt demonstrated the potential of ideological narrative to ignore material circumstances (like physical geography) when nationalist aspirations were at stake.

Remarks on record by US commissioners corroborate these assumptions about Canada's place within this hierarchy of nations. Henry Cabot Lodge opined that the Canadian nominees "were not imposing looking persons, as a matter of fact they were insignificant in appearance, especially Sir Louis Jetté, a little French Canadian of the *chétif* French type and speaking English with a marked accent," and he described Allen Aylesworth as "a round faced, bald headed, rosy, short man, looking amiable and commonplace." The American secretary of the tribunal wrote dismissively that "the Canadians' assistant counsel looked like a set of small country lawyers from remote towns" and that he anticipated trouble from them.[21]

The Alaska Boundary Tribunal's official decision was presented as a compromise of a kind. The British appointee, Lord Alverstone, held the balance of power and voted with the Americans on most issues. Significantly, he did hold out for the priority of "mountain summits" as boundary markers, expanding the territory awarded to Canada considerably from the US position. More controversially, he agreed with the American position that the ten-marine-league limit specified in the treaty as "formed by a line parallel to the windings of the coast" included the *heads* of all inlets, rather than advancing the Canadian argument that it should follow the "general trend of the coast." At the head of the Lynn Canal, for instance, a line ten marine leagues from the coast's "general trend" would have resulted in a border across the Lynn Canal some eighty kilometres south of Skagway, giving the Canadians a much-coveted northern Pacific coast port. The American victory instead pushed the boundary some fifty-five kilometres inland from the head of Lynn Canal. At the south end of the boundary, Dixon Entrance, Alverstone again sided with the American position that the four islands at the mouth of the Portland Canal be divided and distributed, and the outer two be awarded to the United States (essentially blocking Canadian access to the two islands they were awarded). Outvoted, the two Canadians wrote dissenting agreements. Britain's support for a position that cut half of British Columbia off from the ocean left a lasting and bitter impression that Canada's national interests had been sacrificed to Anglo-American harmony.[22]

The International Boundary Commission, 1904

The third body convened to oversee procedures, the 1904 International Boundary Commission, was given the responsibility of actually surveying this mountainous border. Commissioners, still working with an abstractly conceived boundary, identified on maps with the letter "S" the selected summits they had never seen. Of these, Mount Saint Elias was to anchor the northwesterly corner of the boundary. Surveys in 1892 and 1894 had located it on the 141st meridian and 33.3 statute miles from the mouth of the Yahtse River, barely within the ten-marine-league (34.5 mile) limit.[23] One of the Canadian commissioners, Allen Aylesworth, observed that some of the "S" designations being added to "award maps" were moving too far inland, and that American commissioners were ignoring mountains, specifically Mount Fairweather, that had been specified as a boundary marker in the 1825 legislation.[24] The line was adjusted, making Fairweather another linchpin of the new international boundary. Provisional boundaries on the Stikine River and the White and Chilkoot Passes were formalized. At Lynn Canal, the boundary was pushed inland well beyond present-day Haines and Skagway.

The arrival of surveyors rapidly transformed boundary making from abstract mapping to physical emplacement. By 1904, there were 82 "S" points marked on the so-called award map. Survey parties of up to one hundred men spent several months each year locating and measuring these summits, placing conical brass monuments upon them, and adding others as they were identified. When they were physically unable to reach peaks, their instruments allowed them to map by triangulation, locating additional summits with reference to a coastal grid of points already known from prior US coastal surveys. By the time their work was completed in 1918, they had located 187 such boundary points. The dots along what Dall had referred to as a "long caterpillar," slithering its way north through the "sea of mountains," were finally connected (see Map 8).

Legacies remain not just in the inscription of that border but also in the persistent idea that such borders are somehow natural. As Innis reminds us, such practices have intellectual as well as economic consequences. Topographical practices of surveyors and mapmakers were distant from those of Aboriginal residents who must have watched these procedures with amazement. The emplacement of borders had immediate consequences for their trade and subsistence activities, but also longer-term impacts by normalizing concepts of "border" that would come to dominate land claims settlements negotiated a century later.

What is striking about this story so far is the virtual absence of indigenous peoples. They make occasional cameo appearances as "Chilkat guides." More often, though, they are naturalized as part of the landscape, the setting for newcomers' confidence in their own civilizing mission. Arguably, the Tlingits who met the vanguard of surveyors were defending their *passages* between coast and interior rather than specific borders. The Alaska Boundary Tribunal report in 1903 noted that in 1900, Chilkats from Klukwan petitioned to be allowed to continue hunting, fishing, and trading beyond the border that crossed the Chilkat River a mile above their village. The report merely notes that the petition was forwarded to Washington and makes no comment about outcomes.[25]

Inhabited Mountains and Sentient Ecology

To suggest a sharp distinction between sentient myth and scientific measurement is not my intent. Anthropologists have long been skeptical of associating religion with tradition and the secular with modernity. Tim Ingold argues that humans do not acquire ideas about environment from prefigured meanings or from culturally accumulated metaphors. Our understandings more often come from direct engagement with the worlds in which we dwell, and we convey that information to others in stories.[26] Stories, he insists, provide one more source of information, another set of clues to add to the practical business of living in a physical world.

Indigenous oral narratives told from the edges of icefields overwhelmingly convey hints and clues rather than fixed images. Travelling over mountain passes, down rivers, or across glaciers requires close attention to surroundings. In such places, it is crucial to use all of one's senses – hearing, smell, and sight – and sensory clues abound in those stories. The cottonwood tree at Yakutat Bay where travellers could put ear to tree trunk, listening for reverberations that might signal a coming storm, captures one such sensation.[27] The place named "it wiggles like jelly," for the sensory alarm bells set off by quicksand, catches another.[28] At Icy Bay, Topham recorded an account laden with sensory images. In the mid-1800s, he heard, Tlingit people at Icy Bay heard the advancing glacier before they saw it – it travelled across the bay, struck the opposite shore, then turned and continued down the bay, swallowing the village and eventually covering the harbour.[29] But glaciers, as we've heard throughout Chapter 3, are themselves equipped with senses of hearing, sight, and smell, and are quick to respond to any careless indiscretions. Glaciers seem also to have stories about humans. At Yakutat in the late 1930s, John Harrington heard from Tlingits that glaciers resent being scrutinized by strangers wearing dark glasses and may stir up bad weather so that they can "cover up" and turn expeditions back.[30] This might also be interpreted as an early Tlingit reaction to survey parties.

Surveyors and scientists carried tools that were designed to privilege sight, and they were especially attentive to visual clues. Reports fairly bristle with descriptions of instruments they hauled to each summit: transits, sextants, telescopes, chronometers, and prismatic compasses. Lewis Green, who has combed the records left by Alaska boundary surveyors as thoroughly as anyone, expresses regret that human experiences of surveyors so rarely enter the written record.[31] Even personal names are erased from records, in a convention of the times that noted only their surnames and initials, suggesting interchangeable agents in the service of loftier goals. Reports hint at more subjective stories – of terrifying river crossings and fatal accidents – and they are punctuated by occasional terse notes like one in an official report for 1909: "W.F. Ratz ... died in early February at the age of twenty-five after spending four incredibly difficult seasons on the boundary work."[32] Yet once the imagined summits became experienced as places where surveyors were immersed, traces of intense engagement do occasionally make it into written records, often dramatically. Visitors' stories begin to overlap with narratives we have heard before – about the mountains named Saint Elias and Fairweather, about glacier "highways," and about an ever-changing Alsek River axis. As surveyors descended ever deeper into the landscape – from mountains, down to glacier passes, and eventually deep into river valleys, descriptions relying on visual imagery increasingly gave way to other senses. Layered stories accumulate.

Mount Saint Elias and Fairweather

Early European navigators who spotted Mount Saint Elias breaking through cloud and fog refer to its inspirational visual dimensions. More than a century after Vitus Bering gave it the name of a favoured saint in 1741, it gained a (mistaken) reputation as "the highest peak in the world above the snow-line,"[33] exciting a flurry of interest among climbing enthusiasts. Charles Erskine Scott Wood, whom we met briefly in Chapter 5, was travelling north with plans to attempt its first ascent when he stopped to record his description of Glacier Bay in 1877. His plans to go further were thwarted when his Tlingit guide, Tah-ah-nah-klékh, refused to take him beyond Cape Spencer, and pointed to Mount Fairweather. "One mountain is as good as another," he advised Wood. "There is a very big one. Go climb that if you want to."[34] No successful ascents of Mount Saint Elias were reported until after its dimensions were actually "known," in the mathematical sense. American surveyor J.E. McGrath is credited with catapulting it into geodetic certainty in 1892 when he determined its height, and in 1894 when he located its coordinates and it became one anchor of the international boundary. The Italian duke of the Abruzzi, magnificently named Amedeo di Savoia-Aosta, was diverted by plague at the last moment from his goal of climbing Nanga Parbat, one of the highest Himalayan peaks. He came instead to the Gulf of Alaska where, with Italian guides, he made the first documented ascent of Mount Saint Elias in 1897.[35]

Aboriginal residents had their own imaginative appreciation of these "summits of mountains," certified in boundary treaties but mystifying to legislators in Moscow, London, Washington, and Ottawa. Tlingit accounts of world origins assert that when the earth was in flood, the peaks of Mount Saint Elias and Mount Fairweather remained above water and provided refuge for humans and animals.[36] As humans arrived in formerly glaciated regions released at the end of the Little Ice Age, their experiences generated new stories about these two mountains. Both served as compasses for travellers, and both provided guides to weather. We saw in earlier chapters how Ahtna moving south from the Copper River became separated and independently used Mount Saint Elias (Yaas'eita Shaa) to reorient themselves – one group mistaking it for a "rabbit" and the other for a "seagull" as it drifted in and out of view on the horizon. We also heard how Tsalx̱aan remains a weather beacon that provides attentive mariners with clues, tragically missed when their canoes capsized at Lituya Bay shortly before La Pérouse's 1786 arrival. Both mountains were adopted as clan crests because of their crucial roles in human and environmental histories.

These stories, discussed in earlier chapters, initially seem to have more texture than those of the contested "S" symbols marked onto maps by boundary commissioners and mapped onto land by surveyors. American surveyor McGrath's achievement of locating the latitude, longitude, and altitude of Mount Saint Elias was largely technical. Canadian boundary commissioner Allen Aylesworth's rescue of Mount Fairweather as another linchpin, after he observed that American commissioners were ignoring it, was pragmatic rather than poetic.

Surveyors' stories, though, do leak into survey reports. We heard in Chapter 1 about Ahtna foot travellers from Copper River, engulfed in dense fog as they neared Mount Saint Elias. They glimpsed a glacier ramp leading to the north side of the mountain and followed it up to a high ridge where they finally got their bearings and were amazed to see the ocean below. Five American and two Canadian surveyors who set out in 1913 to climb Mount Saint Elias from the north reported a similar experience (see Map 9). They travelled on snowshoes for almost fifty miles south from Logan Glacier before reaching the base of Saint Elias, which they also described as a compass: "In the evening light," wrote A.C. Baldwin, "it recalled a huge white ghost, though in shape it resembled a great sea lion, lying head erect, and facing the east."[37] Like the Ahtna migrants, Baldwin and his companions found that the only accessible route led up a steep glacier to a saddle. These surveyors, like the Ahtna before them, caught their first glimpse of ocean from here, amazed by the visual panorama that greeted them when they reached the crest and made their measurements. "Looking to the south from this camp we could see below us the Malaspina Glacier, and beyond it the Pacific Ocean. The Yahtse River was plainly visible, and in

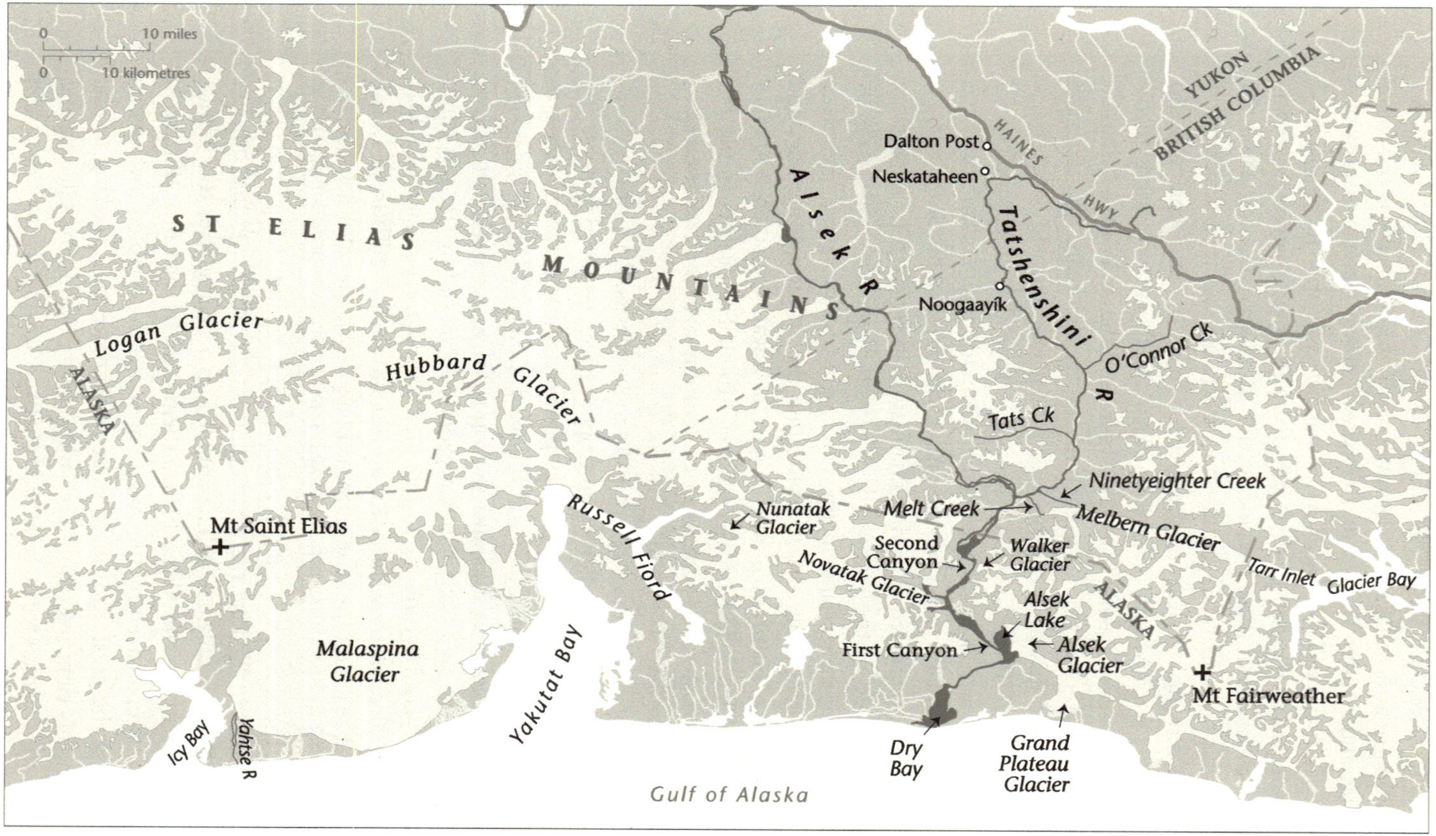

Map 9. Alsek-Tatshenshini river drainage. If the Saint Elias Mountains provide one axis of this region, the Alsek and Tatshenshini drainage provides another. One of the largest river drainages on the west coast of the Americas, it originates on the high Yukon Plateau and drops more than six hundred metres before emptying into the Pacific Ocean. Formerly, the river axis provided a route between interior and coast and was accessible by glaciers from both the east and west.

the sunlight, with every streamlet flashing, it suggested an arm of the sea. Icy Bay was also a noticeable feature, and stretching away to the west side was the Coast Range at about our own level."[38] In every direction, except where their view was blocked by one protruding ridge, they could see for a hundred miles or more, as Baldwin reported enthusiastically. Yet the next morning, 28 June, the valleys flooded with dense fog, and storm flurries moved in. They stopped and waited for a day. Then the weather cleared, and they climbed for nine hours and had reached almost five thousand metres, "when a storm such as is known only at high altitudes, overtook us."[39] And so began their slow and dangerous descent, sounding not unlike the journey made more than a century earlier by descendants of Ahtna and Tlingit, who spoke with Frederica de Laguna at Yakutat..

Glacier Highways

In 1791, Alejandro Malaspina entered Yakutat Bay with two boats, many instruments, and much of the optimism La Pérouse had brought to Lituya Bay five years earlier – a sense that he might be entering the elusive Northwest Passage. Brought up short by a glacier wall in the inner bay, he nevertheless erected his observatory on shore to make final measurements, then hastily transferred his instruments back to the ship when Tlingit showed too spirited an interest in them. He named Yakutat's inner bay Desengaño (Disappointment Bay), and buried a bottle with a note recording that it now belonged to the king of Spain.[40]

More than a century later, two young geologists, Ralph Tarr and Bert Butler, spent the summers of 1905 and 1906 conducting a survey of glaciers at the same Yakutat Bay and became fascinated by another kind of passage. Glaciology was still in its relative infancy as a field study, and these were classificatory moments. Their taxonomic imagination was fired when they identified a kind of glacier "so different from that of the normal glacier valley that it seems to demand a special name." They settled on the term "through glacier," which they defined as "a continuous ice-filled valley from the terminus of one glacier to that of another across a flat divide from which ... ice drainage flows in both directions." As their prototypic "through glacier," they selected "the glacier system which lies between the Russell Fiord and the Alsek River."[41] From the divide, the Nunatak Glacier flows west to Russell Fiord and the Novatak Glacier flows east to the Alsek River in a straight, continuous "highway" (see Map 9). This is the same route that Frederica de Laguna heard described in the 1950s by Yakutat Tlingit whose ancestors travelled from Russell Fiord up the Nunatak Glacier to the icefield where it merges with the Novatak Glacier, and then down that lobe to the Alsek. Though long – this route still stretches fifty kilometres in a straight line – it had the advantage of avoiding unpredictable dangers on the lower Alsek River.[42] Oblivious to its former use by Yakutat Tlingit, Tarr and Butler drew on a more culturally resonant story, noting that some prospectors had apparently chosen this as their route to the Klondike gold rush.

A few years later, and following the judgment of the 1904 International Boundary Commission, a boundary survey party camped at the crest of this same Nunatak/Novatak glacier divide on 28 July 1912, oblivious (like the geologists before them) to its prior use by Tlingit. They too seized upon the more familiar story, describing this glacier pass as one of the routes into the Yukon during the gold rush days, and recording that it was littered from end to end with tin cans, discarded clothes, and sleds.[43] These surveyors had struggled mightily to reach this place – sixteen days cutting trail through eleven miles of dense forest from the Gulf of Alaska coast to Russell Fiord. They encountered torrential rains and their canoe was damaged in transit. They doggedly pursued their assignment, climbing mountains and trying to record visual images required for successful triangulation. But Alaska's Mount Katmai, to the west, had erupted recently and volcanic dust "greatly aggravated the irritation caused by scratches and bites from swarms of black flies and mosquitoes."[44] Visual images, by now one criterion for successful survey, were proving inadequate to the task of representing the land.

De Laguna heard that in order to avoid ascending the Alsek River, hundreds of prospectors dragging sleds travelled this way, but that crevasses later made the route impassable once the glacier began to waste. Consistent with themes we have heard from Tlingit traditions, a Tlingit account from Yakutat, reported by Harrington in undated field notes of 1939-40, explains that when humans die in a glacial crevasse, the glacier will melt. His consultants pointed to the Nunatak Glacier, where at least one prospector fell to his death, as the explanation for the Nunatak's rapid retreat between 1910 and 1940 (see Figure 20).[45]

Alsek River "Highway" and Canyon

The Alsek River, first described in writing by Edward Glave, whose breathless account of safe arrival opened Chapter 6, indeed provided another kind of "highway" to and from the interior. Despite its swift currents, it fostered travel between interior and coast by Tlingit and Athapaskan travellers who portaged the most dangerous sections. It later became a navigational route for surveyors who charted first the international boundary and then the westerly extension of the provincial-territorial boundary.[46] The Alsek, de Laguna learned in 1952, was formerly much more dangerous

Figure 20 Nunatak Glacier, now wasting, was formerly part of a "glacier highway" to the interior. From the divide, the Nunatak Glacier flows west to Russell Fiord and the Novatak flows east to the Alsek River in a straight, continuous line. Yakutat Tlingit traders originally used this route to avoid the difficult and dangerous trip up the lower Alsek, often blocked by glaciers. Prospectors and boundary surveyors later used the same route to the interior (see Map 9). *Photograph by Julie Cruikshank, June 2002*

because glaciers were so much larger, with ice bridges constantly forming and breaking.[47] Again, Deikinaak'w's words at the beginning of this book evoke comparative sensory experience of silently passing through this needle's eye by canoe.

Danger points reported by all river travellers were two canyons, each formed by a rock wall facing an actively calving glacier (see Map 9). At the first, about thirty kilometres upriver from the mouth, an expanded Alsek Glacier formed a vertical wall of ice some sixty metres high, stretching for more than six kilometres and interrupted only by "Gateway Knob," a tall nunatak or promontory from which rocks the size of golf balls rained down.[48] It was here that an ice bridge formed periodically. Sometimes a lake, subject to outbursts, formed just below. Tlingit narrators attributed Gateway Knob's formation to the travelling world-maker, Raven, who distributed geophysical features at the beginning of time. They commented on Raven's wife's dismay whenever she passed beneath this knob's jutting rock face, lest she be killed, and Raven's modest reassurances that rocks would not touch the boat unless some passenger were already fated to die.[49]

When Glave travelled downriver in 1890, he reported the experience of approaching this canyon:

> An enormous glacier [the Alsek Glacier] reaches from the slopes of these mountains and trends away to the river, where its intruding walls of ice are torn asunder by the angry torrent and carried away to the Pacific Ocean.
>
> The stream is now closing together its forces; the towering walls which line each side rapidly come nearer and nearer; on our left an immense wall of ice springs perpendicularly from the water; on our right precipitous granite banks rise almost straight from the stream, banked up by piles of rock. Smaller and smaller becomes the gorge in which the Alsek, now again one deep stream, is shut. Just ahead of us is the dreaded canyon ... Large blocks from the wall of ice toppled over in the water lashing the already wild torrent into a veritable chaos ... The din of the rolling rocks, the roar of the surging stream, and the loud crackling and splashing of falling ice combine in a thundering uproar.[50]

Surveyor Alexander Gillespie travelled in the opposite direction, *upstream* from the mouth of the Alsek, in 1906, sixteen years after Glave passed by. He was twenty-six at the time and had been assigned as assistant to Canadian boundary surveyor Brabazon. Just below the canyon, they found a lake in place (now Alsek Lake), and Gillespie recorded his impressions:

> As we came up near the Glacier, we came into what might almost be called a small lake, formed by an almost right angle bend in the river ... A huge glacier

Figure 21 The Canyon of the Alseck River, sketched by Edward James Glave, appeared in *Frank Leslie's Illustrated Newspaper* 3 January 1891, 414. *Newberry Library, Chicago*

extended along the south side of this small lake and when I entered I noticed a peculiar thing, which was that apparently very recently the lake had been ten or twelve feet higher than at present. This was shown by what was undoubtedly new drift left high up on the sides. There was something rather uncanny about it, so when we made camp that night, we carried our canoe well back from the river and pitched our tent up on the ridge.

That night, when we were sound asleep, we were suddenly awakened by the most awful noise. As I rushed out of the tent, I felt my hair stand on end. The noise was terrifying. I thought at first the great mountain across the river was falling down. Then the waves came roaring across the lake – huge great waves – rushing over the gravel towards us. We then realized what had happened. The Glacier had "calved" and thousands of tons of ice had fallen into the lake. It was a lesson to us, but fortunately, though we had to cross the lake several times, we were only caught in the canoe once when the ice broke. We turned the bow of the canoe into the waves and rode them out.[51]

Above the lake, Gillespie also recorded his impressions of the canyon in a description that echoes Glave's: "On the right bank was a sheer rock cliff,

Figure 22 The Alsek Glacier extending to the Alsek River, 1906. A.J. Brabazon, a Canadian boundary surveyor who made the first topographic map of the region, took this photo from high mountains (now the Brabazon Range), across the Alsek River. The spur in the foreground hides the river canyon. Mount Fairweather rises to the right in this photograph. *Source:* Blackwelder, "Glacial Features of the Alaskan Coast," 427.

hundreds of feet high, and on the left, the ice wall of a hundred feet or more. To make the passing of this canyon even more hazardous, there was an active rockslide down which, at regular intervals all day long, rocks of all sizes came hurtling and plunging into the river. It was a truly nasty place to pass." [52]

Gillespie's co-workers waited three weeks until the water dropped and a gravel bar that seemed safe to cross appeared before they proceeded. He reports, though, that an American survey crew insisted on going ahead and that their canoe was smashed and one member injured.[53] Had there been Tlingit guides, they would have undoubtedly recalled "Raven's work" and his prediction about consequences of falling rocks.

Boundaries, 2003

One way now to glimpse a partial perspective on this massive landscape is to travel by raft from the upper Tatshenshini River down to its intersection with the Alsek River, and from there to the coast. In summer 2003, equipped with Kohklux's 1869 maps as well as laminated copies of Glave's weekly accounts from 1890, and with stories I had heard from women who once lived in this river drainage, I travelled downriver with a group of rafters from Dalton Post (near the old village of Neskataheen) to the Pacific coast.[54] We put in near the site of Dalton Post, where most such raft trips begin. Edward Glave may have written enthusiastically about opening up this region to commerce, but it was his companion on both trips, Jack Dalton, who in the mid-1890s, actually established a modest trading post just upstream from the old village site of Neskataheen.

When Glave began his journey down the Tatshenshini-Alsek from Neskataheen in July 1890, he, Dalton, Koona Ack Sal and his family, and Shank walked downriver for five days because the river was too fast, too shallow, and too rocky for a canoe to navigate safely. This is still the longest section of technical white water on the trip and it is unsafe for canoes (see Map 9). With modern rubber rafts and knowledgeable guides, though, we were able to shoot through the gorge in less than an hour, drenched but still upright by the time we reached the other end. We camped the first night at Silver Creek, where Shank had cached his cottonwood dugout canoe for their 1890 journey. Dalton had modified it by constructing four-inch gunwales on each side, for stabilization and to reduce water intake, lashed to the boat with thong, and they had begun their canoe journey from there.[55]

The first modern boundary we cross, just four kilometres below Silver Creek, divides the Yukon Territory from the Province of British Columbia. A few kilometres on, passing the probable site of Noogaayík, we found the stream clogged by a giant logjam, our first reminder of how dramatically this river changes from year to year. Some days on, as we approached the O'Connor River, the usual shore access vanished and rapid water swept us past a high and crumbling bank that had been a campsite the previous year, a constant reminder of the vagaries of river transformation.

In the mid-1990s, a proposal to build a giant copper mine in the upper Tats Creek was the subject of a major struggle between industry and environmentalists, and the formalization of the Tatshenshini-Alsek Provincial Park was part of a resolution. As the river basin drops ever lower, the forest becomes dense. Splashes of fuchsia high on the mountains emphasized the steady gradient of our descent toward the ocean: where we had begun our trip, fireweed was abundant at ground level. Kohklux's 1869 map shows two village sites along this stretch, one possibly near the mouth of the O'Connor, and another at Melt Creek, though the locations are far from precise. The river runs visibly downhill here, moving at fifteen to twenty kilometres an hour, and spruce trees laden with cones cling to the eroding shore, seemingly desperate to cast seed and reproduce before they are torn loose and swept downriver. These eddies must have challenged Shank and his passengers in their cottonwood canoe.

Once we reached the broad floor of the Alsek valley, the locations of glacier "highways" came into view. Just above the junction of the Tatshenshini and Alsek, a valley opens to the southeast, leading up Melt Creek to the Melbern "through glacier." Following this glacier up and over the Grand Pacific Pass to its snout would take us directly to Tarr Inlet on Glacier Bay. Some narrators suggest that K̲aakex'wtí took this route when he made his trip inland on snowshoes and first met the Athapaskans. Glave speaks of being detained at this junction for a couple of days by wind and rain,[56] and we were also buffeted as coastal storms cycled in and out of range. We camped in a broad bowl, sometimes sunlit, sometimes black with cloud, surrounded by glaciers and always a faint haze of loess or glacial silt blowing through the valley, except when dampened briefly by rain.

Below this junction, the Alsek River almost doubles in size and soon the US border loomed into view, a six-metre-wide survey line, freshly recut in 1998. As we crossed this line from Canada to the United States, we simultaneously moved from Tatshenshini-Alsek Provincial Park to Glacier Bay National Park and Preserve. Borders accumulate.

The unofficially named Walker Glacier seemed grand to us, but much wasted from the one Glave described as standing more than one hundred feet high at the water's edge in 1890.[57] Now set well back from the river, it provides a straightforward ascent for hikers. Looking down and across the river, we saw thickly forested hills where Glave had once observed "facing the glacier, ... an enormous pile of rocks, large and small, which have been displaced."[58] Neoglacial Lake Alsek would have emptied decades before Glave passed, probably stripping away any vegetation that might have escaped glacial grinding. The jungle "verdure" that he so longed for in 1890 and 1891 seems now to be filling the lower Alsek valley.

Fifteen kilometres further down the Alsek, a second, broader valley opens west onto the broad Novatak Glacier, the eastern extension of Nunatak Glacier, Tarr and Butler's taxonomic "through glacier" stretching west as far as the eye can see. The trip from Yakutat to the Alsek River reportedly used to take Tlingit travellers three months, and prospectors four,[59] but from our river's eye view it looked like a stately highway, several miles wide. Below this glacier, we camped on a long sandy spit, just above Gateway Knob, beyond which looms Mount Fairweather, wreathed on this occasion by lenticular clouds.

By the summer of 2003 the alarming canyon no longer existed and the towering ice wall had wasted to two separate glaciers, the Alsek and Grand Plateau, each nestled securely in its own valley, both sedately distant across the now much larger Alsek Lake.[60] The lake has enlarged since Glave's time and is filled with enormous icebergs, inclined to cause turbulence when

Figure 23 The Alsek Glacier, 2003. Comparing this photograph with Figure 22, one sees just how substantially the glacier has wasted. The raft is approaching a mountain that is visible in the 1906 photo only as a small nunatak – a knob of rock – poking through the left side of the glacier at the head of the medial moraine. Enormous icebergs calving from the glacier now fill much of this Alsek Lake. *Photograph by Julie Cruikshank*

they roll over or calve and set lesser bergs adrift. We paddled, careful to keep a respectful distance. The former terrifying channel between the ice wall that encased Gateway Knob and the cliff opposite was almost dry, too shallow for even a raft to float through, so when the lake exit is dammed by bergs, rafters have had to line their vessels through on foot.

Gateway Knob, embedded in Alsek Glacier a century ago, now stands free and high above the lake, a promontory less threatening since the canyon has vanished. Currently it provides a short hiking destination for rafters. We seemed to be camping close to where Gillespie noted distressing evidence of fluctuating lake levels. Exiting the lake the next morning, we shared the river with occasional enormous icebergs less successful than we were at negotiating eddies. Periodically, they capsized and reoriented themselves, hinting at consequences for unskilled river travellers.

Even in places deemed remote, then, human history and human imprints are everywhere. They announce themselves in the work places and waste dumps documented at Nunatak Glacier following the gold rush, and in the broad cut line slicing through forests and across the Alsek River proclaiming an international boundary. Maps chart diverse names, such as "Ninetyeighter Creek," that celebrate some memories, and omit others, such as Nàlùdi (fish stop) Glacier, that quietly document other histories.[61] Glave's early insistence that Tlingit and Southern Tutchone names be retained officially seems to have been largely ignored by those who came after.

An image of patchwork – irregular boundaries securing richly textured narratives – opens this chapter, but it seems in the end rather too relativistic. More apt is the metaphor of an appliqué, a World Heritage site adorning, covering, and ultimately obscuring prior stories (see Map 8). The icefields, though, continue to change. Growing material evidence of human history now melting from glaciers and ice patches is reinvigorating old stories, as we will see in Chapter 8. I will conclude by following contemporary entanglements of boundaries with lives of resident peoples near Canada's northwestern border.

8
Melting Glaciers and Emerging Histories

This book has examined some impacts of glaciers on environmental history and social imagination at the far side of two modern nations. Stories told from the foothills of the Saint Elias Mountains touch on themes resonant elsewhere – colonial encounters, environmental change, sentient landscapes in perpetual motion, and transnational projects shaping boundaries and parks.

Narratives passed on in indigenous communities depict glacier behaviour as occurring within a deeply moral universe where natural-cultural histories are always entangled. Such visions originate in intense engagement with environment, maintained through millennia. When Angela Sidney, Kitty Smith, and Annie Ned spoke about glaciers during the 1970s, they referred to listening, observing, and participating in ritualized respect relations, all themes familiar elsewhere in the circumpolar north.[1] Tim Ingold calls this a "dwelling perspective" so profoundly relational that everyone understands how humans and nature co-produce the world they share.[2]

For successive generations of visitors, too, glaciers provided one striking location where imagination could lodge and nourish inspirational or troubling impressions. Eighteenth-century North Atlantic mariners, inured to nature after months on high seas, were astonished by their initial encounters with North Pacific glaciers. Viewed from the safety of ships, glaciers initially evoked solemn grandeur. Experienced close at hand, they sometimes produced alarming surprises. If La Pérouse imagined glaciers as manifestations of the Sublime – great yet terrible, wondrous yet fearsome – he took comfort in the technology he transported to measure nature's dimensions, tame its uncertainties, and ascertain its physical attributes. A century later, and fresh from Yosemite Valley, John Muir set the bar somewhat differently, with spirit rather than science as his axis. Muir took nature as primary and saw humans as mere fellow travellers in this world. His "glacier gospel" proclaimed nature's transformative potential for souls of humans willing to immerse themselves in glacial landscapes. Edward Glave, emboldened by practices of Victorian region-making,[3] pinned his hopes on locating a river flowing to the sea from "beyond the mountains" and envisioned the Alsek as an imperial conduit to inland commerce, a subarctic Congo River. The Alsek's glacier-swollen shores with their upreared moraines disturbed him though, and in the end he came to view this landscape as "inimical to life." Such shifting sentiments linger and are continually refigured in what Francis Spufford, writing about British polar exploration, refers to as imaginative compost floating through centuries – historic and inherited ideas that eventually stiffen as fixed metaphors, providing convenient receptacles that keep changing their content.[4] Twenty-first-century visitors, for instance, largely view these same landscapes as "scenery."

Transforming landscapes paved the way for unbalanced encounters among humans, between humans and glaciers, and among written records and narratives born of oral tradition. We have seen how stories about such encounters travel, how they are mobilized for different purposes, and how their meanings proliferate. Despite moments of empathy, La Pérouse's meetings with Tlingit at Lituya Bay did not, in the end, guarantee understanding but rather emphasized the incommensurate. French and Tlingit mariners united briefly around their shared losses – members swept oceanward in riptides. Yet La Pérouse ultimately deemed his Tlingit hosts "rude" in the accounts he dispatched to Versailles, and they considered him so forgettable that he comes to mind a century later only as one of "the First Russians." John Muir's fascination with the natural world increasingly drew him to Tlingit philosophies, but his bizarre excursions onto glaciers led Tlingits to speculate that he might be a witch, even as they admired his rhetorical skills. Muir's New York editor at *The Century Magazine*, in turn, chose to excise Muir's most thoughtful observations about Tlingit views of nature, lest they shake up categories already shaping the American environmental movement. Edward Glave's initial openness to indigenous residents on the Tatshenshini River constricted as he began to feel hemmed in by "these colossal heaps of rocks crudely hurled from the mountain heights."[5] He experienced the indifference of glaciers as active hostility, and he longed instead for the jungle. Eventually he extended his unfriendly assessment of glaciers to the humans who inhabited their margins. Yet unanswered questions remain about whether his initial appreciation of Tlingit and Southern Tutchone customs may have contributed to his passionate exposure of what we now call human rights violations once he found himself back in King Leopold's Congo.

Postcolonial theory forces us to look critically at how Enlightenment categories, like nature and culture, were exported from Europe through the expansion of empire to places deemed to be at "the verge of the world," and at how those categories have become sedimented in contemporary practices. Consequences of such dualism continue to cascade internationally through debates about environmentalism, biodiversity, and global climate change. This touchstone of Western rationality – the idea that a measurable natural world might be pried from its cultural moorings – has continued to insinuate itself in locations and landscapes where local understandings were conventionally framed very differently. Drawing on Spufford's image of imaginative compost, it is worth considering how contemporary knowledge continues to fall conveniently into familiar receptacles.

New Stories from Melting Glaciers

The Saint Elias Icefields began to reveal fresh surprises in the 1990s. Three recent events demonstrate just how slippery our views about nature and society continue to be. In 1991, biologist David Hik spotted a rectangular piece of hide roughly one metre in length and half a metre wide melting from a glacier in the upper Kaskawulsh drainage near the centre of what is now Kluane National Park. It had been modified by humans – with slits around the edge and a possible fragment of thong – and looked old. As required by law, he informed Kluane Park staff, who took charge of the hide and then sent it to regional headquarters in Winnipeg where it has remained in a freezer. It appears to have been left by a traveller approximately a thousand years ago.[6] After it was identified as bear hide, park scientists hoped that it might reveal information about genetic relationships and diversity in the Kluane grizzly bear population over time; however, no genetic information has been salvageable because of repeated thawing and freezing. In late 2003, park scientists were preparing a technical report about what has been learned from this skin.[7]

Six years after the hide appeared, in 1997, another biologist hiking near a north-facing alpine basin some 1,830 metres above sea level stumbled on a concentration of caribou droppings, a metre and a half deep and the size of a football field, melting from an alpine ice patch. Artifacts were literally pouring out of melting ice and dung. Subsequent research revealed evidence of caribou harvesting on this mountain, named Thandlät in Southern Tutchone language, for at least eight thousand years. Scientists describe this as a rare opportunity to explore questions about the prehistoric ecology of large caribou populations, implications of climate change for caribou, and human use of high-elevation hunting sites.[8] These droppings contain mitochondrial and nuclear DNA that biologists intend to compare with that of living caribou populations, as well as ancient pollen that may help to reconstruct past climates. Seventy-two ancient alpine ice patches had been identified in the southwest Yukon by 2003, most no more than a square kilometre in size and fifty metres deep. Eighteen of those have yielded tools, and the work continues. Radiocarbon dates for rare wooden tools and other organic material melting from these additional patches demonstrate an enduring relationship between caribou and human hunters at high altitude and latitude for at least eight thousand years, right up until the late nineteenth century.[9] In addition to tools, remains of Dall sheep, mountain goats, elk, bison, and birds have appeared.

Archaeologists working in Athapaskan territories are accustomed to making their inferences from a sparse material record. Subarctic hunters made their tools largely from perishable materials – skin, wood, sinew – used them, left them behind, and remade them as needed, a technology constructed from ingenious principles and carried in the head rather than on the back. Understandably, then, perfectly preserved tools made from organic materials melting from glaciers are spectacularly interesting to scientists as well as to local people, if for different reasons. In their subsequent investigations of Yukon ice patches, archaeologists and Yukon First Nations have formed partnerships, and community members have participated in archaeological field research. Culture camps organized by Champagne-Aishihik First Nation around the theme of ice patches have included visiting scientists who meet with local students.[10] In Alaska, archaeologists are now using GPS (Global Positioning System) instruments to "prospect" for potential melting sites that may be releasing similar evidence on the other side of the Saint Elias range.

The more widely publicized accidental discovery, by sheep hunters in August 1999, was of a young hunter who died in his late teens or early twenties. He was melting from a glacier in the traditional territories of Champagne-Aishihik First Nation (also within Tatshenshini-Alsek Provincial Park). His death was probably accidental. His woven spruce root hat, part of his squirrel fur robe, some tools (including a bone knife with iron stains), and a piece of fish he was carrying were preserved with him. His robe carried traces of spruce and pine pollen and some fish scales. Initial dates obtained from fragments of the robe as well as from his hat, woven from plant fibres, suggest that he died sometime between AD 1415 and 1445.[11] Local elders named him Kwäday Dän Ts'ìnchi (long ago person found) in Southern Tutchone language.

From the beginning, there was close cooperation among scientists and members of the relevant First Nation, Champagne-Aishihik First Nation, without which the scientific research could not have proceeded. Members of the First Nation were interested in learning more about this potential ancestor and about how his travels overlap with their oral histories, and they allowed materials to travel for scientific analysis. Scientists are especially interested in how this rare evidence – flesh and hair as well as bones – might contribute to understandings of health, nutrition, and disease, but also in what his perfectly preserved hat, tools, and fragments of robe may reveal about everyday life from that time.[12] As agreed, the human remains were returned to the community within a specified time frame. The First Nation held a funeral potlatch for him on 21 July 2001, and his cremated remains were returned to the location where he was initially found. Cross-border connections between coastal Tlingit and Champagne-Aishihik First Nations have been strengthened during community negotiations surrounding the research and the funerary arrangements for Kwäday Dän Ts'ínchi.

These events all received wide publicity for a short time – locally, nationally, internationally, and in sources ranging from news media to scientific journals. In such circumstances, scientists and Aboriginal people are encountering concrete, material evidence of the past, but they are also encountering each other at close range. Contemporary encounters fall into new transnational contexts – global climate change, environmentalism, social justice – and again we see how the same evidence produces different interpretations. The piece of bearskin presents scientists with possibilities of learning about ancient grizzly populations and provides local residents with potential evidence of an early ancestor who travelled in the central icefields. Tools pouring from glaciers demonstrate that high-latitude, high-altitude landscapes were intensely shared by humans and caribou for thousands of years. Elders like Annie Ned, born in the 1890s, remembered large herds at the beginning of the twentieth century before caribou moved north. Melting glaciers are revealing material evidence of interest to scientists, but they are also reinvigorating longstanding oral histories about travel and trade near the Saint Elias Mountains. Contemporary tellers do not separate the hat and robe worn by Kwäday Dän Ts'ínchi or his tools from their makers, and they reflect on the mother who might have woven his coastal hat or the grandmother possibly responsible for making his interior gopher skin (arctic ground squirrel) robe. Again, questions arise about where stories told by scientists and elders connect and where they slide apart.

Simon Schama observes in *Landscape and Memory* that "landscape is a work of the mind. Its scenery is built up as much from strata of memory as from layers of rock ... Landscapes are culture before they are nature."[13] We have seen earlier that memories of the Little Ice Age are sedimented both in physical processes studied by scientists – the strata of rock and the bands of grit carried by glaciers – and in memories of long-term residents. Aboriginal residents and archaeologists are now reading new natural-cultural histories from artifacts and organic materials emerging from ice.

Once again, glaciers seem to be playing an active role in negotiating the modern terrain of science, history, and politics in these mountains. Narratives about melting glaciers appear to fall into three interpretive frameworks echoing linked themes that have emerged in this book – environmental change, human encounters, and local knowledge. Environmental-change narratives associated with melting glaciers now concern global warming rather than the Little Ice Age. Stories about human encounters that once depicted Euro-American incursions now address implementation of land claims as one step toward a socially more just society. Local knowledge is again being produced in new contexts and is assuming an expanding role in the rhetorics of co-management policies. In this final chapter, I offer snapshots of such rapidly changing circumstances and conclude with comments about how such interpretative frameworks are continually recast to meet contemporary specifications.

Environmental Change: Climate Warming and Memories of the Little Ice Age

Saint Elias glaciers, created by ice ages and maintained by climate, have long been an active force, ebbing and flowing for thousands of years. Wasting glaciers, routinely reported for Kazakhstan, Nepal, Bolivia, the Himalayas, the Andes, Antarctica, and arctic Canada are becoming a globally recognizable symbol of rapid climate warming. Melting glaciers and ice patches in the Yukon have been reported in both scientific journals and international media as further examples of cryospheric change. For some local residents, though, the unexpected appearance of tools emerging from glaciers calls attention to older stories. The porosity of boundaries between earth and ice resonate, for instance, with oral traditions we have heard about glaciers that are sometimes solid, sometimes liquid, sometimes dens for giant animals, and sometimes alive themselves. Oral traditions from the Yukon and Alaska depict advancing and waning glaciers as shape-shifters capable of responding sharply to humans.

Nineteenth-century North Atlantic visitors also tended to represent glaciers as living beings, whether as Muir's travelling animals "crawling through gorges and valley like monster glittering serpents,"[14] Glave's "weird feature[d] hobgoblins,"[15] or surveyor Baldwin's description of Mount Saint Elias as "a great sea lion, lying head erect, and facing the east."[16] Such language was largely purged from scientific reports by the mid-twentieth century. The resulting chasm now differentiating local narratives – often casually referred to as "myth" or "folklore" – from global narratives of science has so deepened that they rarely intersect in the twentieth century. Yet here, as elsewhere, local and global narratives are now sometimes juxtaposed in discussions about climate change.[17]

Climate change is likely to pose substantial human challenges during coming decades. Subarctic Canadian communities engaged in implementing land claims and self-governance agreements structured around allocation and management of resources – wildlife, fisheries, and forestry – are acutely aware of how dynamics of climate change may affect high latitudes. They also recognize that despite its global dimensions, many responses to climate change will have to occur at a community or regional scale.[18]

Stories told in previous chapters depict nineteenth-century high-latitude mountain environments as risky times and territories. In Chapter 1 we heard accounts of responses to extreme weather events: bone-chilling journeys through mountains in disorienting fog, or struggles to navigate through unexpected storms. Similar stories are told elsewhere in the Yukon. Inland, Rachel Dawson and Angela Sidney each told stories from their grandfathers' time, the mid-nineteenth century, about "a year there was no summer," when old people and children perished.[19]

Gertie Tom, in her role as Tutchone language specialist, transcribed and translated a narrative about men who lost their lives trying to hunt for their families during unusually cold years at a place called Tsändlia Män.[20] Anthropologist Patrick Moore recorded and analyzed Kaska narratives about Hudson's Bay Company traders driven to cannibalism at Pelly Banks in 1850.[21] Coastal Tlingit narrators identify reliable weather guides, as we heard in earlier chapters – like the "weather vane" Tsalx̲aan (Mount Fairweather) or the tree at Yakutat Bay's head where, before crossing the glacier, travellers pressed ear to tree trunk to listen for reverberations of any coming storm. One overriding theme of Little Ice Age variability concerns living with uncertain glacier behaviour – unexpected advances, violent surges, catastrophic floods, and accompanying weather variations. Another concerns human mobility across glacier-filled passes to and from the coast. So the arrival of Kwäday Dän Ts'ínchi both confirms oral traditions in the minds of local people and authenticates, for others, the antiquity of such travel by ancestors. Dates from the mid-1400s AD associated with the young man's clothing suggest that he attempted his glacier crossing near the beginning of the Little Ice Age, when glaciers were re-advancing.

Scientists, though, make a distinction between weather and climate. By definition, they tell us, climate is the statistics of weather, including measurement of means – mean temperature of mean precipitation – and of variance. Climate scientists talk about precise and measurable data – temperature, air pressure, precipitation, and wind speed.[22] As Tim Ingold and Terhi Kurttila reported from their participation in a climate study in northern Finland, oral traditions are unlikely to provide transferable "data" to climate-change scientists, partly because local people are often referring to weather when they talk about environmental change – summer warmth from sun-drenched days or the biting cold of deep river valleys in winter. On the Pacific Northwest coast, weather appears in stories about rain-sodden travel through torrential downpours or the dangers of sudden coastal storms. When the elements sweep inland, they can take the form of chilling boreal winds or nasty hailstorms. More pleasant are spring breezes and long bright summer days. "Climate is recorded," Ingold and Kurttila note succinctly; "weather is experienced." Knowledge about weather, they point out, cannot be transmitted as a set of customary prescriptions or formulae; it is embodied in a lifetime of experience traversing and inhabiting well-known places.[23] Climate science presents a more comprehensive picture than weather. Oral traditions convey understandings that are much broader than data. The two cannot always be conflated, but both reveal experiences of environmental change.

One primary value of local traditions about weather, as others have noted, is to deploy authoritative local traditions in problem-solving during unexpected weather events.[24] Stories that are useful in times of crisis concern proper relations with land and crystallize quick and timely social responses. Those we heard in Chapter 3 about a man falling into a crevasse concern not just technology, like the babiche rope that saved one victim, but also the networks of social relations by which rescues are made. Kwäday Dän Ts'ínchi probably lost his way and his life in an unexpected storm. Stories now surrounding his appearance, his contribution to science, his ceremonial cremation, and his return to the glacier where he was found, point to practices crucial to maintain balance in a moral world. Related oral traditions sometimes equate disastrous effects of environmental change (specifically pollution) with a history of colonialism and its imbalances, rather than viewing these as isolatable physical problems that science might "fix."

Colonial Echoes in "Postcolonial" Worlds: Boundaries and Managers

New encounters fall into twenty-first-century contexts. Material evidence of human history melting from glaciers inevitably calls attention to the inexplicable absence of humans from places now designated "protected wilderness." Terence Ranger traces a conflict-ridden history in Zimbabwe where Matopos Hills, long inhabited, were emptied of African residents and made into a national park (1929-49), then appropriated as "heritage of the world" with UNESCO's World Heritage site designation.[25] Candace Slater raises similar issues in the Amazon now that the concept of "rainforest" has acquired iconic status for international conservation groups, with inhabitants refigured as largely irrelevant. What, she asks, are the thorny issues of justice and injustice that widely disseminated scenes of a marvellous nature too often cloak? Are there ways that our focus on nature is not only narrow, but also politically unjust?[26] What indeed happens when a place like the Saint Elias Mountains, once conceptualized as a moral world where humans and nature are mutually constituted, becomes redefined as a World Heritage site under the stewardship of nature's new managers in Geneva?

UNESCO's World Heritage list sorts the sites given this status into one of three categories: natural, cultural, or mixed properties, reasserting modernist opposition between nature and lived experience. As of November 2004, the 788 properties inscribed on the World Heritage list included 611 sites deemed cultural, 154 classified as natural, and 23 defined as having mixed properties. The awkwardly named "Kluane/Wrangell-Saint Elias/Glacier Bay/Tatshenshini-Alsek" World Heritage site, the first to cross an international boundary, has been allocated to the "natural" category, to the concern of local First Nations. Breaking the bond between people and place along arbitrary lines that separate cultural heritage from natural environment marks a decisive rift. How do management strategies shift with such designations, and with what consequences?

The community of Burwash Landing, situated just east of Kluane National Park between the Alaska Highway and the northwesterly edge of Kluane Lake, offers recent generations of answers (see Map 10). Established as a trading post in 1904 by two enterprising brothers from France, Eugene and Louis Jacquot, Burwash Landing is now headquarters for Kluane First Nation, whose members have been engaged in land claims negotiations with the Government of Canada since the 1970s. One ongoing component of their claim has concerned their exclusion from traditional territories in the Saint Elias foothills after twenty-five thousand square kilometres were set aside in 1942 and made a game sanctuary in 1943. Stretching from the newly constructed highway to the icefields, the entire area was closed to all hunting, including procurement of meat, hides, or furs by Aboriginal peoples who were subsequently relocated to the less productive margins between the highway and the lake.

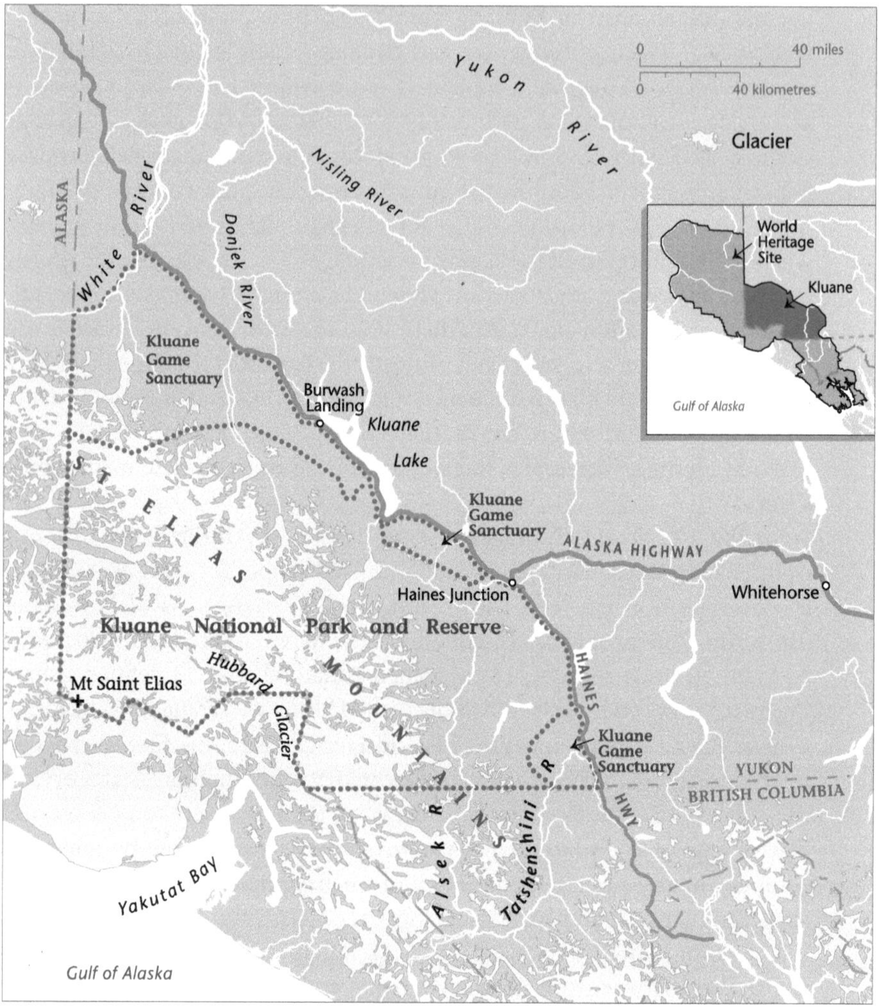

Map 10 Kluane Game Sanctuary was designated in 1943. In 1972 twenty-two thousand square kilometres of that sanctuary were set aside as a national park, officially proclaimed Kluane National Park Reserve in 1976. With the signing of the Champagne and Aishihik First Nations Final Agreements in 1993 the name changed again, to Kluane National Park and Reserve.

This story cuts to the heart of how official acts of boundary-making become normalized as practices that propagate additional boundaries. Ironically, a location that has gathered much of its power as a place where boundaries were always being negotiated (between trading partners, between summer and winter worlds, between glaciers and humans) has now become festooned with international, provincial, territorial, and state borders rather than stories. Prior to the establishment of the game sanctuary, Kluane families occupied the inland slopes of the Saint Elias Mountains, especially the Donjek and upper White rivers.[27] In 1909, a Canadian Boundary Survey party, fifty-one men and eighty-three horses, travelled on foot from Whitehorse to Kluane Lake, then up the Donjek River, and across the divide to the upper White River. They surveyed a line across the White River, allocating the upper drainage to the United States, the lower drainage to Canada, and local Aboriginal family members to two different nation states.[28]

Thirty years later, during the Second World War, the United States anticipated a possible invasion of their country by Japan through Alaska. They conceived the idea of a military highway to connect their distant Alaska territories with the national core, an enormous operation that brought thirty-four thousand workers to construct the road between April 1942 and December 1943. Elderly people who observed this still refer to Alaska Highway construction as the "second rush," reminiscent of the Klondike gold rush. In 1942, the commanding officer for the US Engineer Corps requested that the Yukon government provide special hunting privileges for the US Army and Canadian civilians working on the highway, and with federal encouragement, the Yukon government willingly acceded. Almost immediately, reports began to circulate that animals there were becoming seriously depleted because of both over-hunting during construction and the accessibility provided by the new road. In December 1942, the Governor General of Canada signed an Order-in-Council placing in reserve a substantial portion of the southwest Yukon, west of the new road. Four months later, in spring 1943, the Yukon government moved quickly to designate the area a game sanctuary and prohibited hunting within its margins.[29]

Fundamental to recent human-environmental histories in this region, then, is the transformation of hunting territories to a nature preserve in linked steps that disenfranchised indigenous hunters at the stroke of a pen. New regulations prohibiting hunting within the sanctuary, including subsistence hunting, meant that a hunter who killed a sheep just east of the boundary was deemed a good provider, while someone who took a sheep a few feet west was subject to prosecution. When those boundaries were altered to create Kluane National Park Reserve in 1976, the region joined a national administrative parks network. The layering of a UNESCO-designated World Heritage site across the US/Canadian border in 1979 drew the region into an international agenda. With the signing of Land Claims and Self-Governance Final Agreements by Champagne-Aishihik First Nation (in 1993) and Kluane First Nation (in 2003), allocations have shifted once again and the park name has again changed to Kluane National Park and Reserve.[30]

An international boundary severed people in Alaska from relatives in Canada; a provincial territorial boundary separated families in British Columbia from those in the Yukon; and boundaries placed around Protected Areas locked ancestral territories behind a boundary, or locked people *out* beyond that boundary, depending on point of view. National and international boundaries, as others have noted, proved more formidable than glaciers to negotiate.

During the 1990s, Kluane First Nation petitioned the Government of Canada to hear their case for a Specific Claim[31] concerning the impact of lost access to traditional territories appropriated for "the people of Canada."[32] In February 2002, the Indian Claims Commission held hearings at Kluane Lake, where three generations of community members presented testimony for three days about the social and economic consequences their community experienced following their removal from the Kluane Game Sanctuary and Park. In laying out their claim, speakers argued that exclusion from the sanctuary had deprived them of both economic livelihood and traditional knowledge. Those mountain ranges are a prime location for meat hunting – especially mountain sheep and goats – and the first-hand knowledge gained from hunting there is not easily transferable to other ecological zones where wildlife differs. Loss of access to this region after 1943, they argued, has had long-term social and economic impacts. They further argued that exclusion from these territories sixty years earlier constitutes loss of important knowledge for community members and a rupture in educational strategies.[33]

A crucial problem for those separated by boundaries, then, is how to pass on knowledge about places to young people who never experienced immersion in that landscape. One reason elders whose stories appear in Chapter 3 were so committed to recording these stories and having them written down during the 1970s and 1980s was their concern that young people, deprived of access to these regions after the 1940s, no longer knew such stories in the ways that their elders did. As Paul Nadasdy notes from his extensive ethnographic research with Kluane First Nation:

> People still tell stories about these areas, but to many they are just stories since they themselves have never been there. Kluane people have been trying to reacquaint themselves with the lands in the Kluane Park and Sanctuary; on numerous occasions I accompanied Kluane people on trips to these areas. An important theme on most of these trips was that of exploration, to look for old trails and camps they'd heard stories about and/or just to get a sense of the land and what is on it. These attempts to regain the knowledge of their grandparents are a testament to the continued importance to Kluane people

of knowledge about the land. The effects on the community of the loss of knowledge about these areas, which are some of the richest for hunting in the region, cannot be overestimated.[34]

In his overview of British polar exploration, Francis Spufford[35] argues that once local Inuit knowledge began visibly to undercut the heroism of British exploits in the Arctic – once it became clear that dramatic failures could have been avoided by even the most rudimentary understandings of Inuit domestic skills – the British moved on to the Antarctic, where humans were pleasurably absent. Then British enthusiasts like Robert Falcon Scott went on to make their errors on a polar continent where there was no possibility of local human intercession. In the Saint Elias Icefields, North America seems to have created its own "mini-Antarctic" with inhabitants moved expediently out of the way. Muscular activities like climbing and science continued and expanded. The construction of "wilderness,"[36] a term to which First Nations particularly object because it so thoroughly erases their prior occupancy, proceeded apace. Francis Spufford's image of the Antarctic as a giant "hot cross bun," where national claims radiate from the South Pole, resonates in this World Heritage site with its division into four distinct quadrants. Notably, the official name for one of those four parks, "Tatshenshini-Alsek Wilderness Provincial Park," was changed in 2000 at First Nation insistence to "Tatshenshini-Alsek Provincial Park."

The thousand-year-old bear hide, modified by humans and found in the central icefields, may promise evidence of ancient grizzly population history to scientists but draws different connections for local residents, imprinting locality on landscape.

Local Knowledge as TEK

Melting glaciers have generated partnerships among scientists and First Nations that will inevitably enliven local debates about knowledge. This category of "local knowledge" has become internationalized in the 1990s, both in scholarly scientific debates and as part of everyday conversation surrounding indigenous governance. Terms like "traditional ecological knowledge" and its acronym TEK are ubiquitous in resource management plans in northern Canada and Alaska on topics as diverse as fisheries, wildlife management, forestry, and climate change. If we recall Schwatka's typification of local knowledge as "Native superstition" just over a century ago, summarized in the introduction to this book, we should be persuaded to look at this transformation historically. Is there growing openness to local understandings, or is this some less straightforward process? Throughout this book, I have framed my argument around the importance of tacit local knowledge, continually produced in the context of encounters, yet the "locality" of such knowledge sometimes seems to disappear as prescriptive methodologies to "gather" it proliferate.[37] In the most extreme case, TEK's potential for being "discovered" becomes its defining characteristic, certainly a very old story.

Briefly, the paradox that interests me is this. In much of the resource management literature, there seems to be a growing consensus that indigenous knowledge exists as a kind of distinct epistemology that can be systematized and incorporated into Western management regimes. One of the more trenchant insights from anthropology is that as soon as taken-for-granted, everyday knowledge practices become defined and bounded as "systems" of knowledge, this sets in motion processes that fracture and fragment human experience. Recurring questions concern how knowledge gets identified and authorized in different contexts, and who gets to control it. How, for instance, do different knowledge concepts connect with bureaucratic practices in which much resource management research is now centred?

A critique of the uses and abuses of traditional knowledge identifies several associated problems. One is the underlying premise that different cultural perspectives are bridgeable by concepts in English language (like "sustainable development" or "co-management") and within scientific discourse.[38] Another is the idea that truthful knowledge can somehow be "captured" and recorded in databases; such studies seem to do damage to northern visions when statements by knowledgeable people are stripped from evocative contexts and taped, transcribed, codified, and labelled.[39] Third is the growing recognition that concepts most readily accepted as "tradition" by managers usually reflect ideas compatible with state administration rather than those understood by local people.[40] Natural scientists, as Hugh Raffles notes, have not been shy about naturalizing culture as an endangered object, then selecting data that effectively conflate their own environmental and social agendas.[41]

There are also larger questions about how we come to frame everyday practices as autonomous, homogeneous, internally bounded objects of knowledge, and then set out to analyze them. Much recent scholarship on the history of colonialism traces the social and political conditions under which particular kinds of local knowledge were suppressed and eliminated while other kinds, like Western sciences and humanities, gained authority and then claimed legitimacy to analyze forms of knowledge marginalized in the process. Local knowledge has been framed repeatedly as a foil for concepts of Western rationality that inevitably reflect more about Western ideology than about ways of apprehending the world: as "primitive superstition" (in the nineteenth century), as "ancestral wisdom" (by environmentalists), or as "empirical observation" (TEK). Such formulations seem to deny varieties of local knowledge their own histories. Modernist recasting of "traditional ecological knowledge" continues to present local knowledge as an object for science rather than as intelligence that could inform science.

In the space now called Kluane Park, science and oral history are *both* kinds of local knowledge that share a common history. That history includes authoritative gains for one kind of formulation – science – at the expense of another. Notions of a measurable world decoupled from its cultural moorings emerged from local knowledge traditions flourishing in late-eighteenth-century Europe. Close behind followed the venerable nineteenth-century tradition of scientific reconnaissance and survey in the service of nation-building. In the mid-twentieth century, a multidisciplinary research project in the physical sciences, the Icefield Ranges Research Project, was set in motion in what is now Kluane Park under the institutional sponsorship of the Arctic Institute of North America and the American Geophysical Society. A long record of scientific research at high altitude and high latitude followed, making this a conspicuous site for climate change research. The transformation of most of the Kluane Game Sanctuary into Kluane National Park and Reserve led to government-sponsored management-science. One ironic consequence is that in the early twenty-first century, as part of current co-management policies mandated by modern land claims agreements, indigenous people are now being asked to document their "traditional knowledge" about places from which they were evicted sixty years earlier. In such instances, as Richard White has noted, "our flattery of 'primal peoples' and their knowledge, inevitably deemed to be timeless and ahistorical can be viewed as an act of immense condescension."[42]

In the end, though, data-driven definitions seem much too restrictive. Instead, we need to enlarge spaces for local knowledge by taking into account those generative sources of meaning that make no sharp separation between changing biophysical worlds and changing social worlds. It is worth recalling Bruno Latour's argument in *We Have Never Been Modern*. Despite our best efforts since the Enlightenment to convince ourselves that modernity enables us to firmly distinguish nature from culture, he insists, we have never accomplished this feat. This may seem increasingly self-evident with the proliferation of hybrids like ozone holes, mad cows, and genetically modified crops. It leaves space, however, for the visions of people who have never succumbed to that illusion. Their formulations continue to challenge overly determined environmental narratives with which we are all now familiar.

Entangled Narratives

Stories about glaciers in the Saint Elias Mountains, in constant and uneasy interplay, contribute to a two-century debate about humanity's relationship with the natural world. Regional political and economic practices involved in setting aside protected areas (like parks) now intersect with global practices (like scientific research) that make claims from these spaces. The mountains and glaciers are again being reinvented for new purposes – this time as a hybrid composed of management techniques and measurement practices. Much as narratives of national dreams once normalized practices of mapping and measuring, now global environmental narratives fill that role, bringing primordial wilderness under the human protection of international committees.

Sociologist Adrian Franklin and literary critic Candace Slater each argue, from different starting points, that the nature we are most likely to hear about in the early twenty-first century is increasingly represented as marvellous but endangered, pristine, or bio-diverse. Such depictions, each insists, tend to exclude other ways of seeing and make it more difficult to hear or appreciate unfamiliar points of view.[43] Environmental politics have so normalized our understandings of what "nature" means that we can no longer imagine how other stories might be significant, so we become complicit in processes that make indigenous languages and narratives seem irrelevant to the modern world. As proliferating claims and counter-claims are made in nature's name, areas deemed to be wilderness are re-imagined as uncontaminated by humans. Such views largely exclude other practices, conceptions, and beliefs of people that don't match this vision. Ever-narrowing subsets of nature push humans out, except as subjects for management-science to regulate, effecting a radical purification of nature.

Glacier stories, then, seem well suited to provide alternatives to normalized values that now constrain debates. Always in motion, even when they appear static, the glaciers in these stories encompass both the materiality of the biophysical world and the agency of the non-human, drawing on traditions of thought quite different from those of academic materialism.[44] They are grounded in material circumstances but also carry a multitude of historical, cultural, and social values that are missed when they are relegated uncritically to "nature" as TEK. Works from such diverse historical settings as Africa, the Amazon, and the Arctic suggest that traditions from land-based economies on many continents have their own coherent, globally distributed themes.[45] Local visions passed on in narratives about glaciers, caribou, forests, or rivers seem uniquely important because they place nature and culture in a single social field and graft colonial and environmental histories onto older stories. They draw connections between activities on the land and proper social comportment. They provide rich alternatives to normalized values that now conventionally frame nature as a redeemable object to be "saved."

Narrative recollections and memories about history, tradition, and life experience represent distinct and powerful bodies of local knowledge that have to be appreciated in their totality, rather than fragmented into data, if we are to learn anything from them. Rarely do management-driven studies of TEK or environmentalist parables tap into the range of human engagements with nature – the diverse beliefs, practices, knowledge, and everyday histories of nature that might expand the crisis-ridden focus of environmental politics.[46] Such studies, in fact, often marshal their data to support single arguments that conform to environmentalists' primary concerns about animals, plants, and ecosystems, ignoring what does not fit.[47] What looks similar on the surface often turns out to have different meanings and different aims. Codified as TEK, and engulfed by frameworks of North American management-science, local knowledge shifts its shape. Sentient and social spaces are thus transformed to measurable commodities called "lands" and "resources." Indigenous peoples then face double exclusion, initially by colonial processes that expropriate land, and ultimately by neo-colonial discourses that appropriate and reformulate their ideas. Environmentalist values increasingly shape our understandings of nature (much as science or survey did in the past) but they, too, become entangled with questions of justice working their way through local debates throughout the world.

Environmental change, unbalanced encounters, and the local knowledge emerging in these ambiguous settings have been key themes in this book. Successive visions of Saint Elias Mountains, continuously recast to serve present purposes, become entangled with those of contemporary First Nations whose visions deserve more space in such schema. In the Gulf of Alaska, where European and Aboriginal forms of internationalism have been enmeshed for two centuries, physical places and people have always been entangled. In the future, they are likely to be more entangled than ever before. Local knowledge in northern narratives is *about* unique entanglements of culture and nature, humans and landscapes, objects and their makers. Material evidence of human history – from Kwäday Dän Ts'ínchi, from caribou pellets, or from the modified bear hide, may be naturalized as probable genetic evidence of natural history. But memories covered by appliquéd layers of sanctuary, park, and World Heritage site are also being re-energized as human history emerges from melting glaciers. In both scientific and indigenous communities, melting glaciers will quite probably contribute to new interpretations of the past and present. Annie Ned's advice to "listen for different stories" should claim our attention.

Notes

Introduction

1 The terms "Aboriginal" and "First Nation" are both used in Canada to refer to indigenous peoples. "Aboriginal," the most inclusive term, was selected by the 1990s *Royal Commission on Aboriginal Peoples*, and it encompasses Inuit and Métis, while "First Nation" replaces the administrative term "band," long used by the Government of Canada. "Native" is the more customary inclusive term in Alaska. On both sides of the border, language is increasingly used in self-definition. In this book, the elders referred to are largely speakers of Southern Tutchone and Tagish in the Yukon, and of Tlingit and Ahtna in Alaska. Southern Tutchone and Tagish and Ahtna are three of the more than thirty languages that linguists group within the Athapaskan language family. Tlingit is a distinct language, distantly related to Athapaskan. The grammars, though not the vocabularies, of these two languages are similar.

2 See Thornton, "Tlingit and Toponymies," 295.

3 See Tlen and Moore, "Just Like Being There." I thank Patrick Moore, Daniel Tlen, and John Ritter for helpful discussion on these issues.

4 Povinelli, *Labor's Lot*, 12; and also her paper "Do Rocks Listen?"

5 See, for example, Cronon, "Uses of Environmental History," 4; and Steinberg, "Down to Earth." Other sources that I have found immensely helpful include Ingold, *Perception of the Environment*; Franklin, *Nature and Social Theory*; Slater, *Entangled Edens*; Giles-Vernick, *Cutting the Vines*; and Raffles, *In Amazonia.*

6 Grove, *Little Ice Age*; Fagan, *Little Ice Age.*

7 Ladurie, *Times of Feast*, 147.

8 Strommel and Strommel, "Year without a Summer"; Harington, *Year without a Summer?* (1992).

9 Samuel Taylor Coleridge (1772-1834) included this image in "Hymn before Sunrise, in the Vale of Chamonix"; see Coleridge, *Poems.*

10 Cited in Ladurie, *Times of Feast*, 208-9.

11 Sallnow, *Pilgrims of the Andes*, 224-28; Bolin, "Our Apus Are Dying."

12 Ken Hewitt has generously shared his field notes from October 1961 with me and adds that people living in this region continue with this practice, even when it is not always successful, and can point to small glaciers around the Skardu Basin and elsewhere that they say were planted.

13 Carey, "Confronting Climate Change." Mark Carey, "Managing Melting Glaciers: Climate Change, Society, and the State in Twentieth-Century Peru."

14 For other assessments of current debates about local environmental knowledge, see, for example, Agrawal, "Dismantling the Divide"; Sillitoe, "Development of Indigenous

Knowledge"; Hornborg and Pálsson, *Negotiating Nature*; Ellen et al., *Indigenous Environmental Knowledge*; Milton, *Loving Nature*; Giles-Vernick, *Cutting the Vines.*

15 White, "Discovering Nature."

16 Shelley, *Complete Poems.*

17 Swanton, *Tlingit Myths and Texts*, 67.

18 See Stevens, "Scientists at Work," F1, F6.

19 Daniel Tlen, personal communication, 2004.

20 See especially Comaroff and Comaroff, *Of Revelation and Revolution*, 10-12; Thomas, *Colonialism's Culture*; Raffles, "Uses of Butterflies"; and Brown and Vibert, *Reading beyond Words.*

21 Three geographers who study British Columbia each make these arguments in a slightly different way. See Harris, "How Did Colonialism Dispossess?" as well as his critical study, *Making Native Space*; Clayton, "Absence, Memory and Geography," as well as his *Islands of Truth*; and Braun, *Intemperate Rainforest.*

22 MacEachern, *Natural Selections*, 11-12.

23 For critiques of this representation, see Fienup-Riordan, *Eskimo Essays*, 167-91; Morrow and Hensel, "Hidden Dissension"; Scott "Science for the West"; Cruikshank, *Social Life of Stories*, 45-70; Cooke and Kothari, eds., *Participation: The New Tyranny*; and Nadasdy, *Hunters and Bureaucrats*, 114-46, among others.

24 Beer, *Open Fields*, 2.

25 Williams, *Problems in Materialism*, 67.

26 Milet-Mureau, ed., *A Voyage Round the World*, 367.

27 Latour, *We Have Never Been Modern*. Williams, *Keywords*; Thomas, *Man and the Natural World*; Macnaghten and Urry, *Contested Natures*; Hornborg and Pálsson, *Negotiating Nature*; Castree and Braun, *Social Nature*; and Franklin, *Nature and Social Theory* all provide important overviews of this dualistic view of Nature versus Culture and its consequences.

28 Nadasdy, *Hunters and Bureaucrats* shows how old patterns are replicated when discussions proceed as though these meanings are shared; See especially Chapter 3.

29 See Boyarin, "Space, Time and the Politics of Memory"; Schama, *Landscape and Memory*, 212; Basso, *Wisdom Sits in Places*; and Ingold, "From Culture and Environment to Landscape and Memory."

30 William Cronon's classic paper "The Trouble with Wilderness" discusses the difficulty of recognizing how profoundly human a creation wilderness is, because its naturalness seems so self-evident.

31 Steller, *Journal of a Voyage.*

32 Frederica de Laguna cites Emmons's unpublished notes about this in *Under Mount Saint Elias*, 819.

33 Francis Spufford provides a compelling discussion of "The Sublime" and its role in Arctic exploration in *I May Be Some Time*, 16-40.

34 See 1 Kings 17:1-7 and 19:8-21, and 2 Kings 1:8. I especially thank Jennifer Brown for pointing out these parallels.

35 I thank Marianne de Laet for helping me to frame these encounters in our discussions about La Pérouse's voyages in her edited volume, *Research in Science and Technology Studies.*

36 For insightful discussions of the "first contact" genre, see Wickwire, "Stories from the Margins." Similarly, Tagish accounts of the discovery of Klondike gold centre on the changing lives of Tagish participants and minimize the significance of the "Discovery," now celebrated by a public holiday in the Yukon Territory; see Cruikshank, *Social Life of Stories*, 71-97.

37 Cruikshank, *Social Life of Stories*, 138-59.

38 This was true even when, like E.J. Glave (whom we meet in Chapter 6), they refused to acknowledge how dependent they were on local knowledge.
39 Driver, *Geography Militant.*
40 Schwatka, *Report of a Military Reconnaissance.*
41 Schwatka's journals from this trip were published serially in *The New York Ledger* in 1892, but they faded from view until found a century later by Arland Harris, who published and annotated them in a book in 1996. See Harris, *Schwatka's Last Search,* especially p. 24.
42 Ibid., 168, 169.
43 See also Martindale, *Hunting in the Upper Yukon*, 101-2, for a similar story.
44 Harris, *Schwatka's Last Search*, 169 n. 62.
45 Taussig, "Culture of Terror," 494.
46 Michael Taussig makes this point especially clearly in *Shamanism, Colonialism and the Wild Man*. See also Cohen, *The Combing of History;* Hamilton, *Terrific Majesty*; and White et al., *African Words,* for Africa. For Latin America, Nash, *We Eat the Mines*; Rappaport, *Politics of Memory*; and Muratorio, *Life and Times* (1991) explore this theme, as does Thomas, *Entangled Objects,* for the Pacific.

Chapter 1: Memories of the Little Ice Age

1 International Panel on Climate Change (IPCC), *Climate Change, 2001.*
2 See, for instance, Wenzel, "Warming the Arctic"; Wynne, "May the Sheep Safely Graze?"; Fairhead and Leach, *Misreading the African Landscape*; and Shapin, "Placing the View from Nowhere."
3 Theodore Catton, *Land Reborn*, uses this term to describe emerging lands at Glacier Bay where Little Ice Age glaciers wasted at a spectacular rate.
4 Shapin, *Scientific Revolution*, 58, 78. Intensive international scientific research began in these icefields during the 1960s with the Icefield Ranges Research Project. See Bushnell and Ragle, *Icefield Ranges Research Project,* Vols. 1-3; Bushnell and Marcus, *Icefield Ranges Research Project,* Vol. 4. University-based research continues in southwest Yukon from the Kluane Research Station, administered by the Arctic Institute, University of Calgary.
5 Roots, "Environmental Responses."
6 Overpeck et al., "Arctic Environmental Change," 1252.
7 See, for example, Scott, "Science for the West"; Fienup-Riordan, "Yaqulget Qaillun Pilartat (What the Birds Do)"; Nadasdy, "The Politics of TEK."
8 I have converted measurements, often given in imperial units, to metric units. Mount Saint Elias stands at 5,489 metres and Mount Fairweather at 4,663 metres high.
9 I thank Thomas Thornton for this transcription and translation, personal communication, 2000.
10 Kuklick and Kohler, "Introduction," *Science in the Field*; Hevly, "Heroic Science of Glacier Motion"; Powell, "Intemperate Spaces." See also Beer, *Open Fields.*
11 Ted Chamberlin discusses how overlapping stories about land and its meanings often work from different models of truth telling. The delusion that one reflects reality more accurately than the other is often at the root of conflicts about land. See his book, *If This Is Your Land, Where Are Your Stories?* especially 220-21, 239. Bruce Braun discusses the project of "geologizing nature" that occurred in western Canada under the Geological Survey of Canada during the late nineteenth century in his article "Producing Vertical Territory."
12 Holdsworth, *Mount Logan on CD-ROM.*
13 De Laguna, *Under Mount Saint Elias*, 84, 93.
14 Ibid., 108-11.

15 Vitaliano, *Legends of the Earth*, 104-19.
16 De Laguna, *Under Mount Saint Elias*, 35-55.
17 Russell, "Mount Saint Elias," 46.
18 Tarr and Butler, *Yakutat Bay Region*, 36.
19 De Laguna, *Under Mount Saint Elias*, 85, 86, 91.
20 Russell, "Mount Saint Elias," 171.
21 McClellan, "Intercultural Relations."
22 De Laguna, "Tlingit."
23 Goldschmidt and Haas, *Haa Aaní: Our Land*, 51.
24 Davis, "Prehistory of Southeastern Alaska"; Ames, "The Northwest Coast"; Matson and Coupland, *Prehistory of the Northwest Coast.*
25 De Laguna et al., *Archeology of the Yakutat Bay Area*, 84-87.
26 Miller, *Giant Waves in Lituya Bay*; Ackerman, *Archeology of the Glacier Bay Region.*
27 Goldschmidt and Haas, *Haa Aaní: Our Land*, 46; Thomas Thornton, personal communication, 2000. Goldschmidt and Haas conducted interviews in 1946 and their work was subsequently edited by Thornton, who also provides an introduction and notes.
28 Menzies, *Alaska Travel Journal*, 145.
29 Belcher, *Narrative of a Voyage*, 70-81.
30 Topham, "Visit to the Glaciers of Alaska," 432-33.
31 Tarr and Martin, *Alaska Glacier Studies*, 46-47.
32 De Laguna, *Under Mount Saint Elias*, 97, 286.
33 Klotz, "Notes on Glaciers," 526, 528. A few years earlier, in 1880, John Muir had explored that glacier (then called Taylor Glacier) and recognized that it was advancing, but he made no reference to Vancouver's report. Muir's famous story "An Adventure with a Dog and a Glacier" is set here. Chapter 5 discusses Muir's experiences near Glacier Bay.
34 Swanton, *Tlingit Myths and Texts*, 337-38.
35 Cited in de Laguna, *Under Mount Saint Elias*, 98.
36 Tarr and Butler, *Yakutat Bay Region*, 144.
37 Krauss, *In Honour of Eyak*, 56; de Laguna, *Under Mount Saint Elias*, 59.
38 Krauss, *In Honour of Eyak*, 11-13.
39 Swanton, *Tlingit Myths and Texts*, 352, 355-56, 358.
40 De Laguna, *Under Mount Saint Elias*, 17.
41 Dauenhauer and Dauenhauer, *Haa Shuká, Our Ancestors.*
42 Thornton, "Tlingit and Euro-American Toponymies," and "Know Your Place."
43 McClellan, *My Old People Say.*
44 Cruikshank et al., *Life Lived Like a Story.*
45 Tom, *Èkeyi: Gyò Cho Chú.*
46 Moore, *Dene Gudeji: Kaska Narratives*, and "Point of View in Kaska Oral Narratives."
47 Anthropologists use the term *moiety* to describe an organizational principle whereby everyone is born into one of two groups, in this region named Raven and Eagle on the coast, and Crow and Wolf in the interior. In northwestern North America, descent is traced matrilineally, so that each child inherits the same affiliation as his or her mother. In principle, rules of exogamy are strictly enforced so that each person marries someone from the opposite moiety, though this has changed with time. Consequently, every family is composed of members of both moieties, and alliances are repeatedly forged through marriages, partnerships, and trade. In Tlingit communities, moieties are further subdivided into matrilineal clans.

Clans differ from moieties in claiming a common ancestor, as well as distinctive crests, songs, and formal oral histories. Clans remain primary units of national history and property ownership. Clans mentioned in this book belonging to the Raven group include Deisheetaan, Kaasx̲'gweidí, Kosk!e'dî, Kwáashk'i K̲wáan, Lukaax̲.ádi, L'uknax̲.ádi, and T'ak̲deintaan. Clans grouped as part of the Eagle moiety are Chookaneidí, Dak̲l'aweidí, Kaagwaantaan, L!uq!oe'dî, and Teik̲weidí.

48 Kan, *Memory Eternal*, 14.

49 For a detailed discussion of Swanton's work, see Bringhurst, *A Story as Sharp as a Knife*.

50 Migrants were Ahtna-speaking Athapaskans, and Frederica de Laguna notes that after they arrived at Yakutat Bay, they took an Eyak name, Kwáashk'i (humpback salmon) as their clan name, referring specifically to the Humpback Salmon Creek in the east side of Yakutat Bay (de Laguna, *Under Mount Saint Elias*, 222). Swanton entitles this clan history "Story of the Kwáashk'i K̲wáan," using a phonetic spelling. See Swanton, *Tlingit Myths and Texts*, 347-68; see also Goldschmidt and Haas, *Haa Aaní: Our Land*, 46.

51 De Laguna, *Under Mount Saint Elias*, 349-50.

52 De Laguna and McClellan, "Ahtna," 651-52.

53 De Laguna, *Under Mount Saint Elias*, 232.

54 Ibid., 232, 237, 239, 1226-27.

55 Ibid., 237, 1226-27.

56 Ibid., 235, 236.

57 Swanton, *Tlingit Myths and Texts*, 350-51.

58 Ibid., 352; de Laguna, *Under Mount Saint Elias*, 218, 242.

59 De Laguna, *Under Mount Saint Elias*, 238-39.

60 Swanton, *Tlingit Myths and Texts*, 360.

61 De Laguna, *Under Mount Saint Elias*, 242.

62 Swanton, *Tlingit Myths and Texts*, 361.

63 Ibid., 358.

64 De Laguna, *Under Mount Saint Elias*, 225-26.

65 De Laguna, "Tlingit," 227.

66 De Laguna, *Under Mount Saint Elias*, 277-78; Boyd, *The Coming of the Spirit of Pestilence*, 120-22, 213.

67 Goldschmidt and Haas, *Haa Aaní*, 51.

68 Swanton identified the residents as members of the interior Athapaskan Lukaax̲.ádi Raven clan. He translated their name as "quick people" and described them as "very fast runners" because they moved swiftly, "just like an arrow," and other people "could not catch up with them." See Swanton, *Social Condition*, 400; *Tlingit Myths and Texts*, 356; and de Laguna, *Under Mount Saint Elias*, 223-24. Coastal Lukaax̲.ádi clan members now reject any interpretation that associates their origins with the interior and identify coastal villages further south (including a place named Lukaax̲) as their original homeland (Thomas Thornton, personal communication, 2000). Possibly, two clans with different origins had combined at Dry Bay.

69 Swanton, *Tlingit Myths and Texts*, 1, 326-46. Deikinaak'w actually told one-third of the narratives published in *Tlingit Myths and Texts*, although this is not immediately obvious from the format Swanton uses to present the volume. Of the narratives Deikinaak'w recorded, twenty-eight were told in English, and nine, including this one, were recorded in Tlingit and translated with the help of the bilingual Tlingit man, Don Cameron. Cameron also translated for K̲'áadasteen, whose account of the Copper River migration appeared in the previous section.

70 Swanton, *Tlingit Myths and Texts*, 154-65.

71 Dauenhauer and Dauenhauer, *Haa K̲usteeyí, Our Culture*, 754, identifies this connection.

72 Dauenhauer and Dauenhauer, *Haa Shuká, Our Ancestors*, 152-65. Willie Marks, like the protagonist K̲aakex'wtí, was a member of the Chookaneidí Eagle clan.

73 Dauenhauer and Dauenhauer, *Haa Shuká, Our Ancestors*, 360 n. 1. Swanton entitles the version Deikinaak'w told, "The Story of Kaagwaantaan" in *Tlingit Myths and Texts*,

326-46. In the more recent versions recorded by the Dauenhauers, contemporary elders insist that at that time of their dispersal, Kaagwaantaan was merely a house group of Chookaneidí and became important only later, after the dispersal of both groups from Glacier Bay.

74 Swanton, *Tlingit Myths and Texts*, 329; see also Dauenhauer and Dauenhauer, *Haa Shuká, Our Ancestors*, 153-65; and Thornton, "Know Your Place," 298-300 for reconstructions of his journey.

75 Swanton, *Tlingit Myths and Texts*, 158, 332.

76 Ibid., 162.

77 Inland sources of native copper became important in Aboriginal trade networks and subsequently caused much speculation among miners during the early twentieth century.

78 Swanton, *Tlingit Myths and Texts*, 160, 333.

79 Thornton, "Know Your Place," 300.

80 Swanton, *Tlingit Myths and Texts*, 334-36.

81 Ibid., 337-38.

82 Dauenhauer and Dauenhauer, *Haa Shuká, Our Ancestors*, 244-91, and notes 407-31.

83 Powell, "Role of Physical Sciences in Climate Change."

84 Schroeder, "Historic and Contemporary Tlingit Use of Glacier Bay," 279.

85 Cruikshank, *Athapaskan Women*, 164-67.

86 McClellan, personal communication, 2001.

87 Tom, *Èkeyi: Gyò Cho Chú*, 70-72; Moore, *Dene Gudeji: Kaska Narratives*, 48-53, 246-67; Moore, "Point of View in Kaska Oral Narratives," 165-96.

88 Jacoby and Cook, "Past Temperature Variations."

89 Swanton, *Tlingit Myths and Texts*, 67.

90 De Laguna et al., *Archeology of the Yakutat Bay Area*, 81.

91 McClellan, *My Old People Say*, 446, 447-48.

92 Nyman and Leer, *Gágiwdul.àt'*, 43.

93 Beattie et al., "Kwäday Dän Ts'ínchi."

94 Milet-Mureau, *A Voyage Round the World*, 401, 407.

95 Methods used to reach these dates are discussed in detail in Beattie et al., "Kwäday Dän Ts'ínchi," 135-36.

96 Milet-Mureau, *A Voyage Round the World*, 401.

97 De Laguna, *Under Mount Saint Elias*, 40, 367.

98 Murray, *Journal of the Yukon*; see also the description in McClellan, *My Old People Say*, 302-3.

99 See also McClellan, *My Old People Say*, 71-72.

100 De Laguna, *Under Mount Saint Elias*, 89, 276.

101 McClellan, field notes, 30 March 1963.

102 The Neoglacial is a term given for the period of glacier expansion spanning the last 4000 to 5000 years (encompassing the period referred to in this chapter as the Little Ice Age) but dates given for its onset vary in different parts of the world. In the Pacific Northwest, the Neoglacial is said to have begun about 2800 radiocarbon years ago (Clague and Rampton, "Neoglacial Lake Alsek," 95). Raw radiocarbon measurements are usually reported as years "before present" (BP). This is the number of radiocarbon years before 1950, based on the assumption that the level of carbon-14 in the atmosphere has always been at the 1950 level. Because this is untrue in practice, radiocarbon years do not correspond exactly to calendar years.

103 Clague and Rampton, "Neoglacial Lake Alsek."

104 Daniel Tlen, personal communication, 2004. Daniel Tlen's words contribute to this book's epigraph.

105 McClellan, *My Old People Say*, 26.
106 Ibid., 440-42.
107 Ibid., 20-26.
108 Ibid., 27.
109 Swanton, *Tlingit Myths and Texts*, 154-69, 326-46; McClellan, *My Old People Say*, 27.
110 Ned, in Cruikshank et al., *Life Lived Like a Story*, 280.
111 McClellan, *My Old People Say*, 24.
112 Townsend-Gault, "Circulating Aboriginality."
113 Comaroff and Comaroff, *Of Revelation and Revolution*, 11.
114 One speaker used a particularly effective metaphor to differentiate kinds of glacial surges, comparing the stately movement of one Antarctic glacier to the Sistine Chapel and the fast flow of another to drag racing.

Chapter 2: Constructing Life Stories

1 In both Tlingit and Athapaskan languages, the term for "white people" can be translated as "cloud people" (*k'o* in Southern Tutchone and *gus'* in Tlingit, both derived from the word for "cloud"). De Laguna, *Under Mount Saint Elias*, 217, cites Tlingit translations from Boas, "cloud outside-of people," and from Harrington's notes, "horizon people," "people from where the sky, or clouds, meet the ground," or "horizon-end-of people."
2 Frye, *The Educated Imagination*, 5, 57.
3 Cruikshank in collaboration with Angela Sidney, Kitty Smith, and Annie Ned, *Life Lived Like a Story*.
4 Strictly speaking, these stories don't really have "titles," but the narrators all understand the convention well enough to provide them as a kind of shorthand for referring back to individual narratives.
5 Kitty Smith's mother, Tatl'érma, was a member of the Crow moiety, as was her daughter, and the child was given three successive names – Kàdùhikh, K'algwach, and K'odetéena. Her father, Tákàtà, was a member of the Wolf "side."
6 2 Kings 2:23-24.
7 See Smith, in Cruikshank et al., *Life Lived Like a Story*, 159-262.
8 Annie Ned, like Kitty Smith, was a member of the Crow moiety or "side" and was given the name Ntthenada as a child. Her mother, Tùtalma, also Crow, had the English name Annie, and her daughter was also given that name. Annie Ned's father, Sakuni, was also known as Hutshi Jim, son of Hutshi Chief.
9 See Ned, in Cruikshank et al., *Life Lived Like a Story*, 263-338.
10 Kusawa Glacier was not a surging glacier, but her account suggests that "cooking with grease" was widely regarded as a cause of glacier instability. De Laguna also reports from the coast that Tlingits told her glaciers were repelled by the odour of old clothes burning; de Laguna, *Under Mount Saint Elias*, 819. The English name "Arkell" was given to this lake by members of the *Frank Leslie's Illustrated Newspaper* Expedition when they crossed the glacier in late May 1890. Alfred Shanz named this lake, casually referring to "the discoverer's privilege." Shanz, "Our Alaska Expedition," 466. The lake's name was subsequently changed back to Kusawa, from the Tlingit Koosawu Áa (long lake).
11 Kuzyk et al., "In Pursuit of Prehistoric Caribou"; Mrs. Ned's account appears in Cruikshank, "Contributions to the Oral History."
12 Angela Sidney's parents were La.oos Tláa (Maria) and K̲aajinéek' (Tagish John) and she was given both a Tlingit name Stóow and a Tagish name Ch'óonehte' Má. Her mother was a member of the Tlingit Deisheetaan clan (grouped with the Crow moiety) and her father belonged to the Dak̲l'aweidí clan (Wolf side).

13 Angela Sidney had already worked for years with anthropologist Catharine McClellan and by the 1970s was beginning to document Tagish language with linguist Victor Golla, and Tlingit language with linguist Jeff Leer, so she had clear ideas about how cultural documentation should proceed.
14 See Sidney, in Cruikshank et al., *Life Lived Like a Story*, 37-158; and also Cruikshank, *Social Life of Stories*, 25-44, for a discussion of successive contemporary public uses of an ancient story, and pp. 71-97 for Tagish accounts of the Klondike gold rush.
15 Briggs and Bauman, "Foundation of all Future Researches."
16 Sidney, *Place Names*; *Tagish Tlaagú*; *Haa Shagóon*; Sidney, Smith, and Dawson, *My Stories Are My Wealth*; Smith, *Nindal Kwädindür*; Ned, *Old People in Those Days*. This idea is further expanded in Cruikshank et al., *Life Lived Like a Story*, and Cruikshank, *Social Life of Stories*. I am especially grateful to Frances Pine for discussions we have had on this subject.
17 A case for assessment of historical veracity in oral tradition is made by Vansina, *Oral Tradition as History*. Other disciplinary perspectives are provided by Cronon, "A Place for Stories"; Cohen, *The Combing of History*; and Hinchman and Hinchman, *Memory, Identity, Community*. Philosophical perspectives on the significance of narrative can be found in several sources, including: de Certeau, *The Practice of Everyday Life*; White, *The Content of the Form*; and McIntyre, *After Virtue*.
18 Wolf, *Envisioning Power*, 16.
19 Particularly useful sources relevant to oral history include, for Russia, Khubova et al., "After Glasnost"; for southern Africa, Hofmeyer, *We Spend Our Years*, and Hamilton, "Living by Fluidity"; in Kentucky, Portelli, *Battle of Valle Giulia*, 51-71; from Italy, Passerini, *Fascism and Popular Memory*, and Portelli, *The Order Has Been Carried Out;* and more generally Passerini, *Memory and Totalitarianism*, Watson, "Memory, History and Opposition," and Leydesdorff et al., "Introduction."
20 Morrow, "On Shaky Ground."
21 I am indebted here to Margery Fee's discussion in her paper, "The Social Work of Stories."
22 For a discussion of what I mean by counter-narrative at the Yukon International Storytelling Festival, see Cruikshank, *Social Life of Stories*, 138-59.
23 Innis, *The Fur Trade in Canada*; *The Cod Fisheries*; *Essays in Canadian Economic History*.
24 Innis, *Empire and Communications*; *The Bias of Communication*.
25 Innis, *Essays in Canadian Economic History*, 12-14.
26 Innis, *Empire and Communications*, 64-100; Stamps, *Unthinking Modernity*, 48-51.
27 Innis, *The Bias of Communication*, 8-9.
28 Stamps, *Unthinking Modernity*, 11.
29 Innis, *The Bias of Communication*, 190.
30 Bakhtin, *Rabelais and His World*.
31 Clark and Holquist, *Mikhail Bakhtin*, 9.
32 Bakhtin, *Dialogic Imagination*.
33 Benjamin, "The Storyteller"; Stamps, *Unthinking Modernity*, 23-40.
34 Bakhtin, *Rabelais and His World*.
35 Innis, *The Bias of Communication*, 8-9.
36 See Cruikshank, *Social Life of Stories*, 71-97.
37 McClellan, "Intercultural Relations."
38 Marchand, "Tribal Epidemics in the Yukon."
39 Cruikshank, "The Gravel Magnet."
40 McCandless argues that a federal government initiative to secure parklands was already under way, and that these claims were overstated. See his *Yukon Wildlife*, 75-87.

41 Casey, *Getting Back into Place*; "How to Get from Space to Place." See also Feld and Basso, *Senses of Place*, and Hirsch, "Introduction," for more ethnographic treatments of this same issue.
42 Boyarin, "Space, Time," 3, 4, 15.
43 Sidney, *Place Names*. See also Cruikshank, "Getting the Words Right."
44 This principle is widespread in circumpolar northern regions; see Fienup-Riordan, *Boundaries and Passages*.
45 Basso, *Wisdom Sits in Places*.
46 See Pine, "The Village, the City and the Outside World" for a discussion of these principles in rural Poland.
47 See David Anderson's account of such respect relations in "Reindeer, Caribou."
48 Frye, *The Educated Imagination*, 19.
49 Clague and Rampton, "Neoglacial Lake Alsek," 95.
50 Bear Creek is a tributary of the Dezadeash River, and both flow into the Alsek River (see Map 3).
51 McClellan, field notes, 30 November 1962.
52 Personal communication, Peter Johnson, University of Ottawa, 2001.
53 Gibson, "Smallpox on the Northwest Coast," 73.
54 Personal communication, Garry K.C. Clarke, University of British Columbia, 2000.
55 Anderson, "Reindeer, Caribou."
56 McClellan, *My Old People Say*, 210, 215-16.
57 Lévi-Strauss, *The Way of the Masks*, 111, cites John Swanton's observation that according to coastal Tlingit tradition, humans *should* burn grease to prevent earthquakes. The woman who supports the column on which the world rests shivers when she gets hungry, causing the ground to shake, but she is calmed when she is fed by this grease. Fire, glaciers, earthquakes, and surging glaciers all share transformative spaces in this geophysically active environment.
58 Candace Slater's book *Dance of the Dolphin*, based on work in the Amazon, has been immensely helpful in thinking about these ideas.

Chapter 3: Listening for Different Stories

1 "Outside" is the colloquial expression used in the Yukon to refer to places south of the Territory's southern boundary, the 60th parallel.
2 Welty, *One Writer's Beginnings*, 14.
3 Linguists classify languages spoken in the Yukon Territory as belonging to two language families, Athapaskan and Tlingit. The Athapaskan group encompasses at least thirty distinct languages in northwestern North America as well as several spoken far to the south, including Navajo and Apache. Athapaskan languages still spoken in the Yukon Territory include Gwich'in, Han, Upper Tanana, Tutchone, Southern Tutchone, Kaska, and Tagish. Tlingit is spoken in part of the southern Yukon as well as in Alaska.
4 Cruikshank et al., *Life Lived Like a Story*, 12-20.
5 See Dauenhauer and Dauenhauer, "Oral Literature," 102.
6 Nora and Richard Dauenhauer also argue that the study of oral tradition differs from other kinds of scholarly textual study because it is *embodied*; that is, it occurs in real time, it is performed, it always involves interaction – in their words, "you always have to bother somebody." In northwestern North America it is deeply embedded in clan and community.
7 Mrs. Sidney recorded this story on 10 November 1978, and it appeared first in her booklet, *Tagish Tlaagú*, 21-22, and then as part of her life history in our co-authored book: Cruikshank et al., *Life Lived Like a Story*, 48-49.
8 The term "high person" refers to someone who is economically and socially powerful.

9 Mrs. Smith's version of this story, recorded 13 November 1978, appeared in her booklet *Nindal Kwädindür*, 29-32, and later in Cruikshank et al., *Life Lived Like a Story*, 241-45. For more detailed discussion of "stolen woman" stories, see Cruikshank et al., *Life Lived Like a Story*, 340-46.

10 He encourages her by reminding her that he has many extended family members who can be counted on to help him rescue her.

11 The rescuers are arriving.

12 By "husbands" Mrs. Smith is referring to the captors, two brothers, who have taken her as a wife.

13 The rescuers hear the sound of woodcutting and are able to signal to the young woman that they have arrived.

14 She asks for a separate blanket so she can be more agile when the rescue attack begins.

15 In this story, Mrs. Smith explicitly compares her protagonist and his grandmother with one of her own grandsons and herself. The boy in the story was the first to receive the message that white people, k'och'en, would one day come to the country and bring fundamental changes. She recorded this story on 23 October 1975, and it appeared in her co-authored booklet, Sidney, Smith, and Dawson, *My Stories Are My Wealth*, 113-16, and also in Cruikshank et al., *Life Lived Like a Story*, 254-58.

16 Everyone would expect that he was returning from a transformative experience and had some important new knowledge to impart. His family indicates this by their attentiveness to his requests. And indeed he follows a classic pattern, remaining in a kind of liminal space for seven days and giving instructions to others in the camp. Conventionally, this state would last until the eighth day after his return.

17 She observes that there are fewer Aboriginal people than in the past.

18 Mrs. Sidney recorded this account over several sessions in January 1981. It was published first in her family history, *Haa Shagóon*, xiii-xv, and she subsequently added more details for the version in Cruikshank et al., *Life Lived Like a Story*, 39-41.

19 Den k'e is the Tagish term meaning "in Native language" or "the people" in Tagish language.

20 John Muir heard and summarized a less heroic (or differently gendered) version of the story Angela Sidney tells about travelling under the Stikine Glacier bridge:

> The Indians have a tradition that the river used to run through a tunnel under the united fronts of two large tributary glaciers ... which entered the main cañon from either side; and that on one occasion an Indian, anxious to get rid of his wife, had her sent [sic] adrift in a canoe down through the ice tunnel, expecting that she would trouble him no more. But to his surprise she floated through under the ice in safety. All the evidence connected with the present appearance of these two glaciers indicates that they were united and formed a dam across the river after the smaller tributaries had been melted off and had receded to a greater or lesser height above the valley floor. (Muir, *Travels in Alaska*, 48)

21 Writing in 1887, Canadian geologist George Dawson commented that the use of this route by Tlingit traders was already declining because the journey from the coast to the head of the Takhini River was so difficult; see Dawson, *Report on an Exploration*, 160.

22 McClellan, "Intercultural Relations."

23 Mrs. Ned recorded this version on 25 February 1981 and then again on 27 October 1982. It appeared first in her family history, "Old People in Those Days," 17-21, and again in Cruikshank et al., *Life Lived Like a Story*, 308-10.

24 Mrs. Ned uses three different names for this lake interchangeably: the Tlingit name, Koosawu Aá (long lake); the Athapaskan name, Nakhu, referring to the narrows; and Lake Arkell, the official English name for some years before Kusawa was reinstated.

"Lake Arkell," as we see in Chapter 6, was a name bestowed by members of the *Frank Leslie's Illustrated Newspaper* Expedition.

25 In his liminal state, he is able to hear them and to visualize what is happening. In both this version and Mrs. Smith's version, the food that mourners feed to the fire at the potlatch is transferred directly to the victim and saves his life.

26 Mrs. Smith recorded this version of her story on 28 February 1979. A version appeared in her booklet *Nindal Kwädindür*, 95-97.

27 Angela Sidney is the only one of the three narrators to identify the protagonist in the story as someone she knew personally. A version appeared in her booklet *Tagish Tlaagú*, 88-89.

28 Mrs. Smith told this story over two sessions, on 28 February and 2 March 1979. It appears in her booklet *Nindal Kwädindür*, 87-88, and over the years she added more details included in Cruikshank et al., *Life Lived Like a Story*, 205-8.

29 His "doctor" refers to the source of his shamanic power, his spirit helper.

30 "1016" refers to the old milepost number at Haines Junction, on the Alaska Highway, and is the way people used to refer to place names on that road from Fort St. John, where it begins, to Fairbanks, where it ends.

31 The shorelines of successive lakebeds formed by Neoglacial Lake Alsek are still visible. The hills in this area show clearly demarcated beach ridges, marking levels reached by different fillings.

32 Both the Alsek and Tatshenshini rivers are major rivers, and people often refer to them by the names of their tributaries, where people fished. The main river is much too fast for fishing. See O'Leary, *Salmon and Storage.*

33 She is claiming her authority to speak about events before her lifetime by identifying that this is common knowledge.

34 Mrs. Ned recorded this story on 25 February 1981, and it appears in her booklet we recorded together, *Old People in Those Days,* as well as in Cruikshank et al., *Life Lived Like a Story*, 332-33.

35 They had heard from coastal Tlingit people about such glacier lake fillings.

36 Some elders identify glaciers as dens of giant animals that may emerge when antagonized. Mrs. Ned would expect any listener to understand this relationship.

37 Arctic ground squirrels or "gophers" are numerous near here. The population is subject to cyclical fluctuation, but a flood destroying all the burrows in an area would significantly influence population recovery.

38 This story was also recorded on 25 February 1981 and appears in Mrs. Ned's booklet *Old People in Those Days*, as well as in Cruikshank et al., *Life Lived Like a Story*, 333-36.

39 By pointing to skepticism even from within her own cohort, she builds a strong case for the alarm generated by the events that follow.

40 See Mrs. Ned's previous story, *Bear Creek Glacier.*

41 She is referring to her first husband, Paddy Smith, and points out that her father-in-law's country included Kusawa Lake and upper Takhini River. She discusses her husband's knowledge of this region in Cruikshank et al., *Life Lived Like a Story;* see especially 265, 272-73.

42 Njäl is the Southern Tutchone name for a common house structure in the southern Yukon, the double lean-to, constructed of poles and covered with moss and brush.

43 She is referring to her earlier narrative about a man who fell into a crevasse.

44 Johnny Ned was her first husband's younger brother. Many years later, after Paddy Smith's death, Johnny Ned became Mrs. Ned's second husband. This widespread custom ensures that connections between moieties remain unbroken: at the death of a married man, his brother or his sister's son, or someone who is socially equivalent, would take over the responsibility of providing for and looking after the widow.

45 Older women tend to use the term Old Man, sometimes as a proper name, to refer to a husband.

46 She is referring here to the being that occupies the glacier. In this case, Jack Smith's reckless act of cooking with goat grease causes a huge storm to blow up.

47 They shoot to signal where they are when their fire is drowned, and they are able to guide her husband, Paddy Smith, back to the camp.

48 Johnny Ned was later well known for his special powers of foresight.

49 Mrs. Smith recorded this account on 2 March 1979. I begin by reminding her that she once started to tell me a story about a glacier "whose eyes came out like the sun," and this is her response. It appears in her *Nindal Kwädindür*, 89-91.

50 This seems to set the story during the childhood of a man a generation older than Mrs. Smith, possibly as early as the early 1860s.

51 When Edward Glave travelled through this country in 1890 and 1891, he commented on the absence of moose or caribou in the Tatshenshini valley.

52 Here she is referring to the Tatshenshini River, which passed near Dalton Post, the trading post established by Jack Dalton during the 1890s. Dalton was Edward Glave's travelling companion in 1890 and 1891, and subsequently established a trading post at Neskataheen (see Chapter 6).

53 This is Catharine McClellan's phonetic transcription, *My Old People Say*, 32.

54 Mrs. Smith's story, recorded over two sessions, on 2 March and 20 March 1979, appears in her *Nindal Kwädindür*, 45-47, and again in Cruikshank et al., *Life Lived Like a Story*, 258-62.

55 See McClellan, *My Old People Say*, 108, 170. See also de Laguna, *Under Mount Saint Elias*, 40, 47, who gives the same Tlingit word, but notes in passing that moose arrived on the coast only in the twentieth century. She, in turn, cites Boas as recording Tlingit words for moose and owl that sound very similar.

56 McClellan, *My Old People Say*, 182; and field notes, February 1963. Daniel Tlen makes a similar observation in this book's opening epigraph.

57 Mrs. Smith told this story on 28 February 1979, and it appears in her booklet *Nindal Kwädindür*, 92-94.

Chapter 4: Two Centuries of Stories from Lituya Bay

1 In this chapter, I will be arguing that "the field" is a construct, and that encounters such as the one I describe help to construct the space we call the field; in short, the encounter *makes* the field.

2 Milet-Mureau, *A Voyage Round the World*; Dunmore, *The Journal of Jean-François de Galaup de La Pérouse*.

3 Emmons, "Native Account of the Meeting"; de Laguna, *Under Mount Saint Elias*, 258-59, 273-74, 1159-60; Dauenhauer and Dauenhauer, *Haa Shuká, Our Ancestors*, 293-309.

4 Klotz, "Notes on Glaciers," 526; Miller, *Giant Waves in Lituya Bay*, 54. All measurements were originally given in imperial units and have been converted here to metric units.

5 De Laguna, *Under Mount Saint Elias*, 93.

6 Emmons, "Native Account of the Meeting," 294.

7 Ackerman, *Archeology of the Glacier Bay Region*, 3; see also Miller, *Giant Waves in Lituya Bay*, 51; Fradkin, *Wildest Alaska*.

8 De Laguna, *Under Mount Saint Elias*, 117-19; Goldschmidt and Haas, *Haa Aaní: Our Land*, 45; and Thornton, "Know Your Place," 301, each comment on the extent of activity occurring at Lituya Bay in the late eighteenth century.

9 See Thornton, "Tlingit and Euro-American Toponymies"; and Bohn, *Glacier Bay*, 156-68. Of the 138 official names Dave Bohn documented in the Gulf of Alaska, 63 were explicitly named after individuals, usually early travellers or their patrons, and 4 were named after La Pérouse's crewmembers. Ten others were named after boats (including Astrolabe Bay and Boussole Bay, named for La Pérouse's ships). Three were named for sponsoring universities. Only 37 were minimally descriptive names, like White Glacier, Lone Island, and Pyramid Mountain.

10 See especially Thornton, "Know Your Place," 295, 298, 305. For instance, the mountain Tsalx̠aan (now Mount Fairweather) acts as a weather beacon, providing guidance to wind and weather patterns. However, it also serves as a clan crest that promotes solidarity among Tlingit clan members who were dispersed by the events discussed here, just as the songs associated with the same events may transport listeners to a time when their ancestors were lost in the tragic accident that is described in this chapter.

11 De Laguna, *Under Mount Saint Elias*, 81-91, 98-101, 792-95.

12 Emmons, "Native Account of the Meeting," 297-98.

13 De Laguna, *Under Mount Saint Elias*, 258, 273-74.

14 Ibid., 259.

15 Dauenhauer and Dauenhauer, *Haa Shuká, Our Ancestors*, 295, 297.

16 Ibid., 298. See also Kitty Smith's account of the arrival of k'och'en or "cloud people" from beyond the horizon who arrived in the Tatshenshini River valley: *The First K'och'en*, in Chapter 3.

17 De Laguna, *Under Mount Saint Elias*, 273-74, 1159.

18 Ibid., 274, 1160.

19 Emmons, "Native Account of the Meeting," 295.

20 See, for example, Dunmore, *Pacific Explorer*, 231; Inglis, "Lapérouse 1786," 57; and also the more extensive analyses of this theme on the North Pacific coast by McClellan, "Indian Stories"; and Ruppert, "The Russians Are Coming."

21 Emmons, "Native Account of the Meeting," 296. In another version, two young men were shown a mirror and reported back that they had been shown "a box of our images; we could just see ourselves." Dauenhauer and Dauenhauer, *Haa Shuká, Our Ancestors*, 309.

22 Milet-Mureau, *A Voyage Round the World*, 366-67.

23 Ibid., 370.

24 Ibid., 187.

25 Ibid., 372. Malaspina had a similar experience at Yakutat in 1791 when Tlingit expressed such intense interest in his instruments that he felt compelled to pack up his entire observatory tent and take his instruments on board ship each night; de Laguna, *Under Mount Saint Elias*, 146.

26 Milet-Mureau, *A Voyage Round the World*, 373.

27 Ibid., 374.

28 Ibid., 375.

29 Ibid., 378.

30 Ibid., 387.

31 Ibid., 407.

32 Ibid., 390.

33 Ibid., 390, 399-400.

34 Linnekin, "Ignoble Savages."

35 Milet-Mureau, *A Voyage Round the World*, 396.

36 Inglis, "Lapérouse 1786," 49.

37 Milet-Mureau, *A Voyage Round the World*, xliii.
38 Dunmore, *Pacific Explorer*, 299-303. French filmmaker Yves Bourgeois, working with a team of archaeologists, completed a film for French television, *Le Mystère de Vanikoro*, in 2001. They found evidence that members of the crew may have survived for some time before perishing on the island of Vanikoro; Bourgeois, *Le Mystère de Vanikoro*.
39 I am grateful to Frederica de Laguna for pointing out some of the changes in conceptions about ownership of narratives that she has observed since she began her work at Yakutat in the 1940s. Specifically she notes that ownership of narratives told by an ancestor, describing a personal transformative experience, are now more likely to be distributed among members of that ancestor's clan than they were when they were first told to her. See especially de Laguna, *Under Mount Saint Elias*, 758-90.
40 Several sources provide recent overviews of archaeology on the northern northwest Coast, especially Davis, "Prehistory of Southeastern Alaska," 197; Ames, "The Northwest Coast," 210; and Matson and Coupland, *Prehistory of the Northwest Coast*, 84-87. De Laguna documents changes at Yakutat Bay and Icy Bay in three of her publications: de Laguna et al., *Archeology of the Yakutat Bay Area*, 204-5; *Under Mount Saint Elias*, 26, 97; and "Tlingit," 206. Ackerman has conducted the most detailed archaeological reconnaissance at Lituya Bay; see his *Archeology of the Glacier Bay Region*.
41 Tarr and Butler, *Yakutat Bay Region*, 144.
42 De Laguna, "Tlingit," 206; Dauenhauer and Dauenhauer, *Haa Kusteeyí*, 3.
43 See Catton, *Land Reborn*.
44 De Laguna, *Under Mount Saint Elias*, 84, 93.
45 De Laguna, "Tlingit," 227.
46 Kan, *Memory Eternal*, 8.
47 De Laguna, *Under Mount Saint Elias*, 808; Kan, *Memory Eternal*, 10.
48 Thornton, "Tlingit and Euro-American Toponymies," 295.
49 Ladurie, *Times of Feast*, 170, 209.
50 Strommel and Strommel, "Year without a Summer," and Harington, *Year without a Summer?* discuss the evidence for 1816 as an extremely cold year in some, but not all, regions of the northern hemisphere.
51 Povinelli, *Labor's Lot*, 6.
52 Povinelli, "Do Rocks Listen?"
53 Shapin and Schaffer, *Leviathan and the Air Pump*.
54 Milet-Mureau, *Voyage Round the World*, 187.
55 Sobel, *Longitude*, 90.
56 Sorrenson, "The Ship as a Scientific Instrument," 221.
57 Milet-Mureau, *Voyage Round the World*, 11-44, 118-35, 136-39.
58 Ibid., 19, 24-29.
59 Ibid., 5, 7-8.
60 Ibid., 34, 37.
61 Ibid., i.
62 Ibid., 39-42. La Pérouse may already have given more thought to ethical issues than most of his contemporaries. Four years earlier, in 1782, he was dispatched to Hudson Bay with virtually no maps, through straits choked with icebergs and shrouded in dense fog, with instructions to destroy British forts. Arriving at Fort Churchill, La Pérouse found it undefended and under the supervision of Samuel Hearne who surrendered immediately. La Pérouse and his crew dined with Hearne and his employees at the fort, ushered them aboard a smaller boat, the *Severn*, and sent them back to England, destroying the fort only after everyone was safely aboard. Carrying on to Fort York, 150

miles further, La Pérouse took that fort as well, after bundling all the fort employees onto his own boats this time. Before leaving Fort York, he thoughtfully laid out stashes of food and ammunition for fort traders who had gone inland so that they would not starve later when they returned to find their fort destroyed. Dunmore, *Pacific Explorer*, 63-71. These gestures apparently motivated the British government to offer Cook's two compasses to La Pérouse for his subsequent voyage to the *Pacific Northwest.*

63 Milet-Mureau, *Voyage Round the World*, 182-83.
64 Ibid., 41.
65 Ibid., 38
66 Ibid., 381-86.
67 Ibid., 120, 187.
68 Ibid., 120-24.
69 Ibid., 124, 187-88.
70 Ibid., 126, 136.
71 Ibid., 136-37.
72 Ibid., 393-95.
73 Ibid., 376, 396.
74 Kan, *Memory Eternal*, 44.
75 De Laguna, *Under Mount Saint Elias*, 119.
76 Milet-Mureau, *Voyage Round the World*, 391.
77 Ibid., 125.
78 Ibid., 390.
79 Emmons, *Tlingit Indians*, 376-82.
80 Milet-Mureau, *Voyage Round the World*, 406.
81 Ibid., 398.
82 Shelikov, *A Voyage to America*, 83-105.
83 Emmons, "Native Account of the Meeting."
84 Kuklick and Kohler, "Introduction," 1-14.
85 This issue, raised by Marcel Mauss in *The Gift*, has been taken up and elaborated by Arjun Appadurai in *The Social Life of Things* and by Nicholas Thomas in *Entangled Objects*, works that have contributed greatly to our awareness of the complex relations linking objects with humans.
86 Dunmore, *Pacific Explorer*, 299.
87 Milet-Mureau, *Voyage Round the World*, xxxix. Milet-Mureau also took the opportunity to advocate the standardization of measurement and to make short shrift of the assortment of versts, leagues, metres, and feet that were peppering accounts. La Pérouse's temperatures, for instance, were measured on a Reaumur thermometer (with the freezing point of water as 0°R and the boiling point as 80°R), and he used Paris as his prime meridian, while Cook used Greenwich.
88 Dunmore, *The Journal of Jean-François de Galaup de La Pérouse.*
89 Ibid., 123-31, 132 n. 1.
90 Ibid., 108 n. 2; 110-11 n. 2; 132 n. 2; 144 n. 2.
91 Callon, "Techno-Economic Networks and Irreversibility," see especially 150-51.
92 Dunmore, *The Journal of Jean-François de Galaup de La Pérouse*, 139 n. 3.
93 Dauenhauer and Dauenhauer, Haa *Kusteeyí, Our Culture*, 15. De Laguna, as mentioned in note 39 above, states that this concept has gained new meanings since the 1940s.
94 Dauenhauer and Dauenhauer, *Haa Shuká, Our Ancestors*; *Haa Tuwunáagu Yís, For Healing Our Spirit*; and *Haa Kusteeyí, Our Culture.*
95 See, for example, Watson-Verran and Turnbull, "Science and Other Indigenous Knowledge Systems."

Chapter 5: Bringing Icy Regions Home

1 Dauenhauer and Dauenhauer, *Haa Shuká, Our Ancestors*, 410. When she worked with Susie James, an elder whose story about Glacier Bay we will hear in this chapter, Nora Dauenhauer also recorded the name Gathéeni (Sockeye Salmon River) for the ancient stream that once ran through the valley. The Glacier Bay National Park and Preserve Visitor Center, at Bartlett Cove, Alaska, gives the Tlingit name Teu-ken-hin (Straw River).

2 Menzies, *Alaska Travel Journal*, 162-63 n. 135. Menzies served as naturalist and ship's surgeon on Vancouver's expedition and reported that families were camped in temporary shelters near a creek just west of the ice wall. The ice wall they saw was probably ninety metres high when they arrived; Heacox, "Advances and Retreats," 6.

3 Wood, "Among the Thlinkits," 335. He was travelling north, intending to climb Saint Elias mountain, when he stopped here.

4 Muir, *Travels in Alaska*, 143. Spellings vary, but I follow the convention of using Huna to refer to the people, and Hoonah to identify the contemporary settlement.

5 Young, *Alaska Days*, 66.

6 Goldschmidt and Haas, *Haa Aaní: Our Land*, 54-55.

7 Tarr Inlet was even deeper in 1925 when it briefly crossed the Canadian border, but the Grand Pacific Glacier has advanced slightly since then.

8 Muir reported that eighteen hundred prospectors had already passed through Fort Wrangell in 1879 by the time he arrived in July; Muir, *Travels in Alaska*, 26. Young observed that twenty-five hundred Tlingits were resident there by that year; Young, *Hall Young of Alaska*, 83.

9 By 1879, Glacier Bay dwarfed the smaller nearby Lituya Bay that had so absorbed La Pérouse a century earlier. The two inlets now stood back to back, separated by a distance of only thirty kilometres, with terrestrial access blocked by the immense Fairweather Range (see Map 5).

10 Young, *Alaska Days*, 66, 185.

11 Swanton, *Tlingit Myths and Texts*; Dauenhauer and Dauenhauer, *Haa Shuká, Our Ancestors*.

12 Muir's *Travels in Alaska* appeared in 1915, a year after his death. Young's *Alaska Days with John Muir* was published the same year, 1915, and his crankier *Hall Young of Alaska: "The Mushing Parson"* appeared in 1927, almost fifty years after the men made these two trips.

13 Muir, *Travels in Alaska*, 58, 94, 110, 151.

14 De Laguna, *Story of a Tlingit Community*; Sealaska Corporation, *Angoon: A Century After*; Dauenhauer and Dauenhauer, *Haa K̲usteeyí, Our Culture*, 38.

15 Thomas Thornton, "Know Your Place," 300.

16 Dauenhauer and Dauenhauer, *Haa Shuká, Our Ancestors*, 410. Muir, as we saw, also heard this name for the bay, Sít Eeti G̲eey, and transcribed it as Sit-a-da-kay (Ice Bay).

17 Swanton, *Tlingit Myths and Texts*, 334-38. This event is also noted in Chapter 1.

18 Dauenhauer and Dauenhauer, *Haa Shuká, Our Ancestors*, 244-91.

19 Ibid., 247, 267.

20 Ibid., 271, 273. Notably, scientists have recently detected subglacial earthquakes in southern Alaska that last considerably longer than tectonic earthquakes of similar magnitude. These reportedly produce rapid mass movement in the glacier and a sensation of subglacial churning. See Ekström et al., "Glacial Earthquakes."

21 Dauenhauer and Dauenhauer, *Haa Shuká, Our Ancestors*, 422, 424.

22 Ibid., 253.

23 Ibid., 275.

24 Powell, "Role of Physical Sciences."
25 Muir, *Travels in Alaska*, 58.
26 Wolfe, *Son of the Wilderness*, 204, identifies the missionaries as Sheldon Jackson, Henry Kendall, A.L. Lindsley, and their unnamed wives. Jackson, architect of Alaskan Presbyterianism, subsequently assumed responsibility for Alaska Native education in 1885, when he was named Alaska's General Agent for Education.
27 Cited in Muir, *Travels in Alaska*, 74-75.
28 Young, *Alaska Days*, 16.
29 Muir, *Travels in Alaska*, 97, 101.
30 Ibid., 58, 103.
31 Young's reference to "DDs" refers to doctors of divinity. Muir referred to them more casually as "the Divines."
32 Hinckley, "Early Ministry of S. Hall Young."
33 Young, *Hall Young of Alaska*, 77. Notably, Muir had also heard Jackson speak at Yosemite earlier that year; Muir, *Letters from Alaska*, 20.
34 Muir and Young each wrote accounts of that journey and used different spellings of Tlingit names. Here I follow Muir's spellings for Toyatte and Kadachan; Young recorded them as Tow-a-aat and Kadashan.
35 Muir, *Travels in Alaska*, 115; Young, *Alaska Days*, 68-69.
36 When Swanton came to Wrangell twenty-five years later, in 1904, the majority of texts he recorded there were narrated by this same Kadachan (Swanton spells it Katishan) and his mother, whom Swanton does not name. Swanton, *Tlingit Myths and Texts*, 1; see also Dauenhauer and Dauenhauer, *Haa K̲usteeyí, Our Culture*, 754.
37 Engberg and Merrell, editors of Muir's *Letters from Alaska* provide a good discussion of their two routes with chronology and map; Muir, *Letters from Alaska*, 4, 103-6.
38 Muir, *Travels in Alaska*, 125, identified this as "Klugh-Quan, one of the Kupreanoff Kake villages."
39 Muir's transcription refers to present-day Kootznahoo Inlet, where the village of Angoon is now located. Goldschmidt and Haas, *Haa Aaní: Our Land*, 67.
40 Muir, *Travels in Alaska*, 134-35, 140-41.
41 Young, *Alaska Days*, 74, 127; Muir, *Travels in Alaska*, 204.
42 Missionaries were already christening Tlingit converts with names like Lot, Aaron, and Moses by 1880; Young, *Hall Young of Alaska*, 88.
43 Klotz, "Notes on Glaciers," 526-28.
44 This glacier is the setting for Muir's famous story of the dog "Stickeen," written after he returned from Alaska and published in *The Century Magazine* as "An Adventure with a Dog and a Glacier," then as a best-selling book, *Stickeen*, and later in a slightly different form in Muir's *Travels in Alaska*, 246-57.
45 Young, *Alaska Days*, 74, and *Hall Young of Alaska*, 219. De Laguna notes in *Under Mount Saint Elias*, 184, that Ivan Petroff reproduced Young's bean count in the first official Alaska census, claiming it as his own data, when it is not clear that Petroff ever visited the area.
46 Young, *Hall Young of Alaska*, 96.
47 Ibid., 100.
48 This passage from Muir's unpublished journals is cited in Wolfe, *John of the Mountains*, 273-74.
49 Mary Douglas, *Natural Symbols*, 17.
50 Engberg and Merrell, editors of Muir's *Letters from Alaska*, 65, provide this figure.
51 Wolfe quotes from some of Muir's early letters; Wolfe, *John of the Mountains*, 257, 259, 270-75. When Muir later found garden plots, he seemed almost relieved by this evidence of cultivation. See Muir, *Travels in Alaska*, 125.

52 Muir, *Travels in Alaska*, 123-24.
53 Ibid., 235-36.
54 Ibid., 150, 186. Muir cited this as his Tlingit crew's response to some prospectors who asked why they were out of meat.
55 See, for instance, Fienup-Riordan, *Eskimo Essays*, 161-91, and Wenzel, *Animal Rights*.
56 Muir, *Travels in Alaska*, 235.
57 De Laguna, *Under Mount Saint Elias*, 276, 287.
58 Young, *Alaska Days*, 74; Muir, *Travels in Alaska*, 169.
59 Muir, *Travels in Alaska*, 117.
60 Ibid., 141, 168; Young, *Alaska Days*, 82.
61 Young, *Alaska Days*, 63, 64; Muir, *Travels in Alaska*, 141, 145-46. As noted in Chapter 4, La Pérouse's behaviour seems also to have been interpreted as witchcraft.
62 Muir, *Travels in Alaska*, 201.
63 Ibid., 127.
64 Notably, it is Muir, rather than Young, who records this ambivalence toward misions in his *Travels in Alaska*: at Admiralty Island, pp. 131, 137, at Chilkat, p. 173, at Huna camps, p. 161, and at Hoonah village, p. 259.
65 Muir, *Travels in Alaska*, 171. George Davidson, an American scientist and surveyor, travelled to Klukwan, Alaska, in 1869 to observe a solar eclipse on 7 August. He and his party were thoroughly outfitted with the latest scientific instruments and made something of a stir as they passed through; hence the questions to Muir. While there, Davidson met the Chilkat chief Kohklux, also known as Shotridge, and the relative to whom Kadachan traced his northern connection in 1879. We will hear more about this expedition in Chapter 7.
66 Muir, *Travels in Alaska*, 221.
67 Ibid., 130, 163.
68 Ibid., 172, 173.
69 Branch, "Telling Nature's Story," suggests that Muir's contribution to Transcendentalism and Romanticism was his insistence that his goal was to "tell nature's story" rather than his own.
70 Young, *Alaska Days*, 100-2.
71 Ibid., 107.
72 Ibid., 138.
73 Muir, *Travels in Alaska*, 182.
74 Young, *Hall Young of Alaska*, 217; Muir's account of the same event is more subdued in *Travels in Alaska*, 192-93.
75 Muir, *Travels in Alaska*, 24; Young, *Alaska Days*, 174.
76 Young, *Alaska Days*, 178-82.
77 Fox, *John Muir and His Legacy*; see also two collections edited by Miller, *John Muir, Life and Work*; and *John Muir in Historical Perspective*.
78 See especially the work of Hinckley, "Early Ministry of S. Hall Young," and *The Canoe Rocks*.
79 Muir's article "The Alaska Trip" was directed specifically to this audience. Engberg and Morrell, editors of Muir's *Letters from Alaska* cite this figure of five thousand. Kimes and Kimes, *John Muir*, reproduce a travel brochure from this era that includes Muir's strong endorsement.
80 Cooper continued his long-term study of Glacier Bay throughout his career, and his series of three "Recent Ecological History" articles document this vegetative succession.
81 Young, *Alaska Days*, 188.
82 See Muir, "Discovery of Glacier Bay," and Catton's critical assessment in "Glacier Bay National Monument."

83 Limbaugh, *John Muir's "Stickeen."* Limbaugh is former Director of the John Muir Center for Regional Studies at the University of the Pacific in Stockton, CA.
84 Johnson, a former editor with *Scribner's*, came to *The Century Magazine* as associate editor in 1889, about the time he first met Muir. On this subject, see also Wolfe, *Son of the Wilderness*, 244-46.
85 Limbaugh, *John Muir's "Stickeen,"* 77, 86. Such ideas emerge most clearly in Muir's well-known story of being lost on Brady Glacier with the small dog Stickeen.
86 Ibid., 130.
87 Muir, cited in ibid., 85-86.
88 Muir, cited in ibid., 110.
89 Ibid., 66. Muir was elected president at the founding meeting of the Sierra Club, in 1892, and held that position for the rest of his life.
90 Muir, *Travels in Alaska*, 293.
91 See Goetzmann and Sloan, *Looking Far North*, 162-68, for a description and photographs documenting this event.
92 Cited in Dauenhauer and Dauenhauer, *Haa Kusteeyí, Our Culture*, 55-56.
93 Catton, *Inhabited Wilderness.*
94 Dauenhauer and Dauenhauer, *Haa Kusteeyí, Our Culture* 67.
95 Dauenhauer and Dauenhauer, *Haa Kusteeyí, Our Culture,* includes accounts of recent confrontations among elders and park officials, 160-61, and 457-58.
96 Ibid., 37, 50.
97 For a longer account of Mr. Hammond's presentation that day, see Cruikshank, *Social Life of Stories*, 145-47. When I visited Mr. Hammond at his home a year earlier with Clara Schenkel and Sharon Jacobs, two Yukon First Nation educators, he showed us the threatening letter, framed and hanging on his wall, that Nichols had written to Daanawáak, five years after Muir's visit:

> U.S. Pinta, Portage Bay, May 18, 1885
> To: Chief Donnawaak and Chief Clanaat and the Chilkoot Indians
>
> I have come here because the white men have told me that you had ordered them to go away and had threatened to kill them if they did not go. Better counsels have since prevailed and I am glad to find that the white men have gone about their business. This country is free to all white men to go through in the presence of their business; it is for your interest to have them there because they bring you wealth by your contracts to work for them. If any of the white men desire to do their own packing they must not be interfered with. The chief of the tribe and the headmen of families are by me held responsible for the good conduct of their people, and the white chief who governs the whole country is very angry with you for ill-treatment of peacable [sic] people passing through your country. Should their [sic] hereafter be any complaints or should there be any disturbances or outrages that call for my interference I shall punish the offenders to the full extent of the law.
>
> Henry E. Nichols
> Lt. Commander, U.S. Navy, and Senior Naval Officer, Alaska

98 Clifford, "Interview."
99 Hunn et al., "Huna Tlingit Environmental Knowledge."
100 Cronon, "The Trouble with Wilderness."
101 Spufford maintains that early British travellers were particularly prone to this view, and that they "almost all anthropomorphized ice, seeing its bleakness as a kind of geographical misery affecting the extremes of the earth." Spufford, *I May Be Some Time*, 14-15.

Chapter 6: Edward James Glave, the Alsek, and the Congo

1 Glave, "Our Alaska Expedition," 20 December 1890, 376.

2 De Laguna, *Under Mount Saint Elias*, 86.

3 Glave, "Our Alaska Expedition," 27 December 1890, 396-97. Their canoe journey began on the river local people then called "Alseck," the name Glave recorded. Subsequent visitors were less careful and sometimes redistributed the names then in use to refer to other rivers. The river Glave refers to as "Alseck" is now officially named the Tatshenshini and flows into a larger river, now named the Alsek. The earliest map of the region, drawn by the Tlingit Chief Kohklux in 1869, redrawn by scientist George Davidson in 1901, and discussed in Chapter 7, gives the name "Kaskarwurlsh" to the contemporary Alsek River, the name "All-segh" to the present-day Tatshenshini, and the name "Ta-tchan-seena" to the present Blanchard River. See Davidson, "Explanation of an Indian Map." See Figure 19.

4 Glave, "Our Alaska Expedition," 10 January 1891, 438.

5 Glave, "Our Alaska Expedition," 3 January 1891, 414.

6 Comaroff and Comaroff, *Of Revelation and Revolution*, 10.

7 Glave always refers to this as "Alaska." At the time he was writing, the location of this international boundary was much in dispute, and he was writing for an American weekly newspaper.

8 Glave, "Pioneer Packhorses in Alaska: 2. The Return," 870.

9 Riffenburgh, *Myth of the Explorer*, 112.

10 See Robbins, "Scribner's Monthly." Gilder was the editor-in-chief of *The Century Magazine* (successor to *Scribner's Monthly*) from 1881 until his death in 1909. We have seen in Chapter 5 how Robert Underwood Johnson, associate editor at *The Century Magazine*, edited John Muir's submissions. Johnson replaced Gilder as editor-in-chief in 1909.

11 Glave's diaries for 1890-91 are housed at the Elmer E. Rasmuson Library, University of Alaska. A copy produced by Elmer E. Rasmuson Micrographics is available at the Yukon Archives, Whitehorse, Yukon.

12 Glave, *Six Years*, 16.

13 Russell, "Glave's Career."

14 Gilder, "Death of Glave," 952.

15 Shanz, "Our Alaska Expedition," 28 June 1890, 440. Tlingit still largely controlled the passes to the interior, though a few small parties had managed to make the crossing; see McClellan, *My Old People Say*, 5.

16 Glave, "Pioneer Packhorses in Alaska: 1. The Advance," 672, 679, discusses rates the following year: two dollars per day or sixty dollars a month "and board." A few years later, Tlingit packers were able to raise their own rates dramatically when the Klondike gold rush attracted thousands of prospectors.

17 See Shanz, "Our Alaska Expedition," 5 July 1890, 466. The party expressed delight when a competitor, British alpinist Heywood Seton-Karr, who was three days ahead of them on the trail, informed them just before turning back himself, that he had named a tributary of the Chilkat River "Welleslie," a tongue-twisting honorific to salute both their expedition's leader (Wells) and its sponsor (Leslie).

18 Glave, "Our Alaska Expedition," 22 November 1890, 286. While Glave largely adheres to this principle, he seems to have been unable to resist the practice of naming entirely, reporting in this same series of articles names he gave to "Frederick Lake ... in loving memory of my brother who died a few years ago," 15 November 1890, 266; "Stanley Range," after his mentor Henry Morton Stanley, 22 November 1890, 286; and Harrison Range after the US president, 27 December 1890, 396. The renaming of Koosaa Aak (Kusawa Lake) by one of his companions to "Lake Arkell" provides one example of the confusion that resulted from such practices. The Tlingit name was Koosawu Áa (long

lake) reflecting their trading orientation; Athapaskans who congregated there to fish at the shallow narrows named the lake for those narrows, "Nakhu." When Mrs. Annie Ned, a Southern Tutchone elder explained this etymology, though, she still referred to it as "Lake Arkell" in English, even though "Kusawa" is again the official name. See Mrs. Ned's story, *Lake Arkell Glacier*, in Chapter 3.

19 Shanz, "Our Alaska Expedition," 5 July 1890, 466.

20 Ibid.

21 Glave, "Our Alaska Expedition," 9 August 1890, 572.

22 Shanz, "Our Alaska Expedition," 5 July 1890, 466-67.

23 Glave, "Our Alaska Expedition," 9 August 1890, 572.

24 In a letter to George Davidson, written 5 January 1891, Glave complains that a San Francisco reporter had written a newspaper article accusing Glave and Dalton of having "left the main party owing to some 'unexplained difference.'" Glave vigorously denied this charge, insisting that he had *written* instructions to explore the Alseck [sic] River to the coast. Glave, letter to George Davidson, Davidson collection, Bancroft Library, University of California, Berkeley. We hear more of Davidson in Chapter 7. I thank Linda Johnson for bringing this letter to my attention.

25 Glave, "Our Alaska Expedition," 15 November 1890, 266.

26 Glave, "Our Alaska Expedition," 22 November 1890, 286. These are Glave's transcriptions.

27 Glave, "Our Alaska Expedition," 9 August 1890, 572.

28 Glave, "Our Alaska Expedition," 22 November 1890, 286. Archaeologist Beth O'Leary, *Salmon and Storage,* conducted a thorough survey of sites in this region in the 1970s. She suggests that when Glave noted these "absences," he may have been travelling through a woodlot used as a source for firewood and house timbers, and that the people he failed to see on the Tatshenshini River may have been fishing on tributaries rather than along the fast-moving main branch. O'Leary, personal communication, 2003.

29 Glave, "Our Alaska Expedition," makes this point in several of his articles: 22 November 1890, 286; 29 November 1890, 310; and 6 December 1890, 332. Catharine McClellan learned in the 1940s and 1950s that this distinction was the chief local classification that Southern Tutchone people still used to differentiate "Fish people" living at Champagne, who relied chiefly on salmon, from "Hill people" living near Kluane Lake, who relied more heavily on meat, particularly sheep. McClellan, *My Old People Say*, 15, 98.

30 Glave, "Our Alaska Expedition," 22 November 1890, 286-87.

31 Glave, "Our Alaska Expedition," 20 December 1890, 376.

32 Glave, "Our Alaska Expedition," 6 December 1890, 332.

33 Glave, "Our Alaska Expedition," 13 December 1890, 352.

34 McClellan, *My Old People Say*, 23, 28.

35 Glave, "Our Alaska Expedition," 15 November 1890, 266.

36 Glave, "Our Alaska Expedition," 10 January 1891, 438.

37 Glave, "Our Alaska Expedition," 3 January 1891, 414.

38 Glave's two articles have the same title, "Pioneer Packhorses in Alaska," and different subtitles, "1. The Advance," and "2. The Return to the Coast." They were published in *The Century Magazine*, volumes 44, 5 and 44, 6 in 1892.

39 Glave, "Pioneer Packhorses in Alaska: 1. The Advance," 679.

40 Glave, "Unpublished Diaries," 1 August 1891, 186.

41 Glave, "Pioneer Packhorses in Alaska: 1. The Advance," 671, 673, 674. Leland Donald, in his book *Aboriginal Slavery* notes that Northwest Coast slavery diminished markedly in the second half of the nineteenth century, largely because of the disastrous population decline associated with epidemics.

42 Glave, "Our Alaska Expedition," 6 September 1890, 86; "Pioneer Packhorses in Alaska: 1. The Advance," 679.

43 Glave, "Pioneer Packhorses in Alaska: 2. The Return," 869.
44 Glave, "Unpublished Diaries," 11 June 1891, 103.
45 Glave, "Pioneer Packhorses in Alaska: 1. The Advance," 672.
46 See Gilder, "Death of Glave," 952.
47 Glave, "Pioneer Packhorses in Alaska: 1. The Advance," 676-77.
48 Ibid., 682.
49 Russell, "Glave's Career," 867.
50 McClellan, "Indian Stories," 125; Smith in Cruikshank et al., *Life Lived Like a Story*, 202-3. People do remember Dalton, by name, because he seized this entrepreneurial opportunity and returned later to establish a trading post at Neskataheen during the Klondike gold rush a few years later.
51 Mrs. Grace Johnson, personal communication, Burwash Landing, February 2002.
52 Glave, "Pioneer Packhorses in Alaska: 2. The Return," 872.
53 Ibid., 872.
54 Ibid., 873.
55 The Dezadeash River joins the Kaskawulsh River (flowing from Kaskawulsh Glacier) to produce the river now called the Alsek. Glave and Dalton probably crossed near the confluence.
56 Glave, "Pioneer Packhorses in Alaska: 2. The Return," 876.
57 Ibid., 878.
58 Glave, "Unpublished Diaries," 8 August 1891, 208; 12 August 1891, 214.
59 For Schwatka's details, see Harris, *Schwatka's Last Search*, Map C, p. 112, Map D, p. 160, and Log, p. 261. Glave's dates come from his own diaries, cited above (see note 11).
60 Glave, "Unpublished Diaries," 2 August 1891, 186. He also made this comment a year earlier in "Our Alaska Expedition," 9 August 1890, 572.
61 Harris, *Schwatka's Last Search*, 168.
62 Ironically in his published report, Glave states that they "found" the canoe in the bushes. Repeatedly in his accounts, Glave mentions the "scrupulous honesty" of his hosts and contrasts their behaviour with that in London and New York where to leave a personal article behind would probably result in its disappearance; see, for instance, Glave, "Our Alaska Expedition," 13 December 1890, 352. His own use (and then loss) of this canoe seems to confirm his point.
63 Glave, "Pioneer Packhorses in Alaska: 2. The Return," 878-79.
64 Ibid., 879.
65 Glave, "Unpublished Diaries," 5 September 1891.
66 The American edition of Glave's book was entitled *In Savage Africa, or Six Years of Adventure in Congo-Land*. The British edition omitted the first four words. All references here are to the 1893 British edition.
67 Glave, *Six Years*, 32-33.
68 Ibid., 45.
69 Harms, *River of Wealth*, 221.
70 Glave, *Six Years*, 43.
71 On the Alsek, Glave likewise praised as "remarkable ... the quiet and orderly conduct existing throughout the whole line of camps." Glave, "Our Alaska Expedition," 13 December 1890, 352.
72 Glave, *Six Years*, 69.
73 Robert Harms in *River of Wealth*, 92, 126-27, notes that while Bobangi began as one of many localized languages in this region, by the nineteenth century it had become the major language of traders for some nine hundred miles on this stretch of the Congo River. Fabian, *Language and Colonial Power*, discusses the significance of Swahili as a trade language in the eastern Congo.

74 Glave, *Six Years*, 44; "Pioneer Packhorses in Alaska: 1. The Advance," 673.
75 Glave, *Six Years*, 49.
76 Ward, *Voice from the Congo*, 218.
77 Glave, *Six Years*, 91-93.
78 Ibid., 133.
79 Ibid., 57.
80 Spellings all follow Harms, *River of Wealth*, except when quoting directly from Glave.
81 Glave, *Six Years*, 191. Harms, *River of Wealth*, 23-30, 36, says that no such group as Lofembé has ever been identified and suggests "lofembé" (Glave's "lufembé") may have been a general word for war. He argues that one paradoxical consequence of British efforts to end the overseas slave trade was that the internal slave trade in the Congo River basin actually intensified after 1839.
82 Glave imagined that he was buying their freedom, but because most slaves were transported far from home to remove them from kinship networks, he was probably endangering them. Living as unprotected individuals was out of the question, so the only option for a freed slave was to look for a new master. Harms, *River of Wealth*, 148-50.
83 Glave, *Six Years*, 229. Nancy Rose Hunt, in her book *Colonial Lexicon*, 39-42, notes that in the 1850s, Zanzibari traders from eastern Africa were moving westward into Central Africa in search of ivory, and that by the 1870s, Tippu Tip had become the dominant trader on the upper Congo River in both ivory and human slaves, making alliances with local big men.
84 Glave, *Six Years*, 209.
85 Riffenburgh, *Myth of the Explorer*, 2.
86 Driver, *Geography Militant*, 121.
87 This speech is cited in Russell, "Glave's Career," 867.
88 Gilder, "Death of Glave," 952.
89 Gilder, "Glave's Last Letter."
90 Lindqvist, in his book *Exterminate All the Brutes*, 23, focuses on this inconsistency and takes it for irresolution, but seems to have read only Glave's final article, "Cruelty in the Congo."
91 Glave's first episode, "Glave in Nyassaland," covers the period from mid-July 1893 until the end of March 1894 and was published posthumously in 1896. Five episodes were serialized in *The Century Magazine* in 1896 and 1897.
92 Glave, "Glave in Nyassaland," 606.
93 In his book *King Leopold's Ghost*, 228-29, Adam Hochschild cites an order Jules Jacques once issued to a subordinate after learning that villagers had cut some rubber vines to extract sap more quickly in order to meet their rubber quotas: "Decidedly, these people of [Inongo] are a bad lot ... We must fight them until their absolute submission has been obtained, or their complete extermination ... Inform the natives that if they cut another single vine, I will exterminate them to the last man."
94 Entries from late April until early July 1894 were published under Glave's authorship, as "Glave's Journey to the Livingstone Tree," in 1896.
95 Glave, "Glave's Journey to the Livingstone Tree," 769.
96 Records from mid-July until mid-September 1894 appeared under Glave's name as "Glave in the Heart of Africa," in 1896.
97 Glave, "Glave in the Heart of Africa," 925.
98 Ibid., 927.
99 Glave's notes from September 1894 until January 1895 appear as "New Conditions in Central Africa," in 1897.
100 Glave, "New Conditions in Central Africa," 905.
101 Ibid., 909.

102 Entitled "Cruelty in the Congo Free State," Glave's best-known article from this journey was published in *The Century Magazine,* 1897.
103 Glave, "Cruelty in the Congo Free State," 699. Possibly this is the man that Hochschild, *King Leopold's Ghost,* 229, identifies as Lemaire, whose diaries are self-incriminating.
104 Glave, "Cruelty in the Congo Free State," 704.
105 Ibid., 705-6.
106 Ibid., 709.
107 Ibid., 706. Firchow, *Envisioning Africa,* 230 n. 4, notes that Rom was assigned to Stanley Falls from 26 April 1894 until 1 November 1895.
108 Courtney, "An Experiment in Commercial Expansion."
109 Morel's book *Red Rubber,* credited as one of the key documents exposing Belgian practices in the Congo, cites Glave prominently. Morel, *Red Rubber,* 41.
110 Cookey, *Britain and the Congo Question,* 48.
111 Lindqvist, *Exterminate All the Brutes,* 21-29; Hochschild, *King Leopold's Ghost,* 140-45; Firchow, *Envisioning Africa,* 128-74. Lindqvist and Hochschild, though, rely only on Glave's last published diary entries, so their assessments of him are slender.
112 Firchow, *Envisioning Africa,* 128-47, and notes 229-33.
113 Ibid., 138.
114 Glave, "Cruelty in the Congo Free State," 709.
115 Vansina, "King Leopold's Congo," 358.
116 Ibid., 330; Hochschild, *King Leopold's Ghost,* 233.
117 Vansina, "King Leopold's Congo," 337, 358.
118 Ibid., 331.
119 Campbell, "Two Journals"; Glave, "Our Alaska Expedition," 29 November 1890, 310; 13 December 1890, 352.
120 Glave, "Our Alaska Expedition," 22 November 1890, 286.
121 Fortuine, *Chills and Fevers,* 230-33.
122 McClellan, *My Old People Say,* 24.
123 Glave, "Our Alaska Expedition," 20 December 1890, 376.
124 McClellan, *My Old People Say,* 28.
125 Ibid., 26 suggests that there were probably several raids. Linguistic anthropologist Patrick Moore has examined gender differences in the way narratives are framed by nearby Kaska speakers. He notes that accounts of warfare show well-defined differences between men's and women's accounts, with men likely to inflate mortality figures and women more likely to focus on causes of conflict and concern for victims, so this may also have influenced diverse accounts of raids at Dezadeash. See Moore, "Point of View in Kaska Oral Narratives," 139-63.
126 Davis, *Late Victorian Holocausts,* 12.
127 See Taussig, "Culture of Terror"; and also his *Shamanism, Colonialism and the Wild Man.*
128 See also Briggs and Mantini-Briggs, *Stories in the Time of Cholera.*
129 Cookey, *Britain and the Congo Question,* 65.
130 Taussig, "Culture of Terror," 472.
131 Casement visited Glave's grave at Matadi and noted in his diary on 16 August 1903, "poor old Ted Glave ... with all his memories around him." See Singleton-Gates and Girodias, *The Black Diaries,* 157.
132 Glave, *Six Years,* 98.
133 Glave, "Our Alaska Expedition," 20 December 1890, 396, my emphasis.
134 Ibid., 396.
135 The lower Alsek looked very different in 1890 from today. First, two of the glaciers Glave described as calving directly into the Tatshenshini (now known as the Walker Glacier and the Grand Plateau Glacier) are dramatically reduced in size and stand well

back from the river, though giant moraines loom as testimony to their size when Glave described them as calving directly into the river. Second, the catastrophic emptying of Neoglacial Lake Alsek some forty years earlier would have stripped the lower Alsek of any vegetation during Glave's day. Today, some of the locations he described as desolate wastelands are covered with rich and impenetrable vegetation.

136 Forfeitt, "Letter to the Editor," *The Times* (London), 3 January 1896.

137 Topham, "Visit to the Glaciers of Alaska," 425, is reported in de Laguna, *Under Mount Saint Elias*, 86, 89. Frederica de Laguna describes this arch as extending from a portion of the Grand Pacific Glacier that flows from Mount Fairweather and periodically crossed the Alsek in the past.

138 De Laguna, *Under Mount Saint Elias*, 87. See also Angela Sidney's account, *My Father's Dak̲l'aweidí History*, in Chapter 3.

Chapter 7: Mapping Boundaries

1 McClellan, "Intercultural Relations."

2 Adrian Franklin speaks compellingly about the role of such "primordial glue" in Australian nation-building in "Nation, Nature and Naturalisation."

3 Muir, *Travels in Alaska*, 171.

4 The Hudson's Bay Company had sponsored Robert Campbell's attempt to establish Fort Selkirk in 1848 near the junction of the Yukon and Pelly rivers in an early effort to push westward the border of British North America.

5 Davidson, "Explanation of an Indian Map"; see also Davidson, *The Alaska Boundary*, 13-16.

6 The story of locating the maps is itself an encounter narrative. Linda Johnson, then Yukon Archivist, had made inquiries to the Bancroft Library, which holds Davidson's papers, about whether the original Kohklux map was among them, and learned that they had no such map. On a subsequent visit to the library in 1984, she spoke to the map archivist who told her that the original owner of the papers had just recently located and donated two maps. The library subsequently agreed to lend the Yukon Archives these maps for a Yukon-Alaska conference that brought together coastal Tlingit, interior Tutchone, and Southern Tutchone speakers. Layers of stories resulting from this conference are described in a Yukon Historical and Museums Association publication, *The Kohklux Map* (1995), which includes full-size copies of both maps.

7 Glave, "Our Alaska Expedition," 6 September 1890, 86.

8 McClellan, "Before Boundaries." See also work done by Angela Sidney, *Place Names*; Gertie Tom, *Ekeyí: Gyò Cho Chú*; Margaret Workman, *Kwäday Kwändür*; Daniel Tlen and Patrick Moore, "Just Like Being There"; and others in their ongoing documentation of place names.

9 Lewis Green's compelling book *The Boundary Hunters*, now out of print, draws on archival documents – official reports, letters of participants, and unpublished manuscripts – to tell a story that is layered with political intrigue. Green also documents the physical labour that contributed to the surveying of Canada's northwestern border. I draw extensively on Green's work in this chapter.

10 "Treaty between Great Britain and Russia, Signed at St. Petersburg, February 28/16, 1825." The full text appears in the International Boundary Commission, *Joint Report* (1918), Appendix 1, 202-5.

11 Ibid.

12 "Treaty concerning the Cession of the Russian Possessions in North America by His Majesty the Emperor of all the Russians to the United States of America." Full text also appears in the International Boundary Commission, *Joint Report* (1918), Appendix 1, 208-11.

13 Schwatka, *Report of a Military Reconnaissance.*
14 Klotz, "Notes on Glaciers."
15 Dawson, *Report on an Exploration.*
16 Green, *Boundary Hunters*, 19-45.
17 Ibid., 50.
18 Ibid., 63.
19 Ibid., 79.
20 Ibid., 83.
21 Ibid., 84.
22 Cole, "Allen Aylesworth."
23 International Boundary Commission, *Joint Report* (1918), 87-88; *Joint Report* (1952), 250-52.
24 Cole, "Allen Aylesworth," 475-76.
25 Green, *Boundary Hunters*, 76.
26 Ingold, *Perception of the Environment*, especially 189-90.
27 Swanton, *Tlingit Myths and Texts*, 360.
28 De Laguna, *Under Mount Saint Elias*, 83.
29 Cited in ibid., 286.
30 Cited in ibid., 819.
31 Green, *Boundary Hunters*, 101.
32 Ibid., 123.
33 Wood, "Among the Thlinkits," 323.
34 Ibid., 332.
35 International Boundary Commission, *Joint Report* (1918), 88-89. See also Filippi, *Ascent of Mount St. Elias.*
36 De Laguna, *Under Mount Saint Elias*, 235.
37 International Boundary Commission, *Joint Report* (1918), 93.
38 Ibid., 96.
39 Ibid., 97.
40 Olson, *Through Spanish Eyes*, 345-46.
41 Tarr and Butler, *Yakutat Bay Region*, 35-36.
42 De Laguna, *Under Mount Saint Elias*, 86.
43 International Boundary Commission, *Joint Report* (1952), 106.
44 Ibid. In fact, Mount Katmai *imploded*, and the volcanic ash came from a nearby volcano known as Novarupta; however, some scientists think that the Novarupta eruption was directly triggered by the implosion of Mount Katmai. Rozell, "Sudden Disappearance."
45 Cited in de Laguna, *Under Mount Saint Elias*, 818-19.
46 British Columbia – Yukon – Northwest Territories Boundary Commission, *Report*, 19-21.
47 De Laguna, *Under Mount Saint Elias*, 85-86.
48 Blackwelder, "Glacial Features," 430. According to Blackwelder's report, which includes some of surveyor A.J. Brabazon's photos, Gateway Knob was at this time embedded in the ice wall (see Figure 22). For other vivid descriptions, see Farewell, "Heroism on the Alsek"; and Robson, "Conquest of the Alsek," 168-69.
49 De Laguna, *Under Mount Saint Elias*, 87.
50 Glave, "Our Alaska Expedition," 3 January 1891, 414.
51 Gillespie, *Journey*, 45.
52 Gillespie describes it as one hundred feet in 1906 and Robson as two hundred feet four years later, indicating how difficult it is to make visual estimates in such circumstances. See Robson, "Conquest of the Alsek," 168-69.
53 The incident was also reported in the International Boundary Commission, *Joint Report* (1952), 58.

54 This was a commercial raft trip run by James Katz, and I thank him enormously for including me to provide views from human history for other members of the group in 2003 and again in 2004.
55 Glave, "Our Alaska Expedition," 13 December 1890, 352.
56 Glave, "Our Alaska Expedition," 27 December 1890, 396.
57 Ibid., 396.
58 Ibid., 396.
59 De Laguna, *Under Mount Saint Elias*, 86.
60 This lake is not to be confused with Neoglacial Lake Alsek, which formed behind the Lowell Glacier, Nàlùdi, well upriver on the Alsek River (see Map 3).
61 Ninetyeighter Creek, the official name for a tributary of the Tatshenshini flowing from the Melbern Glacier, commemorates the gold rush. Nàlùdi has been renamed Lowell Glacier.

Chapter 8: Melting Glaciers and Emerging Histories

1 See Anderson, "Reindeer, Caribou," for a circumpolar perspective on these issues.
2 Ingold, *Perception of the Environment*, especially 153-56.
3 Hugh Raffles provides an elegant discussion of Victorian notions of "region" in his paper on naturalist Henry Walter Bates, "Uses of Butterflies," and expands its implications in his book *In Amazonia*.
4 Spufford, *I May Be Some Time*, 267-68. Spufford attributes his notion of "the stiffening metaphor" in turn to nineteenth-century anthropologist Edward Tylor.
5 Glave, "Our Alaska Expedition," 27 December 1890, 396.
6 David Hik, personal communication, 1991; Krajick, "Nunataks," 70.
7 The most recent dates are 1110 BP +/- 50, based on AMS scanning and calibrated to account for fluctuations of C14 in the atmosphere. David Arthurs, personal communication, 2 October 2003.
8 Kuzyk et al., "In Pursuit of Prehistoric Caribou." Mrs. Ned's orally narrated accounts about caribou in this region early in the twentieth century were cited in that paper.
9 Hare, "Out of the Northern Ice"; Krajick, "Melting Glaciers." The most detailed and current discussion of this to date comes from articles by Hare et al., "Ethnographic and Archaeological Investigations," and Farnell et al. "Multidisciplinary Investigations."
10 Pringle, "High Spirits."
11 A detailed discussion of methods used to arrive at these dates appears in Beattie et al., "Kwäday Dän Ts'ínchi," 135-36.
12 Beattie et al., "Kwäday Dän Ts'ínchi"; Monsalve et al., "Brief Communication." So far, DNA indicates only that the young man had closer connections with other Native Americans than with populations in Asia or Greenland. Botanists have determined more about his diet from bone samples. See Dickson et al., "Kwäday Dän Ts'ìnchí." In late 2003, tests are still continuing. A more general account appears in Pringle, "Out of the Ice."
13 Schama, *Landscape and Memory*, 5, 61.
14 Muir, *Travels in Alaska*, 94.
15 Glave, "Our Alaska Expedition," 27 December 1890, 396.
16 International Boundary Commission, *Joint Report* (1918), 93.
17 See, for example, Wynne, "May the Sheep Safely Graze"; Togola, "Memories, Abstractions and Conceptualizations"; Krupnik and Jolly, *Earth Is Faster Now*.
18 McIntosh et al., *The Way the Wind Blows*.
19 These stories are recorded in Cruikshank, *Athapaskan Women*, 164-67.
20 Tom, *Èkeyi: Gyò Cho Chú*, 70-72. This lake drains to the Thirty Mile River, which in turn enters the Yukon River at Hootalinqua.
21 Moore, "Point of View in Kaska Oral Narratives," 165-96.

22 Weaver, "Science of Climate Change."
23 Ingold and Kurttila, "Perceiving the Environment," 187.
24 See for example, McIntosh et al., *The Way the Wind Blows.*
25 Ranger, *Voices from the Rocks.*
26 Slater, *Entangled Edens*, 3-7.
27 McClellan, *My Old People Say*, 4, 17, 31; Nadasdy, *Hunters and Bureaucrats*, Chapter 1.
28 International Boundary Commission, *Joint Report* (1918), 43-45, 258.
29 McCandless, *Yukon Wildlife*; see also Cruikshank, "The Gravel Magnet."
30 For a detailed discussion of this history, see Nadasdy, *Hunters and Bureaucrats,* Chapter 1.
31 Under policies established for comprehensive land claims negotiations in Canada, Kluane First Nation raised this as a "Specific Claim," arguing that the Government of Canada was negligent in failing to carry out its lawful obligation to Aboriginal peoples when decisions about boundaries were made. Throughout the late 1990s, they argued their case to the Indian Claims Commission, an independent body established by Order in Privy Council to inquire into and report on disputes between First Nations and the Government of Canada. I participated in the role of expert witness at the invitation of Kluane First Nation during three days of Indian Claims Commission hearings in Burwash Landing during February 2002. Conclusions from that process were incorporated into ongoing land claims negotiations. On 18 October 2003, the Kluane First Nation, the Government of the Yukon, and the Government of Canada signed the Kluane First Nation Final and Self-Government Agreement.
32 MacEachern documents parallel processes in the Maritimes in his book *Natural Selections.*
33 Indian Claims Commission, "Kluane First Nation."
34 Nadasdy, *Hunters and Bureaucrats*, 273 n. 18.
35 Spufford, *I May Be Some Time.*
36 Matz, "World Heritage Wilderness."
37 For a fuller discussion, see Cruikshank, "Yukon Arcadia," in *Social Life of Stories*, 45-70.
38 Morrow and Hensel, "Hidden Dissension."
39 David Anderson makes this point in his general assessment of knowledge claims made in the circumpolar north. See Anderson, "Reindeer, Caribou."
40 Ingold and Kurttila, "Perceiving the Environment"; Nadasdy, *Hunters and Bureaucrats*, Chapter 3.
41 Raffles, *In Amazonia*, 152.
42 White, "Using the Past," 218.
43 Franklin, *Nature and Social Theory*; Slater, *Entangled Edens.*
44 Raffles explores different but related issues with reference to the Amazon River, and I draw on his perceptive insights from *In Amazonia*, 38, 181.
45 See Descola, "Societies of Nature"; Ingold and Kurttila, "Perceiving the Environment"; Giles-Vernick, *Cutting the Vines*; and Raffles, *In Amazonia.*
46 Franklin's argument about environmentalism is equally valid for TEK studies; see his *Nature and Social Theory*, 12.
47 Slater, *Entangled Edens*, 150.

Bibliography

Ackerman, Robert E. *The Archeology of the Glacier Bay Region, Southeastern Alaska.* Washington State University, Laboratory of Anthropology. Report of Investigations, No. 44. Pullman, WA: Washington State University, 1968.

Agrawal, Arun. "Dismantling the Divide between Indigenous and Scientific Knowledge." *Development and Change* 26 (1995): 413-49.

Ames, Kenneth M. "The Northwest Coast: Complex Hunter-Gatherers, Ecology, and Social Complexity." *Annual Review of Anthropology* 23 (1994): 209-29.

Anderson, David G. "Reindeer, Caribou and 'Fairy Stories' of State Power." In *Cultivating Arctic Landscapes: Knowing and Managing Animals in the Circumpolar North,* edited by David G. Anderson and Mark Nuttall, 1-16. Oxford: Berghahn, 2004.

Appadurai, Arjun. *The Social Life of Things: Commodities in Cultural Perspective.* Cambridge: Cambridge University Press, 1986.

Bakhtin, Mikhail. *The Dialogic Imagination.* Edited by Michael Holquist, and translated by Caryl Emerson and Michael Holquist. Austin: University of Texas Press, 1981.

–. *Rabelais and His World.* Translated by Helene Iswolsky. Bloomington: Indiana University Press, 1984.

Basso, Keith. *Wisdom Sits in Places: Landscape and Language among the Western Apache.* Albuquerque: University of New Mexico Press, 1996.

Beattie, Owen, Brian Apland, Eric W. Blake, James A. Cosgrove, Sarah Gaunt, Sheila Greer, Alexander P. Mackie, Kjerstin E. Mackie, Dan Straathof, Valerie Thorp, and Peter M. Troffe. "The Kwäday Dän Ts'ínchi Discovery from a Glacier in British Columbia." *Canadian Journal of Archaeology* 24 (2000): 129-47.

Beer, Gillian. *Open Fields: Science in Colonial Encounter.* Oxford: Clarendon Press, 1996.

Belcher, Edward. *Narrative of a Voyage Round the World Performed in Her Majesty's Ship Sulphur during the Years 1836-1842.* London: Henry Colburn, 1843.

Benjamin, Walter. "The Storyteller." In *Illuminations,* edited by Hannah Arendt, and translated by Harry Zohn, 82-109. New York: Schocken, 1969.

Blackwelder, Eliot. "Glacial Features of the Alaskan Coast between Yakutat Bay and the Alsek River." *Journal of Glaciology* 15, 5 (1907): 415-33.

Bohn, Dave. *Glacier Bay: The Land and the Silence.* San Francisco: Sierra Club, 1967.

Bolin, Inge. "'Our Apus Are Dying' – Glacier Retreat and Its Consequences for Life in the Andes." Paper delivered at American Anthropological Association Meetings, Chicago, November 2003.

Bourgeois, Yves. *Le Mystère de Vanikoro.* Documentary film. 2001.

Boyarin, Jonathan. "Space, Time and the Politics of Memory." In *Remapping Memory: The Politics of TimeSpace*, edited by Jonathan Boyarin, 1-37. Minneapolis: University of Minnesota Press, 1994.

Boyd, Robert. *The Coming of the Spirit of Pestilence: Introduced Infectious Diseases and Population Decline among Northwest Coast Indians, 1774-1874.* Vancouver: UBC Press/ Washington: University of Washington Press, 1999.

Branch, Michael. "Telling Nature's Story: John Muir and the Decentering of the Romantic Self." In *John Muir in Historical Perspective*, edited by Sally M. Miller, 99-122. New York: Peter Long Publishing, 1999.

Braun, Bruce. *The Intemperate Rainforest: Nature, Culture, and Power on Canada's West Coast.* Minneapolis: University of Minnesota Press, 2002.

–. "Producing Vertical Territory: Geology and Governmentality in Late Victorian Canada." *Ecumene* 7, 1 (2000): 7-46.

Briggs, Charles L., and Richard Bauman. "'The Foundation of All Future Researches': Franz Boas, George Hunt, Native American Texts and the Construction of Modernity." *American Quarterly* 51, 3 (1999): 479-528.

Briggs, Charles L., with Clara Mantini-Briggs. *Stories in the Time of Cholera.* Berkeley: University of California Press, 2003.

Bringhurst, Robert. *A Story as Sharp as a Knife: The Classical Haida Mythtellers and Their World.* Vancouver: Douglas and McIntyre, 1999.

British Columbia – Yukon – Northwest Territories Boundary Commission. *Report of the Commission to Delimit the Boundary between the Province of British Columbia and the Yukon and Northwest Territories.* Ottawa: Queen's Printer, 1966.

Brown, Jennifer S.H., and Elizabeth Vibert, eds. *Reading beyond Words: Contexts for Native History.* 2nd edition. Peterborough, ON: Broadview Press, 2003.

Bushnell, Vivian C., and M.G. Marcus. *Icefield Ranges Research Project: Scientific Results.* Vol. 4. New York and Montreal: American Geophysical Society and Arctic Institute of North America, 1974.

Bushnell, Vivian C., and Richard H. Ragle. *Icefield Ranges Research Project: Scientific Results.* Vols. 1-3. New York and Montreal: American Geophysical Society and Arctic Institute of North America, 1969, 1970, 1972.

Callon, Michel. "Techno-Economic Networks and Irreversibility." In *A Sociology of Monsters: Essays on Power, Technology and Domination,* edited by J. Law, 132-61. London and New York: Routledge, 1991.

Campbell, Robert. "Two Journals of Robert Campbell, 1808-1853." Limited Edition. Mimeographed typescript at Yukon Archives, Whitehorse, dated at Seattle, WA, 1958.

Carey, Mark. "Confronting Climate Change, Glacier Retreat and Outburst Floods in Peru: Local People's Views of Scientists and Their Science." Paper presented at the 84th Annual Meeting of the American Meteorological Society Annual Meeting, Seattle, WA, 13 January 2004.

–. "Managing Melting Glaciers: Climate Change, Society, and the State in Twentieth-Century Peru." PhD diss., Department of History, University of California, Davis, in progress.

Casey, Edward S. *Getting Back into Place: Toward a Renewed Understanding of the Place-World.* Bloomington: Indiana University Press, 1993.

–. "How to Get from Space to Place in a Fairly Short Stretch of Time." In *Senses of Place*, edited by Steven Feld and Keith H. Basso, 13-52. Santa Fe: School of American Research, 1996.

Castree, Noel, and Bruce Braun, eds. *Social Nature: Theory, Practice, and Politics.* Malden, MA: Blackwell, 2001.

Catton, Theodore. "Glacier Bay National Monument, the Tlingit, and the Artifice of Wilderness." *The Northern Review* 11 (1993): 56-82.
–. *Inhabited Wilderness: Indians, Eskimos and National Parks in Alaska*. Albuquerque: University of New Mexico Press, 1997.
–. *Land Reborn: A History of Administration and Visitor Use in Glacier Bay National Park and Preserve*. Anchorage, AK: National Parks Service, 1995.
Chamberlin, J. Edward. *If This Is Your Land, Where Are Your Stories? Finding Common Ground*. Toronto: Alfred A. Knopf Canada, 2003.
Clague, John J., and V.N. Rampton. "Neoglacial Lake Alsek." *Canadian Journal of Earth Sciences* 19 (1982): 94-117.
Clark, Katerina, and Michael Holquist. *Mikhail Bakhtin*. Cambridge, MA: Harvard University Press, 1984.
Clayton, Daniel. "Absence, Memory and Geography." *BC Studies*, 132 (2001-2): 65-79.
–. *Islands of Truth: The Imperial Fashioning of Vancouver Island*. Vancouver: UBC Press, 2000.
Clifford, James. "Interview with Brian Wallis." *Art in America* (July 1989): 86-87, 152-53.
Cohen, David William. *The Combing of History*. Chicago: University of Chicago Press, 1994.
Cole, Douglas. "Allen Aylesworth on the Alaska Boundary Award." *Canadian Historical Review* 52 (1971): 472-77.
Coleridge, Samuel. *The Poems of Samuel Coleridge*. London: William Pickering, 1848.
Comaroff, Jean, and John Comaroff. *Of Revelation and Revolution: Christianity, Colonialism and Consciousness in South Africa*. Chicago and London: University of Chicago Press, 1991.
Cooke, Bill, and Uma Kothari, eds. *Participation: The New Tyranny?* London: Zed Books, 2001.
Cookey, Sylvanus John Sodieye. *Britain and the Congo Question: 1885-1913*. London: Longmans, Green and Company, 1968.
Cooper, William S. "The Recent Ecological History of Glacier Bay, Alaska: I. The Interglacial Forests of Glacier Bay." *Ecology* 4, 2 (1923): 93-128.
–. "The Recent Ecological History of Glacier Bay, Alaska: II. The Present Vegetation Cycle." *Ecology* 4, 3 (1923): 223-46.
–. "The Recent Ecological History of Glacier Bay, Alaska: III. Permanent Quadrants at Glacier Bay: An Initial Report upon a Long-Period Study." *Ecology* 4, 4 (1923): 355-65.
Courtney, Leonard H. "An Experiment in Commercial Expansion." The Annual Address of the Right Hon. Leonard H. Courtney MA, MP, President of the Royal Statistical Society, Session 1898-99. In *Journal of the Royal Statistical Society* 61, 4 (1898): 640-67.
Cronon, William. "A Place for Stories: Nature, History and Narrative." *The Journal of American History* 78, 4 (1992): 1347-76.
–. "The Trouble with Wilderness: Or, Getting Back to the Wrong Nature." In *Uncommon Ground: Toward Reinventing Nature*, edited by William Cronon, 69-90. New York: W.W. Norton, 1995.
–. "The Uses of Environmental History." *Environmental History Review* 17, 3 (1993): 1-22.
Cruikshank, Julie. *Athapaskan Women: Lives and Legends*. Canadian Ethnology Service, Paper No. 57. Ottawa: National Museums of Canada, 1979.
–. "Contributions to the Oral History of the Kusawa Lake Region, Yukon Territory, from Mrs. Annie Ned." Report prepared for the Archaeological Survey of Canada, National Museum of Man, National Museums of Canada, 1985.

–. "Getting the Words Right: Perspectives on Naming and Places in Athapaskan Oral History." *Arctic Anthropology* 27, 1 (1990): 52-65.

–. "Glaciers and Climate Change: Perspectives from Oral Tradition." *Arctic* 54, 4 (2001): 377-93.

–. "The Gravel Magnet: Some Social Impacts of the Alaska Highway on Yukon Indians." In *The Alaska Highway: Papers of the 40th Anniversary Symposium*, edited by Kenneth Coates, 172-87. Vancouver: UBC Press, 1985.

–. *The Social Life of Stories: Narrative and Knowledge in the Yukon Territory.* Lincoln: University of Nebraska Press/Vancouver: UBC Press, 1998.

Cruikshank, Julie, in collaboration with Angela Sidney, Kitty Smith, and Annie Ned. *Life Lived Like a Story: Life Stories of Three Yukon Native Elders.* Lincoln: University of Nebraska Press/Vancouver: UBC Press, 1990.

Dauenhauer, Richard, and Nora Marks Dauenhauer. *Haa K̲usteeyí, Our Culture: Tlingit Life Stories.* Seattle: University of Washington Press/Juneau: Sealaska Heritage Foundation, 1994.

–. *Haa Shuká, Our Ancestors: Tlingit Oral Narratives.* Seattle: University of Washington Press/Juneau: Sealaska Heritage Foundation, 1987.

–. *Haa Tuwunáagu Yís, For Healing Our Spirit: Tlingit Oratory.* Seattle: University of Washington Press/Juneau: Sealaska Heritage Foundation, 1990.

–. "Oral Literature Embodied and Disembodied." In *Aspects of Oral Communication*, edited by M. Quasthoff, 91-111. Berlin: de Gruyter, 1995.

Davidson, George. *The Alaska Boundary.* San Francisco: Alaska Packers Association, 1903.

–. "Explanation of an Indian Map of the Rivers, Lakes, Trails and Mountains from the Chilkaht to the Yukon Drawn by the Chilkaht Chief, Kohklux in 1869." *Mazama* (April 1901): 71-82.

Davis, Mike. *Late Victorian Holocausts: El Niño Famines and the Making of the Third World.* London: Verso, 2001.

Davis, Stanley D. "Prehistory of Southeastern Alaska." In *Handbook of North American Indians.* Vol. 7, *Northwest Coast*, edited by Wayne Suttles, 197-202. Washington, DC: Smithsonian Institution, 1990.

Dawson, George. *Report on an Exploration in the Yukon District, N.W.T. and Adjacent Northern Portion of British Columbia, 1887, with Extracts Relating to the Yukon District from Report on an Exploration in the Yukon and Mackenzie Basins, 1887-88, by R.G. McConnell.* Ottawa: Geological Survey of Canada, 1898.

de Certeau, Michel. *The Practice of Everyday Life.* Translated by Stephen Rendall. Berkeley: University of California Press, 1984.

de Laet, Marianne, ed. *Research in Science and Technology Studies: Knowledge and Technology Transfer.* Vol. 13 of *Knowledge and Society.* Oxford, UK: Elsevier, 2002.

de Laguna, Frederica. *The Story of a Tlingit Community: A Problem in the Relationship between Archeological, Ethnological and Historical Methods.* Bureau of American Ethnology Bulletin 172. Washington, DC: Smithsonian Institution, 1960.

–. "Tlingit." In *Handbook of North American Indians.* Vol. 7, *Northwest Coast,* edited by Wayne Suttles, 203-28. Washington, DC: Smithsonian Institution, 1990.

–. *Under Mount Saint Elias: The History and Culture of the Yakutat Tlingit.* 3 vols. Smithsonian Contributions to Anthropology 7. Washington, DC: Smithsonian Institution Press, 1972.

de Laguna, Frederica, and Catharine McClellan. "Ahtna." In *Handbook of North American Indians.* Vol. 6, *Subarctic,* edited by June Helm, 641-63. Washington, DC: Smithsonian Institution, 1981.

de Laguna, Frederica, Francis A. Riddell, Donald F. McGeein, Kenneth S. Lane, and J. Arthur Freed. *Archeology of the Yakutat Bay Area, Alaska.* Smithsonian Institution

Bureau of American Ethnology, Bulletin 192. Washington, DC: US Government Printing Office, 1964.
Descola, Philippe. "Societies of Nature and the Nature of Society." In *Conceptualizing Society*, edited by Adam Kuper, 107-26. London, New York: Routledge, 1992.
Descola, Philippe, and Gísli Pálsson, eds. *Nature and Society: Anthropological Perspectives*. London, New York: Routledge, 1996.
Dickson, James H., Michael P. Richards, Richard J. Hebda, Petra J. Mudie, Owen Beattie, Susan Ramsay, Nancy J. Turner, Bruce J. Leighton, John M. Webster, Niki R. Hobischak, Gail. S. Anderson, Peter M. Troffe, and Rebecca J. Wigen. "Kwäday Dän T'sìnchí." *The Holocene* 14, 4 (2004): 481-86.
Donald, Leland. *Aboriginal Slavery on the Northwest Coast of North America*. Berkeley: University of California Press, 1997.
Douglas, Mary. *Natural Symbols: Exploration in Cosmology*. 1973. Reprint, with a new introduction, New York: Vintage Books, 1996.
Driver, Felix. *Geography Militant: Cultures of Exploration and Empire*. Oxford: Blackwell, 2001.
Dunmore, John. *The Journal of Jean-François de Galaup de La Pérouse, 1785-1788*. Vol. 1. London: Hakluyt Society, 1994.
–. *Pacific Explorer: The Life of Jean-François de Lapérouse*. Palmerston, NZ: Dunmore Press, 1985.
Dunmore, John, and Maurice de Brossard. *Le Voyage de Lapérouse, 1785-1788*. 2 vols. Paris: Imprimerie Nationale, 1985.
Ekström, Göan, Meredith Nettles, and Geoffrey A. Abers. "Glacial Earthquakes." *Science* 302 (2003): 622-24.
Ellen, Roy, Peter Parkes, and Alan Bicker, eds. *Indigenous Environmental Knowledge and Its Transformations: Critical Anthropological Perspectives*. Amsterdam: Harwood Academic Publishers, 2000.
Emmons, George Thornton. "Native Account of the Meeting between La Pérouse and the Tlingit." *American Anthropologist* 13 (1911): 294-98.
–. *The Tlingit Indians*. Edited with additions by Frederica de Laguna. Vancouver: Douglas and McIntyre, in association with the American Museum of Natural History, 1991.
Fabian, Johannes. *Language and Colonial Power: The Appropriation of Swahili in the Former Belgian Congo, 1880-1938*. Cambridge: Cambridge University Press, 1986.
–. *Out of Our Minds: Reason and Madness in the Exploration of Central Africa*. Berkeley: University of California Press, 2000.
–. *Remembering the Present: Painting and Popular History in Zaire*. Berkeley: University of California Press, 1996.
Fagan, Brian. *The Little Ice Age: How Climate Made History, 1300-1850*. New York: Basic Books, 2000.
Fairhead, James, and Melissa Leach. *Misreading the African Landscape: Society and Ecology in a Forest-Savanna Mosaic*. Cambridge: Cambridge University Press, 1996.
Farewell, George E. "Heroism on the Alsek." *Sunset Magazine* 22, 5 (1909): 531-36.
Farnell, Richard, P. Gregory Hare, Erik Blake, Vandy Bower, Charles Schweger, Sheila Greer, and Ruth Gotthardt. "Multidisciplinary Investigations of Alpine Ice Patches in Southwest Yukon, Canada: Paleoenviromental and Paleobiological Investigations." *Arctic* 57, 3 (2004): 247-59.
Fee, Margery. "The Social Work of Stories." *ZKS: Zeitschrift für Kanada-Studien* (2000): 1-13.
Feld, Steven, and Keith H. Basso, eds. *Senses of Place*. Santa Fe: School of American Research, 1996.

Fienup-Riordan, Ann. *Boundaries and Passages: Rule and Ritual in Yup'ik Eskimo Oral Tradition*. Norman, OK: University of Oklahoma Press, 1994.
–. *Eskimo Essays: Yup'ik Lives and How We See Them*. New Brunswick, NJ: Rutgers University Press, 1990.
–. "Yaqulget Qaillun Pilartat (What the Birds Do): Yup'ik Eskimo Understanding of Geese and Those Who Study Them." *Arctic* 52, 1 (1999): 1-22.
Filippi, Filippo de. *The Ascent of Mount St. Elias (Alaska) by Prince Luigi Amedeo di Savoia, Duke of the Abruzzi*. Westminster: Archibald Constable and Co., 1900.
Firchow, Peter Edgerly. *Envisioning Africa: Racism and Imperialism in Conrad's "Heart of Darkness."* Lexington: University of Kentucky Press, 2000.
Forfeitt, Lawson. "Letter to the Editor." *The Times* (London), 3 January 1896, 8.
Fortuine, Robert. *Chills and Fevers: Health and Disease in the Early History of Alaska*. Fairbanks: University of Alaska Press, 1989.
Fox, Stephen R. *John Muir and His Legacy: The American Conservation Movement*. Boston: Little, Brown, 1981.
Fradkin, Philip L. *Wildest Alaska: Journeys of Great Peril in Lituya Bay*. Berkeley: University of California Press, 2001.
Franklin, Adrian. "Nation, Nature and Naturalisation: The Case of Australia." Presentation to Department of Social Anthropology, University of Oslo, 10 October 2001.
–. *Nature and Social Theory*. London: Sage, 2002.
Frye, Northrop. *The Educated Imagination*. Toronto: Canadian Broadcasting Corporation, 1963.
Gibson, James R. "Smallpox on the Northwest Coast, 1835-38." *BC Studies*, 56 (1982-83): 61-81.
Gilder, Richard Watson. "The Death of Glave." *The Century Magazine* 50, 6 (1895): 951-52.
–. "Glave's Last Letter and His Death." *The Century Magazine* 54, 5 (1897): 796-98.
–. "The Heart of Dr. Livingstone." *The Century Magazine* 50, 1 (1895): 100-2.
Giles-Vernick, Tamara. *Cutting the Vines of the Past: Environmental Histories of the Central African Rain Forest*. Charlottesville: University Press of Virginia, 2002.
Gillespie, Alexander. *Journey through Life*. Victoria, BC: Victoria Press, 1954.
Glave, Edward James. "Cruelty in the Congo Free State: Concluding Extracts from the Journals of the Late E.J. Glave." *The Century Magazine* 54, 5 (1897): 699-715.
–. "Glave in Nyassaland. British Raids on the Slave Traders." *The Century Magazine* 52, 4 (1896): 589-606.
–. "Glave in the Heart of Africa. Peace and War between Lakes Bangweolo and Tanganyika." *The Century Magazine* 52, 6 (1896): 918-33.
–. "Glave's Journey to the Livingstone Tree: Glimpses of Life in Africa from the Journals of the Late E.J. Glave." *The Century Magazine* 52, 5 (1896): 765-81.
–. "New Conditions in Central Africa." *The Century Magazine* 53, 6 (1897): 900-15.
–. "Our Alaska Expedition." *Frank Leslie's Illustrated Newspaper* 70: 510-11 (19 July 1890); 572 (9 August 1890); 86-87 (6 September 1890); 266 (15 November 1890); 286-87 (22 November 1890); 310 (29 November 1890); 332 (6 December 1890); 352 (13 December 1890); 376 (20 December 1890); 396-97 (27 December 1890); vol. 71: 414 (3 January 1891); 438 (10 January 1891).
–. "Pioneer Packhorses in Alaska: 1. The Advance." *The Century Magazine* 44, 5 (1892): 671-82.
–. "Pioneer Packhorses in Alaska: 2. The Return to the Coast." *The Century Magazine* 44, 6 (1892): 869-81.
–. *Six Years of Adventure in Congo-Land*. London: Samson, Marston and Company, 1893.

–. "Unpublished Diaries 1890-91." Elmer E. Rasmuson Library, University of Alaska. Copied as Elmer E. Rasmuson Micrographics, Yukon Archives, Whitehorse, Yukon.

Goetzmann, William, and Kay Sloan. *Looking Far North: The Harriman Expedition to Alaska, 1899.* New York: Viking Press, 1982.

Goldschmidt, Walter R., and Theodore H. Haas. *Haa Aaní: Our Land. Tlingit and Haida Land Rights and Use.* Edited with an introduction by Thomas F. Thornton. Seattle: University of Washington Press, 1998.

Green, Lewis. *The Boundary Hunters: Surveying the 141st Meridian and the Alaska Panhandle.* Vancouver: UBC Press, 1982.

Grove, Jean. *The Little Ice Age.* London: Methuen, 1988.

Hamilton, Carolyn. "'Living by Fluidity': Oral Histories, Material Custodies and the Politics of Archiving." In *Refiguring the Archive*, edited by Carolyn Hamilton, Verne Harris, Jane Taylor, Michele Pickover, Graeme Reid, and Razia Saleh, 209-27. Dordrecht, Boston, and London: Kluwer Academic Publishers, 2002.

–. *Terrific Majesty: The Powers of Shaka Zulu and the Limits of Historical Invention.* Cambridge, MA: Harvard University Press, 1998.

Hare, Greg. "Out of the Northern Ice." In *Glaciers of Alaska*, edited by Bruce Molnia. Special issue. *Alaska Geographic* 28, 2 (2001): 42-44.

Hare, P. Gregory, Sheila Greer, Ruth Gotthardt, Richard Farnell, Vandy Bower, Charley Schweger, and Diane Strand. "Ethnographic and Archaeological Investigations of Alpine Ice Patches in Southwest Yukon, Canada." *Arctic* 57, 3 (2004): 260-72.

Harington, C. Richard, ed. *The Year without a Summer? World Climate in 1816.* Ottawa: Canadian Museum of Nature, 1992.

Harms, Robert W. *River of Wealth, River of Sorrow: The Central Zaire Basin in the Era of the Slave and Ivory Trade, 1500-1891.* New Haven, CT, and London: Yale University Press, 1981.

Harris, Arland S., ed. *Schwatka's Last Search: The New York Ledger Expedition through Unknown Alaska and British America.* Fairbanks: University of Alaska Press, 1996.

Harris, Cole. "How Did Colonialism Dispossess? Comments from an Edge of Empire." *Annals of the Association of American Geographers* 94, 1 (2004): 165-82.

–. *Making Native Space: Colonialism, Resistance, and Reserves in British Columbia.* Vancouver: UBC Press, 2002.

Heacox, Kim S. "Advances and Retreats at Glacier Bay." *Pacific Discovery* 36, 4 (1983): 4-17.

Hevly, Bruce. "The Heroic Science of Glacier Motion." In *Osiris*, Vol. 11: *Science in the Field*, 2nd series, edited by Henrika Kuklick and Robert E. Kohler, 66-86. Chicago: University of Chicago Press Journals Division, 1996.

Hinchman, Lewis P., and Sandra K. Hinchman, eds. *Memory, Identity, Community: The Idea of Narrative in the Human Sciences.* Albany: State University of New York Press, 1998.

Hinckley, Ted C. *The Canoe Rocks: Alaska's Tlingit and the Euramerican Frontier, 1800-1912.* Lanham, MD: University Press of America, 1996.

–. "The Early Ministry of S. Hall Young, 1878-1888." In *An Alaska Anthology: Interpreting the Past*, edited by Stephen W. Haycox and Mary Childers Mangusso, 34-155. Seattle: University of Washington Press, 1996.

Hirsch, Eric. "Introduction: Landscape; Between Place and Space." In *The Anthropology of Landscape: Perspectives on Place and Space*, edited by Eric Hirsch and Michael O'Hanlon, 1-29. Oxford: Clarendon, 1995.

Hochschild, Adam. *King Leopold's Ghost.* Boston: Houghton Mifflin, 1998.

Hofmeyer, Isabel. *We Spend Our Years as a Tale That Is Told: Oral Historical Narrative in a South African Chiefdom.* Johannesburg: Witwatersrand University Press, 1994.

Holdsworth, Gerald. *Mount Logan on CD-ROM*. Vol. 1. Calgary: Arctic Institute of North America, 1999.

Hornborg, Alf, and Gísli Pálsson, eds. *Negotiating Nature: Culture, Power and Environmental Argument*. Lund, Sweden: Lund University Press, 2000.

Hunn, Eugene S., Darryll R. Johnson, Priscilla N. Russell, and Thomas F. Thornton. "Huna Tlingit Environmental Knowledge, Conservation, and the Management of a 'Wilderness' Park." *Current Anthropology* 44, Supplement (December 2003): S79-S103.

Hunt, Nancy Rose. *A Colonial Lexicon of Birth Ritual, Medicalization and Mobility in the Congo*. Durham and London: Duke University Press, 1999.

Indian Claims Commission. "Kluane First Nation: Kluane National Park and Game Sanctuary Specific Claim." Proceedings Held in Jacquot Building, Burwash Landing, Yukon Territory, 6-8 February 2002.

Inglis, Richard. "Lapérouse 1786: A French Naval Visit to Alaska." In *Enlightenment and Exploration in the North Pacific 1741-1805*, edited by Stephen Haycox, James Barnett, and Caedmon Liburd, 49-64. Seattle: University of Washington Press, 1997.

Ingold, Tim. "From Culture and Environment to Landscape and Memory." In *Negotiating Nature: Culture, Power and Environmental Argument*, edited by Alf Hornborg and Gísli Pálsson, 213-24. Lund, Sweden: Lund University Press, 2000.

–. *The Perception of the Environment*. London and New York: Routledge, 2000.

Ingold, Tim, and Terhi Kurttila. "Perceiving the Environment in Finnish Lapland." *Body and Society* 6, 3-4 (2000): 183-96.

Innis, Harold. *The Bias of Communication*. Toronto: University of Toronto Press, 1951.

–. *The Cod Fisheries: The History of an International Economy*. Toronto: University of Toronto Press, 1940.

–. *Empire and Communications*. Oxford: Clarendon, 1950.

–. *Essays in Canadian Economic History*. Toronto: University of Toronto Press, 1956.

–. *The Fur Trade in Canada*. Toronto: University of Toronto Press, 1930.

Intergovernmental Panel on Climate Change (IPCC). *Climate Change, 2001: The Scientific Basis*. Edited by J.T. Houghton. Cambridge: Cambridge University Press, 2001.

International Boundary Commission. *Joint Report upon the Survey and Demarcation of the International Boundary between the United States and Canada along the 141st Meridian from the Arctic Ocean to Mount Saint Elias*. Ottawa and Washington: King's Printer and Government Printing Office, 1918.

–. *Joint Report upon the Survey and Demarcation of the International Boundary between the United States and Canada from Tongass Passage to Mount St. Elias*. Ottawa and Washington: King's Printer and Government Printing Office, 1952.

Jacoby, G.R., and E.R. Cook. "Past Temperature Variations Inferred from a 400-Year Tree-Ring Chronology from Yukon Territory, Canada." *Arctic and Alpine Research* 13, 4 (1981): 409-18.

Kan, Sergei. *Memory Eternal: Tlingit Culture and Russian Orthodox Christianity through Two Centuries*. Seattle: University of Washington Press, 1999.

Khubova, Daria, Andrei Ivankiev, and Tania Sharova, eds. "After Glasnost: Oral History in the Soviet Union." In *Memory and Totalitarianism*, edited by Luisa Passerini, 89-101. Oxford: Oxford University Press, 1992.

Kimes, William F., and Maymie B. Kimes, eds. *John Muir: A Reading Bibliography*. Palo Alto: W.P. Wreden, 1977.

Klotz, Otto Julius. "Notes on Glaciers of Southeastern Alaska and Adjoining Territory." *Geographical Journal* 14 (1899): 523-34.

Krajick, Kevin. "Melting Glaciers Release Ancient Relics." *Science* 296 (2002): 454-56.

–. "Nunataks: Icebound Islands of Life." *National Geographic* 194, 6 (1998): 60-71.

Krauss, Michael E., ed. *In Honor of Eyak: The Art of Anna Nelson Harry.* Fairbanks: Alaska Native Language Center, 1982.

Krupnik, Igor, and Dyanna Jolly. *The Earth Is Faster Now: Indigenous Observations of Arctic Environmental Change.* Fairbanks: Arctic Consortium of the United States, 2002.

Kuklick, Henrika, and Robert E. Kohler. "Introduction." In *Osiris,* Vol. 11: *Science in the Field,* 2nd series, edited by Henrika Kuklick and Robert E. Kohler, 1-14. Chicago: University of Chicago Press Journals Division, 1996.

Kuzyk, Gerald W., Donald E. Russell, Richard S. Farnell, Ruth M. Gotthardt, P. Gregory Hare, and Erik Blake. "In Pursuit of Prehistoric Caribou on Thandlät, Southern Yukon." *Arctic* 52, 2 (1999): 214-19.

Ladurie, Emmanuel LeRoy. *Times of Feast, Times of Famine: A History of Climate Since the Year 1000.* New York: Doubleday, 1971.

Latour, Bruno. *We Have Never Been Modern.* Cambridge, MA: Harvard University Press, 1993.

Lévi-Strauss, Claude. *The Way of the Masks.* Translated by Sylvia Modelski. Seattle/Vancouver: University of Washington Press/Douglas and McIntyre, 1982.

Leydesdorff, Selma, Luisa Passerini, and Paul Thompson. "Introduction." In *Gender and Memory,* edited by Selma Leydesdorff, Luisa Passerini, and Paul Thompson, 1-16. Oxford: Oxford University Press, 1996.

Limbaugh, Ronald. *John Muir's "Stickeen" and the Lessons of Nature.* Fairbanks: University of Alaska Press, 1996.

Lindqvist, Sven. *Exterminate All the Brutes.* Translated by Joan Tate. London: Granta Books, 1996.

Linnekin, Jocylyn. "Ignoble Savages and Other European Views: The La Pérouse Affair in Samoan History." *The Journal of Pacific History* 26, 1 (1991): 3-26.

Lord, Nancy. *Green Alaska: Dreams from the Far Coast.* Washington, DC: Counterpoint, 1999.

McCandless, Robert. *Yukon Wildlife: A Social History.* Edmonton: University of Alberta Press, 1985.

McClellan, Catharine. "Before Boundaries: Peoples of Yukon/Alaska." In *Borderlands: A Conference on the Alaska-Yukon Border, Whitehorse, Yukon, 2-4 June 1989,* 8-34. Proceedings. Whitehorse: Yukon Historical and Museums Association, 1992.

–. "Indian Stories about the First Whites in Northwestern North America." In *Ethnohistory in Southwestern Alaska and the Southern Yukon: Method and Content,* edited by Margaret Lantis, 103-33. Lexington: University Press of Kentucky, 1970.

–. "Intercultural Relations and Cultural Change in the Cordillera." In *Handbook of North American Indians.* Vol. 6, *Subarctic,* edited by June Helm, 387-401. Washington, DC: Smithsonian Institution, 1981.

–. *My Old People Say: An Ethnographic Survey of Southern Yukon Territory.* 2 vols. Mercury Series, Canadian Ethnology Service Paper 137. 1975. Reprint, Ottawa: Canadian Museum of Civilization, 2001.

MacEachern, Alan. *Natural Selections: National Parks in Atlantic Canada, 1935-1970.* Montreal and Kingston: McGill-Queen's University Press, 2001.

McIntosh, Roderick J., Joseph A. Tainter, and Susan Keech McIntosh, eds. *The Way the Wind Blows: Climate, History, and Human Action.* New York: Columbia University Press, 2000.

McIntyre, Alisdair. *After Virtue: A Study in Moral Theory*. Notre Dame, IN: University of Notre Dame Press, 1981.
Macnaghten, Phil, and John Urry. *Contested Natures*. London: Sage, 1998.
Marchand, John. "Tribal Epidemics in the Yukon." *Journal of the American Medical Association* 123 (1943): 1019-20.
Martindale, Thomas. *Hunting in the Upper Yukon*. Philadelphia: G.W. Jacobs and Co., 1913.
Matson, R.G., and Gary Coupland. *The Prehistory of the Northwest Coast*. New York: Academic Press, 1995.
Matz, George, ed. "World Heritage Wilderness: From the Wrangells to Glacier Bay." Special issue of *Alaska Geographic* 26, 2 (1999).
Mauss, Marcel. *The Gift*. 1924. Reprint, London: Routledge, 1966.
Menzies, Archibald. *The Alaska Travel Journal of Archibald Menzies, 1793-1794*. Edited by Wallace M. Olson. Fairbanks: University of Alaska Press, 1993.
Milet-Mureau, Louis Antoine, ed. *A Voyage Round the World, Performed in the Years 1785, 1786, 1787 and 1788 by the Boussole and Astrolabe under the Command of J.F.G. de La Pérouse*. London: G.G. and J. Robinson, 1799.
Miller, Don J. *Giant Waves in Lituya Bay, Alaska*. US Geological Survey Professional Paper, 354-C, 51-86. Washington, DC: Government Printing Office, 1960.
Miller, Sally M., ed. *John Muir in Historical Perspective*. New York: Peter Long, 1999.
–, ed. *John Muir, Life and Work*. Albuquerque: University of New Mexico Press, 1993.
Milton, Kay. *Loving Nature: Towards an Ecology of Emotion*. London and New York: Routledge, 2002.
Monsalve, M. Victoria, Anne C. Stone, Cecil M. Lewis, Allan Rempel, Michael Richards, Dan Straathof, and Dana V. Devine. "Brief Communication: Molecular Analysis of the Kwäday Dän Ts'ìnchi Ancient Remains Found in a Glacier in Canada." *American Journal of Physical Anthropology* 119 (2002): 288-91.
Moore, Patrick. *Dene Gudeji: Kaska Narratives*. Whitehorse: Kaska Tribal Council, 1999.
–. "Point of View in Kaska Oral Narratives." PhD diss., Department of Anthropology, Indiana University, 2002.
Morel, Edward. *Red Rubber: The Story of the Rubber Trade Which Flourished in the Congo for Twenty Years, 1890-1910*. New and revised edition. Manchester: National Labour Press, 1919.
Morrow, Phyllis. "On Shaky Ground: Folklore, Collaboration and Problematic Outcomes." In *When Our Words Return: Writing, Hearing and Remembering Oral Traditions of Alaska and the Yukon*, edited by Phyllis Morrow and William Schneider, 27-51. Logan: Utah State University Press, 1995.
Morrow, Phyllis, and Chase Hensel. "Hidden Dissension: Minority-Majority Relationships and the Uses of Contested Terminology." *Arctic Anthropology* 29, 1 (1992): 38-53.
Muir, John. "An Adventure with a Dog and a Glacier." *The Century Magazine* 54, 5 (1897): 769-76.
–. "The Alaska Trip." *The Century Magazine* 54, 4 (1897): 513-26.
–. "The Discovery of Glacier Bay." *The Century Magazine* 50, 2 (1895): 234-47.
–. *Letters from Alaska*, edited by Robert Engberg and Bruce Merrell. Madison: University of Wisconsin Press, 1993.
–. *Stickeen*. Boston: Houghton Mifflin, 1909.
–. *Travels in Alaska*. Introduction by Edward Way Teale. 1915. Reprint, with a foreword by David Rains Wallace, Boston: Houghton Mifflin, 1998.

Muratorio, Blanca. *The Life and Times of Grandfather Alonso: Culture and History in the Upper Amazon*. New Brunswick, NJ: Rutgers University Press, 1991.

Murray, Alexander Hunter. *Journal of the Yukon, 1847-48*. Ottawa: Government Printing Bureau, 1910.

Nadasdy, Paul. *Hunters and Bureaucrats: Power, Knowledge, and Aboriginal-State Relations in the Southwest Yukon*. Vancouver: UBC Press, 2003.

–. "The Politics of TEK: Power and the 'Integration' of Knowledge." *Arctic Anthropology* 36, 1-2 (1999): 1-18.

Nash, June. *We Eat the Mines and the Mines Eat Us: Dependency and Exploitation in Bolivian Tin Mines*. New York: Columbia University Press, 1979.

Ned, Annie. *Old People in Those Days, They Told Their Story All the Time*. Edited by Julie Cruikshank. Whitehorse: Yukon Native Languages Project, 1984.

Nyman, Elizabeth, and Jeff Leer, *Gágiwdul.àt: Brought Forth to Reconfirm: The Legacy of a Taku River Tlingit Clan*. Whitehorse: Yukon Native Language Centre/Fairbanks: Alaska Native Language Center, 1993.

O'Leary, Beth. *Salmon and Storage: Southern Tutchone Use of an "Abundant" Resource*. Whitehorse: Yukon Heritage Branch, Government of the Yukon, 1992.

Olson, Wallace M. *Through Spanish Eyes: Spanish Voyages to Alaska, 1774-1792*. Auke Bay, AK: Heritage Research, 2002.

Overpeck, J., K. Hughen, D. Hardey, R. Bradley, R. Case, M. Douglas, B. Finney, C. Gajewski, G. Jacoby, A. Jennings, S. Lamoureaux, A. Lasca, G. MacDonald, J. Moore, M. Reteile, S. Smith, A. Wolfe, and G. Zielinski. "Arctic Environmental Change of the Last Four Centuries." *Science* 278 (1997): 1251-56.

Passerini, Luisa. *Fascism and Popular Memory*. Cambridge: Cambridge University Press, 1987.

–, ed. *Memory and Totalitarianism*. Oxford: Oxford University Press, 1992.

Peterson, David L., and Darryll R. Johnson. "Human Ecology and Climate Change at Northern Latitudes." In *Human Ecology and Climate Change: People and Resources in the Far North*, edited by David L. Peterson and Darryll R. Johnson, 3-15. Washington, DC: Taylor and Francis, 1995.

Pine, Frances. "The Village, the City and the Outside World: Integration and Exclusion in Two Regions of Rural Poland." In *Post-Socialist Peasant? Rural and Urban Constructions of Identity in Eastern Europe, East Asia and the Former Soviet Union*, edited by Pamela Leonard and Deema Kaneff, 160-79. New York: Palgrave, 2002.

Portelli, Alessandro. *The Battle of Valle Giulia: Oral History and the Art of Dialogue*. Madison: University of Wisconsin Press, 1997.

–. *The Order Has Been Carried Out: History, Memory, and Meaning of a Nazi Massacre in Rome*. New York: Palgrave MacMillan, 2003.

Povinelli, Elizabeth. "Do Rocks Listen? The Cultural Politics of Apprehending Australian Aboriginal Law." *American Anthropologist* 97, 3 (1995): 505-18.

–. *Labor's Lot: The Power, History and Culture of Aboriginal Action*. Chicago: University of Chicago Press, 1993.

Powell, Richard. "Intemperate Spaces: Field Practices and Environmental Science in the Canadian Arctic, 1995-2000." PhD diss., University of Cambridge, 2004.

Powell, Ross D. "Role of Physical Sciences in Global Change Research at Glacier Bay National Park and Preserve." In *Proceedings of the Third Glacier Bay Science Symposium, 1993*, edited by Daniel R. Engstrom, 1-4. Anchorage: National Park Service, 1995.

Pringle, Heather. "High Spirits." *Canadian Geographic* 122, 4 (2002): 68-74.

–. "Out of the Ice." *Canadian Geographic* 122, 4 (2002): 56-64.

Raffles, Hugh. *In Amazonia: A Natural History*. Princeton: Princeton University Press, 2002.

–. "The Uses of Butterflies." *American Ethnologist* 28, 3 (2001): 513-48.

Ranger, Terence. *Voices from the Rocks: Nature, Culture and History in the Matopos Hills of Zimbabwe*. Bloomington: Indiana University Press, 1999.

Rappaport, Joanne. *The Politics of Memory: Native Historical Interpretation in the Colombian Andes*. Cambridge: Cambridge University Press, 1990.

Riffenburgh, Beau. *The Myth of the Explorer: The Press, Sensationalism and Geographical Discovery*. Cambridge and Belhaven: Scott Polar Research Institute, University of Cambridge, 1993.

Robbins, Fred W. "Scribner's Monthly." In *American Literary Magazines: The Eighteenth and Nineteenth Centuries*, edited by Edward E. Chielens, 364-69. New York: Greenwood Press, 1986.

Robson, Ralph E. "The Conquest of the Alsek." *Alaska-Yukon Magazine* 10 (1910): 163-73.

Roots, Fred. "Environmental Responses of High-Latitude Mountainous Areas to Global Change, and Likely Socio-Economic Consequences." *Abstract, EuroMAB IV*, Zakopane, Poland, 6-11 September 1993.

Rozell, Ned. "The Sudden Disappearance of Mount Katmai." *Alaska Science Forum*, no. 1551 (16 July 2001). Alaska Geophysical Institute website, University of Alaska, <http://www.gi.alaska.edu/ScienceForum>.

Ruppert, James. "The Russians Are Coming, the Russians Are Dead: Myth and Historical Consciousness in Two Contact Narratives." *Studies in American Indian Literatures*, 2nd series, 2, 1 (1990): 1-10.

Russell, Israel Cook. "Mount Saint Elias and Its Glaciers." *American Journal of Science*, 3rd series, 43 (1892): 169-82.

Russell, Robert Howard. "Glave's Career." *The Century Magazine* 50, 6 (1895): 865-68.

Sallnow, Michael J. *Pilgrims of the Andes: Regional Cults in Cusco*. Washington, DC: Smithsonian Institution Press, 1987.

Satterfield, Terre. *Anatomy of a Conflict: Identity, Knowledge and Emotion in Old-Growth Forests*. Vancouver: UBC Press, 2002.

Schama, Simon. *Landscape and Memory*. London: Harper Collins, 1995.

Schroeder, Robert F. "Historic and Contemporary Tlingit Use of Glacier Bay." In *Proceedings of the Third Glacier Bay Science Symposium, 1993*, edited by Daniel R. Engstrom, 278-93. Anchorage: National Park Service, 1995.

Schwatka, Frederick. *Report of a Military Reconnaissance in Alaska Made in 1883*. Washington, DC: Government Printing Office, 1885.

Scott, Colin. "Science for the West, Myth for the Rest? The Case of James Bay Cree Knowledge Construction." In *Naked Science: Anthropological Inquiry into Boundaries, Power and Knowledge*, edited by Laura Nader, 69-86. London: Routledge, 1996.

Sealaska Heritage Foundation. *Angoon: A Century After*. Juneau: Sealaska, 1982.

Shanz, Alfred B. "Our Alaska Expedition." *Frank Leslie's Illustrated Newspaper* 70 (1890): 440, 466-67.

Shapin, Steven. "Placing the View from Nowhere: Historical and Sociological Problems in the Location of Science." *Transactions of the British Geographers*, n.s., 23 (1998): 5-12.

–. *The Scientific Revolution*. Chicago and London: University of Chicago Press, 1996.

Shapin, Steven, and S. Simon Schaffer. *Leviathan and the Air Pump: Hobbes, Boyle and the Experimental Life*. Princeton: Princeton University Press, 1985.

Shelikov, Grigorii I. *A Voyage to America 1783-1786*. Translated by M. Ramsay, and edited by Richard A. Pierce. Kingston, ON: Limestone Press, 1981.

Shelley, Percy. *The Complete Poems of Percy Shelley, with Notes by Mary Shelley*. New York: Modern Library, 1994.

Sidney, Angela. *Haa Shagóon/Our Family History*. Compiled by Julie Cruikshank. Whitehorse: Yukon Native Languages Project, 1983.

–. *Place Names of the Tagish Region, Southern Yukon*. Whitehorse: Yukon Native Languages Project, 1980.

–. *Tagish Tlaagú: Tagish Stories*. Recorded by Julie Cruikshank. Whitehorse: Council for Yukon Indians and Government of Yukon, 1982.

Sidney, Angela, Kitty Smith, and Rachel Dawson. *My Stories Are My Wealth*. Recorded by Julie Cruikshank. Whitehorse: Council for Yukon Indians, 1977.

Sillitoe, Paul. "The Development of Indigenous Knowledge: A New Applied Anthropology." *Current Anthropology* 39, 2 (1998): 223-52.

Singleton-Gates, Peter, and Maurice Girodias. *The Black Diaries: An Account of Roger Casement's Life and Times with a Collection of His Diaries and Public Writings*. London: Sidgwick and Jackson, 1959.

Slater, Candace. *Dance of the Dolphin: Transformation and Disenchantment in the Amazonian Imagination*. Chicago: University of Chicago Press, 1994.

–. *Entangled Edens: Visions of the Amazon*. Berkeley and London: University of California Press, 2002.

Smith, Kitty. *Nindal Kwädindür: I'm Going to Tell You a Story*. Recorded by J. Cruikshank. Whitehorse: Council for Yukon Indians and Government of Yukon, 1982.

Sobel, Dana. *Longitude*. London: Penguin, 1995.

Sorrenson, Richard. "The Ship as a Scientific Instrument in the Eighteenth Century." In *Osiris*, Vol. 11: *Science in the Field*, 2nd series, edited by Henrika Kuklick and Robert E. Kohler, 221-36. Chicago: University of Chicago Press Journals Division, 1996.

Spittles, Brian. *Joseph Conrad, Text and Context*. London: Macmillan, 1992.

Spufford, Francis. *I May Be Some Time: Ice and the English Imagination*. London: Faber and Faber, 1996.

Stamps, Judith. *Unthinking Modernity: Innis, McLuhan and the Frankfurt School*. Montreal: McGill-Queen's University Press, 1995.

Steinberg, Ted. "Down to Earth: Nature, Agency and Power in History." *The American Historical Review* 107, 3 (2002): 798-820.

Steller, Georg Wilhelm. *Journal of a Voyage with Bering, 1741-1742*. Edited, with an introduction by O.W. Frost, and translated by Margritt A. Engel and O.W. Frost. Stanford: Stanford University Press, 1998.

Stevens, William K. "Scientists at Work, Wallace Broecker: Iconoclastic Guru of the Climate Debate." *New York Times*, 17 March 1998, F1, F6.

Strommel, Henry, and Elizabeth Strommel. "The Year without a Summer." *Scientific American* 240, 6 (1979): 134-40.

Swanton, John Reed. *Social Condition, Beliefs and Linguistic Relationship of the Tlingit Indians*. Bureau of American Ethnology, 26th Annual Report (1908), 391-485.

–. *Tlingit Myths and Texts*. Washington, DC: Bureau of American Ethnology Bulletin 39 (1909).

Tarr, Ralph, and Bert S. Butler. *The Yakutat Bay Region, Alaska*. Washington, DC: Government Printing Office, 1909.

Tarr, Ralph, and Lawrence Martin. *Alaska Glacier Studies*. Washington, DC: National Geographical Society, 1914.

Taussig, Michael. "Culture of Terror – Space of Death: Roger Casement's Putumayo Report and the Explanation of Torture." *Comparative Studies in Society and History* 26 (1984): 467-97.

–. *Shamanism, Colonialism and the Wild Man: A Study in Terror and Healing*. Chicago and London: University of Chicago Press, 1987.

Thomas, Keith. *Man and the Natural World: Changing Attitudes in England, 1500-1800*. London: Penguin, 1983.

Thomas, Nicholas. *Colonialism's Culture: Anthropology, Travel and Government*. Princeton, NJ: Princeton University Press, 1994.

–. *Entangled Objects: Exchange, Material Culture and Colonialism in the Pacific*. Cambridge, MA: Harvard University Press, 1991.

Thornton, Thomas. "Know Your Place: The Organization of Tlingit Geographic Knowledge." *Ethnology* 36, 4 (1997): 295-307.

–. "Tlingit and Euro-American Toponymies in Glacier Bay." In *Proceedings of the Third Glacier Bay Science Symposium, 1993*, edited by Daniel R. Engstrom, 294-301. Anchorage: National Park Service, 1995.

Tlen, Daniel, and Patrick Moore. "'Just Like Being There': The Use of Deictic Directionals in Southern Tutchone Narratives." Forthcoming.

Togola, Téréba. "Memories, Abstractions and Conceptualizations of Ecological Crisis in the Mande World." In *The Way the Wind Blows: Climate, History and Human Action*, edited by Roderick J. McIntosh, Joseph A. Tainter, and Susan Keech McIntosh, 181-92. New York: Columbia University Press, 2000.

Tom, Gertie. *Èkeyi: Gyò Cho Chú. My Country: Big Salmon River*. Whitehorse: Yukon Native Language Centre, 1987.

Topham, Harold W. "A Visit to the Glaciers of Alaska and Mount Saint Elias." *Proceedings of the Royal Geographical Society* 11 (1889): 424-33.

Townsend-Gault, Charlotte. "Circulating Aboriginality." *Journal of Material Culture* 9, 2 (2004): 183-202.

Vansina, Jan. "King Leopold's Congo, 1886-1908: Occupation and Administration of the State." In *The Cambridge History of Africa*. Vol. 6, *1870-1905*, edited by Roland Oliver and G.N. Sanderson, 327-58. Cambridge: Cambridge University Press, 1985.

–. *Oral Tradition as History*. Madison: University of Wisconsin Press, 1985.

Vitaliano, Dorothy B. *Legends of the Earth: Their Geologic Origins*. Bloomington: Indiana University Press, 1973.

Wallace, Bronwen. *The Stubborn Particulars of Grace*. Toronto: McClelland and Stewart, 1987.

Ward, Herbert. *A Voice from the Congo: Comprising Stories, Anecdotes and Descriptive Notes*. London: Heinemann, 1910.

Watson, Rubie. "Memory, History and Opposition under State Socialism: An Introduction." In *Memory, History and Opposition under State Socialism*, edited by Rubie S. Watson. Santa Fe: School of American Research, 1994.

Watson-Verran, Helen, and David Turnbell. "Science and Other Indigenous Knowledge Systems." In *Handbook of Science and Technology Studies*, edited by Sheila Jasanoff, Gerald E. Markle, James C. Peterson, and Trevor Pinch, 115-39. Thousand Oaks, CA, London, and New Delhi: Sage, 1994.

Weaver, Andrew J. "The Science of Climate Change." *Geoscience Canada* 30, 3 (2003): 91-109.

Wells, E.H. "Our Alaska Expedition." *Frank Leslie's Illustrated Newspaper* 70 (1890): 419.

Welty, Eudora. *One Writer's Beginnings*. Cambridge, MA: Harvard University Press, 1984.

Wenzel, George. *Animal Rights, Human Rights: Ecology, Economy and Ideology in the Canadian Arctic*. London: Bellhaven, 1991.

–. "Warming the Arctic: Environmentalism and Canadian Inuit." In *Human Ecology and Climate Change: People and Resources in the Far North*, edited by Darryll R. Johnson and David L. Peterson, 169-84. Washington, DC: Taylor and Francis, 1995.

White, Hayden. *The Content of the Form: Narrative Discourse and Historical Representation*. Baltimore: Johns Hopkins University Press, 1987.

White, Luise, Stephan F. Miescher, and David William Cohen, eds. *African Words, African Voices: Critical Practices in Oral History*. Bloomington: Indiana University Press, 2001.

White, Richard. "Discovering Nature in North America." *The Journal of American History* 79, 3 (1992): 874-91.

–. "Using the Past: History and Native American Studies." In *Studying Native America*, edited by Russell Thornton, 217-43. Madison: University of Wisconsin Press, 1998.

Wickwire, Wendy. "To See Ourselves as the Other's Other: Nlaka'pamux Contact Narratives." *Canadian Historical Review* 75, 1 (1994): 1-20.

–. "Stories from the Margins: Toward a More Inclusive B.C. Historiography." *Journal of American Folklore* 118, 470 (2005).

Williams, Raymond. *Keywords: A Vocabulary of Culture and Society*. New York: Oxford University Press, 1976.

–. *Problems in Materialism and Culture: Selected Essays*. London: Verso, 1980.

Wilson, Eric G. *The Spiritual History of Ice: Romanticism, Science and the Imagination*. New York: Palgrave, 2003.

Wolf, Eric R. *Envisioning Power: Ideologies of Dominance and Crisis*. Berkeley: University of California Press, 1999.

Wolfe, Linnie Marsh. *John of the Mountains: The Unpublished Journals of John Muir*. Madison: University of Wisconsin Press, 1979.

–. *Son of the Wilderness: The Life of John Muir*. Madison: University of Wisconsin Press, 1978.

Wood, Charles Erskine Scott. "Among the Thlinkits in Alaska." *The Century Magazine* 24, 3 (1882): 323-39.

Workman, Margaret, compiler and translator. *Kwäday Kwändür: Traditional Southern Tutchone Narratives*. Whitehorse: Yukon Native Language Centre, 2000.

Wynne, Brian. "May the Sheep Safely Graze? A Reflexive View of the Expert-Lay Knowledge Divide." In *Risk, Environment and Modernity: Towards a New Ecology*, edited by Scott Lash, Bronislaw Szerszynski, and Brian Wynne, 44-83. London and Thousand Oaks, CA: Sage, 1996.

Young, Samuel Hall. *Alaska Days with John Muir*. New York: Fleming H. Revell Co., 1915.

–. *Hall Young of Alaska: "The Mushing Parson."* New York: Fleming H. Revell Co., 1927.

Yukon Historical and Museums Association. *The Kohklux Map*. Whitehorse: Yukon Historical and Museums Association, 1995.

Index

Note: Page numbers in italics refer to illustrations.

Printed and bound in Canada

Anniversary Edition

Set in Galliard and Univers by Robert Pietrobon

Cover designer: George Kirkpatrick

Cover image: Unnamed valley glacier in the Donjek Ranges, Yukon Territory; photo by Christian Schoof

Original Edition

Set in Galliard and Univers by Artegraphica Design Co. Ltd.

Copy editor: Andy Carroll

Proofreader: Deborah Kerr

Indexer: Christine Jacobs

Cartographer: Eric Leinberger

Authorized Representative: Easy Access System Europe – Mustamäe tee 50, 10621 Tallinn, Estonia, gpsr.requests@easproject.com